Fuzzy Logic Applications in Traffic and Transportation Engineering

Fuzzy Logic Applications in Traffic and Transportation Engineering

Guest Editors

Momčilo Dobrodolac
Stefan Jovčić
Marjana Čubranić-Dobrodolac

Basel • Beijing • Wuhan • Barcelona • Belgrade • Novi Sad • Cluj • Manchester

Guest Editors

Momčilo Dobrodolac
Faculty of Transport and
Traffic Engineering
University of Belgrade
Belgrade
Serbia

Stefan Jovčić
Faculty of Transport
Engineering
University of Pardubice
Pardubice
Czech Republic

Marjana
Čubranić-Dobrodolac
Faculty of Transport and
Traffic Engineering
University of Belgrade
Belgrade
Serbia

Editorial Office
MDPI AG
Grosspeteranlage 5
4052 Basel, Switzerland

This is a reprint of the Special Issue, published open access by the journal *Mathematics* (ISSN 2227-7390), freely accessible at: https://www.mdpi.com/si/mathematics/Fuzzy_Logic_Traffic.

For citation purposes, cite each article independently as indicated on the article page online and as indicated below:

Lastname, A.A.; Lastname, B.B. Article Title. *Journal Name* **Year**, *Volume Number*, Page Range.

ISBN 978-3-7258-4021-2 (Hbk)
ISBN 978-3-7258-4022-9 (PDF)
https://doi.org/10.3390/books978-3-7258-4022-9

© 2025 by the authors. Articles in this book are Open Access and distributed under the Creative Commons Attribution (CC BY) license. The book as a whole is distributed by MDPI under the terms and conditions of the Creative Commons Attribution-NonCommercial-NoDerivs (CC BY-NC-ND) license (https://creativecommons.org/licenses/by-nc-nd/4.0/).

Contents

About the Editors vii

Momčilo Dobrodolac, Marjana Čubranić-Dobrodolac and Stefan Jovčić
Special Issue: "Fuzzy Logic Applications in Traffic and Transportation Engineering"
Reprinted from: *Mathematics* 2025, 13, 1313, https://doi.org/10.3390/math13081313 1

Marjana Čubranić-Dobrodolac, Stefan Jovčić, Sara Bošković and Darko Babić
A Decision-Making Model for Professional Drivers Selection: A Hybridized
Fuzzy–AROMAN–Fuller Approach
Reprinted from: *Mathematics* 2023, 11, 2831, https://doi.org/10.3390/math11132831 6

Ivana Nikolić, Jelena Milutinović, Darko Božanić and Momčilo Dobrodolac
Using an Interval Type-2 Fuzzy AROMAN Decision-Making Method to Improve the
Sustainability of the Postal Network in Rural Areas
Reprinted from: *Mathematics* 2023, 11, 3105, https://doi.org/10.3390/math11143105 30

Nenad Marković, Tijana Ivanišević, Svetlana Čičević and Aleksandar Trifunović
Fuzzy Logic Model for Assessing Accident Proneness Based on Passenger Vehicle Speed in Real
and Virtual Traffic Conditions
Reprinted from: *Mathematics* 2024, 12, 421, https://doi.org/10.3390/math12030421 56

Vukašin Pajić, Milan Andrejić, Marijana Jolović and Milorad Kilibarda
Strategic Warehouse Location Selection in Business Logistics: A Novel Approach Using IMF
SWARA–MARCOS—A Case Study of a Serbian Logistics Service Provider
Reprinted from: *Mathematics* 2024, 12, 776, https://doi.org/10.3390/math12050776 76

Panayotis Christidis, Juan Carlos Martín and Concepción Román
Analysing the Hidden Relationship between Long-Distance Transport and Information and
Communication Technology Use through a Fuzzy Clustering Eco-Extended Apostle Model
Reprinted from: *Mathematics* 2024, 12, 791, https://doi.org/10.3390/math12060791 98

**Dejan Andjelković, Gordan Stojić, Nikola Nikolić, Dillip Kumar Das, Marko Subotić
and Željko Stević**
A Novel Data-Envelopment Analysis Interval-Valued Fuzzy-Rough-Number Multi-Criteria
Decision-Making (DEA-IFRN MCDM) Model for Determining the Efficiency of Road Sections
Based on Headway Analysis
Reprinted from: *Mathematics* 2024, 12, 976, https://doi.org/10.3390/math12070976 119

Adham Salih, Joseph Gabbay and Amiram Moshaiov
Transferability of Multi-Objective Neuro-Fuzzy Motion Controllers: Towards Cautious and
Courageous Motion Behaviors in Rugged Terrains
Reprinted from: *Mathematics* 2024, 12, 992, https://doi.org/10.3390/math12070992 138

Snežana Tadić, Mladen Krstić, Miloš Veljović, Olja Čokorilo and Milica Milovanović
Risk Analysis of the Use of Drones in City Logistics
Reprinted from: *Mathematics* 2024, 12, 1250, https://doi.org/10.3390/math12081250 157

Boldizsár Tüű-Szabó, Péter Földesi and László T. Kóczy
An Efficient Tour Construction Heuristic for Generating the Candidate Set of the Traveling
Salesman Problem with Large Sizes
Reprinted from: *Mathematics* 2024, 12, 2960, https://doi.org/10.3390/math12192960 174

Qiong Bao, Minghao Gao, Jianming Chen and Xu Tan
Location and Size Planning of Charging Parking Lots Based on EV Charging Demand Prediction and Fuzzy Bi-Objective Optimization
Reprinted from: *Mathematics* **2024**, *12*, 3143, https://doi.org/10.3390/math12193143 . . . . **195**

Sadegh Niroomand, Tofigh Allahviranloo, Ali Mahmoodirad, Alireza Amirteimoori, Leo Mršić and Sovan Samanta
Solving a Fully Intuitionistic Fuzzy Transportation Problem Using a Hybrid Multi-Objective Optimization Approach
Reprinted from: *Mathematics* **2024**, *12*, 3898, https://doi.org/10.3390/math12243898 . . . . **216**

About the Editors

Momčilo Dobrodolac

Dr. Momčilo Dobrodolac is a Full Professor at the Faculty of Transport and Traffic Engineering, University of Belgrade, Serbia. He was born in Ljubljana, Slovenia, in 1979. He received his B.S., M.S., and Ph.D. degrees in transport and traffic engineering from the Faculty of Transport and Traffic Engineering, University of Belgrade, Serbia, in 2003, 2008, and 2011, respectively. From 2004 to 2011, he was a Research and Teaching Assistant with the Department of Postal and Telecommunication Traffic, Faculty of Transport and Traffic Engineering, University of Belgrade. From 2011 to 2016, he was an Assistant Professor, and from 2016 to 2022, he was an Associate Professor at the University of Belgrade. He is the author of three books and more than 100 articles. He has participated in several research projects and was the team leader of two projects that defined the directions of strategic development of the postal sector in Serbia. His research interests include postal strategy, postal technology, postal services, and optimization algorithms.

Stefan Jovčić

Dr. Stefan Jovčić is a Research and Teaching Assistant with the Management, Marketing, and Logistics Department, Faculty of Transport Engineering, University of Pardubice. He was born in Vranje, Serbia, in 1992. He received his Ph.D. degree in transportation engineering [A decision-making model for third-party logistics (3PL) provider selection] from the University of Pardubice, Czech Republic, in 2021. He has published approximately 40 articles, out of which 15 are in high-impact scientific journals. His research interests include city logistics and postal traffic. He has the knowledge and expertise to solve various multi-criteria decision-making (MCDM) issues that are related to transportation, city logistics, freight distribution, last-mile delivery (LMD), electric vehicles (EVs), 3PL evaluation and selection, and civil engineering.

Marjana Čubranić-Dobrodolac

Dr. Marjana Čubranić-Dobrodolac is an Assistant Professor at the Faculty of Transport and Traffic Engineering, University of Belgrade, Serbia. She graduated in psychology from the Faculty of Philosophy, University of Belgrade. She defended her doctoral dissertation entitled "A Decision-Making Model for Explaining Driver Behavior" at the Faculty of Transport Engineering, University of Pardubice, Czech Republic. She has been employed at the Faculty of Transport and Traffic Engineering, University of Belgrade, since 2005. During her academic career, she has published 75 scientific and professional papers, of which 13 papers are in international journals indexed in *Web of Science*. As a team member, she has participated in the execution of nine research projects. She has participated in reviewing papers for several scientific and professional journals and conferences. She is a member of the Editorial Board of the journal *Perner's Contacts*. In her professional and scientific work, she has addressed issues related to the perception and behavior of drivers, as well as other road users.

Editorial

Special Issue: "Fuzzy Logic Applications in Traffic and Transportation Engineering"

Momčilo Dobrodolac [1,2,*], Marjana Čubranić-Dobrodolac [2] and Stefan Jovčić [3]

[1] Department of Mathematics SIMATS Engineering, Saveetha Institute of Mechanical and Technical Sciences, Chennai 602105, Tamil Nadu, India
[2] Faculty of Transport and Traffic Engineering, University of Belgrade, 11000 Belgrade, Serbia; marjana@sf.bg.ac.rs
[3] Faculty of Transport Engineering, University of Pardubice, Studentská 95, 532 10 Pardubice, Czech Republic; stefan.jovcic@upce.cz
* Correspondence: m.dobrodolac@sf.bg.ac.rs

1. Introduction

Traffic and transportation engineering involves the application of scientific principles to the planning, design, and operation of facilities for any mode of transportation and to human resource management in industry, which are required to enable the safe, efficient, economical, and environmentally compatible movement of people and goods. Bearing in mind the complexity of the processes at work in transportation engineering, fuzzy logic is a convenient tool for the modeling of these processes. A detailed description of the mathematics of fuzzy set theory was presented by Zadeh [1] in 1975. Fuzzy logic is based on human-like reasoning that is approximate rather than precise, which provides various possibilities for applications in the transportation field, a domain characterized by constant transformations that often lead to uncertainty and imprecision. A particular advantage of fuzzy systems is the ability to include multiple goals in calculations and, using adequate optimization algorithms, to achieve a high level of similarity to real-world phenomena.

This Special Issue of the journal *Mathematics*, titled "Fuzzy Logic Applications in Traffic and Transportation Engineering", is devoted to examples of implementing fuzzy logic to solve various traffic and transportation engineering problems, for all modes of transportation, including road, rail, air, and waterborne transport, the postal and logistics industries, and telecommunications. The Special Issue's Guest Editors were inspired by the current gap in the literature regarding this topic and the realization of the enormous potential of fuzzy logic for applications within the field of transportation. The Guest Editors' previous research within this field of study involved modeling driver behavior using fuzzy inference systems and optimizing them using metaheuristic algorithms. Additionally, previous research has incorporated fuzzy sets into decision-making theory.

2. Contributions

This Special Issue contains 11 papers. The 46 authors represent 15 countries, with 4 authors listing multiple affiliations. The research results were obtained on three continents: Africa, Asia, and Europe. The authors' geographical distribution is shown in Table 1. A notable contribution of this Special Issue is its facilitation of collaboration between authors from multiple countries.

Table 1. Geographic distribution of authors by country.

Country	Number of Authors
Serbia	21
China	4
Hungary	3
Iran	3
Israel	3
Spain	3
Croatia	2
Czech Republic	2
Bosnia and Herzegovina	1
India	1
Italy	1
Republic of Korea	1
Slovenia	1
South Africa	1
Turkey	1

Contribution 1 introduces a hybridized decision-making model, which combines fuzzy logic, Alternative Ranking Order Method Accounting for Two-Step Normalization (AROMAN), and Fuller methods to enhance the selection process for professional drivers. It identifies 14 criteria for driver evaluation through a literature review and expert interviews, then narrows them down to the seven most important using the Decision Making Trial and Evaluation Laboratory (DEMATEL) method and Fuller's pairwise comparisons. The model integrates these criteria into a fuzzy environment for the first time, demonstrating its applicability with a case study involving bus drivers. The proposed approach aims to improve traffic safety and reduce financial costs for transportation companies by selecting the most suitable candidates. Additionally, it offers a general framework that can be applied to various multi-criteria decision-making problems beyond driver selection.

Contribution 2 is related to the postal services. It introduces an interval type-2 fuzzy AROMAN decision-making method to optimize the sustainability of postal networks in rural areas. It identifies and prioritizes key criteria for postal network optimization through expert interviews and the Full Consistency Method (FUCOM). The proposed model is applied to a case study in Serbia, demonstrating its effectiveness in ranking postal units for reorganization. This approach provides a robust tool for policymakers to enhance service provision in rural areas, ensuring equitable access to essential services.

Contribution 3 presents a fuzzy logic model used to assess accident proneness based on passenger-vehicle speed perception in real and virtual traffic conditions. It highlights the significant impact of speed on road crashes and explores how different environments affect speed estimation accuracy. The study involves an experimental setup with 87 participants, analyzing their speed perception at various speeds and from various perspectives. The results show statistically significant differences in speed estimation based on gender, driving experience, and frequency of driving. The proposed model can be used to predict the likelihood of road crashes, offering valuable insights for improving road safety measures.

Contribution 4 is from the field of logistics. It introduces a novel hybrid multi-criteria decision-making model combining improved fuzzy Step-Wise Weight Assessment Ratio Analysis (IMF SWARA) and Measurement Alternatives and Ranking according to Compromise Solution (MARCOS) methods to select optimal warehouse locations for a logistics service provider in Serbia. It identifies seven key criteria for evaluation and assesses five potential locations, emphasizing the importance of factors such as land cost, infrastructure access, and workforce availability. The proposed model offers a systematic approach to decision-making, enhancing the efficiency and cost-effectiveness of supply chain operations. The study demonstrates the model's robustness through sensitivity analysis and validation against other Multi-Criteria Decision-Making (MCDM) methods. This approach provides valuable insights for logistics professionals and can be adapted to various industries and geographical contexts.

Contribution 5 examines the hidden relationship between long-distance transport (LDT) and information and communication technology (ICT) use among European Union (EU) citizens, utilizing a fuzzy clustering eco-extended apostle model. It reveals that the majority of EU citizens neither travel long distances nor frequently use ICT for transport, while a minority engages in both activities extensively. The study highlights significant socio-demographic influences on these patterns, such as gender, age, education, and employment status. The novel methodology provides deeper insights into the complex interactions between LDT and ICT use, offering a robust framework for future research. This approach enhances the understanding of how ICT adoption impacts travel behavior and vice versa.

Contribution 6 is related to road transportation engineering. It introduces a novel multi-criteria decision-making model, which integrates data envelopment analysis (DEA) with interval-valued fuzzy-rough-numbers (IFRN) and Weighted Aggregated Sum Product Assessment (WASPAS) methods. The model is named DEA-IFRN WASPAS. This model is applied to evaluate the efficiency of 14 road sections based on headway analysis, incorporating criteria such as annual average daily traffic (AADT) and road gradient. The study's main contribution lies in the development of the IFRN WASPAS method, which enhances decision-making under uncertainty. The results provide valuable insights for infrastructure managers and traffic experts to optimize road section efficiency and improve traffic flow.

Contribution 7 investigates the development of neuro-fuzzy motion controllers for autonomous vehicles navigating rugged terrains, focusing on cautious, intermediate, and courageous behaviors. It introduces a sequential transfer optimization approach, utilizing multiple bi-objective source problems to enhance the evolution of controllers. The study demonstrates that edge solutions from Pareto fronts provide better transferability than center solutions, substantiating this hypothesis through extensive experimental analysis. This research contributes to the efficient design of versatile neuro-fuzzy controllers capable of adapting to various environmental challenges.

Contribution 8 proposes a hybrid multi-criteria decision-making (MCDM) model combining fuzzy factor relationship (FARE) and axial distance-based aggregated measurement (ADAM) methods to assess the risks associated with using different types of drones in city logistics. This model identifies the least risky drone type by evaluating nine alternatives based on seven criteria, ultimately selecting the single-rotor microdrone as the optimal solution. The study introduces a comprehensive framework for assessing drones optimized for urban logistics applications, emphasizing risk mitigation. Additionally, the paper validates the robustness of the proposed model through sensitivity analysis and comparison with other MCDM methods. This research contributes to safer and more efficient logistics operations in urban environments.

Contribution 9 introduces a novel heuristic for generating candidate sets for large-scale instances of the traveling salesman problem (TSP) using fuzzy clustering. This method significantly improves the efficiency and quality of candidate sets, outperforming traditional techniques in terms of time complexity and solution quality. Extensive testing on benchmark instances demonstrates that the heuristic covers nearly all edges of optimal solutions and produces smaller candidate sets, enhancing the performance of subsequent improvement methods like the Lin–Kernighan heuristic. Overall, this approach offers a robust solution for effectively solving large-scale instances of the TSP.

Contribution 10 proposes a novel framework for the location and size planning of charging parking lots (CPLs) based on electric vehicle (EV) charging demand prediction and fuzzy bi-objective optimization. It introduces a method to predict the spatial–temporal distribution of EV charging demand using real vehicle usage data and a fuzzy logic inference system. The study then develops a bi-objective optimization model to minimize EV users' charging waiting time and maximize CPL operators' profits, solved using a fuzzy genetic algorithm. The proposed approach is validated using a case study, demonstrating its effectiveness in reducing travel and waiting times while controlling construction costs. This research provides a practical solution for the efficient planning and management of EV charging infrastructure.

Contribution 11 introduces a novel approach to solving fully intuitionistic fuzzy transportation problems without using ranking functions, thereby addressing the shortcomings of existing methods. It transforms the problem into a crisp multi-objective form and proposes a new hybrid multi-objective solution procedure. The effectiveness of this approach is demonstrated through computer experiments with benchmark problems, showing superior results compared to existing methods. Additionally, the study highlights practical applications in real-world scenarios where demand, supply, and transportation costs are vague and inadequate.

3. Conclusions

The Guest Editors would like to thank all the authors for presenting their research results in the Special Issue "Fuzzy Logic Applications in Traffic and Transportation Engineering". Furthermore, we are extremely grateful to all the reviewers for their timely and insightful reports, and to the staff of the Editorial Office for their support in preparing this Special Issue. We hope that this Special Issue will inspire other researchers to carry out new research using fuzzy logic in solving practical problems in the field of transportation engineering.

Conflicts of Interest: The authors declare no conflicts of interest.

List of Contributions

1. Čubranić-Dobrodolac, M.; Jovčić, S.; Bošković, S.; Babić, D. A Decision-Making Model for Professional Drivers Selection: A Hybridized Fuzzy–AROMAN–Fuller Approach. *Mathematics* **2023**, *11*, 2831. https://doi.org/10.3390/math11132831.
2. Nikolić, I.; Milutinović, J.; Božanić, D.; Dobrodolac, M. Using an Interval Type-2 Fuzzy AROMAN Decision-Making Method to Improve the Sustainability of the Postal Network in Rural Areas. *Mathematics* **2023**, *11*, 3105. https://doi.org/10.3390/math11143105.
3. Marković, N.; Ivanišević, T.; Čičević, S.; Trifunović, A. Fuzzy Logic Model for Assessing Accident Proneness Based on Passenger Vehicle Speed in Real and Virtual Traffic Conditions. *Mathematics* **2024**, *12*, 421. https://doi.org/10.3390/math12030421.
4. Pajić, V.; Andrejić, M.; Jolović, M.; Kilibarda, M. Strategic Warehouse Location Selection in Business Logistics: A Novel Approach Using IMF SWARA–MARCOS—A Case Study of a Serbian Logistics Service Provider. *Mathematics* **2024**, *12*, 776. https://doi.org/10.3390/math12050776.
5. Christidis, P.; Martín, J.C.; Román, C. Analysing the Hidden Relationship between Long-Distance Transport and Information and Communication Technology Use through a Fuzzy Clustering Eco-Extended Apostle Model. *Mathematics* **2024**, *12*, 791. https://doi.org/10.3390/math12060791.
6. Andjelković, D.; Stojić, G.; Nikolić, N.; Das, D.K.; Subotić, M.; Stević, Ž. A Novel Data-Envelopment Analysis Interval-Valued Fuzzy-Rough-Number Multi-Criteria Decision-Making (DEA-IFRN MCDM) Model for Determining the Efficiency of Road Sections Based on Headway Analysis. *Mathematics* **2024**, *12*, 976. https://doi.org/10.3390/math12070976.

7. Salih, A.; Gabbay, J.; Moshaiov, A. Transferability of Multi-Objective Neuro-Fuzzy Motion Controllers: Towards Cautious and Courageous Motion Behaviors in Rugged Terrains. *Mathematics* **2024**, *12*, 992. https://doi.org/10.3390/math12070992.
8. Tadić, S.; Krstić, M.; Veljović, M.; Čokorilo, O.; Milovanović, M. Risk Analysis of the Use of Drones in City Logistics. *Mathematics* **2024**, *12*, 1250. https://doi.org/10.3390/math12081250.
9. Tüű-Szabó, B.; Földesi, P.; Kóczy, L.T. An Efficient Tour Construction Heuristic for Generating the Candidate Set of the Traveling Salesman Problem with Large Sizes. *Mathematics* **2024**, *12*, 2960. https://doi.org/10.3390/math12192960.
10. Bao, Q.; Gao, M.; Chen, J.; Tan, X. Location and Size Planning of Charging Parking Lots Based on EV Charging Demand Prediction and Fuzzy Bi-Objective Optimization. *Mathematics* **2024**, *12*, 3143. https://doi.org/10.3390/math12193143.
11. Niroomand, S.; Allahviranloo, T.; Mahmoodirad, A.; Amirteimoori, A.; Mršić, L.; Samanta, S. Solving a Fully Intuitionistic Fuzzy Transportation Problem Using a Hybrid Multi-Objective Optimization Approach. *Mathematics* **2024**, *12*, 3898. https://doi.org/10.3390/math12243898.

Reference

1. Zadeh, L.A. The Concept of a Linguistic Variable and Its Application to Approximate Reasoning—I. *Inf. Sci.* **1975**, *8*, 199–249. [CrossRef]

Disclaimer/Publisher's Note: The statements, opinions and data contained in all publications are solely those of the individual author(s) and contributor(s) and not of MDPI and/or the editor(s). MDPI and/or the editor(s) disclaim responsibility for any injury to people or property resulting from any ideas, methods, instructions or products referred to in the content.

Article

A Decision-Making Model for Professional Drivers Selection: A Hybridized Fuzzy–AROMAN–Fuller Approach

Marjana Čubranić-Dobrodolac [1,*], Stefan Jovčić [2], Sara Bošković [2] and Darko Babić [3]

1. Faculty of Transport and Traffic Engineering, University of Belgrade, 11000 Belgrade, Serbia
2. Faculty of Transport Engineering, University of Pardubice, 532 10 Pardubice, Czech Republic; stefan.jovcic@upce.cz (S.J.); sara.boskovic@student.upce.cz (S.B.)
3. Faculty of Transport and Traffic Sciences, University of Zagreb, 10000 Zagreb, Croatia; darko.babic@fpz.unizg.hr
* Correspondence: marjana@sf.bg.ac.rs

Citation: Čubranić-Dobrodolac, M.; Jovčić, S.; Bošković, S.; Babić, D. A Decision-Making Model for Professional Drivers Selection: A Hybridized Fuzzy–AROMAN–Fuller Approach. *Mathematics* 2023, 11, 2831. https://doi.org/10.3390/math11132831

Academic Editor: Hsien-Chung Wu

Received: 27 May 2023
Revised: 18 June 2023
Accepted: 22 June 2023
Published: 24 June 2023

Copyright: © 2023 by the authors. Licensee MDPI, Basel, Switzerland. This article is an open access article distributed under the terms and conditions of the Creative Commons Attribution (CC BY) license (https:// creativecommons.org/licenses/by/ 4.0/).

Abstract: Professional drivers play a crucial role in many businesses and the lives of people. They are responsible for transferring people and goods between distant points, enabling safe and efficient flows. The road traffic death rate is from 8.3 to 27.5 per 100,000 inhabitants in the countries globally. Because professional drivers spend a significant amount of time on the road, their appropriate selection may contribute to general traffic safety. In addition, an adequate selection of candidates significantly impacts the financial costs of the employing company. However, the recruitment procedure is a very complex task where multiple criteria should be considered. By its nature, this is a typical multi-criteria decision-making problem. The purpose of this paper is twofold: to contribute to the methodological, as well as to the professional field. Considering the professional, we propose a decision-making tool in the procedure of professional driver selection. There are several methodological contributions. By reviewing the literature, we identified 14 criteria for candidate selection. In the proposed model, by using expert opinion and implementing DEMATEL and Fuller's pairwise comparisons, we ranked these criteria and determined the seven most important for further calculation procedure. Here, we introduced an original approach for measuring the reliability of obtained answers. Then, to rank the candidates, the fuzzy AROMAN approach is applied for the first time in the literature. The input data were obtained in the form of a survey, where the experts evaluated the importance of criteria and their interrelation. We used MS Excel and MATLAB for data processing. An additional methodological contribution of this study is an advancement of the AROMAN method by the proposal of an algorithm for the calculation of parameter λ used in the final ranking formula. To illustrate the applicability of the proposed model, a case study is provided. Based on the results, we can conclude that the new methodological approaches can be successfully used in the procedure of professional driver selection, as well as in solving other multi-criteria decision-making problems.

Keywords: recruitment procedure; personnel selection; road safety; transportation companies; professional drivers; fuzzy logic; AROMAN; Fuller's triangle; DEMATEL

MSC: 03E72; 47S40; 90B50

1. Introduction

Road traffic accidents are one of the leading causes of death and serious injuries for people all across the world. Based on a report by the World Health Organization, the road traffic death rate is from 8.3 in high-income countries, to 27.5 per 100,000 inhabitants in low- and middle-income countries. In total, there are around 1.35 million deaths and 50 million injured on the roads each year [1]. Many problems in transportation, such as traffic congestion, road blockage, and road accidents, can be solved to a certain extent by the digitization of roads and vehicles [2]; however, the impact of the human factor is still of crucial importance as well. In the literature, there are three main categories of factors that contribute to road traffic accident occurrence: human factors, vehicle factors, and the factor related to road design and construction. Human factors are by far the most represented cause of accidents. Around 90 to 95% of all traffic accidents involve human error [3–5]. Based on this, it is evident that adequate educational programs for drivers can contribute to improved traffic safety. In addition, particular attention should be placed on the recruitment procedures for professional drivers having in mind their constant and widespread presence on the roads.

A professional driver represents a driver who drives a transport vehicle as a paid employee. In this study, we are focused on road transport, and the case study is related to bus drivers. However, the proposed methodology is general and can be implemented for other types of drivers, such as truck drivers, train drivers, sea captains, or airline pilots, as well as in general cases, for any personnel selection problem.

Professional drivers, depending on the type of driving vehicle, are responsible for goods of high value that are transported, and even more importantly, for the lives of people that travel by different means of public transport. This job is very demanding, both from the physical and mental standpoint [6]. These are the reasons why particular attention should be placed on the selection procedure, to employ candidates that are capable of responding to all of the challenges of this work. It is evident that various criteria influence the assessment procedure of candidates and one of the aims of this paper is to investigate the literature and systemize the criteria used in the process of professional driver selection.

The main aim of this paper is to propose a methodological framework for solving the problem of professional driver selection. Having in mind, on the one hand, that certain criteria should be minimized or maximized in decision-making depending on their nature, and on the other hand, that the candidates can be considered as alternatives, it can be concluded that this is a typical multi-criteria decision-making (MCDM) problem. There are numerous MCDM techniques in the literature [7–9]; however, to contribute both to the professional and scientific fields, we propose an extension of a relatively new MCDM method: An alternative ranking order method accounting for two-step normalization—AROMAN [10,11]. Because certain criteria in the process of professional driver selection are hard to describe numerically, we introduce fuzzy logic in the model. The main motive for applying the AROMAN method is that it is a very new MCDM method and we intend to further test its applicability. Aside from this, our crucial goal is to test this method in a fuzzy environment. Therefore, the main contribution of this study can be structured as follows: (i) We identified the criteria for the selection of professional drivers by a comprehensive literature review, (ii) We measured the relevance ranks of the set criteria by interviewing the experts from the field and by implementing Fuller's triangle method, (iii) We implemented the AROMAN method in the fuzzy environment for the first time in the literature, (iv) We proposed an extension of the AROMAN method by integrating the relevance ranks of the set criteria obtained by Fuller's triangle method with the calculation of alternatives ranks.

The rest of the paper is structured as follows: Section 2 is a review of the literature to identify the criteria for professional driver selection. Section 3 explains the methodology of the research. To illustrate the applicability of the proposed model, in Section 4 there is an illustrative case study. Finally, Section 5 represents a conclusion.

2. Literature Review

This section investigates the current knowledge in the field of professional drivers. The main research source for this study was the Web of Science (WoS) database. There are two subsections. The first is related to the review of different topics considered in this field and the second is devoted to the identification of criteria used for the professional driver evaluation.

2.1. Literature on Professional Drivers

In the last decade, there have been numerous papers addressing the issue of professional drivers. Here, we will mention just a few to demonstrate the diversity of considered problems in the field. For instance, Zaranka et al. [12] evaluated the factors affecting the behavior of road users and investigated the impact of fatigue on road users. Maslać et al. [13] compared the behaviors of professional and non-professional drivers in the Republic of Serbia. Rosso et al. [14] conducted a cross-sectional questionnaire survey to investigate obesity among professional drivers in Italy. Chen et al. [15] investigated the difference between professional and non-professional drivers in terms of the effectiveness of the compensatory strategy adopted by older drivers. Wu et al. [16] carried out research related to the effectiveness of eco-driving training for male professional and non-professional drivers.

Öz et al. [17] considered professional and non-professional drivers' stress reactions and risky driving. Nordfaern et al. [18] investigated safety attitudes, behavior, anxiety, and perceived control among professional and non-professional drivers. Serrano-Fernández et al. [19] addressed the most important predictive variables for sleep quality in professional drivers. Chen et al. [20] conducted a driving simulator study regarding the safety of professional drivers in an aging society. Meng et al. [21] investigated driving fatigue in professional taxi and truck drivers in Beijing. Han and Jianyou [22] tackled driver behavior and traffic accident involvement among professional urban bus drivers in China. Hernández-Rodríguez et al. [23] estimated psychosocial risk and job satisfaction in professional drivers. Serrano-Fernández et al. [24] considered variables that predict attitudes toward safety regulations in professional drivers. Llamazares et al. [25] investigated commuting accidents of Spanish professional drivers when the occupational risk exceeds the workplace. The related research papers are summarized in Table 1.

Table 1. Studies related to professional drivers.

Year	Authors	Considered Problem
2010	Öz, Özkan and Lajunen [17]	Professional and non-professional drivers' stress reactions and risky driving
2012	Nordfaern, Jorgensen and Rundmo [18]	Safety attitudes, behavior, anxiety, and perceived control among professional and non-professional drivers
2015	Rosso, Perotto, Feola, Bruno and Caramella [14]	Obesity among professional drivers
2015	Meng, Li, Cao, Li, Peng, Wang and Zhang [21]	Driving fatigue among professional taxi and truck drivers
2018	Maslać, Antić, Lipovac, Pešić and Milutinović [13]	Comparison of the professional and non-professional drivers considering rules violations
2018	Wu, Zhao, Rong and Zhang [16]	Effectiveness of eco-driving training for male professional and non-professional drivers
2019	Chen, Sze and Bai [20]	Safety of professional drivers in an ageing society
2020	Han and Zhao [22]	Driver behavior and traffic accident involvement among professional urban bus drivers in China
2020	Serrano-Fernández, Tàpia-Caballero, Boada-Grau and Araya-Castillo [24]	Variables that predict attitudes toward safety regulations in professional drivers
2021	Zaranka, Pečeliunas and Žuraulis [12]	Factors affecting the behavior of road users
2021	Serrano-Fernández, Boada-Grau, Robert-Sentís and Vigil-Colet [19]	Predictive variables for sleep quality in professional drivers
2021	Chen, Sze, Newnam and Bai [15]	Difference between professional and non-professional drivers in terms of the effectiveness
2021	Llamazares, Useche, Montoro and Alonso [25]	Commuting accidents of professional drivers when the occupational risk exceeds the workplace
2022	Hernández-Rodríguez, Maeso-González, Gutiérrez-Bedmar and García-Rodríguez [23]	Psychosocial risk and job satisfaction in professional drivers

As can be noticed from this part of the literature review, various forms of studies tackling professional drivers have been conducted by researchers around the globe. However, the research gap in the literature is that there is a lack of studies considering the professional driver evaluation and selection problem. Having the stated in mind, this paper aims to address the professional driver evaluation and selection issue using a multicriteria decision-making approach combined with fuzzy logic. More concretely, this paper applies the recently developed AROMAN method, coupled with the fuzzy logic to effectively evaluate and select the most appropriate professional driver. As a starting point to perform this procedure, the evaluation criteria should be set. The next subchapter is devoted to this task, where the criteria are identified by the review of current publications.

2.2. Criteria for Professional Drivers Evaluation

In this subsection, a summarized overview of the considered criteria for professional driver evaluation is offered, along with the applied methodology in the related papers (Table 2). Professional drivers need to maintain their attention on many traffic circumstances while driving. Cvahte Ojsteršek and Topolšek [26] analyzed the influence of drivers' visual and cognitive attention on their perception of changes in the traffic environment. Further, Milošević and Gajić [27] considered how different situations in traffic impacts the perception of road signs.

Table 2. Criteria for professional driver evaluation.

No.	Criteria	Authors	Used Methodology
1.	Attention	- Cvahte Ojsteršek and Topolšek [26] - Milošević and Gajić [27]	- Statistical analysis - Statistical analysis
2.	Fatigue resistance	- Milosevic [28] - Brown, Farias Zuniga, Mulla, Mendonca, Keir and Bray [29]	- Statistical analysis - Statistical analysis
3.	Reaction time	- Poliak, Svabova, Benus and Demirci [30] - Čulík, Kalašová and Štefancová [31]	- Statistical analysis - Statistical analysis
4.	Visual abilities	- Anstey, Horswill, Wood and Hatherly [32] - Lacherez, Au and Wood [33]	- Statistical analysis - Statistical analysis
5.	Speed estimation	- Chen, Wei and Gao [34] - Čubranić-Dobrodolac, Švadlenka, Čičević, Trifunović and Dobrodolac [35]	- Fuzzy AHP - Fuzzy inference system
6.	Physical fitness	- Caragata, Tuokko and Damini [36] - Gilson, Mielke, Coombes, Feter, Smith, Duncan, Wallis and Brown [37]	- Statistical analysis - Statistical analysis
7.	Driving experience	- Ku Khalif, Gegov and Abu Bakar [38] - Mueller and Trick [39]	- Fuzzy TOPSIS - Statistical analysis
8.	Risk assessment	- Wang, Chen, Chen, Deng, Chen [40] - Al-Garawi, Dalhat and Aga [41]	- Statistical analysis - Statistical analysis
9.	Impulsiveness	- Cubranic-Dobrodolac, Svadlenka, Markovic and Dobrodolac [42] - Smorti and Guarnieri [43]	- Fuzzy inference system - Statistical analysis
10.	Aggressiveness	- Cubranic-Dobrodolac, Svadlenka, Markovic and Dobrodolac [42] - Rodriguez Gonzalez, Wilby, Vinagre Diaz and Sanchez Avila [44]	- Fuzzy inference system - Statistical analysis
11.	Self-assessment of driving ability	- Tronsmoen [45] - Sundström [46]	- Statistical analysis - Statistical analysis
12.	Space capabilities	- Čubranić-Dobrodolac, Švadlenka, Čičević, Trifunović and Dobrodolac [47]	- Fuzzy inference system
13.	Intelligence	- Petrović and Petrović [48] - Li, Lai and Kao [49]	- Fuzzy TOPSIS - TOPSIS
14.	Morality	- Zaranka, Pečeliunas and Žuraulis [12] - Li, Lai and Kao [49]	- Statistical analysis - TOPSIS

Milosevic [28] examined the fatigue resistance in a group of city bus drivers, by measuring heart rate by electro-cardio recorder before and after driving. It is interesting to notice that mental fatigue can cause negative effects on physical performance as well [29].

Drivers' reaction time is related to the amount of time needed to process important information and act in emergencies. Poliak et al. [30] evaluated the impact of age on the reaction time of professional drivers. Čulík et al. [31] investigated if gender, practice, or alcohol significantly affected the reaction time of drivers.

Anstey et al. [32] proposed a model to measure the capacity to drive safely based on assessing visual functions. Lacherez et al. [33] examined an association between indices of driving safety and low-level changes in visual function.

Papers that deal with the selection procedure of professional drivers by using a multi-criteria decision-making approach are very rare in the literature. One of them is by Chen et al. [34] where speed estimation is taken as an evaluation criterion. The research by Čubranić-Dobrodolac et al. [35] confirms that a level of speed perception capabilities is related to the occurrence of road traffic accidents.

In the literature, an interdependence between physical fitness and driving skills is proven [36]. Since professional drivers often drive even during the night, resulting in a lack of sleep, this segment is of particular importance in the selection procedure [37].

Inexperience is one of the strongest predictors of crashes [39]. Therefore, work experience is often taken as an evaluation criterion in the staff recruitment process [38], as well as risk assessment [40]. Driver's improper driving behavior is often related to poor risk assessment [40,41].

Examples of driver aggression are related to driving at excessive speed, intimidation of other road users, improper following, improper lane changing and passing, and similar. It is proven that aggressiveness positively correlates with road accident occurrence [42,44].

Aside from aggression, similar behavior represents impulsiveness. There is evidence in the literature that elevated impulsiveness is associated with other forms of inappropriate behavior in traffic, such as drink-driving, drug-driving offenses, using a mobile phone behind the wheel, etc. [43,50].

A higher level of self-assessment of driving ability can be found in drivers with a lower level of involvement in crashes [45]. A comprehensive review of methods for measuring subjective driving ability can be found in [46]. Another ability that contributes to safe driving relates to space assessment capability [47].

Intelligence is an innate ability that is very often considered in the recruitment procedure, in the field of transportation, and many others [48,49]. Zaranka et al. [12] introduce a social component in the recruitment procedure of professional drivers, where the first things considered are morality, social fit, and interpersonal skills [49,51].

3. Methods

After an extensive literature review to identify criteria for professional driver evaluation, further research methodology can be structured into two parts. The first aim of reducing the number of identified criteria to simplify the calculation process in the second part relates to the ranking of candidates. In the first part, we apply two methods, DEMATEL and the Fuller triangle method. Interdependence between the criteria is calculated by DEMATEL, while the level of importance of each criterion to the decision-making process is determined by the Fuller triangle method. The second part of the methodology is related to the proposal of the Fuzzy–AROMAN–Fuller approach for ranking the alternatives. The research structure is presented in Figure 1.

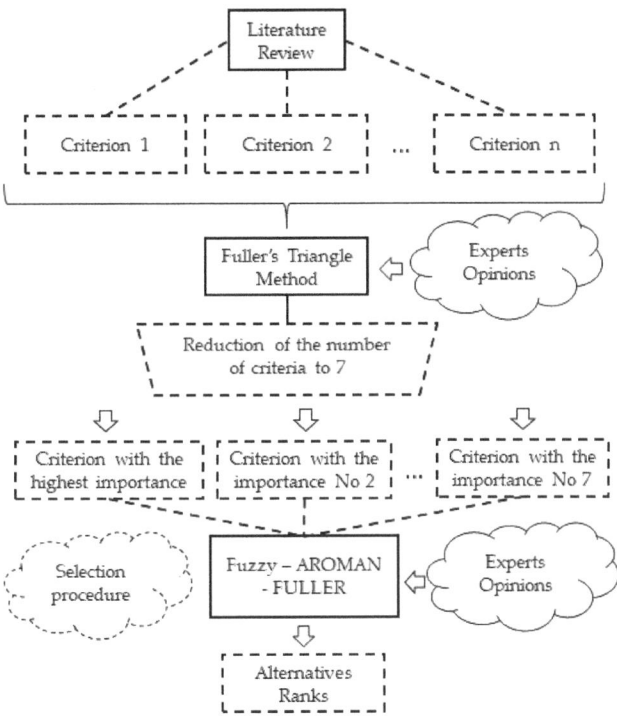

Figure 1. Research structure.

3.1. Determination of Interdependence between the Criteria by the DEMATEL Method

The DEMATEL method can be structured into four main steps. They relate to generating the direct-relation matrix by interviewing the experts, normalization of the direct-relation matrix, calculating the total-relation matrix, and producing a causal diagram. In the following text, the procedure is explained in more detail.

Step 1. *Generate the direct-relation matrix.*

The direct-relation matrix is created by using a comparison scale:

- 0 = No influence;
- 1 = Low influence;
- 2 = Medium influence;
- 3 = High influence;
- 4 = Very high influence.

An expert answers the questions considering the degree of influence of one criterion over another. Let a_{ij} denotes a pair-wise comparison score between two criteria. If there are n criteria, and all the comparisons are obtained, the direct-relation matrix $A = [a_{ij}]_{nxn}$ can be formed. If there are more experts $A^1, A^2, \ldots, A^m$, the final direct-relation matrix can be generated by Equation (1) [52].

$$A = \frac{1}{m}\sum_{k=1}^{m} A_{ij}^k \qquad (1)$$

Step 2. *Normalize the direct-relation matrix.*

The normalized direct-relation matrix X, $X = [x_{ij}]_{nxn}$ and $0 \leq x_{ij} \leq 1$, can be calculated by Equations (2) and (3). It should be noted that all diagonal elements are equal to zero [52].

$$X = S * A \tag{2}$$

$$S = \frac{1}{\max_{1 \leq i \leq n} \sum_{j=1}^{n} A_{ij}}, i,j = 1, 2, \ldots, n \tag{3}$$

Step 3. *Calculate the total-relation matrix.*

The total-relation matrix T can be obtained by applying Equation (4). Here, the matrix I indicates the identity matrix [52].

$$T = X * (I - X)^{-1} \tag{4}$$

Step 4. *Create a causal diagram.*

To interpret the results, the important variables are D and R. They are calculated by Equations (6) and (7) [52].

$$T = t_{ij}, \ i,j = 1, 2, \ldots, n \tag{5}$$

$$D = \sum_{j=1}^{n} t_{ij} \tag{6}$$

$$R = \sum_{i=1}^{n} t_{ij} \tag{7}$$

A causal diagram can be obtained by mapping the pairs $(D + R, D - R)$. The first dimension gives information about the impact of a particular criterion over others, while the second dimension describes the nature of this impact, i.e., is a criterion in the cause (positive values) or effect group (negative values).

3.2. Determination of the Criteria Relevance by the Fuller Triangle Method

To reduce the number of criteria identified by the literature review, we will determine their relevance and rank them according to the method named the Fuller triangle method [53–55]. The Fuller method is in the group of the subjective weighting methods, such as the Analytic Hierarchy Process—AHP [56], Best–Worst Method—BWM [57], Full Consistency Method—FUCOM [58], or Stepwise Weight Assessment Ratio Analysis—SWARA [59]. The procedure of the Fuller triangle method is explained in the following text.

Step 1. *The Fuller method starts with forming a triangular structure as shown in Figure 2. The first two rows relate to the pairwise comparison of Criterion 1 with all other criteria. Accordingly, in the first row, there are $n - 1$ columns with Criterion 1 and the same number of all other criteria from Criterion 2 to n. A decision maker should choose which of the considered criteria in each pair is more important than the other and mark it. The same procedure should be performed for all other comparisons; however, each of the subsequent two rows is shorter by one column, and at the end, there is just a comparison of one pair, between Criterion $n - 1$ and n. The number of all pairs being compared is equal to N, calculated by Equation (8), where n is the total number of compared criteria.*

$$N = \frac{n(n-1)}{2} \tag{8}$$

Step 2. *After all comparisons are carried out, it can be considered that each criterion that "win" as the more important one in the pairwise comparison receives one point. If a decision is made that they are of equal significance, the criteria achieve half of a point each. The points awarded to criteria should be summed up per each criterion, and the sums represent their relevance rank.*

Step 3. *In the third step, the relevance ranks (w_j) should be normalized according to Equation (9) [53]. v_j represents the number of preferences, i.e., the number of points each criterion received, and in the denominator is the total number of all preferences.*

$$w_j = \frac{v_j}{\sum_{k=1}^{n} v_k}; j = 1, 2, \ldots, n \qquad (9)$$

Step 4. *If there is a criterion that did not receive any points, in this case, in the previous formula, the numerator should be increased by 1 to avoid the relevance rank being equal to zero. Then, the relevance ranks should be calculated by Equation (10).*

$$w_j = \frac{v_j + 1}{n + \sum_{k=1}^{n} v_k}; j = 1, 2, \ldots, n \qquad (10)$$

If the evaluation of relevance ranks is carried out by more than one expert, an arithmetic mean value of all input values should be calculated. To aggregate opinions from more experts, other methods can be used as well, such as geometric mean [60] or centroid [61]. However, the arithmetic mean is the most commonly used.

| C1 | C1 | C1 | .... | C1 |
| C2 | C3 | C4 | ... | Cn |

C2	C2		C2
C3	C4	...	Cn
		...	

...	...
Cn-2	Cn-2
Cn-1	Cn

| Cn-1 |
| Cn |

Figure 2. Illustration of starting procedure in Fuller triangle method.

An important issue considering subjective methods, such is the Fuller triangle method, is measuring the reliability of collected answers. For example, in the AHP method, there is a well-known approach where the rate of inconsistency is calculated, and it should be lower than 0.1 to conclude satisfactory reliability. However, this approach cannot be applied in the case of the Fuller triangle method, and in addition, by reviewing the literature, we did not find any convenient approach that could be implemented here. This was an inspiration for the authors to propose a new technique to assess the reliability of experts' opinions.

The procedure implies a second round of interviewing the experts. Without knowing the results of the first round where they gave opinions about the pair-wise comparisons of criteria importance, they were asked to give additional assessments. They were told to imagine the scale from 0 to 100% and to determine the percentage importance of each criterion for the recruitment process of selecting the professional driver. This should be carried out in the way that all 14 assessments give the sum of 100%. Finally, the results of the second round should be compared with the first round to conclude about the reliability of answers. If we denote the answers from the second round by p_j, and previously we marked the obtained weight in the first round by w_j, then the rate of inconsistency (RI) can be calculated as explained in Equation (11).

$$RI = \frac{\sum_{j=1}^{n} |w_j * 100 - p_j|}{100} \qquad (11)$$

3.3. Ranking Alternatives Using a Hybridized Fuzzy-AROMAN-FULLER Approach

As previously mentioned, the AROMAN method is for the first time implemented in a fuzzy environment in this paper. Therefore, it is useful to provide some preliminaries on fuzzy arithmetic.

3.3.1. Preliminaries on Fuzzy Arithmetic

In the following text, we briefly present some basic definitions of fuzzy sets and numbers [62].

Definition 1. *A fuzzy set $\tilde{A}$ in a universe of discourse X is characterized by a membership function $\mu_{\tilde{A}}(x)$ which associates with each element x in X a real number in the interval $[0, 1]$. The function value $\mu_{\tilde{A}}(x)$ represents the grade of membership of x in $\tilde{A}$ [62].*

Definition 2. *A fuzzy set $\tilde{A}$ of the universe of discourse X is convex if and only if for all x_1, x_2 in X,*

$$\mu_{\tilde{A}}(\gamma x_1 + (1-\gamma) x_2) \geq \text{Min}(\mu_{\tilde{A}}(x_1), \mu_{\tilde{A}}(x_2)), \qquad (12)$$

where $\in [0, 1]$ [62].

Definition 3. *A fuzzy set $\tilde{A}$ of the universe of discourse X is called a normal fuzzy set implying that $\exists x_i \in X$, $\mu_{\tilde{A}}(x_i) = 1$ [62].*

Definition 4. *A fuzzy number is a fuzzy subset in the universe of discourse X that is both convex and normal. An example of a triangular fuzzy number is given in Figure 3.*

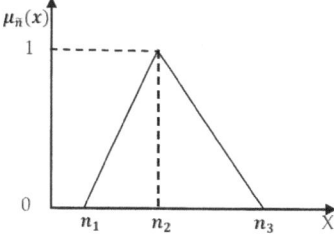

Figure 3. A triangular fuzzy number $\tilde{n}$.

Definition 5. *The α-cut of fuzzy number $\tilde{n}$ is defined*

$$\tilde{n}^\alpha = \left\{ x_i : \mu_{\tilde{n}}(x_i) \geq \alpha, x_i \in X \right\}, \qquad (13)$$

where $\alpha \in [0, 1]$ [62].

$\tilde{n}^\alpha$ is a non-empty bounded closed interval contained in X and it can be denoted by $\tilde{n}^\alpha = \left[\tilde{n}_l^\alpha, \tilde{n}_u^\alpha\right]$, where $\tilde{n}_l^\alpha$ and $\tilde{n}_u^\alpha$ are the lower and upper bounds of the closed interval, respectively. Figure 4 shows a fuzzy number $\tilde{n}$ with α-cuts, where

$$\tilde{n}^{\alpha 1} = \left[\tilde{n}_l^{\alpha 1}, \tilde{n}_u^{\alpha 1}\right], \tilde{n}^{\alpha 2} = \left[\tilde{n}_l^{\alpha 2}, \tilde{n}_u^{\alpha 2}\right]. \qquad (14)$$

From Figure 4 we can see that if $\alpha_2 \geq \alpha_1$, then $\tilde{n}_l^{\alpha 2} \geq \tilde{n}_l^{\alpha 1}$ and $\tilde{n}_u^{\alpha 1} \geq \tilde{n}_u^{\alpha 2}$.

Definition 6. *A triangular fuzzy number $\tilde{n}$ can be defined by a triplet (n_1, n_2, n_3) shown in Figure 3. The membership function $\mu_{\tilde{n}}(x)$ is defined as [62]:*

$$\mu_{\tilde{n}}(x) = \begin{cases} 0, & x < n_1 \\ \frac{x-n_1}{n_2-n_1}, & n_1 \leq x \leq n_2 \\ \frac{n_3-x}{n_3-n_2}, & n_2 \leq x \leq n_3 \\ 0, & x > n_3 \end{cases} \quad (15)$$

Definition 7. *If $\tilde{n}$ is a fuzzy number and $\tilde{n}_l^\alpha > 0$ for $\alpha \in [0,1]$, then $\tilde{n}$ is called a positive fuzzy number.*

Given any two positive fuzzy numbers $\tilde{m}, \tilde{n}$ and a positive real number r, the α-cut of two fuzzy numbers are $\tilde{m}^\alpha = [m_l^\alpha, m_u^\alpha]$ and $\tilde{n}^\alpha = [n_l^\alpha, n_u^\alpha]$ ($\alpha \in [0,1]$), respectively. According to the interval of confidence, some main operations of positive fuzzy numbers $\tilde{m}$ and $\tilde{n}$ can be expressed as follows [62]:

$$\left(\tilde{m}(+)\tilde{n}\right)^\alpha = [m_l^\alpha + n_l^\alpha, m_u^\alpha + n_u^\alpha], \quad (16)$$

$$\left(\tilde{m}(-)\tilde{n}\right)^\alpha = [m_l^\alpha - n_u^\alpha, m_u^\alpha - n_l^\alpha], \quad (17)$$

$$\left(\tilde{m}(\cdot)\tilde{n}\right)^\alpha = [m_l^\alpha \cdot n_l^\alpha, m_u^\alpha \cdot n_u^\alpha], \quad (18)$$

$$\left(\tilde{m}(:)\tilde{n}\right)^\alpha = \left[\frac{m_l^\alpha}{n_u^\alpha}, \frac{m_u^\alpha}{n_l^\alpha}\right], \quad (19)$$

$$(\tilde{m}^\alpha)^{-1} = \left[\frac{1}{m_u^\alpha}, \frac{1}{m_l^\alpha}\right], \quad (20)$$

$$\left(\tilde{m}(\cdot)r\right)^\alpha = [m_l^\alpha \cdot r, m_u^\alpha \cdot r], \quad (21)$$

$$\left(\tilde{m}(:)r\right)^\alpha = \left[\frac{m_l^\alpha}{r}, \frac{m_u^\alpha}{r}\right], \quad (22)$$

where r is a constant.

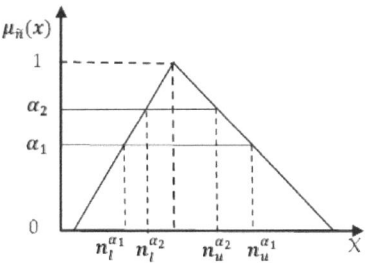

Figure 4. Fuzzy number $\tilde{n}$ with α cuts.

3.3.2. Fuzzy–AROMAN–Fuller Approach

An extension of the AROMAN method [10,11] to the fuzzy environment is proposed in this part. The method is very convenient for solving MCDM problems where more experts are involved in the decision-making process. The procedure will be explained in steps.

Step 1. *Determine the initial decision-making matrix with the input data.*

A fuzzy MCDM problem can be presented in matrix format as:

$$\tilde{D} = \begin{bmatrix} \tilde{x}_{11} & \cdots & \tilde{x}_{1j} & \cdots & \tilde{x}_{1n} \\ \tilde{x}_{21} & \cdots & \tilde{x}_{2j} & \cdots & \tilde{x}_{2n} \\ \vdots & \ddots & \vdots & \ddots & \vdots \\ \tilde{x}_{m1} & \cdots & \tilde{x}_{mj} & \cdots & \tilde{x}_{mn} \end{bmatrix}, i = 1, 2, \ldots, m, j = 1, 2, \ldots, n.$$

where $\tilde{x}_{ij}$ are linguistic variables.

To rate the qualitative criteria, the inputs are linguistic variables. These linguistic variables can be expressed as triangular fuzzy numbers. The scale is offered in Table 3.

Table 3. Linguistic variables for the ratings of criteria.

Linguistic Variable	Fuzzy Number
Very low (VL)	(0,0,1)
Low (L)	(0,1,3)
Medium-low (ML)	(1,3,5)
Medium (M)	(3,5,7)
Medium-high (MH)	(5,7,9)
High (H)	(7,9,10)
Very High (VH)	(9,10,10)

If there are K experts that evaluate the alternatives based on set criteria, then the ratings can be calculated as:

$$\tilde{x}_{ij} = \frac{1}{K}\left[\tilde{x}_{ij}^1(+)\tilde{x}_{ij}^2(+)\ldots(+)\tilde{x}_{ij}^K\right]. \quad (23)$$

In the further procedure, the normalization of data should be carried out. The AROMAN method implies two types of normalization, as explained in Steps 2 and 3.

Step 2. *Normalization No. 1.*

$$\tilde{t}_{ij} = \frac{\tilde{x}_{ij} - \min_i \tilde{x}_{ij}}{\max_i \tilde{x}_{ij} - \min_i \tilde{x}_{ij}}, i = 1, 2, \ldots, m; j = 1, 2, \ldots, n; \quad (24)$$

Step 3. *Normalization No. 2.*

$$\tilde{t}_{ij}^* = \frac{\tilde{x}_{ij}}{\sqrt{\sum_{i=1}^m \tilde{x}_{ij}^2}}; i = 1, 2, \ldots, m; j = 1, 2, \ldots, n; \quad (25)$$

As it is generally known, in MCDM problems certain criteria should be minimized, also known as cost criteria, and the others should be maximized, often named as benefit criteria. The normalization procedure in Steps 2 and 3 should be applied for both criteria types (min and max).

Step 4. *Aggregated normalization.*

The aggregated normalization is obtained by Equation (25).

$$\tilde{t}_{ij}^{norm} = \frac{\beta \tilde{t}_{ij} + (1-\beta)\tilde{t}_{ij}^*}{2}; i = 1, 2, \ldots, m; j = 1, 2, \ldots, n; \quad (26)$$

where $\tilde{t}_{ij}^{norm}$ denotes the aggregated averaged normalization. β is a weighting factor for each type of normalization varying from 0 to 1.

Step 5. *Weighted aggregated normalized decision-making matrix.*

In this step, the aggregated normalized decision-making (DM) matrix should be multiplied by the criteria weights to obtain a weighted DM matrix. Here, the weights of criteria are determined by the previously explained Fuller triangle method.

$$\hat{\tilde{t}}_{ij} = W_{ij} \cdot \tilde{t}_{ij}^{norm} \quad ; i = 1, 2, \ldots, m; j = 1, 2, \ldots, n; \tag{27}$$

Step 6. *Summation of weighted aggregated normalized DM per the criteria type.*

Further procedure relates to a summation of the normalized weighted values separately for the criteria type min $(\tilde{L}_i)$ and the type max $(\tilde{A}_i)$.

$$\tilde{L}_i \sum_{j=1}^{n} \hat{\tilde{t}}_{ij}^{(min)} \quad ; i = 1, 2, \ldots, m; j = 1, 2, \ldots, n; \tag{28}$$

$$\tilde{A}_i \sum_{j=1}^{n} \hat{\tilde{t}}_{ij}^{(max)} \quad ; i = 1, 2, \ldots, m; j = 1, 2, \ldots, n; \tag{29}$$

Step 7. *Raise the obtained $\tilde{L}_i$ and $\tilde{A}_i$ values to the degree of λ.*

$$\hat{\tilde{L}}_i = \tilde{L}_i^{\lambda} = \left(\sum_{j=1}^{n} \hat{\tilde{t}}_{ij}^{(min)} \right)^{\lambda} \quad ; i = 1, 2, \ldots, m; j = 1, 2, \ldots, n; \tag{30}$$

$$\hat{\tilde{A}}_i = \tilde{A}_i^{1-\lambda} = \left(\sum_{j=1}^{n} \hat{\tilde{t}}_{ij}^{(max)} \right)^{1-\lambda} \quad ; i = 1, 2, \ldots, m; j = 1, 2, \ldots, n; \tag{31}$$

where λ represents the coefficient degree of the criterion type. Parameter λ can be determined in different ways; however, we propose using the weights obtained by the Fuller triangle method. If we mark the weights of the criteria of min type by w_j^{min}, then the parameter λ can be obtained by Equation (31).

$$\lambda = \sum_{j=1}^{n} w_j^{min}; j = 1, 2, \ldots, n \tag{32}$$

Step 8. *Calculate the final ranking.*

To obtain the final ranking of alternatives (R_i), the difference between the values $\hat{\tilde{A}}_i$ and $\hat{\tilde{L}}_i$ should be calculated and the final ranking equation applied.

$$R_i = e^{(\hat{\tilde{A}}_i - \hat{\tilde{L}}_i)}; i = 1, 2, \ldots, m \tag{33}$$

4. Case Study

To demonstrate the applicability of the proposed methodology, we provide an illustrative numerical example. Let us suppose that the task to be solved is to select the most appropriate bus driver from the three candidates who applied for the job. The candidates can be considered the alternatives in the MCDM process, and we denote them as A1, A2, and A3. The criteria that are used for the evaluation of candidates are identified in the literature. According to the model, the number of criteria should be reduced to seven. This will be completed by interviewing the experts from the field and implementing the Fuller triangle method which gives the importance rank for each considered criterion. However, additional information about the criteria and their interdependence can be obtained by the DEMATEL method.

Since both the DEMATEL and the Fuller triangle method belong to the group of subjective methods, the first task in their implementation is to identify and interview the appropriate experts. In this case study, we collected the answers from three experts. The first is from the field of Traffic psychology and the other two are experts in Road traffic safety. All experts have more than 15 years of professional experience. They also possess Ph.D. degrees.

4.1. The Results of the DEMATEL Method

As explained in the methodology section, there are four steps in the DEMATEL implementation.

Step 1. The experts assessed the interdependence between the criteria in the pair-wise comparisons and gave marks from 0 to 4 depending on the type of relation. Their answers are presented in Tables A1, A3 and A5 in Appendices A–C. Based on these answers, we formed the direct-relation matrix, as shown in Table 4.

Table 4. The direct-relation matrix.

	C1	C2	C3	C4	C5	C6	C7	C8	C9	C10	C11	C12	C13	C14
C1	0.00	1.33	1.00	0.00	1.00	0.00	0.67	1.00	0.67	0.67	0.67	1.33	0.67	0.67
C2	1.67	0.00	2.33	0.67	0.67	0.67	0.33	0.67	0.67	1.00	1.33	0.67	0.33	0.00
C3	0.67	0.67	0.00	0.33	1.00	0.67	0.00	0.00	0.00	0.00	0.00	1.00	0.67	0.00
C4	0.00	0.67	2.67	0.00	1.00	1.00	0.67	1.00	0.00	0.00	1.00	0.67	0.00	0.00
C5	1.00	1.33	2.33	0.67	0.00	0.00	0.33	1.67	0.67	0.67	2.33	1.00	0.67	0.00
C6	0.00	1.00	1.33	0.67	0.67	0.00	0.00	0.33	0.33	0.33	1.00	0.00	0.00	0.00
C7	0.67	0.67	0.33	0.67	0.67	0.00	0.00	1.67	1.00	0.67	1.67	1.00	0.00	0.00
C8	1.00	0.67	0.33	1.00	2.33	0.00	0.33	0.00	1.67	2.33	2.00	1.67	0.33	0.33
C9	0.67	0.67	0.00	0.00	1.00	0.67	0.67	1.67	0.00	2.67	0.67	0.00	0.00	0.67
C10	0.67	1.00	0.00	0.00	1.00	0.00	0.67	2.00	2.67	0.00	1.00	0.00	0.00	0.67
C11	0.67	0.67	1.00	1.00	1.67	0.67	0.00	1.67	0.67	0.67	0.00	1.00	0.67	0.67
C12	0.33	0.67	1.33	1.00	1.00	0.00	0.67	1.67	0.00	0.00	1.00	0.00	1.67	0.00
C13	0.67	0.67	0.67	0.00	1.00	0.00	0.00	0.67	0.00	0.00	1.00	1.33	0.00	0.00
C14	0.33	0.33	0.00	0.00	0.00	0.00	0.00	0.67	1.33	1.33	1.33	0.00	0.00	0.00

Step 2. The normalized direct-relation matrix X is calculated according to Equations (2) and (3). The resulting matrix is in Table 5.

Table 5. The normalized direct-relation matrix.

	C1	C2	C3	C4	C5	C6	C7	C8	C9	C10	C11	C12	C13	C14
C1	0.00	0.10	0.07	0.00	0.07	0.00	0.05	0.07	0.05	0.05	0.05	0.10	0.05	0.05
C2	0.12	0.00	0.17	0.05	0.05	0.05	0.02	0.05	0.05	0.07	0.10	0.05	0.02	0.00
C3	0.05	0.05	0.00	0.02	0.07	0.05	0.00	0.00	0.00	0.00	0.00	0.07	0.05	0.00
C4	0.00	0.05	0.19	0.00	0.07	0.07	0.05	0.07	0.00	0.00	0.07	0.05	0.00	0.00
C5	0.07	0.10	0.17	0.05	0.00	0.00	0.02	0.12	0.05	0.05	0.17	0.07	0.05	0.00
C6	0.00	0.07	0.10	0.05	0.05	0.00	0.00	0.02	0.02	0.02	0.07	0.00	0.00	0.00
C7	0.05	0.05	0.02	0.05	0.05	0.00	0.00	0.12	0.07	0.05	0.12	0.07	0.00	0.00
C8	0.07	0.05	0.02	0.07	0.17	0.00	0.02	0.00	0.12	0.17	0.14	0.12	0.02	0.02
C9	0.05	0.05	0.00	0.00	0.07	0.05	0.05	0.12	0.00	0.19	0.05	0.00	0.00	0.05
C10	0.05	0.07	0.00	0.00	0.07	0.00	0.05	0.14	0.19	0.00	0.07	0.00	0.00	0.05
C11	0.05	0.05	0.07	0.07	0.12	0.05	0.00	0.12	0.05	0.05	0.00	0.07	0.05	0.05
C12	0.02	0.05	0.10	0.07	0.07	0.00	0.05	0.12	0.00	0.00	0.07	0.00	0.12	0.00
C13	0.05	0.05	0.05	0.00	0.07	0.00	0.00	0.05	0.00	0.00	0.07	0.10	0.00	0.00
C14	0.02	0.02	0.00	0.00	0.00	0.00	0.00	0.05	0.10	0.10	0.10	0.00	0.00	0.00

Step 3. We calculated the total-relation matrix (Table 6) by using MATLAB software. It is applied also to create a causal diagram in the fourth step.

Table 6. The total-relation matrix.

	C1	C2	C3	C4	C5	C6	C7	C8	C9	C10	C11	C12	C13	C14
C1	0.11	0.21	0.22	0.08	0.23	0.04	0.10	0.24	0.16	0.18	0.22	0.22	0.12	0.09
C2	0.23	0.14	0.33	0.13	0.23	0.10	0.08	0.23	0.16	0.19	0.26	0.18	0.10	0.05
C3	0.10	0.11	0.09	0.06	0.15	0.07	0.03	0.08	0.05	0.05	0.09	0.13	0.09	0.02
C4	0.09	0.15	0.32	0.07	0.21	0.11	0.08	0.20	0.08	0.09	0.21	0.16	0.07	0.03
C5	0.21	0.25	0.36	0.15	0.23	0.07	0.09	0.33	0.19	0.21	0.37	0.24	0.15	0.05
C6	0.07	0.14	0.19	0.09	0.14	0.03	0.03	0.12	0.08	0.09	0.16	0.07	0.04	0.02
C7	0.16	0.17	0.18	0.13	0.22	0.05	0.06	0.30	0.19	0.19	0.29	0.20	0.08	0.05
C8	0.23	0.23	0.26	0.19	0.41	0.07	0.11	0.28	0.30	0.35	0.39	0.29	0.13	0.09
C9	0.16	0.18	0.15	0.08	0.24	0.09	0.11	0.30	0.16	0.33	0.23	0.12	0.06	0.10
C10	0.17	0.20	0.16	0.09	0.26	0.05	0.11	0.34	0.33	0.18	0.26	0.13	0.07	0.10
C11	0.17	0.19	0.25	0.16	0.30	0.10	0.06	0.30	0.18	0.19	0.20	0.21	0.13	0.09
C12	0.13	0.16	0.25	0.15	0.23	0.05	0.09	0.27	0.10	0.11	0.23	0.13	0.19	0.03
C13	0.12	0.13	0.16	0.06	0.18	0.03	0.03	0.16	0.07	0.08	0.18	0.18	0.06	0.02
C14	0.09	0.10	0.08	0.04	0.11	0.03	0.04	0.16	0.18	0.19	0.19	0.07	0.04	0.03

Step 4. A causal diagram is formed based on D and R values calculated by Equations (6) and (7) and obtained values are in Table 7. Finally, a causal diagram is shown in Figure 5.

Table 7. D and R values.

Criterion	D Values	R Values	$D + R$	$D - R$
C1	2.2332	2.0404	4.2736	0.1928
C2	2.3986	2.3421	4.7407	0.0565
C3	1.1113	3.0015	4.1129	−1.8902
C4	1.8706	1.4894	3.3600	0.3813
C5	2.8875	3.1333	6.0208	−0.2458
C6	1.2819	0.8855	2.1674	0.3964
C7	2.2486	1.0195	3.2681	1.2292
C8	3.3333	3.3073	6.6406	0.0259
C9	2.3082	2.2282	4.5364	0.0800
C10	2.4422	2.4269	4.8691	0.0153
C11	2.5329	3.2905	5.8234	−0.7577
C12	2.1374	2.3323	4.4697	−0.1949
C13	1.4515	1.3153	2.7668	0.1362
C14	1.3436	0.7686	2.1122	0.5750

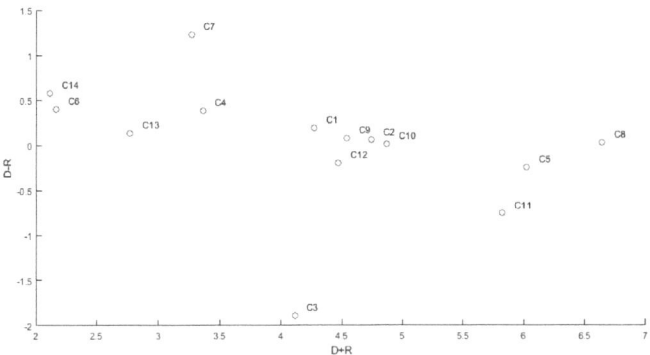

Figure 5. A causal diagram.

As can be noticed from Figure 5, criteria C3, C5, C11, and C12 belong to the effect group, while the others are in the cause group. Since we can conclude about a relatively low interdependence between the criteria, this is a good prerequisite to conducting the Fuller triangle method.

4.2. The Results of the Fuller Triangle Method

The procedure is carried out according to the previous methodological explanation.

Step 1. We formed a triangular structure where 14 criteria were involved. Such a form was offered to the experts and they were asked to make pairwise comparisons of criteria in the case of the bus driver selection problem. Their answers are presented in Tables A2, A4 and A6 in Appendices A–C. The fields marked with green color are their choices.

Step 2. Further procedure implies counting the collected answers. In Table 8, Columns 3, 5, and 7, are the point that each criterion received by experts 1, 2, and 3, respectively.

Step 3. The relevance ranks (w_j) are calculated for each criterion and each expert and presented in Table 8, Columns 4, 6, and 8.

Step 4. The final relevance ranks are obtained. They are presented in the final column of Table 8, as well as in Figure 6, where they are aligned in descending order to easier notice the first seven that will be used in the further calculations.

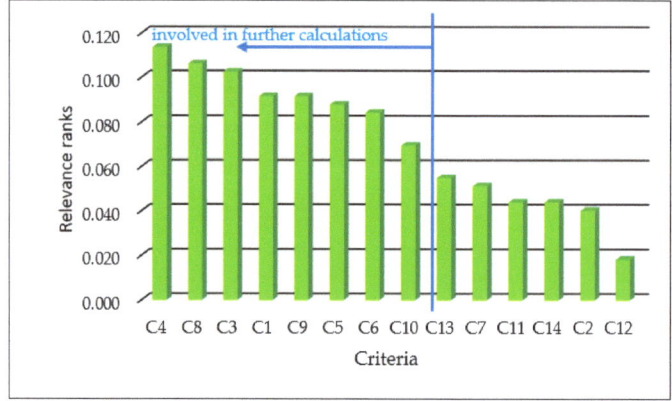

Figure 6. Descending order of the relevance ranks of criteria.

Table 8. The relevance ranks of criteria obtained by the Fuller triangle method.

No.	Criteria	Number of Preferences by Expert 1	w_j Based on Expert 1	Number of Preferences by Expert 2	w_j Based on Expert 2	Number of Preferences by Expert 3	w_j Based on Expert 3	Final w_j
1.	Attention	9	0.099	8	0.088	8	0.088	0.092
2.	Fatigue resistance	1	0.011	4	0.044	6	0.066	0.040
3.	Reaction time	9	0.099	9	0.099	10	0.110	0.103
4.	Visual abilities	10	0.110	10	0.110	11	0.121	0.114
5.	Speed estimation	8	0.088	8	0.088	8	0.088	0.088
6.	Physical fitness	8	0.088	7	0.077	8	0.088	0.084
7.	Driving experience	4	0.044	4	0.044	6	0.066	0.051
8.	Risk assessment	9	0.099	10	0.110	10	0.110	0.106
9.	Impulsiveness	9	0.099	8	0.088	8	0.088	0.092
10.	Aggressiveness	6	0.066	7	0.077	6	0.066	0.070
11.	Self-assessment of driving ability	6	0.066	4	0.044	2	0.022	0.044
12.	Space capabilities	2	0.022	2	0.022	1	0.011	0.018
13.	Intelligence	6	0.066	6	0.066	3	0.033	0.055
14.	Morality	4	0.044	4	0.044	4	0.044	0.044
	Total	91	1	91	1	91	1	1

To check the reliability of the obtained results, we interviewed the experts in the second round to collect information about the percentage distribution of criteria importance. The results are shown in Table 9. As it can be concluded, the rate of inconsistency is below 0.1 ($RI = 0.07$), which means that reliability is satisfactory.

Table 9. Calculation of the rate of inconsistency.

Criteria	w_j	Expert 1 [%]	Expert 2 [%]	Expert 3 [%]	Average Assessment—p_j	$\|w_j*100 - p_j\|$	RI_j
C1	0.092	12	10	13	11.667	1.777	0.0178
C2	0.040	2	1	3	2.000	0.901	0.0090
C3	0.103	10	10	8	9.333	0.557	0.0056
C4	0.114	10	12	11	11.000	0.011	0.0001
C5	0.088	9	9	10	9.333	0.542	0.0054
C6	0.084	8	9	9	8.667	0.125	0.0012
C7	0.051	5	4	5	4.667	0.271	0.0027
C8	0.106	9	10	9	9.333	0.557	0.0056
C9	0.092	9	10	10	9.667	0.223	0.0022
C10	0.070	6	6	8	6.667	0.073	0.0007
C11	0.044	6	7	5	6.000	0.593	0.0059
C12	0.018	3	2	2	2.333	0.136	0.0014
C13	0.055	7	6	4	5.667	0.927	0.0093
C14	0.044	4	4	3	3.667	0.729	0.0073
							$RI = 0.0742$

4.3. The Results of a Hybridized Fuzzy–AROMAN–Fuller Approach

As we mentioned, the subject of the case study is a bus-operating company that needs to hire a bus driver. Three potential candidates are marked by A1, A2, and A3, the interviewed experts by E1, E2, and E3, and set evaluation criteria from C1 to C14, where only seven of them are considered in this part of the model. The structure of the considered MCDM problem is shown in Figure 7.

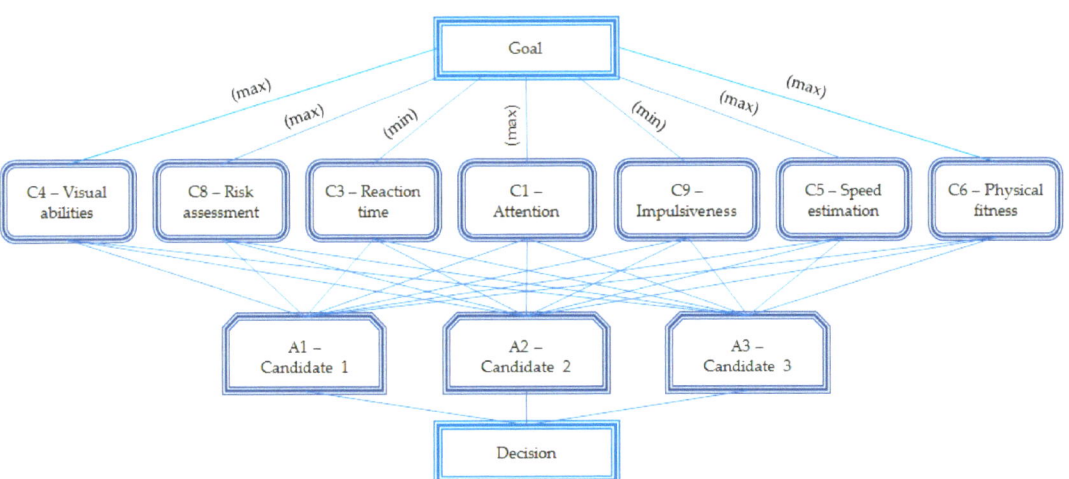

Figure 7. The structure of the MCDM problem.

The implementation of the Fuzzy–AROMAN–Fuller approach for solving the mentioned problem is presented in steps, as previously explained in the methodological section.

Step 1. *Let us suppose that the experts use linguistic variables to evaluate the alternatives and that their answers form the initial decision-making matrix as shown in Table 10. The linguistic inputs are converted to fuzzy numbers following the rules presented in Table 3. The fuzzy decision matrix that is averaged by Equation (23) is shown in Table 11.*

Table 10. The ratings of candidates.

Criteria	Candidates	Experts		
		E1	E2	E3
C4	A1	H	M	M
	A2	VH	H	H
	A3	H	H	MH
C8	A1	M	MH	M
	A2	MH	H	H
	A3	ML	M	M
C3	A1	H	MH	MH
	A2	L	VL	L
	A3	M	ML	ML
C1	A1	H	MH	M
	A2	M	H	H
	A3	VH	H	H
C9	A1	M	M	M
	A2	MH	M	M
	A3	H	MH	MH
C5	A1	MH	M	M
	A2	H	MH	H
	A3	VH	H	MH
C6	A1	M	ML	ML
	A2	M	H	MH
	A3	MH	M	MH

Table 11. The fuzzy decision matrix.

	C4	C8	C3	C1	C9	C5	C6
A1	(4.33, 6.33, 8)	(3.67, 5.67, 7.67)	(5.67, 7.67, 9.33)	(5, 7, 8.67)	(3, 5, 7)	(3.67, 5.67, 7.67)	(1.67, 3.67, 5.67)
A2	(7.67, 9.33, 10)	(6.33, 8.33, 9.67)	(0, 0.67, 2.33)	(5.67, 7.67, 9)	(3.67, 5.67, 7.67)	(6.33, 8.33, 9.67)	(5, 7, 8.67)
A3	(6.33, 8.33, 9.67)	(2.33, 4.33, 6.33)	(1.67, 3.67, 5.67)	(7.67, 9.33, 10)	(5.67, 7.67, 9.33)	(7, 8.67, 9.67)	(4.33, 6.33, 8.33)

Step 2. *Normalization No. 1 is performed and the obtained results are shown in Table 12.*

Table 12. Normalization No. 1 of the fuzzy decision matrix.

	C4	C8	C3	C1	C9	C5	C6
A1	(0, 0.35, 0.65)	(0.18, 0.45, 0.73)	(0.61, 0.82, 1)	(0, 0.4, 0.73)	(0, 0.32, 0.63)	(0, 0.33, 0.67)	(0, 0.28, 0.57)
A2	(0.59, 0.88, 1)	(0.54, 0.82, 1)	(0, 0.07, 0.25)	(0.13, 0.53, 0.8)	(0.11, 0.42, 0.74)	(0.44, 0.78, 1)	(0.48, 0.76, 1)
A3	(0.35, 0.71, 0.94)	(0, 0.27, 0.55)	(0.18, 0.39, 0.61)	(0.53, 0.87, 1)	(0.42, 0.74, 1)	(0.56, 0.83, 1)	(0.38, 0.67, 0.95)

Step 3. *Normalization No. 2 is complete and the obtained results are in Table 13.*

Table 13. Normalization No. 2 of the fuzzy decision matrix.

	C4	C8	C3	C1	C9	C5	C6
A1	(0.27, 0.45, 0.74)	(0.26, 0.52, 0.99)	(0.51, 0.90, 1.58)	(0.31, 0.50, 0.81)	(0.21, 0.46, 0.95)	(0.23, 0.43, 0.76)	(0.13, 0.36, 0.83)
A2	(0.48, 0.67, 0.92)	(0.45, 0.76, 1.26)	(0, 0.08, 0.39)	(0.35, 0.55, 0.84)	(0.26, 0.53, 1.04)	(0.40, 0.63, 0.95)	(0.38, 0.69, 1.27)
A3	(0.39, 0.59, 0.89)	(0.17, 0.39, 0.82)	(0.14, 0.43, 0.96)	(0.48, 0.67, 0.93)	(0.41, 0.71, 1.26)	(0.47, 0.65, 0.95)	(0.32, 0.63, 1.22)

Step 4. *The aggregated normalization is calculated by Equation (26), where we considered the parameter β to be 0.5. The results are in Table 14.*

Table 14. Aggregated normalization of the fuzzy decision matrix.

	C4	C8	C3	C1	C9	C5	C6
A1	(0.14, 0.40, 0.69)	(0.22, 0.49, 0.86)	(0.55, 0.86, 1.29)	(0.16, 0.45, 0.77)	(0.21, 0.46, 0.95)	(0.12, 0.38, 0.71)	(0.06, 0.32, 0.70)
A2	(0.53, 0.77, 0.96)	(0.50, 0.79, 1.13)	(0, 0.07, 0.32)	(0.24, 0.54, 0.82)	(0.26, 0.53, 1.04)	(0.42, 0.70, 0.98)	(0.43, 0.73, 1.14)
A3	(0.37, 0.65, 0.92)	(0.08, 0.33, 0.68)	(0.16, 0.41, 0.78)	(0.51, 0.77, 0.96)	(0.41, 0.71, 1.26)	(0.50, 0.74, 0.98)	(0.35, 0.65, 1.09)

Step 5. *Next, the weighted fuzzy decision-making matrix is formed. We used the weights obtained by the Fuller triangle method; however, since the number of criteria is reduced from 14 to 7, we arranged the sum of the remaining 7 weights to be equal to 1. The resulting weighted matrix is shown in Table 15.*

Table 15. The weighted fuzzy decision matrix.

	C4	C8	C3	C1	C9	C5	C6
A1	(0.02, 0.07, 0.12)	(0.03, 0.08, 0.14)	(0.08, 0.13, 0.20)	(0.02, 0.06, 0.10)	(0.01, 0.05, 0.10)	(0.02, 0.05, 0.09)	(0.01, 0.04, 0.09)
A2	(0.09, 0.13, 0.16)	(0.08, 0.12, 0.18)	(0, 0.01, 0.05)	(0.03, 0.07, 0.11)	(0.02, 0.06, 0.12)	(0.06, 0.09, 0.13)	(0.05, 0.09, 0.14)
A3	(0.06, 0.11, 0.15)	(0.01, 0.05, 0.11)	(0.02, 0.06, 0.12)	(0.07, 0.10, 0.13)	(0.06, 0.10, 0.15)	(0.06, 0.10, 0.13)	(0.04, 0.08, 0.13)

Step 6. *In this step, the summation of the weighted aggregated normalized fuzzy decision-making matrix should be completed per the criteria type. In our case, the min type criteria are C3 and C9, while the max type criteria are C4, C8, C1, C5, and C6.*

Step 7. *The sums from Step 6 should be raised to the degree of λ, which is in our case, according to Equation (32) equal to 0.29. The obtained values are in Table 16.*

Table 16. Summation of weighted fuzzy decision matrix per the criteria type.

	$\tilde{L}_i^\wedge$	$\tilde{A}_i^\wedge$
A1	(0.52, 0.61, 0.71)	(0.20, 0.42, 0.64)
A2	(0.35, 0.48, 0.60)	(0.43, 0.62, 0.79)
A3	(0.49, 0.59, 0.69)	(0.38, 0.56, 0.74)

Step 8. *In the final step, we calculate the final ranking by Equation (33). As shown in Table 17, the results of implemented method indicate that the best candidate is A2, followed by A3 and A1.*

Table 17. Final ranking.

	R_i
A1	0.82
A2	1.15
A3	0.97

5. Conclusions

The problem of personnel selection is very complex, bearing in mind that multiple criteria should be considered in the candidate evaluation process. The task is even more complicated when it comes to demanding jobs, such is the job of a professional driver. There is often a need to manipulate uncertain or imprecise data. In this paper, we demonstrated how a hybridized Fuzzy–AROMAN–Fuller approach can be successfully used to solve the considered problem.

This research resulted in several contributions. First of all, by reviewing the literature from the field of traffic psychology, road safety, and personnel selection, we identified the criteria that should be used in the process of professional driver selection. Further, we interviewed the experts to determine the relevance ranks of the set criteria. We interviewed three eminent experts from the field of road traffic safety and traffic psychology; however, a direction for future research can be to include more experts in the research and to compare the results. Finally, for the first time in the literature, we applied the AROMAN method in a fuzzy environment. We further couple it with the Fuller triangle method. By solving a numerical example, we demonstrated the applicability of the proposed model. Additional paths for future research can be directed toward comparing the obtained results with some other MCDM approaches. For example, the criteria weights can be determined by AHP and coupled with the AROMAN method, or the final ranking of alternatives can be performed by some other MCDM method and be compared with the AROMAN.

Although we demonstrated the proposed model on the example of a professional driver selection problem, this model is general and can be applied to many other problems. These problems can relate to personnel selection in other fields; however, a hybridized Fuzzy–AROMAN–Fuller approach can be implemented for solving any other MCDM problem.

Author Contributions: Conceptualization, M.Č.-D. and S.J.; methodology, M.Č.-D., S.J. and S.B.; software, D.B.; validation, M.Č.-D., S.J. and S.B.; formal analysis, M.Č.-D. and S.B.; investigation, S.J. and S.B.; resources, M.Č.-D.; data curation, M.Č.-D. and D.B.; writing—original draft preparation, M.Č.-D. and S.J.; writing—review and editing, S.B. and D.B.; visualization, S.J.; supervision, M.Č.-D.; project administration, D.B. All authors have read and agreed to the published version of the manuscript.

Funding: This work was supported in part by the Research Program SGS_2023_017.

Data Availability Statement: All research data are presented in this paper, in the main part and appendices as well.

Acknowledgments: The authors are grateful for the valuable comments of the Editors, and the two anonymous reviewers, who helped to improve the manuscript greatly.

Conflicts of Interest: The authors declare no conflict of interest.

Appendix A. Answers from Expert 1

Table A1. Answers related to the DEMATEL method from Expert 1.

	C1	C2	C3	C4	C5	C6	C7	C8	C9	C10	C11	C12	C13	C14
C1	0	2	1	0	1	0	1	1	1	1	1	1	1	1
C2	2	0	2	1	1	1	1	1	1	1	2	1	1	0
C3	1	1	0	1	1	1	0	0	0	0	0	1	1	0
C4	0	1	3	0	1	1	1	1	0	0	1	1	0	0
C5	1	1	2	1	0	0	1	2	1	1	2	1	0	0
C6	0	1	1	1	0	0	0	0	0	0	1	0	0	0
C7	0	1	0	1	2	0	0	2	1	1	2	1	0	0
C8	1	1	0	1	2	0	1	0	2	2	2	2	1	1
C9	1	1	0	0	1	2	1	2	0	3	1	0	0	1
C10	1	1	0	0	1	0	1	2	3	0	1	0	0	1
C11	1	0	1	1	2	1	0	2	1	1	0	1	1	1
C12	1	1	1	1	1	0	1	2	0	0	1	0	2	0
C13	1	1	1	0	1	0	0	1	0	0	1	2	0	0
C14	0	0	0	0	0	0	0	1	1	1	1	0	0	0

Table A2. Answers related to the Fuller triangle method from Expert 1.

C1	**C1**	**C1**	**C1**	**C1**	**C1**	**C1**	**C1**	**C1**	**C1**	**C1**	**C1**	**C1**	**C1**
C2	C3	C4	C5	C6	C7	C8	C9	C10	C11	C12	C13	C14	
C2	**C2**	**C2**	**C2**	**C2**	**C2**	**C2**	**C2**	**C2**	**C2**	**C2**	**C2**		
C3	C4	C5	C6	C7	C8	C9	C10	C11	C12	C13	C14		
C3	C3	C3	C3	C3	C3	C3	C3	**C3**	**C3**				
C4	C5	C6	C7	C8	C9	C10	C11	C12	C13	**C14**			
C4	C4	C4	**C4**	**C4**	**C4**	**C4**	**C4**	**C4**					
C5	C6	C7	C8	C9	C10	C11	C12	C13	C14				
C5	C5	C5	C5	**C5**	**C5**	**C5**	**C5**						
C6	C7	C8	C9	C10	C11	C12	C13	**C14**					
C6	C6	C6	**C6**	C6	**C6**	**C6**							
C7	C8	C9	C10	C11	C12	C13	**C14**						
C7	C7	C7	C7	C7	**C7**								
C8	C9	C10	C11	C12	C13	**C14**							
C8	C8	C8	C8	C8									
C9	C10	C11	C12	C13	**C14**								
C9	**C9**												
C10	C11	C12	C13	**C14**									
C10	C10	C10	C10										
C11	C12	C13	**C14**										
C11	C11	C11											
C12	C13	**C14**											
C12	C12												
C13	**C14**												
C13													
C14													

The green color indicates the answer of the expert, i.e., which criterion is more important in a pair-wise comparison.

Appendix B. Answers from Expert 2

Table A3. Answers related to the DEMATEL method from Expert 2.

	C1	C2	C3	C4	C5	C6	C7	C8	C9	C10	C11	C12	C13	C14
C1	0	1	1	0	1	0	0	1	0	0	0	2	0	0
C2	1	0	2	1	1	0	0	1	1	1	0	0	0	0
C3	0	0	0	0	1	0	0	0	0	0	0	1	1	0
C4	0	0	2	0	1	1	1	1	0	0	1	0	0	0
C5	1	2	3	0	0	0	0	2	1	1	3	1	1	0
C6	0	1	1	0	1	0	0	0	1	1	1	0	0	0
C7	1	0	0	1	0	0	0	2	1	0	1	1	0	0
C8	1	0	1	1	3	0	0	0	2	2	2	2	0	0
C9	0	0	0	0	1	0	0	1	0	4	0	0	0	1
C10	0	1	0	0	1	0	0	2	4	0	1	0	0	1
C11	0	1	1	1	2	1	0	2	1	1	0	1	1	1
C12	0	1	1	1	1	0	1	2	0	0	1	0	2	0
C13	1	1	0	0	1	0	0	1	0	0	1	2	0	0
C14	0	0	0	0	0	0	0	0	1	1	1	0	0	0

Table A4. Answers related to the Fuller triangle method from Expert 2.

Col 1	Col 2	Col 3	Col 4	Col 5	Col 6	Col 7	Col 8	Col 9	Col 10	Col 11	Col 12	Col 13	Col 14
C1	C1	C1	C1	C1	C1	C1	C1	C1	C1	C1	C1	C1	C1
C2	C3	C4	**C5**	**C6**	C7	C8	C9	C10	C11	C12	**C13**	C14	
C2	C2	C2	C2	C2	C2	C2	C2	C2	C2	C2	C2		
C3	**C4**	**C5**	C6	C7	C8	C9	C10	C11	C12	C13	C14		
C3	**C3**	**C3**	**C3**	**C3**	**C3**	**C3**	**C3**	**C3**	**C3**				
C4	**C5**	**C6**	C7	C8	C9	C10	C11	C12	C13	C14			
C4	**C4**	**C4**	**C4**	**C4**	**C4**	**C4**	**C4**	**C4**					
C5	**C6**	**C7**	C8	C9	C10	C11	C12	**C13**	C14				
C5	**C5**	**C5**	**C5**	**C5**	**C5**	**C5**	**C5**						
C6	C7	**C8**	C9	C10	C11	C12	C13	C14					
C6	**C6**	**C6**	**C6**	**C6**	**C6**	**C6**							
C7	**C8**	**C9**	C10	C11	C12	C13	C14						
C7	**C7**	**C7**	**C7**	**C7**	**C7**	**C7**							
C8	C9	C10	C11	C12	C13	C14							
C8	**C8**	**C8**	**C8**	**C8**									
C9	C10	C11	C12	C13	C14								
C9	**C9**	**C9**	**C9**										
C10	C11	C12	C13	C14									
C10	**C10**	**C10**	**C10**										
C11	C12	C13	C14										
C11	**C11**	**C11**											
C12	C13	C14											
C12	**C12**												
C13	**C14**												
C13													
C14													

The green color indicates the answer of the expert, i.e. which criterion is more important in a pair-wise comparison.

Appendix C. Answers from Expert 3

Table A5. Answers related to the DEMATEL method from Expert 3.

	C1	C2	C3	C4	C5	C6	C7	C8	C9	C10	C11	C12	C13	C14
C1	0	1	1	0	1	0	1	1	1	1	1	1	1	1
C2	2	0	3	0	0	1	0	0	0	1	2	1	0	0
C3	1	1	0	0	1	1	0	0	0	0	0	1	0	0
C4	0	1	3	0	1	1	0	1	0	0	1	1	0	0
C5	1	1	2	1	0	0	0	1	0	0	2	1	1	0
C6	0	1	2	1	1	0	0	1	0	0	1	0	0	0
C7	1	1	1	0	0	0	0	1	1	1	2	1	0	0
C8	1	1	0	1	2	0	0	0	1	3	2	1	0	0
C9	1	1	0	0	1	0	1	2	0	1	1	0	0	0
C10	1	1	0	0	1	0	1	2	1	0	1	0	0	0
C11	1	1	1	1	1	0	0	1	0	0	0	1	0	0
C12	0	0	2	1	1	0	0	1	0	0	1	0	1	0
C13	0	0	1	0	1	0	0	0	0	0	1	0	0	0
C14	1	1	0	0	0	0	0	1	2	2	2	0	0	0

Table A6. Answers related to the Fuller triangle method from Expert 3.

C1	C1	C1	C1	C1	C1	C1	C1	C1	C1	C1	C1	C1	C1
C2	C3	C4	C5	C6	C7	C8	C9	C10	C11	C12	C13	C14	
C2	C2	C2	C2	C2	C2	C2	C2	C2	C2	C2	C2	C2	
C3	C4	C5	C6	C7	C8	C9	C10	C11	C12	C13	C14		
C3	C3	C3	C3	C3	C3	C3	C3	C3	C3	C3	C3		
C4	C5	C6	C7	C8	C9	C10	C11	C12	C13	C14			
C4	C4	C4	C4	C4	C4	C4	C4	C4					
C5	C6	C7	C8	C9	C10	C11	C12	C13	C14				
C5	C5	C5	C5	C5	C5	C5	C5						
C6	C7	C8	C9	C10	C11	C12	C13	C14					
C6	C6	C6	C6	C6	C6	C6							
C7	C8	C9	C10	C11	C12	C13	C14						
C7	C7	C7	C7	C7	C7	C7							
C8	C9	C10	C11	C12	C13	C14							
C8	C8	C8	C8	C8									
C9	C10	C11	C12	C13	C14								
C9	C9	C9	C9										
C10	C11	C12	C13	C14									
C10	C10	C10	C10										
C11	C12	C13	C14										
C11	C11	C11											
C12	C13	C14											
C12	C12												
C13	C14												
C13													
C14													

The green color indicates the answer of the expert, i.e. which criterion is more important in a pair-wise comparison.

References

1. World Health Organization. *Global Status Report on Road Safety 2018*; World Health Organization: Geneva, Switzerland, 2018.
2. Debnath, P. A QGIS-Based Road Network Analysis for Sustainable Road Network Infrastructure: An Application to the Cachar District in Assam, India. *Infrastructures* **2022**, *7*, 114. [CrossRef]
3. Cai, Q. Cause Analysis of Traffic Accidents on Urban Roads Based on an Improved Association Rule Mining Algorithm. *IEEE Access* **2020**, *8*, 75607–75615. [CrossRef]
4. Čubranić-Dobrodolac, M.; Švadlenka, L.; Čičević, S.; Dobrodolac, M. Modelling Driver Propensity for Traffic Accidents: A Comparison of Multiple Regression Analysis and Fuzzy Approach. *Int. J. Inj. Contr. Saf. Promot.* **2019**, *27*, 156–167. [CrossRef] [PubMed]
5. Čubranić-Dobrodolac, M.; Lipovac, K.; Čičević, S.; Antić, B. A Model for Traffic Accidents Prediction Based on Driver Personality Traits Assessment. *Promet—TrafficTransport.* **2017**, *29*, 631–642. [CrossRef]
6. Crizzle, A.M.; Bigelow, P.; Adams, D.; Gooderham, S.; Myers, A.M.; Thiffault, P. Health and Wellness of Long-Haul Truck and Bus Drivers: A Systematic Literature Review and Directions for Future Research. *J. Transp. Health* **2017**, *7*, 90–109. [CrossRef]
7. Stojčić, M.; Zavadskas, E.K.; Pamučar, D.; Stević, Ž.; Mardani, A. Application of MCDM Methods in Sustainability Engineering: A Literature Review 2008–2018. *Symmetry* **2019**, *11*, 350. [CrossRef]
8. Hezam, I.M.; Rahman, K.; Alshamrani, A.; Božanić, D. Geometric Aggregation Operators for Solving Multicriteria Group Decision-Making Problems Based on Complex Pythagorean Fuzzy Sets. *Symmetry* **2023**, *15*, 826. [CrossRef]
9. Svadlenka, L.; Simic, V.; Dobrodolac, M.; Lazarevic, D.; Todorovic, G. Picture Fuzzy Decision-Making Approach for Sustainable Last-Mile Delivery. *IEEE Access* **2020**, *8*, 209393–209414. [CrossRef]
10. Boskovic, S.; Svadlenka, L.; Jovcic, S.; Dobrodolac, M.; Simic, V.; Bacanin, N. An Alternative Ranking Order Method Accounting for Two-Step Normalization (AROMAN); A Case Study of the Electric Vehicle Selection Problem. *IEEE Access* **2023**, *11*, 39496–39507. [CrossRef]
11. Bošković, S.; Švadlenka, L.; Dobrodolac, M.; Jovčić, S.; Zanne, M. An Extended AROMAN Method for Cargo Bike Delivery Concept Selection. *Decis. Mak. Adv.* **2023**, *1*, 1–9. [CrossRef]
12. Zaranka, J.; Pečeliunas, R.; Žuraulis, V. A Road Safety-Based Selection Methodology for Professional Drivers: Behaviour and Accident Rate Analysis. *Int. J. Environ. Res. Public Health* **2021**, *18*, 12487. [CrossRef]
13. Maslać, M.; Antić, B.; Lipovac, K.; Pešić, D.; Milutinović, N. Behaviours of Drivers in Serbia: Non-Professional versus Professional Drivers. *Transp. Res. Part F Traffic Psychol. Behav.* **2018**, *52*, 101–111. [CrossRef]
14. Rosso, G.L.; Perotto, M.; Feola, M.; Bruno, G.; Caramella, M. Investigating Obesity among Professional Drivers: The High Risk Professional Driver Study. *Am. J. Ind. Med.* **2015**, *58*, 212–219. [CrossRef]

15. Chen, T.; Sze, N.N.; Newnam, S.; Bai, L. Effectiveness of the Compensatory Strategy Adopted by Older Drivers: Difference between Professional and Non-Professional Drivers. *Transp. Res. Part F Traffic Psychol. Behav.* **2021**, *77*, 168–180. [CrossRef]
16. Wu, Y.; Zhao, X.; Rong, J.; Zhang, Y. The Effectiveness of Eco-Driving Training for Male Professional and Non-Professional Drivers. *Transp. Res. Part D Transp. Environ.* **2018**, *59*, 121–133. [CrossRef]
17. Öz, B.; Özkan, T.; Lajunen, T. Professional and Non-Professional Drivers' Stress Reactions and Risky Driving. *Transp. Res. Part F Traffic Psychol. Behav.* **2010**, *13*, 32–40. [CrossRef]
18. Nordfaern, T.; Jorgensen, S.H.; Rundmo, T. Safety Attitudes, Behaviour, Anxiety and Perceived Control among Professional and Non-Professional Drivers. *J. Risk Res.* **2012**, *15*, 875–896. [CrossRef]
19. Serrano-Fernández, M.-J.; Boada-Grau, J.; Robert-Sentís, L.; Vigil-Colet, A. Predictive Variables for Sleep Quality in Professional Drivers. *An. Psicol.* **2021**, *37*, 393–401. [CrossRef]
20. Chen, T.; Sze, N.N.; Bai, L. Safety of Professional Drivers in an Ageing Society—A Driving Simulator Study. *Transp. Res. Part F Traffic Psychol. Behav.* **2019**, *67*, 101–112. [CrossRef]
21. Meng, F.; Li, S.; Cao, L.; Li, M.; Peng, Q.; Wang, C.; Zhang, W. Driving Fatigue in Professional Drivers: A Survey of Truck and Taxi Drivers. *Traffic Inj. Prev.* **2015**, *16*, 474–483. [CrossRef]
22. Han, W.; Zhao, J. Driver Behaviour and Traffic Accident Involvement among Professional Urban Bus Drivers in China. *Transp. Res. Part F Traffic Psychol. Behav.* **2020**, *74*, 184–197. [CrossRef]
23. Hernández-Rodríguez, V.; Maeso-González, E.; Gutiérrez-Bedmar, M.; García-Rodríguez, A. Psychosocial Risk and Job Satisfaction in Professional Drivers. *Front. Psychol.* **2022**, *13*, 5660. [CrossRef] [PubMed]
24. Serrano-Fernández, M.J.; Tàpia-Caballero, P.; Boada-Grau, J.; Araya-Castillo, L. Variables That Predict Attitudes Toward Safety Regulations in Professional Drivers. *J. Transp. Health* **2020**, *19*, 100967. [CrossRef]
25. Llamazares, J.; Useche, S.A.; Montoro, L.; Alonso, F. Commuting Accidents of Spanish Professional Drivers: When Occupational Risk Exceeds the Workplace. *Int. J. Occup. Saf. Ergon.* **2021**, *27*, 754–762. [CrossRef]
26. Cvahte Ojsteršek, T.; Topolšek, D. Influence of Drivers' Visual and Cognitive Attention on Their Perception of Changes in the Traffic Environment. *Eur. Transp. Res. Rev.* **2019**, *11*, 45. [CrossRef]
27. Milošević, S.; Gajić, R. Presentation Factors and Driver Characteristics Affecting Road-Sign Registration. *Ergonomics* **2007**, *29*, 807–815. [CrossRef]
28. Milosevic, S. Drivers' Fatigue Studies. *Ergonomics* **1997**, *40*, 381–389. [CrossRef]
29. Brown, D.M.Y.; Farias Zuniga, A.; Mulla, D.M.; Mendonca, D.; Keir, P.J.; Bray, S.R. Investigating the Effects of Mental Fatigue on Resistance Exercise Performance. *Int. J. Environ. Res. Public Health* **2021**, *18*, 6794. [CrossRef]
30. Poliak, M.; Svabova, L.; Benus, J.; Demirci, E. Driver Response Time and Age Impact on the Reaction Time of Drivers: A Driving Simulator Study among Professional-Truck Drivers. *Mathematics* **2022**, *10*, 1489. [CrossRef]
31. Čulík, K.; Kalašová, A.; Štefancová, V. Evaluation of Driver's Reaction Time Measured in Driving Simulator. *Sensors* **2022**, *22*, 3542. [CrossRef]
32. Anstey, K.J.; Horswill, M.S.; Wood, J.M.; Hatherly, C. The Role of Cognitive and Visual Abilities as Predictors in the Multifactorial Model of Driving Safety. *Accid. Anal. Prev.* **2012**, *45*, 766–774. [CrossRef]
33. Lacherez, P.; Au, S.; Wood, J.M. Visual Motion Perception Predicts Driving Hazard Perception Ability. *Acta Ophthalmol.* **2014**, *92*, 88–93. [CrossRef]
34. Chen, X.M.; Wei, Z.H.; Gao, L. Professional Driver Suitability Evaluation. *Procedia Eng.* **2011**, *15*, 5222–5226. [CrossRef]
35. Čubranić-Dobrodolac, M.; Švadlenka, L.; Čičević, S.; Trifunović, A.; Dobrodolac, M. A Bee Colony Optimization (BCO) and Type-2 Fuzzy Approach to Measuring the Impact of Speed Perception on Motor Vehicle Crash Involvement. *Soft Comput.* **2021**, *26*, 4463–4486. [CrossRef]
36. Caragata, G.E.; Tuokko, H.; Damini, A. Fit to Drive: A Pilot Study to Improve the Physical Fitness of Older Drivers. *Act. Adapt. Aging* **2009**, *33*, 240–255. [CrossRef]
37. Gilson, N.D.; Mielke, G.I.; Coombes, J.S.; Feter, N.; Smith, E.; Duncan, M.J.; Wallis, G.; Brown, W.J. VO2peak and 24-Hour Sleep, Sedentary Behavior, and Physical Activity in Australian Truck Drivers. *Scand. J. Med. Sci. Sports* **2021**, *31*, 1574–1578. [CrossRef]
38. Ku Khalif, K.M.N.; Gegov, A.; Abu Bakar, A.S. Hybrid Fuzzy MCDM Model for Z-Numbers Using Intuitive Vectorial Centroid. *J. Intell. Fuzzy Syst.* **2017**, *33*, 791–805. [CrossRef]
39. Mueller, A.S.; Trick, L.M. Driving in Fog: The Effects of Driving Experience and Visibility on Speed Compensation and Hazard Avoidance. *Accid. Anal. Prev.* **2012**, *48*, 472–479. [CrossRef]
40. Wang, T.; Chen, B.; Chen, Y.; Deng, S.; Chen, J. Traffic Risk Assessment Based on Warning Data. *J. Adv. Transp.* **2022**, *2022*, 11. [CrossRef]
41. Al-Garawi, N.; Dalhat, M.A.; Aga, O. Assessing the Road Traffic Crashes among Novice Female Drivers in Saudi Arabia. *Sustainability* **2021**, *13*, 8613. [CrossRef]
42. Cubranic-Dobrodolac, M.; Svadlenka, L.; Markovic, G.Z.; Dobrodolac, M. A Decision Support Model for Transportation Companies to Examine Driver Behavior. *IEEE Trans. Eng. Manag.* **2021**. [CrossRef]
43. Smorti, M.; Guarnieri, S. Do Aggressive Driving and Negative Emotional Driving Mediate the Link between Impulsiveness and Risky Driving among Young Italian Drivers? *J. Soc. Psychol.* **2016**, *156*, 669–673. [CrossRef] [PubMed]
44. Rodriguez Gonzalez, A.B.; Wilby, M.R.; Vinagre Diaz, J.J.; Sanchez Avila, C. Modeling and Detecting Aggressiveness from Driving Signals. *IEEE Trans. Intell. Transp. Syst.* **2014**, *15*, 1419–1428. [CrossRef]

45. Tronsmoen, T. Associations between Self-Assessment of Driving Ability, Driver Training and Crash Involvement among Young Drivers. *Transp. Res. Part F Traffic Psychol. Behav.* **2008**, *11*, 334–346. [CrossRef]
46. Sundström, A. Self-Assessment of Driving Skill—A Review from a Measurement Perspective. *Transp. Res. Part F Traffic Psychol. Behav.* **2008**, *11*, 1–9. [CrossRef]
47. Čubranić-Dobrodolac, M.; Švadlenka, L.; Čičević, S.; Trifunović, A.; Dobrodolac, M. Using the Interval Type-2 Fuzzy Inference Systems to Compare the Impact of Speed and Space Perception on the Occurrence of Road Traffic Accidents. *Mathematics* **2020**, *8*, 1548. [CrossRef]
48. Petrović, I.; Petrović, J. Personality Traits in Selection of Military, Civil and Sports' Pilots: Hybridized-IT2FS-MCDM Approach. *Int. J. Traffic Transp. Eng.* **2021**, *12*, 1–20. [CrossRef]
49. Li, Y.M.; Lai, C.Y.; Kao, C.P. Building a Qualitative Recruitment System via SVM with MCDM Approach. *Appl. Intell.* **2011**, *35*, 75–88. [CrossRef]
50. Čubranić-Dobrodolac, M.; Čičević, S.; Dobrodolac, M.; Nešić, M. The Risks Associated with Using a Mobile Phone by Young Drivers. *Transport* **2013**, *28*, 381–388. [CrossRef]
51. Gottwald, D.; Jovčić, S.; Lejsková, P. Multi-Criteria Decision-Making Approach in Personnel Selection Problem—A Case Study at the University of Pardubice. *Econ. Comput. Econ. Cybern. Stud. Res.* **2022**, *56*, 149–164. [CrossRef]
52. Wu, W.W.; Lee, Y.T. Developing Global Managers' Competencies Using the Fuzzy DEMATEL Method. *Expert Syst. Appl.* **2007**, *32*, 499–507. [CrossRef]
53. Stopka, O.; Stopková, M.; Ľupták, V.; Krile, S. Application of the Chosen Multi-Criteria Decision-Making Methods to Identify the Autonomous Train System Supplier. *Transp. Probl.* **2020**, *15*, 45–57. [CrossRef]
54. Agarski, B.; Budak, I.; Kosec, B.; Hodolic, J. An Approach to Multi-Criteria Environmental Evaluation with Multiple Weight Assignment. *Environ. Model. Assess.* **2012**, *17*, 255–266. [CrossRef]
55. Agarski, B.; Hadzistevic, M.; Budak, I.; Moraca, S.; Vukelic, D. Comparison of Approaches to Weighting of Multiple Criteria for Selecting Equipment to Optimize Performance and Safety. *Int. J. Occup. Saf. Ergon.* **2017**, *25*, 228–240. [CrossRef]
56. Dobrodolac, M.; Lazarević, D.; Švadlenka, L.; Živanović, M. A Study on the Competitive Strategy of the Universal Postal Service Provider. *Technol. Anal. Strateg. Manag.* **2016**, *28*, 935–949. [CrossRef]
57. Alshamrani, A.; Majumder, P.; Das, A.; Hezam, I.M.; Božanić, D. An Integrated BWM-TOPSIS-I Approach to Determine the Ranking of Alternatives and Application of Sustainability Analysis of Renewable Energy. *Axioms* **2023**, *12*, 159. [CrossRef]
58. Pamučar, D.; Lukovac, V.; Božanić, D.; Komazec, N. Multi-Criteria Fucom-Mairca Model for the Evaluation of Level Crossings: Case Study in the Republic of Serbia. *Oper. Res. Eng. Sci. Theory Appl.* **2018**, *1*, 108–129. [CrossRef]
59. Karabasevic, D.; Stanujkic, D.; Urosevic, S. The MCDM Model for Personnel Selection Based on SWARA and ARAS Methods. *Manag. J. Theory Pract. Manag.* **2015**, *20*, 43–52. [CrossRef]
60. Mariani, F.; Ciommi, M. Aggregating Composite Indicators through the Geometric Mean: A Penalization Approach. *Computation* **2022**, *10*, 64. [CrossRef]
61. Lazarević, D.; Dobrodolac, M.; Švadlenka, L.; Stanivuković, B. A Model for Business Performance Improvement: A Case of the Postal Company. *J. Bus. Econ. Manag.* **2020**, *21*, 564–592. [CrossRef]
62. Chen, C.T. Extensions of the TOPSIS for Group Decision-Making under Fuzzy Environment. *Fuzzy Sets Syst.* **2000**, *114*, 1–9. [CrossRef]

Disclaimer/Publisher's Note: The statements, opinions and data contained in all publications are solely those of the individual author(s) and contributor(s) and not of MDPI and/or the editor(s). MDPI and/or the editor(s) disclaim responsibility for any injury to people or property resulting from any ideas, methods, instructions or products referred to in the content.

Article

Using an Interval Type-2 Fuzzy AROMAN Decision-Making Method to Improve the Sustainability of the Postal Network in Rural Areas

Ivana Nikolić [1], Jelena Milutinović [2], Darko Božanić [3] and Momčilo Dobrodolac [1,*]

[1] Faculty of Transport and Traffic Engineering, University of Belgrade, Vojvode Stepe 305, 11000 Belgrade, Serbia; i.nikolic@sf.bg.ac.rs
[2] ICT College of Vocational Studies, Academy of Technical and Art Applied Studies Belgrade, Zdravka Čelara 16, 11000 Belgrade, Serbia; jelena.milutinovic@ict.edu.rs
[3] Military Academy, University of Defence in Belgrade, Veljka Lukica Kurjaka 33, 11000 Belgrade, Serbia; darko.bozanic@va.mod.gov.rs
* Correspondence: m.dobrodolac@sf.bg.ac.rs

Abstract: One of the crucial pillars of each state's development strategy relates to service provision in rural areas. An adequate scope of these services is a prerequisite for uniform regional progress. Postal operators play a key role in supporting these development policies, by providing postal, financial and transportation services to each citizen in a state, regardless of place of residence. The postal network represents one of the biggest logistics networks worldwide. However, since it is not financially justified to provide services to all citizens, even to those that live in the most remote areas, the question of how to optimize the postal network is always topical. This problem is very complex because the postal units' existence in rural areas cannot be considered just from an economic standpoint; many other criteria should be considered. The model proposed in this paper can be considered a decision-making tool designed to support policymakers in planning the postal network. First, we identify the criteria that should be considered in decision-making by an extensive literature review. We then apply the FUCOM method to determine the importance of individual criteria. Finally, we propose an Interval Type-2 Fuzzy AROMAN approach to determine which postal unit should be reorganized.

Keywords: multi-criteria decision-making; AROMAN; FUCOM; postal services; last-mile delivery; service networks; rural areas

MSC: 03E72; 47S40; 90B50

1. Introduction

Most rural residents are engaged in food production, which is a crucial pillar of human civilization [1,2]. However, the quality of life in rural areas is an intricate issue in numerous countries [3,4]. The appropriate infrastructure and availability of services are mostly lacking in these areas [5,6]. Many factors may have caused this problem; however, one of the main policy pillars of each government should be to contribute to the development of rural areas [7–9].

Individual countries define "rural areas" differently, the scope ranging from definitions in terms of dispersed population, agricultural-based economy, distance from major urban centers, and, as a direct consequence, lack of access to major services [10,11]. At the international level, the most frequently used approach is that proposed by the Organisation for Economic Co-operation and Development—OECD. The OECD has established a regional typology according to which regions have been classified as predominantly rural (PR), intermediate (IR), and predominantly urban (PU). This typology is based on a combination of three criteria: the population density, the percentage of the population of a region living in rural communities, and the presence of large urban centers in such a region. As shown in Figure 1, among the considered 1348 regions in the EU-28, some 367 were classified as predominantly urban, 553 as intermediate, and 428 as predominantly rural regions in the year 2016 [12].

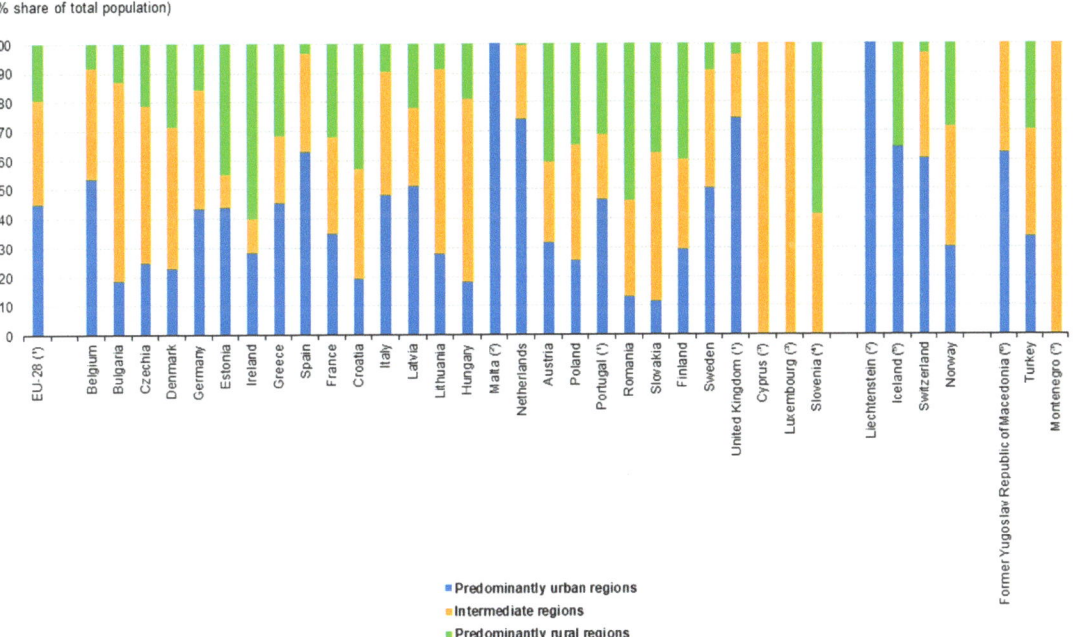

Figure 1. Population structure, by urban–rural topology (% share of the total population) [12].

The integration of developing countries into the modern world economy was in the past associated with a population migration tendency reflected mainly in the direction of rural to urban areas [13]. Along with a process of de-agriculturalization of rural households, there is also increasing development of new non-agricultural activities in rural areas, such as manufacturing, tourism, housing expansion, and new consumption patterns, connected to leisure and recreation that have increased demand for labor [14–16]. The nature of rural areas includes more than the production of agricultural products and rural areas are diversifying. Earlier, rural communities were almost isolated from various influences, but there is now a large degree of variability among rural residents. New social groups are emerging, and the result is a change in demand for services because new groups have new habits. Rural development is less and less associated with underdevelopment and more and more with the lack of attractiveness of these areas. Rural households have difficulties accessing food stores, banking and postal services, health and education, and public transport [17].

Postal services are of particular interest for regional growth, and this is the reason why the states consider them as services of general economic interest [18]. As a consequence, at the global level, the concept of universal postal obligation is introduced in the sector, which implies the existence of certain scope of postal services in every community [19,20]. Such an extensive network of postal units represents one of the biggest logistics infrastructures worldwide [21]. However, since it is not profitable to offer the services at each point of a state, the problem of optimization of the postal network is one the most crucial in this industry [22,23].

In this paper, we propose a methodological approach for the optimization of the postal network at a micro level, considering just a handful of postal units. We demonstrate the application of the model on a small number of units (6 in our case), but we can repeat this analysis many times (6 + 6 + ...) and analyze the whole postal network by this (more thousand units). The concept of analysis implies assessing several postal units in a certain rural region, where the result of the implemented methodology should give the rank of the considered postal units. The unit with the lowest rank should be somehow reorganized. While assessing the importance rank of each unit, multiple criteria should be included in the analysis. Accordingly, the considered problem is a typical multi-criteria decision-making (MCDM) problem. Various techniques could be used for solving this kind of problem while providing ways to deal with uncertainty in data, using the theory of fuzzy or rough sets [24,25]. In this paper, we decided to propose the implementation of an alternative ranking order method accounting for two-step normalization—AROMAN [26–28]—in a type-2 fuzzy environment. According to the authors' knowledge, this is the first time in the literature that an interval type-2 fuzzy AROMAN has been proposed and implemented. The most important contributions of this study are as follows: (i) based on an in-depth literature review, we discovered the attributes for optimization of the postal network; (ii) the set of twenty identified attributes is reduced to seven criteria by grouping them into seven clusters; (iii) we determined the relevance ranks of the criteria by interviewing the experts from the postal industry and by applying the FUCOM method; (iv) we implemented the AROMAN method in the type-2 fuzzy environment for the first time in the literature; (v) we offered the proposal for reorganization of the lowest ranked postal units.

2. Literature Review on the Criteria for the Postal Network Assessment

This section reveals the criteria that various authors used to evaluate the efficiency of the postal and related sectors. The summarized overview is shown in Table 1.

Closing a postal network unit (PNU) has the most detrimental effect on sensitive population groups. These categories are characterized by limited mobility due to illness or commuting difficulties. Every relocation has an impact on their inability to access postal services or their overall experience with the postal network. Such a change also creates additional expenses for people with low income or problems with daily schedules to organize the additional commute required for gaining access to postal services [22,29,30].

One of the important attributes is the number of legal entities in the territory covered by PNU. Closing a PNU has a significant effect on the local business community as well. This slows down the information flow, causes delays and additional expenses for gas to reach alternative PNU, and leads to negative ecological effects [31,32].

Ralevic et al. [33] used the Data Envelopment Analysis (DEA) approach for public postal operators' profit efficiency measurement. They used different approaches and different inputs and outputs. It is also interesting that this method may be applied at different levels—an individual postal operator and its network; city level; regional, national, or for example, European postal market. For example, Filippini and Zola [34] use the econometrical approach for determining the cost efficiency of the Swiss Post. The analysis was carried out in the Italian-speaking area of Switzerland and included 47 small local post offices. Most studies that measure the efficiency of the postal network take the number of employees as one of the main inputs [18]. Dobrodolac et al. [35] proposed a model for the comparison of business units in the postal industry based on the stress level of employees.

Klingenberg et al. [36] analyzed the United States Postal Service, which possesses the largest retail network in the United States with over 30,000 retail locations. The authors consider various factors, such as geographical diversity, population density, Internet broadband access, diversity of transportation modes, transit routes or parking regulations, quality of retail counter service/employee helpfulness, constraints related to the existing retail network, changes in population and employment over time, changes in the use of postal services over time, changes in demographic profile over time, changes in transportation networks and transit routes over time and accuracy of input data. For customers from underdeveloped and remote areas, the postal infrastructure is the only medium to ensure access to information [37].

Mizutani and Uranishi [38] analyze whether and to what extent the competition affects a reduction in expenses and overall productivity. The sample refers to the organizations that deliver parcels in Japan—one of them is state-owned, and the others are private operators.

The quality of service is an intricate question in the postal sector. This is because postal services should be provided to every citizen in a state due to universal service obligations, which are very costly and demanding [39].

Human capital is of crucial importance for each company, particularly in the service sector. Speaking about the expertise of employees, experienced workers are an advantage in complex systems such as the postal system [40]. The companies also implement various programs to stimulate their satisfaction, expecting that this would lead to increased kindness toward customers [41].

The interior and exterior of the post office also have a significant impact on user satisfaction. Accordingly, postal operators invest significant funds in the repair and improvement of their facilities [42]. Further, opening hours significantly affect the accessibility of public service delivery [43]. The researchers, and customers as well, assess the efficiency of service by analyzing the average waiting times [44]. A range of postal services and corresponding quality issues offered to rural communities generate constant debate in the postal sector [19,23].

The proximity of an alternative post office is a valuable attribute when considering reducing the postal network. The study by Vaishar et al. [45] showed that postal branches in Europe should be accessible to users in rural areas within a shorter time than 30 min. Accordingly, customers in rural areas often use various transportation modes to reach the post office [46].

The number of delivery points, i.e., the number of households that are served by a PNU, is an important attribute that gives information about the significance of a particular postal unit [47]. A similar attribute relates to the covered area by a PNU [48]. Even though the goal of many studies is to minimize capital resources, such as vehicles [49], here, we should maximize this criterion because the PNU that covers a wider area can be considered more important for the fulfillment of universal service obligations.

All services offered in a PNU are normalized, which makes it possible to use the number of services by type to determine the overall realized norm minutes for a certain period, which represents a productivity measure of a PNU. The number of norm minutes per month is a measure directly associated with the costs of a PNU, as one of the most important criteria in decision-making [50]. The higher values of norm minutes bring lower costs per provided service.

Based on the literature review, twenty attributes are identified. The authors of the paper concluded that these attributes, also named potential criteria, can be grouped into clusters which would be the final criteria used in the decision-making process (Figure 2). The grouping is carried out as follows: the first cluster includes vulnerable groups and access for people with disabilities; the second legal entities, covered area, number of mailboxes, number of routes and number of norm minutes per month; the third efficiency, quality of postal services and waiting time in the line; the fourth employees, the expertise of employees and the kindness of employees; the fifth mobile and Internet network coverage; the sixth competition and the proximity of an alternative post office; and the seventh interior and exterior of the post office, appropriate working hours, range of services, and easiness of access.

Table 1. Attributes of the postal network identified from the relevant literature.

Attributes or Potential Criteria (PC)	Type of Attribute	Definition	Authors
Vulnerable groups—PC1	maximization	The number of people from vulnerable groups (older people, people with a lack of mobility, low-income people, single parents, etc.)	Milutinović, Marković, Stanivuković, Švadlenka, Dobrodolac [22]; Hamilton [29]
Legal entities—PC2	maximization	Number of legal entities in the territory covered by the observed PNU	Cabras, Lau [31]; Christiaanse, Haartsen [32]
Efficiency—PC3	maximization	The efficiency of a PNU as a ratio of the average monthly PNU incomes and the average monthly PNU outcomes	Ralevic, Dobrodolac, Markovic, Mladenovic [33]; Filippini, Zola [34]
Employees—PC4	maximization	Number of employees in the observed PNU	Ralević, Dobrodolac, Marković [18] Dobrodolac, Švadlenka, Čubranić-Dobrodolac, Čičević, Stanivuković [35]
Mobile and Internet network coverage—PC5	minimization	Mobile and internet network coverage in the area of observed PNU	Klingenberg, Bzhilyanskaya, Ravnitzky [36] Budziewicz-Guźlecka, Drab-Kurowska [37]
Competition—PC6	minimization	The number of competing organizations providing similar services	Mizutani, Uranishi [38]
Quality of postal services—PC7	maximization	User assessment of the provided service quality	Klingenberg, Bzhilyanskaya, Ravnitzky [36] Matúšková, Madleňáková [39]
The expertise of employees—PC8	maximization	User assessment of the expertise of employees	Neupane, Kyrönlahti, Prakash, Siukola, Kosonen, Lumme-Sandt, Nikander, Nygård [40]
The kindness of employees—PC9	maximization	User assessment of the kindness of employees	Drašković, Průša, Čičević, Jovčić [41]
Interior and exterior of the post office—PC10	maximization	Interior and exterior attractiveness of the observed PNU	Minami [42]
Appropriate working hours—PC11	maximization	Availability of the system at the daily and weekly level	Neutens, Delafontaine, Schwanen, van de Weghe [43]
Range of services—PC12	maximization	The range of services should be adjusted to customer needs	Dobrodolac, Ralević, Švadlenka, Radojičić [19]
Waiting time in the line—PC13	minimization	User perception of waiting time get access to post office counter	Doble [44]
Easiness of access—PC14	maximization	Easy access to the observed PNU (parking, bus station, …)	Mostarac, Kavran, Rakić [46]
Access for people with disabilities—PC15	maximization	Width of the entrance, step-free access, assistance, low-level counters, portable PIN pads, hearing loops, staff interaction	Shergold, Parkhurst [30]
The proximity of an alternative post office—PC16	minimization	The proximity of an alternative post office in case of shutting down the observed PNU	Vaishar, Šťastná, Ilaria, Kataishi, Akhavan, Senjyu [45]

Table 1. Cont.

Attributes or Potential Criteria (PC)	Type of Attribute	Definition	Authors
Covered area—PC17	maximization	Delivery area of the observed PNU	Çakır, Perçin, Min [48]
Number of mailboxes—PC18	maximization	Number of delivery points/number of households	Mostarac, Mostarac, Kavran, Šarac [47]
Number of routes—PC19	maximization	Number of routes in the delivery area of a PNU	Nebro, García-Nieto, Berlí, Warchulski, Kozdrowski [49]
Number of norm minutes per month—PC20	maximization	The overall realized norm minutes for a certain period, which represents a productivity measure of a PNU	de Araújo, Dos Reis, da Silva, Aktas [50]

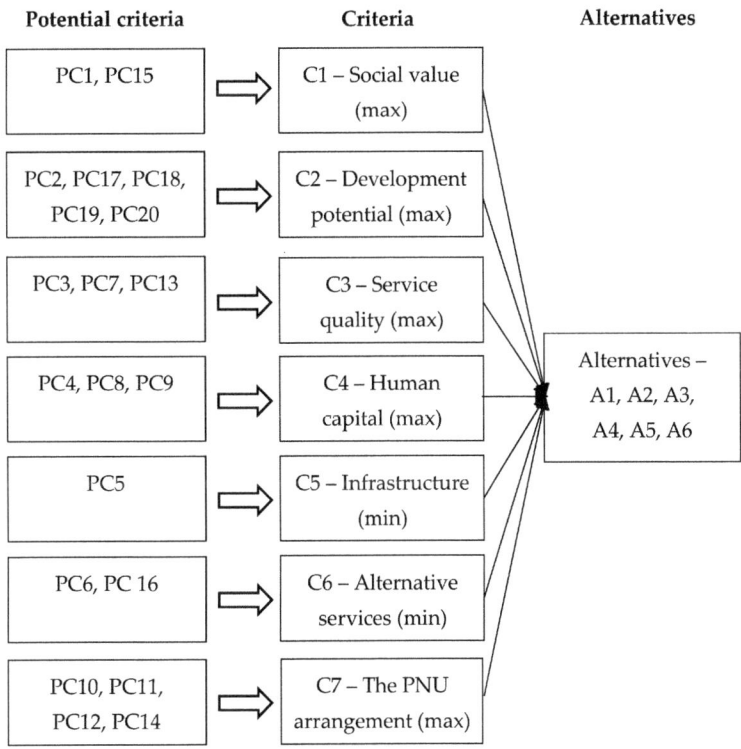

Figure 2. Structure of decision-making problem of postal network optimization.

3. Methods

Based on an extensive literature review, we identified twenty potential criteria for postal network optimization. We then further structured them into seven clusters representing the final criteria in the decision-making process. The following research methodology can be structured into two parts: determination of criteria weights and alternative ranking. For the first part, we apply the FUCOM method, while for the second we propose an implementation of the type-2 fuzzy AROMAN method. The research configuration is shown in Figure 3.

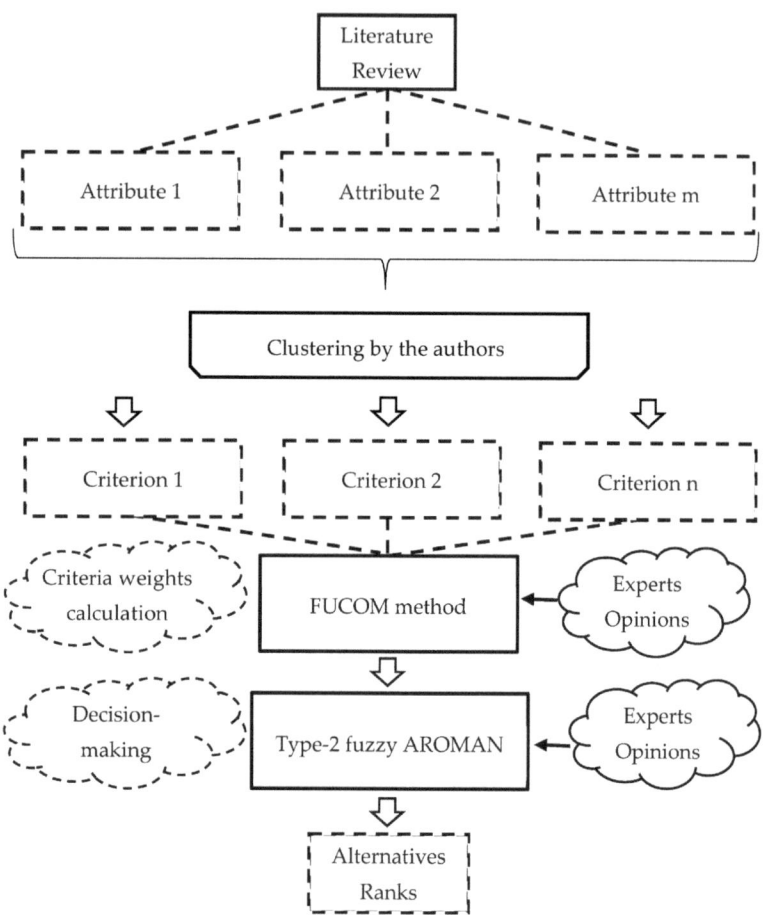

Figure 3. Research configuration.

3.1. Determination of Criteria Weights by the FUCOM Method

In this paper, we use the Full Consistency Method (FUCOM) to determine the weights of identified criteria. FUCOM is a relatively new method proposed by Pamučar et al. [51] in 2018.

A typical MCMD model can be described by the equation $max[\,f_1(x),\,f_2(x),\,\ldots,\,f_n(x)]$, $n \geq 2$, where $x \in A = [a_1,\,a_2,\,\ldots,\,a_m]$; n is the number of the criteria, m is the number of the alternatives, f_j represents the criteria ($j = 1,\,2,\,\ldots,\,n$) and A represents the set of the alternatives a_i ($i = 1,\,2,\,\ldots,\,m$). The values f_{ij} of each considered criterion f_j for each considered alternative a_i are known, namely $f_{ij} = f_j(a_i)$, $\forall (i,\,j); i = 1,\,2,\,\ldots,\,m;\,j = 1,\,2,\,\ldots,\,n$, where each value of the attribute depends on the j-th criterion and the i-th alternative.

Commonly, real-life problems are not described by criteria of the same degree of importance, and deciding the relative weights of criteria in MCDM models is a specific problem that includes subjectivity. This FUCOM method enables the calculation of the weight coefficients of all of the elements mutually compared at a certain level of the hierarchy, simultaneously satisfying the conditions of comparison consistency [51].

FUCOM reduces the possibility of errors in comparison to the least possible extent due to (1) a small number of comparisons ($n - 1$) and (2) the constraints defined when calculating the optimal values of criteria. FUCOM offers the possibility to validate the model by calculating the error for the obtained weight vectors by determining DFC. In the following text, the procedure of the FUCOM method is explained in more detail.

Step 1: In the first step, the criteria from the predefined set of evaluation criteria $C = \{C_1, C_2, \ldots, C_n\}$ are ranked. The ranking is performed according to the significance of the criteria; i.e., starting from the criterion that is expected to have the highest weight coefficient to the criterion of the least significance. Thus, the criteria ranked according to the expected values of the weight coefficients are obtained [51]:

$$C_{j(1)} > C_{j(2)} > \ldots > C_{j(k)} \tag{1}$$

where k represents the rank of the observed criterion. If there is a judgment of the existence of two or more criteria with the same significance, the sign of equality is placed instead of ">" between these criteria in the expression (1).

Step 2: Further comparison of the ranked criteria is carried out by determining the comparative priority ($\varphi_{k/(k+1)}$, $k = 1, 2, \ldots, n$, where k represents the rank of the criteria). The comparative priority of the evaluation criteria ($\varphi_{k/(k+1)}$) is an advantage of the criterion of the $C_{j(k)}$ rank compared to the criterion of the $C_{j(k+1)}$ rank. Thus, the vectors of the comparative priorities of the evaluation criteria are obtained, as in expression (2) [51]:

$$\Phi = \left(\varphi_{1/2}, \varphi_{2/3}, \ldots, \varphi_{k/(k+1)}\right) \tag{2}$$

where $\varphi_{k/(k+1)}$ represents the significance (priority) that the criterion of the $C_{j(k)}$ rank has been compared to the criterion of the $C_{j(k+1)}$ rank.

The comparative priority of the criteria is assessed in one of two ways: (a) according to their preferences, decision-makers define the comparative priority $\varphi_{k/k+1}$ among the observed criteria. When solving real problems, decision-makers compare the ranked criteria based on internal knowledge, so they determine the comparative priority $\varphi_{k/k+1}$ based on subjective preferences. If the decision-maker thinks that the criterion of the $C_{j(k)}$ rank has the same significance as the criterion of the $C_{j(k+1)}$ rank, then the comparative priority is $\varphi_{k/k+1} = 1$. (b) Based on a predefined scale for the comparison of criteria, decision-makers compare the criteria and thus determine the significance of each criterion in the expression (1). The comparison is made concerning the first-ranked (the most significant) criterion. Thus, the significance of the criteria $\omega_{C_{j(k)}}$ for all of the criteria ranked in Step 1 is obtained. Since the first-ranked criterion is compared with itself (its significance is $\omega_{C_{j(1)}} = 1$), it means that the $n - 1$ comparison of the criteria should be performed.

The FUCOM model allows the pairwise comparison of the criteria employing integer, decimal values, or the values from the predefined scale for the pairwise comparison of the criteria [52].

Step 3: The final values of the weight coefficients should be calculated in Step 3 (ω_1, $\omega_2, \ldots, \omega_n)^T$. These values should satisfy the two conditions:

(1) that the ratio of the weight coefficients is equal to the comparative priority among the observed criteria ($\varphi_{k/(k+1)}$) defined in Step 2; i.e., that the following condition is met [51]:

$$\frac{\omega_k}{\omega_{k+1}} = \varphi_{k/(k+1)} \tag{3}$$

(2) In addition to condition (3), the final values of the weight coefficients should satisfy the condition of mathematical transitivity; i.e., that $\varphi_{k/(k+1)} \otimes \varphi_{(k+1)/(k+2)} = \varphi_{k/(k+2)}$. Since $\varphi_{k/(k+1)} = \frac{\omega_k}{\omega_{k+1}}$ and $\varphi_{(k+1)/(k+2)} = \frac{\omega_{k+1}}{\omega_{k+2}}$, the condition that $\frac{\omega_k}{\omega_{k+1}} \otimes \frac{\omega_{k+1}}{\omega_{k+2}} = \frac{\omega_k}{\omega_{k+2}}$ is obtained. Thus, yet another condition that the final values of the weight coefficients of the evaluation criteria need to meet is obtained, namely [51]:

$$\frac{\omega_k}{\omega_{k+2}} = \varphi_{k/(k+1)} \otimes \varphi_{(k+1)/(k+2)} \tag{4}$$

Full consistency, i.e., minimum DFC (χ) is satisfied only if transitivity is fully respected, i.e., when the conditions of $\frac{\omega_k}{\omega_{k+1}} = \varphi_{k/(k+1)}$ and $\frac{\omega_k}{\omega_{k+2}} = \varphi_{k/(k+1)} \otimes \varphi_{(k+1)/(k+2)}$ are met. In that way, the requirement for maximum consistency is fulfilled, i.e., DFC is $\chi = 0$ for the obtained values of the weight coefficients. For the conditions to be met, it is necessary that the values of the weight coefficients $(\omega_1, \omega_2, \ldots, \omega_n)^T$ meet the condition of $\left|\frac{\omega_k}{\omega_{k+1}} - \varphi_{k/(k+1)}\right| \leq \chi$ and $\left|\frac{\omega_k}{\omega_{k+2}} - \varphi_{k/(k+1)} \otimes \varphi_{(k+1)/(k+2)}\right| \leq \chi$ with the minimization of the value χ. In that manner, the requirement for maximum consistency is satisfied.

Based on the defined settings, the final model for determining the final values of the weight coefficients of the evaluation criteria can be defined [51].

$$\begin{aligned}
& \min \chi \\
& \text{s.t.} \\
& \left|\frac{\omega_{j(k)}}{\omega_{j(k+1)}} - \varphi_{k/(k+1)}\right| \leq \chi, \forall j \\
& \left|\frac{\omega_{j(k)}}{\omega_{j(k+2)}} - \varphi_{k/(k+1)} \otimes \varphi_{(k+1)/(k+2)}\right| \leq \chi, \forall j \\
& \sum_{j=1}^{n} \omega_j = 1, \forall j \\
& \omega_j \geq 0, \forall j
\end{aligned} \qquad (5)$$

By solving model (5), the final values of the evaluation criteria $(\omega_1, \omega_2, \ldots, \omega_n)^T$ and the degree of DFC (χ) are generated [53].

3.2. Ranking Alternatives Using a Type-2 Fuzzy AROMAN Method

The type-2 fuzzy AROMAN method is, for the first time in the literature, implemented in this paper. First, we will provide some preliminaries on type-2 fuzzy arithmetic.

3.2.1. Preliminaries on Type-2 Fuzzy Arithmetic

In this section, we provide the definitions concerning the type-2 fuzzy sets and principles of type-2 fuzzy arithmetic that will be used in calculations related to the type-2 fuzzy AROMAN method.

Definition 1. *A type-2 fuzzy set $\tilde{\tilde{A}}$ in the universe of discourse X can be represented by a type-2 membership function $\mu_{\tilde{\tilde{A}}}$, shown as follows [54]:*

$$A = \{((x, u), \mu_A(x, u)) | \forall x \in X, \forall u \in J_X \subseteq [0, 1], 0 \leq \mu_A(x, u) \leq 1\} \qquad (6)$$

where J_X denotes an interval in $[0, 1]$. Moreover, the type-2 fuzzy set A can also be represented as follows [54]:

$$A = \int_{x \in X} \int_{u \in J_X} \mu_A(x, u)/(x, u), \qquad (7)$$

where $J_X \subseteq [0, 1]$ and $\int\int$ denotes union over all admissible x and u.

Definition 2. *Let $\tilde{\tilde{A}}$ be a type-2 fuzzy set in the universe of discourse X represented by the type-2 membership function $\mu_{\tilde{\tilde{A}}}$. If all $\mu_{\tilde{\tilde{A}}}(x, u) = 1$, then $\tilde{\tilde{A}}$ is called an interval type-2 fuzzy set [54]. An interval type-2 fuzzy set $\tilde{\tilde{A}}$ can be regarded as a special case of a type-2 fuzzy set, represented as follows [54]:*

$$A = \int_{x \in X} \int_{u \in J_X} 1/(x, u), \qquad (8)$$

where $J_X \subseteq [0, 1]$.

Definition 3. *The upper membership function and the lower membership function of an interval type-2 fuzzy set are type-1 membership functions, respectively. In this paper, we propose the* application of interval type-2 fuzzy sets for solving fuzzy MCDM problems, where the points with maximum membership degrees of the upper and the lower membership functions of interval type-2 fuzzy sets are used to characterize interval type-2 fuzzy sets. Figure 4 illustrates a trapezoidal interval type-2 fuzzy set $\tilde{\tilde{A}} = \left(\tilde{A}_i^U, \tilde{A}_i^L\right) = ((a_{i1}^U, a_{i2}^U, a_{i3}^U, a_{i4}^U; H_1\left(\tilde{A}_i^U\right), H_2\left(\tilde{A}_i^U\right)), (a_{i1}^L, a_{i2}^L, a_{i3}^L, a_{i4}^L; H_1\left(\tilde{A}_i^L\right), H_2\left(\tilde{A}_i^L\right))$ where $\tilde{A}_i^U$ and $\tilde{A}_i^L$ are type-1 fuzzy sets, $a_{i1}^U, a_{i2}^U, a_{i3}^U, a_{i4}^U, a_{i1}^L, a_{i2}^L, a_{i3}^L$ and a_{i4}^L are the reference points of the interval type-2 fuzzy set $\tilde{\tilde{A}}_i$, $H_j\left(\tilde{A}_i^U\right)$ denotes the membership value of the element $a_{i(j+1)}^U$ in the upper trapezoidal membership function $\tilde{A}_i^U$, $1 \leq j \leq 2$, $H_j\left(\tilde{A}_i^L\right)$ denotes the membership value of the element $a_{i(j+1)}^L$ in the lower trapezoidal membership function $\tilde{A}_i^L$, $1 \leq j \leq 2$, $H_1\left(\tilde{A}_i^U\right) \in [0,1]$, $H_2\left(\tilde{A}_i^U\right) \in [0,1]$, $H_1\left(\tilde{A}_i^L\right) \in [0,1]$, $H_2\left(\tilde{A}_i^L\right) \in [0,1]$, and $1 \leq i \leq n$.

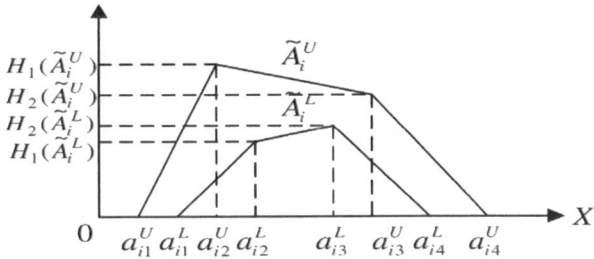

Figure 4. The upper and lower trapezoidal membership functions of the interval type-2 fuzzy set.

Definition 4. *The addition operation between the trapezoidal interval type-2 fuzzy sets* $\tilde{\tilde{A}}_1 = (\tilde{A}_1^U, \tilde{A}_1^L) = ((a_{11}^U, a_{12}^U, a_{13}^U, a_{14}^U; H_1(\tilde{A}_1^U), H_2(\tilde{A}_1^U)), (a_{11}^L, a_{12}^L, a_{13}^L, a_{14}^L; H_1(\tilde{A}_1^L), H_2(\tilde{A}_1^L)))$ *and* $\tilde{\tilde{A}}_2 = (\tilde{A}_2^U, \tilde{A}_2^L) = ((a_{21}^U, a_{22}^U, a_{23}^U, a_{24}^U; H_1(\tilde{A}_2^U), H_2(\tilde{A}_2^U)), (a_{21}^L, a_{22}^L, a_{23}^L, a_{24}^L; H_1(\tilde{A}_2^L), H_2(\tilde{A}_2^L)))$ *is defined as follows [54–56]:*

$$\tilde{\tilde{A}}_1 \oplus \tilde{\tilde{A}}_2 = (\tilde{A}_1^U, \tilde{A}_1^L) \oplus (\tilde{A}_2^U, \tilde{A}_2^L) = ((a_{11}^U + a_{21}^U, a_{12}^U + a_{22}^U, a_{13}^U + a_{23}^U, a_{14}^U + a_{24}^U; \\ \min(H_1(\tilde{A}_1^U), H_1(\tilde{A}_2^U)), \min(H_2(\tilde{A}_1^U), H_2(\tilde{A}_2^U))), \\ (a_{11}^L + a_{21}^L, a_{12}^L + a_{22}^L, a_{13}^L + a_{23}^L, a_{14}^L + a_{24}^L; \\ \min(H_1(\tilde{A}_1^L), H_1(\tilde{A}_2^L)), \min(H_2(\tilde{A}_1^L), H_2(\tilde{A}_2^L)))). \tag{9}$$

Definition 5. *The subtraction operation between the trapezoidal interval type-2 fuzzy sets* $\tilde{\tilde{A}}_1 = (\tilde{A}_1^U, \tilde{A}_1^L) = ((a_{11}^U, a_{12}^U, a_{13}^U, a_{14}^U; H_1(\tilde{A}_1^U), H_2(\tilde{A}_1^U)), (a_{11}^L, a_{12}^L, a_{13}^L, a_{14}^L; H_1(\tilde{A}_1^L), H_2$

$(\tilde{A}_1^L)))$ and $\tilde{\tilde{A}}_2 = (\tilde{A}_2^U, \tilde{A}_2^L) = ((a_{21}^U, a_{22}^U, a_{23}^U, a_{24}^U; H_1(\tilde{A}_2^U), H_2(\tilde{A}_2^U)), (a_{21}^L, a_{22}^L, a_{23}^L, a_{24}^L; H_1(\tilde{A}_2^L), H_2(\tilde{A}_2^L)))$ is defined as follows [54–56]:

$$\begin{aligned}
\tilde{\tilde{A}}_1 \ominus \tilde{\tilde{A}}_2 &= (\tilde{A}_1^U, \tilde{A}_1^L) \ominus (\tilde{A}_2^U, \tilde{A}_2^L) = ((a_{11}^U - a_{24}^U, a_{12}^U - a_{23}^U, a_{13}^U - a_{22}^U, a_{14}^U - a_{21}^U; \\
&\quad \min(H_1(\tilde{A}_1^U), H_1(\tilde{A}_2^U)), \min(H_2(\tilde{A}_1^U), H_2(\tilde{A}_2^U))), \\
&\quad (a_{11}^L - a_{24}^L, a_{12}^L - a_{23}^L, a_{13}^L - a_{22}^L, a_{14}^L - a_{21}^L; \\
&\quad \min(H_1(\tilde{A}_1^L), H_1(\tilde{A}_2^L)), \min(H_2(\tilde{A}_1^L), H_2(\tilde{A}_2^L)))).
\end{aligned} \qquad (10)$$

Definition 6. *The multiplication operation between the trapezoidal interval type-2 fuzzy sets* $\tilde{\tilde{A}}_1 = (\tilde{A}_1^U, \tilde{A}_1^L) = ((a_{11}^U, a_{12}^U, a_{13}^U, a_{14}^U; H_1(\tilde{A}_1^U), H_2(\tilde{A}_1^U)), (a_{11}^L, a_{12}^L, a_{13}^L, a_{14}^L; H_1(\tilde{A}_1^L), H_2(\tilde{A}_1^L)))$ *and* $\tilde{\tilde{A}}_2 = (\tilde{A}_2^U, \tilde{A}_2^L) = ((a_{21}^U, a_{22}^U, a_{23}^U, a_{24}^U; H_1(\tilde{A}_2^U), H_2(\tilde{A}_2^U)), (a_{21}^L, a_{22}^L, a_{23}^L, a_{24}^L; H_1(\tilde{A}_2^L), H_2(\tilde{A}_2^L)))$ *is defined as follows [54–56]:*

$$\begin{aligned}
\tilde{\tilde{A}}_1 \otimes \tilde{\tilde{A}}_2 &= (\tilde{A}_1^U, \tilde{A}_1^L) \otimes (\tilde{A}_2^U, \tilde{A}_2^L) = ((a_{11}^U \times a_{21}^U, a_{12}^U \times a_{22}^U, a_{13}^U \times a_{23}^U, a_{14}^U \times a_{24}^U; \\
&\quad \min(H_1(\tilde{A}_1^U), H_1(\tilde{A}_2^U)), \min(H_2(\tilde{A}_1^U), H_2(\tilde{A}_2^U))), \\
&\quad (a_{11}^L \times a_{21}^L, a_{12}^L \times a_{22}^L, a_{13}^L \times a_{23}^L, a_{14}^L \times a_{24}^L; \\
&\quad \min(H_1(\tilde{A}_1^L), H_1(\tilde{A}_2^L)), \min(H_2(\tilde{A}_1^L), H_2(\tilde{A}_2^L)))).
\end{aligned} \qquad (11)$$

Definition 7. *The division operation between the trapezoidal interval type-2 fuzzy sets* $\tilde{\tilde{A}}_1 = (\tilde{A}_1^U, \tilde{A}_1^L) = ((a_{11}^U, a_{12}^U, a_{13}^U, a_{14}^U; H_1(\tilde{A}_1^U), H_2(\tilde{A}_1^U)), (a_{11}^L, a_{12}^L, a_{13}^L, a_{14}^L; H_1(\tilde{A}_1^L), H_2(\tilde{A}_1^L)))$ *and* $\tilde{\tilde{A}}_2 = (\tilde{A}_2^U, \tilde{A}_2^L) = ((a_{21}^U, a_{22}^U, a_{23}^U, a_{24}^U; H_1(\tilde{A}_2^U), H_2(\tilde{A}_2^U)), (a_{21}^L, a_{22}^L, a_{23}^L, a_{24}^L; H_1(\tilde{A}_2^L), H_2(\tilde{A}_2^L)))$ *is defined as follows [54–56]:*

$$\begin{aligned}
\tilde{\tilde{A}}_1 \oslash \tilde{\tilde{A}}_2 &= (\tilde{A}_1^U, \tilde{A}_1^L) \oslash (\tilde{A}_2^U, \tilde{A}_2^L) = ((\tfrac{a_{11}^U}{a_{24}^U}, \tfrac{a_{12}^U}{a_{23}^U}, \tfrac{a_{13}^U}{a_{22}^U}, \tfrac{a_{14}^U}{a_{21}^U}; \\
&\quad \min(H_1(\tilde{A}_1^U), H_1(\tilde{A}_2^U)), \min(H_2(\tilde{A}_1^U), H_2(\tilde{A}_2^U))), \\
&\quad (\tfrac{a_{11}^L}{a_{24}^L}, \tfrac{a_{12}^L}{a_{23}^L}, \tfrac{a_{13}^L}{a_{22}^L}, \tfrac{a_{14}^L}{a_{21}^L}; \min(H_1(\tilde{A}_1^L), H_1(\tilde{A}_2^L)), \min(H_2(\tilde{A}_1^L), H_2(\tilde{A}_2^L)))).
\end{aligned} \qquad (12)$$

Definition 8. *The arithmetic operations between the trapezoidal interval type-2 fuzzy sets* $\tilde{\tilde{A}}_1 = (\tilde{A}_1^U, \tilde{A}_1^L) = ((a_{11}^U, a_{12}^U, a_{13}^U, a_{14}^U; H_1(\tilde{A}_1^U), H_2(\tilde{A}_1^U)), (a_{11}^L, a_{12}^L, a_{13}^L, a_{14}^L; H_1(\tilde{A}_1^L), H_2(\tilde{A}_1^L)))$ *and the crisp value k is defined as follows [54–56]:*

$$\begin{aligned}
k\tilde{\tilde{A}}_1 &= ((k \times a_{11}^U, k \times a_{12}^U, k \times a_{13}^U, k \times a_{14}^U; .H_1(\tilde{A}_1^U), H_2(\tilde{A}_1^U)), \\
&\quad (k \times a_{11}^L, k \times a_{12}^L, k \times a_{13}^L, k \times a_{14}^L; .H_1(\tilde{A}_1^L), H_2(\tilde{A}_1^L)), \\
\tfrac{\tilde{\tilde{A}}_1}{k} &= ((\tfrac{1}{k} \times a_{11}^U, \tfrac{1}{k} \times a_{12}^U, \tfrac{1}{k} \times a_{13}^U, \tfrac{1}{k} \times a_{14}^U; .H_1(\tilde{A}_1^U), H_2(\tilde{A}_1^U)), \\
&\quad (\tfrac{1}{k} \times a_{11}^L, \tfrac{1}{k} \times a_{12}^L, \tfrac{1}{k} \times a_{13}^L, \tfrac{1}{k} \times a_{14}^L; .H_1(\tilde{A}_1^L), H_2(\tilde{A}_1^L)), \\
&\text{where } k > 0.
\end{aligned} \qquad (13)$$

3.2.2. Type-2 Fuzzy AROMAN Method

An extension of the AROMAN method [26–28] to the type-2 fuzzy environment is proposed in this section. The procedure is described in the following steps.

Step 1: Determine the initial decision-making matrix with the input data.
A type-2 fuzzy MCDM problem can be shown in the matrix format as:

$$\tilde{\tilde{D}} = \begin{bmatrix} \tilde{\tilde{x}}_{11} & \cdots & \tilde{\tilde{x}}_{1j} & \cdots & \tilde{\tilde{x}}_{1n} \\ \tilde{\tilde{x}}_{21} & \cdots & \tilde{\tilde{x}}_{2j} & \cdots & \tilde{\tilde{x}}_{2n} \\ \vdots & \ddots & \vdots & \ddots & \vdots \\ \tilde{\tilde{x}}_{m1} & \cdots & \tilde{\tilde{x}}_{mj} & \cdots & \tilde{\tilde{x}}_{mn} \end{bmatrix}, i = 1, 2, \ldots, m, j = 1, 2, \ldots, n.$$

where $\tilde{\tilde{x}}_{ij}$ are linguistic variables.

To rate the qualitative criteria, the inputs are linguistic variables. These linguistic variables can be expressed as type-2 trapezoidal fuzzy numbers. The scale is offered in Table 2.

Table 2. Linguistic variables for the ratings of criteria.

Linguistic Variable	Type-2 Fuzzy Numbers
Very low (VL)	(0, 0, 0, 1; 1, 1), (0, 0, 0, 0.5; 0.9, 0.9)
Low (L)	(0, 1, 1, 3; 1, 1), (0.5, 1, 1, 2; 0.9, 0.9)
Medium-low (ML)	(1, 3, 3, 5; 1, 1), (2, 3, 3, 4; 0.9, 0.9)
Medium (M)	(3, 5, 5, 7; 1, 1), (4, 5, 5, 6; 0.9, 0.9)
Medium-high (MH)	(5, 7, 7, 9; 1, 1), (6, 7, 7, 8; 0.9, 0.9)
High (H)	(7, 9, 9, 10; 1, 1), (8, 9, 9, 9.5; 0.9, 0.9)
Very High (VH)	(9, 10, 10, 10; 1, 1), (0.95, 10, 10, 10; 0.9, 0.9)

If there are K experts that evaluate the alternatives based on set criteria, then the ratings can be calculated as:

$$\tilde{\tilde{x}}_{ij} = \frac{1}{K} \left[\tilde{\tilde{x}}_{ij}^1 (+) \tilde{\tilde{x}}_{ij}^2 (+) \ldots (+) \tilde{\tilde{x}}_{ij}^K \right]. \quad (14)$$

Next, the normalization of data should be carried out. The AROMAN method implies two types of normalization, as explained in Steps 2 and 3.

Step 2: Normalization No. 1.

$$\tilde{\tilde{t}}_{ij} = \frac{\tilde{\tilde{x}}_{ij} - \min_i \tilde{\tilde{x}}_{ij}}{\max_i \tilde{\tilde{x}}_{ij} - \min_i \tilde{\tilde{x}}_{ij}}, i = 1, 2, \ldots, m; j = 1, 2, \ldots, n; \quad (15)$$

Step 3: Normalization No. 2.

$$\tilde{\tilde{t}}_{ij}^* = \frac{\tilde{\tilde{x}}_{ij}}{\sqrt{\sum_{i=1}^m \tilde{\tilde{x}}_{ij}^2}}; i = 1, 2, \ldots, m; j = 1, 2, \ldots, n; \quad (16)$$

The normalization procedure in Steps 2 and 3 should be applied for both criterion types (min and max).

Step 4: Aggregated normalization.
The aggregated normalization is obtained by Equation (17).

$$\tilde{\tilde{t}}_{ij}^{norm} = \frac{\beta \tilde{\tilde{t}}_{ij} + (1-\beta) \tilde{\tilde{t}}_{ij}^*}{2}; i = 1, 2, \ldots, m; j = 1, 2, \ldots, n; \quad (17)$$

where $\tilde{\tilde{t}}_{ij}^{norm}$ denotes the aggregated averaged normalization. β is a weighting factor for each type of normalization varying from 0 to 1.

Step 5: Weighted aggregated normalized decision-making matrix.

The aggregated normalized decision-making (DM) matrix should be multiplied by the criteria weights to obtain a weighted DM matrix.

$$\tilde{\tilde{t}}_{ij} = W_{ij} \cdot \tilde{\tilde{t}}_{ij}^{norm}; \quad i = 1, 2, \ldots, m; j = 1, 2, \ldots, n; \tag{18}$$

Step 6: Summation of weighted aggregated normalized DM per the criteria type.

Further procedure relates to a summation of the normalized weighted values separately for the criteria type min ($\tilde{\tilde{L}}_i$) and the type max ($\tilde{\tilde{A}}_i$).

$$\tilde{\tilde{L}}_i = \sum_{j=1}^{n} \tilde{\tilde{t}}_{ij}^{(min)}; \quad i = 1, 2, \ldots, m; j = 1, 2, \ldots, n; \tag{19}$$

$$\tilde{\tilde{A}}_i = \sum_{j=1}^{n} \tilde{\tilde{t}}_{ij}^{(max)}; \quad i = 1, 2, \ldots, m; j = 1, 2, \ldots, n; \tag{20}$$

Step 7: Raise the obtained $\tilde{\tilde{L}}_i$ and $\tilde{\tilde{A}}_i$ values to the degree of λ.

$$\hat{\tilde{\tilde{L}}}_i = \tilde{\tilde{L}}_i^{\lambda} = (\sum_{j=1}^{n} \tilde{\tilde{t}}_{ij}^{(min)})^{\lambda}; \quad i = 1, 2, \ldots, m; j = 1, 2, \ldots, n; \tag{21}$$

$$\hat{\tilde{\tilde{A}}}_i = \tilde{\tilde{A}}_i^{1-\lambda} = (\sum_{j=1}^{n} \tilde{\tilde{t}}_{ij}^{(max)})^{1-\lambda}; \quad i = 1, 2, \ldots, m; j = 1, 2, \ldots, n; \tag{22}$$

where λ represents the coefficient degree of the criterion type. Parameter λ can be set in different ways; however, here, we apply the weights obtained by the FUCOM method. If we mark the weights of the criteria of min type by w_j^{min}, then the parameter λ can be obtained by Equation (23).

$$\lambda = \sum_{j=1}^{n} w_j^{min}; \quad j = 1, 2, \ldots, n \tag{23}$$

Step 8: Calculate the final ranking.

To obtain the final ranking of alternatives (R_i), the difference between the values $\hat{\tilde{\tilde{A}}}_i$ and $\hat{\tilde{\tilde{L}}}_i$ should be calculated and the final ranking equation applied. To transform the type-2 fuzzy numbers to crisp values, we will apply the approach proposed by Lee and Chen [57] for ranking values of trapezoidal interval type-2 fuzzy sets.

Let A_i be an interval type-2 fuzzy set shown in Figure 4, where $A_i = (\tilde{A}_i^U, \tilde{A}_i^L)$ $= (a_{i1}^U, a_{i2}^U, a_{i3}^U, a_{i4}^U; H_1(\tilde{A}_i^U), H_2(\tilde{A}_i^U)) \cdot, (a_{i1}^L, a_{i2}^L, a_{i3}^L, a_{i4}^L; H_1(\tilde{A}_i^L), H_2(\tilde{A}_i^L)))$. The ranking value Rank(A_i) of the trapezoidal interval type-2 fuzzy set A_i is defined as follows [57]:

$$\begin{aligned}\text{Rank } \tilde{\tilde{A}}_i = & M_1(\tilde{A}_i^U) + M_1(\tilde{A}_i^L) + M_2(\tilde{A}_i^U) + M_2(\tilde{A}_i^L) + M_3(\tilde{A}_i^U) + M_3(\tilde{A}_i^L) \\ & - \tfrac{1}{4}(S_1(\tilde{A}_i^U) + S_1(\tilde{A}_i^L) + S_2(\tilde{A}_i^U) + S_2(\tilde{A}_i^L) + S_3(\tilde{A}_i^U) + S_3(\tilde{A}_i^L) \\ & + S_4(\tilde{A}_i^U) + S_4(\tilde{A}_i^L)) + H_1(\tilde{A}_i^U) + H_1(\tilde{A}_i^L) + H_2(\tilde{A}_i^U) + H_2(\tilde{A}_i^L),\end{aligned} \tag{24}$$

where $M_p(\tilde{A}_i^j)$ denotes the average of the elements a_{ip}^j and $a_{i(p+1)}^j$, $M_p(\tilde{A}_i^j) = \frac{a_{ip}^j + a_{i(p+1)}^j}{2}$, $1 \leq p \leq 3$, $S_q(\tilde{A}_i^j)$ denotes the standard deviation of the elements a_{iq}^j and $a_{i(q+1)}^j$, $S_q(\tilde{A}_i^j) = \sqrt{\tfrac{1}{2}\sum_{k=q}^{q+1}(a_{ik}^j - \tfrac{1}{2}\sum_{k=q}^{q+1}a_{ik}^j)^2}$, $1 \leq q \leq 3$, $S_4(\tilde{A}_i^j)$ denotes the standard deviation of the elements $a_{i1}^j, a_{i2}^j, a_{i3}^j, a_{i4}^j$, $S_4(\tilde{A}_i^j) = \sqrt{\frac{1}{4}\sum_{k=1}^{4}(a_{ik}^j - \frac{1}{4}\sum_{k=1}^{4}a_{ik}^j)^2}$, $H_p(\tilde{A}_i^j)$ denotes the membership value of the element $a_{i(q+1)}^j$ in the trapezoidal membership function $\tilde{A}_i^j$, $1 \leq p \leq 2, j \in \{U, L\}$, and $1 \leq i \leq n$.

In Equation (24), the summation of $M_1(\tilde{A}_i^U), M_1(\tilde{A}_i^L), M_2(\tilde{A}_i^U), M_2(\tilde{A}_i^L), M_3(\tilde{A}_i^U)$, $M_3(\tilde{A}_i^L), H_1(\tilde{A}_i^U), H_1(\tilde{A}_i^L), H_2(\tilde{A}_i^U)$ and $H_2(\tilde{A}_i^L)$ is called the basic ranking score, where we deduct the average of $S_1(\tilde{A}_i^U), S_1(\tilde{A}_i^L), S_2(\tilde{A}_i^U), S_2(\tilde{A}_i^L), S_3(\tilde{A}_i^U), S_3(\tilde{A}_i^L), S_4(\tilde{A}_i^U)$ and $S_4(\tilde{A}_i^L)$ from the basic ranking score to give the dispersive interval type-2 fuzzy set a penalty, where $1 \leq i \leq n$.

Accordingly, the final equation for the calculation of alternative ranks is as follows:

$$R_i = e^{Rank(\hat{\tilde{A}}_i - \hat{\tilde{L}}_i)}; \, i = 1, 2, \ldots, m \qquad (25)$$

4. Case Study—Optimization of the Rural Postal Network in the Region of Bajina Bašta, Serbia

To illustrate the applicability of the proposed methodology, we present a real-life case study in this section. The task will be to determine the importance ranks of six postal branches of the rural postal network in the region of Bajina Bašta, Serbia. In the considered region, there is just one post office in the urban area, 31250 Bajina Bašta, while the remaining six, which are the subjects of a case study and can be considered as alternatives, are in rural areas, and their names are:

- 31251 Mitrovac—alternative 1 (A1);
- 31253 Zlodol—alternative 2 (A2);
- 31254 Kostojevići—alternative 3 (A3);
- 31255 Rogačica—alternative 4 (A4);
- 31256 Perućac—alternative 5 (A5);
- 31258 Bačevci—alternative 6 (A6).

The number before the name of the location of the post office represents its postal code. The position of the Bajina Bašta region on the map of Europe is presented in Figure 5. A layout of post offices in the considered region is shown in Figure 6, where the red point is an urban post office and the remaining six in green are post offices in rural areas. The numbers correspond to the serial number of each alternative. The visual impression of the buildings where post offices are located is presented in Figure 7.

After we identified seven criteria, as previously explained in the section concerning the literature review, and six alternatives, we started the procedure by interviewing experts. The experts were interviewed twice: the first time to obtain the criteria weights by the FUCOM method, and the second time to implement the type-2 fuzzy AROMAN method. In this case study, we collected the answers from three experts from the postal industry. All experts have more than 20 years of professional experience. Moreover, two of them possess Ph.D. degrees, while the remaining one is a postal technology engineer.

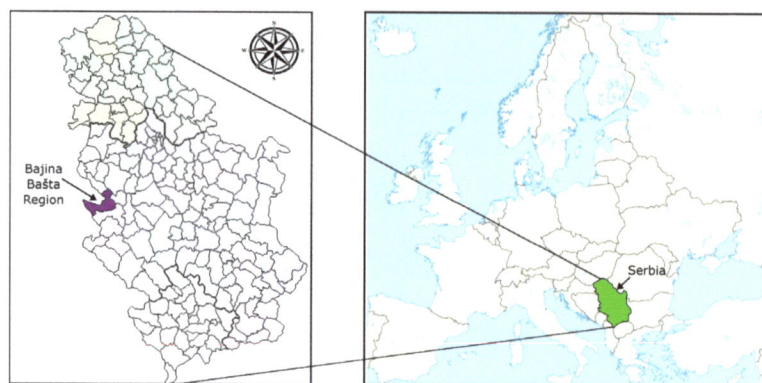

Figure 5. Position of the Bajina Bašta region on the map of Europe.

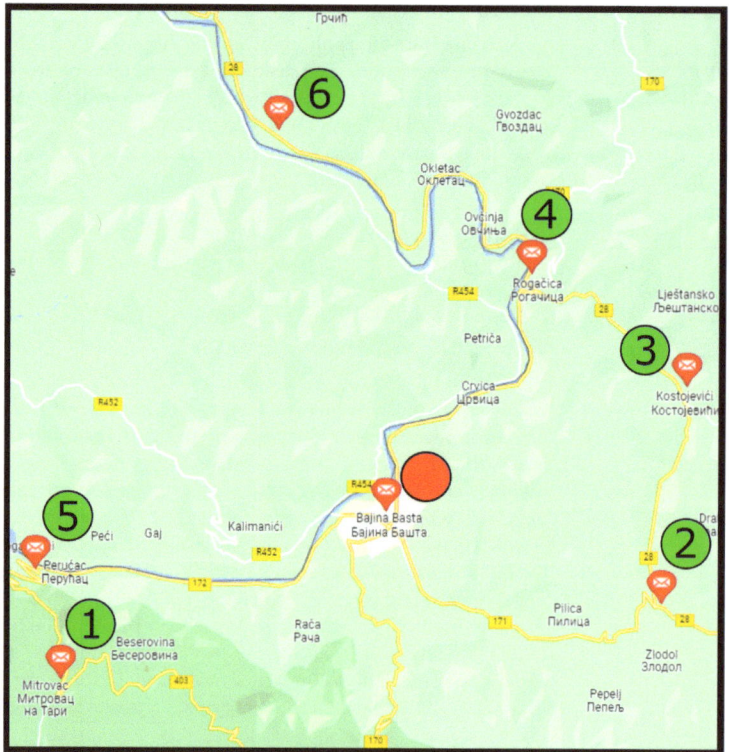

Figure 6. Layout of post offices in the region of Bajina Bašta. 1—31251 Mitrovac; 2—31253 Zlodol; 3—31254 Kostojevići; 4—31255 Rogačica; 5—31256 Perućac; 6—31258 Bačevci. Red Circle is an urban post office.

Figure 7. The appearance of the considered post offices. 1—31251 Mitrovac; 2—31253 Zlodol; 3—31254 Kostojevići; 4—31255 Rogačica; 5—31256 Perućac; 6—31258 Bačevci.

4.1. The Results of the FUCOM Method

Step 1: The initial interrelation between the criteria is examined by using the numbers from 1 to 7. The criteria ranked 1 are the most important, while the criteria marked 7 are the least important. The results of evaluations by five experts are presented in Table 3.

Table 3. The answers of experts about the initial interrelation between the criteria.

	Criterion 1	Criterion 2	Criterion 3	Criterion 4	Criterion 5	Criterion 6	Criterion 7
Expert 1	3	1	4	6	5	2	7
Expert 2	3	1	4	7	5	2	6
Expert 3	4	2	3	7	5	1	6

Step 2: Further comparison of the ranked criteria is carried out by determining the comparative priority, and the answers are in Table 4.

Table 4. The answers of experts about the comparative priority of the criteria.

	Criterion 1	Criterion 2	Criterion 3	Criterion 4	Criterion 5	Criterion 6	Criterion 7
Expert 1	2.8	1	2.9	3.5	3.2	2.1	3.9
Expert 2	1.8	1	2.4	4	2.9	1.2	3.5
Expert 3	3	2	2.1	6	4	1	4.5

Step 3: According to the explanation of Step 3 in the methodological part, we calculated the criteria weights. The achieved results are presented in Table 5. These results will be further used in the procedure of type-2 fuzzy AROMAN implementation.

Table 5. The final values of the weight coefficients.

	Criterion 1	Criterion 2	Criterion 3	Criterion 4	Criterion 5	Criterion 6	Criterion 7
Expert 1	0.118	0.330	0.114	0.094	0.103	0.157	0.085
Expert 2	0.151	0.271	0.113	0.068	0.094	0.226	0.078
Expert 3	0.113	0.170	0.162	0.057	0.085	0.339	0.075
Average	0.127	0.257	0.129	0.073	0.094	0.241	0.079

The results of the FUCOM method implementation indicate that the most important criterion for the optimization of the postal network is Criterion 2—development potential (Figure 8). This can be explained by the significant benefits that the attributes relating to Criterion 2 might bring to the rural area. For example, the presence of legal entities in certain areas can generate new demand for services and products produced by local community members. The second-ranked criterion is C6—alternative services. It is described by the attributes competition and the proximity of an alternative post office. The high importance of this criterion is logical, keeping in mind that the potential closing of a post office is very difficult to overcome if the alternative solutions are not available.

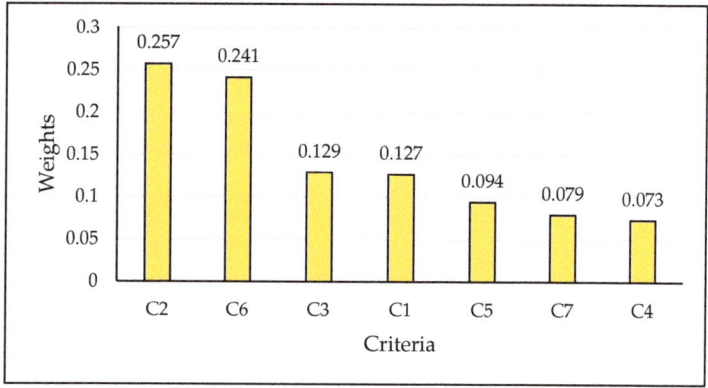

Figure 8. The result of ranking the criteria importance.

The third-ranked criterion is C3—service quality. It involves attributes such as the efficiency, quality of the provided postal services or waiting time in the line. Unlike the previous two criteria, which can be considered as external or non-dependent from the efforts of managers in the postal branch, C3 is mostly dependent. Therefore, these managers should be aware of the relatively high impact of their business efforts on the long-term existence of their postal branch. The social value, Criterion 1, relates to the number of inhabitants that belong to vulnerable groups. This should remind the policymakers that post offices in rural areas are important for more than just providing postal services. Indeed, they can be considered as entities supporting vulnerable groups in different ways, from providing financial aid and representing a medium for supplying basic necessities to acting as the main pillar of social life and interconnection of these people with the community.

The fifth-ranked criterion is C5—infrastructure, in terms of mobile and Internet network coverage. Developed infrastructure can replace certain needs for postal services, however, not in total, especially as it cannot replace the post office as a unit of social value.

The sixth-ranked criterion is Criterion 7—the postal network unit arrangement. This criterion includes the attributes: interior and exterior of the post office, appropriate working hours, range of services, and easiness of access. The last-ranked criterion, C4, is closely related to the previous one, since both are internal criteria, depending mostly on the managers and employees in the postal branch. C4 involves the expertise and kindness of employees.

4.2. The Results of a Type-2 Fuzzy AROMAN Method

The procedure of type-2 fuzzy AROMAN starts by interviewing experts about the values considering each criterion, per each considered alternative. In this case study, we collected the answers as shown in Table 6, in this way forming the initial decision-making matrix. Then, the linguistic inputs are converted into type-2 fuzzy numbers following the rules presented in Table 2. The results are averaged for all three experts and presented in Table 7.

Table 6. The ratings of alternatives.

Criteria	Alternatives	Experts		
		E1	E2	E3
C1	A1	M	MH	MH
	A2	MH	H	H
	A3	M	ML	M
	A4	VH	H	VH
	A5	L	ML	ML
	A6	VL	L	L
C2	A1	L	ML	ML
	A2	M	ML	M
	A3	MH	M	M
	A4	H	H	VH
	A5	ML	ML	ML
	A6	MH	M	MH
C3	A1	L	L	ML
	A2	VH	H	H
	A3	VH	H	VH
	A4	H	H	MH
	A5	ML	M	M
	A6	MH	M	M
C4	A1	L	L	ML
	A2	H	H	MH
	A3	H	H	MH
	A4	VH	H	H
	A5	H	H	MH
	A6	L	L	ML
C5	A1	ML	M	M
	A2	MH	MH	M
	A3	ML	M	M
	A4	H	MH	H
	A5	ML	M	M
	A6	MH	M	M
C6	A1	MH	M	M
	A2	M	MH	M
	A3	ML	M	M
	A4	MH	MH	H
	A5	ML	M	M
	A6	ML	M	ML
C7	A1	M	MH	MH
	A2	M	MH	M
	A3	ML	M	M
	A4	MH	H	H
	A5	M	ML	M
	A6	ML	M	M

Table 7. The type-2 fuzzy decision matrix.

Criteria	Alternatives	Experts (Average)
C1	A1	(4.33, 6.33, 6.33, 8.33; 1, 1), (5.33, 6.33, 6.33, 7.33; 0.9, 0.9)
	A2	(6.33, 8.33, 8.33, 9.67; 1, 1), (7.33, 8.33, 8.33, 9.00; 0.9, 0.9)
	A3	(2.33, 4.33, 4.33, 6.33; 1, 1), (3.33, 4.33, 4.33, 5.33; 0.9, 0.9)
	A4	(8.33, 9.67, 9.67, 10.00; 1, 1), (9.00, 9.67, 9.67, 9.83; 0.9, 0.9)
	A5	(0.67, 2.33, 2.33, 4.33; 1, 1), (1.50, 2.33, 2.33, 3.33; 0.9, 0.9)
	A6	(0.00, 0.67, 0.67, 2.33; 1, 1), (0.33, 0.67, 0.67, 1.50; 0.9, 0.9)
C2	A1	(0.67, 2.33, 2.33, 4.33; 1, 1), (1.50, 2.33, 2.33, 3.33; 0.9, 0.9)
	A2	(2.33, 4.33, 4.33, 6.33; 1, 1), (3.33, 4.33, 4.33, 5.33; 0.9, 0.9)
	A3	(3.67, 5.67, 5.67, 7.67; 1, 1), (4.67, 5.67, 5.67, 6.67; 0.9, 0.9)
	A4	(7.67, 9.33, 9.33, 10.00; 1, 1), (8.50, 9.33, 9.33, 9.67; 0.9, 0.9)
	A5	(1.00, 3.00, 3.00, 5.00; 1, 1), (2.00, 3.00, 3.00, 4.00; 0.9, 0.9)
	A6	(4.33, 6.33, 6.33, 8.33; 1, 1), (5.33, 6.33, 6.33, 7.33; 0.9, 0.9)
C3	A1	(0.33, 1.67, 1.67, 3.67; 1, 1), (1.00, 1.67, 1.67, 2.67; 0.9, 0.9)
	A2	(7.67, 9.33, 9.33, 10.00; 1, 1), (8.50, 9.33, 9.33, 9.67; 0.9, 0.9)
	A3	(8.33, 9.67, 9.67, 10.00; 1, 1), (9.00, 9.67, 9.67, 9.83; 0.9, 0.9)
	A4	(6.33, 8.33, 8.33, 9.67; 1, 1), (7.33, 8.33, 8.33, 9.00; 0.9, 0.9)
	A5	(2.33, 4.33, 4.33, 6.33; 1, 1), (3.33, 4.33, 4.33, 5.33; 0.9, 0.9)
	A6	(3.67, 5.67, 5.67, 7.67; 1, 1), (4.67, 5.67, 5.67, 6.67; 0.9, 0.9)
C4	A1	(0.33, 1.67, 1.67, 3.67; 1, 1), (1.00, 1.67, 1.67, 2.67; 0.9, 0.9)
	A2	(6.33, 8.33, 8.33, 9.67; 1, 1), (7.33, 8.33, 8.33, 9.00; 0.9, 0.9)
	A3	(6.33, 8.33, 8.33, 9.67; 1, 1), (7.33, 8.33, 8.33, 9.00; 0.9, 0.9)
	A4	(7.67, 9.33, 9.33, 10.00; 1, 1), (8.50, 9.33, 9.33, 9.67; 0.9, 0.9)
	A5	(6.33, 8.33, 8.33, 9.67; 1, 1), (7.33, 8.33, 8.33, 9.00; 0.9, 0.9)
	A6	(0.33, 1.67, 1.67, 3.67; 1, 1), (1.00, 1.67, 1.67, 2.67; 0.9, 0.9)
C5	A1	(2.33, 4.33, 4.33, 6.33; 1, 1), (3.33, 4.33, 4.33, 5.33; 0.9, 0.9)
	A2	(4.33, 6.33, 6.33, 8.33; 1, 1), (5.33, 6.33, 6.33, 7.33; 0.9, 0.9)
	A3	(2.33, 4.33, 4.33, 6.33; 1, 1), (3.33, 4.33, 4.33, 5.33; 0.9, 0.9)
	A4	(6.33, 8.33, 8.33, 9.67; 1, 1), (7.33, 8.33, 8.33, 9.00; 0.9, 0.9)
	A5	(2.33, 4.33, 4.33, 6.33; 1, 1), (3.33, 4.33, 4.33, 5.33; 0.9, 0.9)
	A6	(3.67, 5.67, 5.67, 7.67; 1, 1), (4.67, 5.67, 5.67, 6.67; 0.9, 0.9)
C6	A1	(3.67, 5.67, 5.67, 7.67; 1, 1), (4.67, 5.67, 5.67, 6.67; 0.9, 0.9)
	A2	(3.67, 5.67, 5.67, 7.67; 1, 1), (4.67, 5.67, 5.67, 6.67; 0.9, 0.9)
	A3	(2.33, 4.33, 4.33, 6.33; 1, 1), (3.33, 4.33, 4.33, 5.33; 0.9, 0.9)
	A4	(5.67, 7.67, 7.67, 9.33; 1, 1), (6.67, 7.67, 7.67, 8.50; 0.9, 0.9)
	A5	(2.33, 4.33, 4.33, 6.33; 1, 1), (3.33, 4.33, 4.33, 5.33; 0.9, 0.9)
	A6	(1.67, 3.67, 3.67, 5.67; 1, 1), (2.67, 3.67, 3.67, 4.67; 0.9, 0.9)
C7	A1	(4.33, 6.33, 6.33, 8.33; 1, 1), (5.33, 6.33, 6.33, 7.33; 0.9, 0.9)
	A2	(3.67, 5.67, 5.67, 7.67; 1, 1), (4.67, 5.67, 5.67, 6.67; 0.9, 0.9)
	A3	(2.33, 4.33, 4.33, 6.33; 1, 1), (3.33, 4.33, 4.33, 5.33; 0.9, 0.9)
	A4	(6.33, 8.33, 8.33, 9.67; 1, 1), (7.33, 8.33, 8.33, 9.00; 0.9, 0.9)
	A5	(2.33, 4.33, 4.33, 6.33; 1, 1), (3.33, 4.33, 4.33, 5.33; 0.9, 0.9)
	A6	(2.33, 4.33, 4.33, 6.33; 1, 1), (3.33, 4.33, 4.33, 5.33; 0.9, 0.9)

The results of Steps 2, 3, and 4 will not be displayed here to keep the length of the article reasonable. However, the results of the weighted aggregated normalized decision-making matrix that need to be calculated in Step 5 are shown in Table 8.

Table 8. The weighted aggregated normalized type-2 fuzzy decision matrix.

Criteria	Alternatives	Type-2 Fuzzy Numbers—Average Experts' Answers
C1	A1	(0.03, 0.04, 0.04, 0.06; 1, 1), (0.03, 0.04, 0.04, 0.05; 0.9, 0.9)
	A2	(0.04, 0.06, 0.06, 0.07; 1, 1), (0.05, 0.06, 0.06, 0.06; 0.9, 0.9)
	A3	(0.02, 0.03, 0.03, 0.04; 1, 1), (0.02, 0.03, 0.03, 0.04; 0.9, 0.9)
	A4	(0.05, 0.06, 0.06, 0.07; 1, 1), (0.06, 0.07, 0.07, 0.07; 0.9, 0.9)
	A5	(0.00, 0.02, 0.02, 0.03; 1, 1), (0.01, 0.01, 0.01, 0.02; 0.9, 0.9)
	A6	(0.00, 0.00, 0.00, 0.02; 1, 1), (0.00, 0.00, 0.00, 0.01; 0.9, 0.9)

Table 8. Cont.

Criteria	Alternatives	Type-2 Fuzzy Numbers—Average Experts' Answers
C2	A1	(0.00, 0.02, 0.02, 0.06; 1, 1), (0.00, 0.01, 0.01, 0.03; 0.9, 0.9)
	A2	(0.02, 0.05, 0.05, 0.09; 1, 1), (0.03, 0.05, 0.05, 0.07; 0.9, 0.9)
	A3	(0.04, 0.07, 0.07, 0.11; 1, 1), (0.05, 0.07, 0.07, 0.09; 0.9, 0.9)
	A4	(0.10, 0.13, 0.13, 0.14; 1, 1), (0.11, 0.13, 0.13, 0.14; 0.9, 0.9)
	A5	(0.01, 0.03, 0.03, 0.07; 1, 1), (0.01, 0.03, 0.03, 0.04; 0.9, 0.9)
	A6	(0.05, 0.08, 0.08, 0.12; 1, 1), (0.06, 0.08, 0.08, 0.10; 0.9, 0.9)
C3	A1	(0.00, 0.01, 0.01, 0.02; 1, 1), (0.00, 0.01, 0.01, 0.01; 0.9, 0.9)
	A2	(0.05, 0.06, 0.06, 0.07; 1, 1), (0.06, 0.06, 0.06, 0.07; 0.9, 0.9)
	A3	(0.05, 0.06, 0.06, 0.07; 1, 1), (0.06, 0.07, 0.07, 0.07; 0.9, 0.9)
	A4	(0.04, 0.06, 0.06, 0.07; 1, 1), (0.05, 0.06, 0.06, 0.06; 0.9, 0.9)
	A5	(0.01, 0.03, 0.03, 0.04; 1, 1), (0.02, 0.03, 0.03, 0.03; 0.9, 0.9)
	A6	(0.02, 0.04, 0.04, 0.05; 1, 1), (0.03, 0.04, 0.04, 0.04; 0.9, 0.9)
C4	A1	(0.00, 0.01, 0.01, 0.01; 1, 1), (0.00, 0.00, 0.00, 0.01; 0.9, 0.9)
	A2	(0.02, 0.03, 0.03, 0.04; 1, 1), (0.03, 0.03, 0.03, 0.04; 0.9, 0.9)
	A3	(0.02, 0.03, 0.03, 0.04; 1, 1), (0.03, 0.03, 0.03, 0.04; 0.9, 0.9)
	A4	(0.03, 0.04, 0.04, 0.04; 1, 1), (0.03, 0.04, 0.04, 0.04; 0.9, 0.9)
	A5	(0.02, 0.03, 0.03, 0.04; 1, 1), (0.03, 0.03, 0.03, 0.04; 0.9, 0.9)
	A6	(0.00, 0.01, 0.01, 0.01; 1, 1), (0.00, 0.00, 0.00, 0.01; 0.9, 0.9)
C5	A1	(0.00, 0.01, 0.01, 0.03; 1, 1), (0.00, 0.01, 0.01, 0.02; 0.9, 0.9)
	A2	(0.01, 0.03, 0.03, 0.04; 1, 1), (0.02, 0.03, 0.03, 0.04; 0.9, 0.9)
	A3	(0.00, 0.01, 0.01, 0.03; 1, 1), (0.00, 0.01, 0.01, 0.02; 0.9, 0.9)
	A4	(0.03, 0.04, 0.04, 0.05; 1, 1), (0.03, 0.04, 0.04, 0.05; 0.9, 0.9)
	A5	(0.00, 0.01, 0.01, 0.03; 1, 1), (0.00, 0.01, 0.01, 0.02; 0.9, 0.9)
	A6	(0.01, 0.02, 0.02, 0.04; 1, 1), (0.01, 0.02, 0.02, 0.03; 0.9, 0.9)
C6	A1	(0.03, 0.07, 0.07, 0.11; 1, 1), (0.04, 0.07, 0.07, 0.09; 0.9, 0.9)
	A2	(0.03, 0.07, 0.07, 0.11; 1, 1), (0.04, 0.07, 0.07, 0.09; 0.9, 0.9)
	A3	(0.01, 0.04, 0.04, 0.08; 1, 1), (0.02, 0.04, 0.04, 0.06; 0.9, 0.9)
	A4	(0.07, 0.10, 0.10, 0.14; 1, 1), (0.09, 0.11, 0.11, 0.13; 0.9, 0.9)
	A5	(0.01, 0.04, 0.04, 0.08; 1, 1), (0.02, 0.04, 0.04, 0.06; 0.9, 0.9)
	A6	(0.00, 0.03, 0.03, 0.07; 1, 1), (0.00, 0.02, 0.02, 0.05; 0.9, 0.9)
C7	A1	(0.01, 0.02, 0.02, 0.04; 1, 1), (0.01, 0.02, 0.02, 0.03; 0.9, 0.9)
	A2	(0.01, 0.02, 0.02, 0.03; 1, 1), (0.01, 0.02, 0.02, 0.03; 0.9, 0.9)
	A3	(0.00, 0.01, 0.01, 0.02; 1, 1), (0.00, 0.01, 0.01, 0.02; 0.9, 0.9)
	A4	(0.02, 0.03, 0.03, 0.04; 1, 1), (0.03, 0.04, 0.04, 0.04; 0.9, 0.9)
	A5	(0.00, 0.01, 0.01, 0.02; 1, 1), (0.00, 0.01, 0.01, 0.02; 0.9, 0.9)
	A6	(0.00, 0.01, 0.01, 0.02; 1, 1), (0.00, 0.01, 0.01, 0.02; 0.9, 0.9)

In Step 6, the summation of the weighted aggregated normalized type-2 fuzzy decision-making matrix should be carried out per the criterion type. In our case, the min type criteria are C5 and C6, while the max type criteria are C1, C2, C3, C4, and C7. The results are shown in Table 9.

Table 9. Summation of weighted type-2 fuzzy decision matrix per the criteria type.

	$\tilde{\tilde{L}}_i$	$\tilde{\tilde{A}}_i$
A1	(0.03, 0.08, 0.08, 0.14; 1, 1), (0.04, 0.08, 0.08, 0.11; 0.9, 0.9)	(0.04, 0.10, 0.10, 0.19; 1, 1), (0.05, 0.09, 0.09, 0.13; 0.9, 0.9)
A2	(0.05, 0.09, 0.09, 0.15; 1, 1), (0.06, 0.09, 0.09, 0.13; 0.9, 0.9)	(0.15, 0.22, 0.22, 0.29; 1, 1), (0.17, 0.22, 0.22, 0.25; 0.9, 0.9)
A3	(0.01, 0.06, 0.06, 0.11; 1, 1), (0.02, 0.05, 0.05, 0.08; 0.9, 0.9)	(0.14, 0.21, 0.21, 0.28; 1, 1), (0.16, 0.20, 0.20, 0.24; 0.9, 0.9)
A4	(0.09, 0.14, 0.14, 0.19; 1, 1), (0.12, 0.15, 0.15, 0.18; 0.9, 0.9)	(0.25, 0.31, 0.31, 0.36; 1, 1), (0.28, 0.32, 0.32, 0.35; 0.9, 0.9)
A5	(0.01, 0.06, 0.06, 0.11; 1, 1), (0.02, 0.05, 0.05, 0.08; 0.9, 0.9)	(0.05, 0.12, 0.12, 0.20; 1, 1), (0.06, 0.10, 0.10, 0.15; 0.9, 0.9)
A6	(0.01, 0.06, 0.06, 0.11; 1, 1), (0.01, 0.04, 0.04, 0.08; 0.9, 0.9)	(0.08, 0.14, 0.14, 0.22; 1, 1), (0.09, 0.13, 0.13, 0.17; 0.9, 0.9)

In Step 7, we should raise the obtained values from Step 6 to the degree of λ. We calculated λ as explained in the methodological part, and in our case, $\lambda = 0.335$. The obtained results from Step 7 are in Table 10.

Table 10. The results of Step 7 of the type-2 fuzzy AROMAN method.

	$\tilde{\tilde{L}}_i^{\wedge}$	$\tilde{\tilde{A}}_i^{\wedge}$
A1	(0.32, 0.43, 0.43, 0.51; 1, 1), (0.35, 0.42, 0.42, 0.47; 0.9, 0.9)	(0.12, 0.22, 0.22, 0.33; 1, 1), (0.14, 0.20, 0.20, 0.26; 0.9, 0.9)
A2	(0.36, 0.45, 0.45, 0.53; 1, 1), (0.39, 0.45, 0.45, 0.50; 0.9, 0.9)	(0.28, 0.37, 0.37, 0.44; 1, 1), (0.31, 0.36, 0.36, 0.40; 0.9, 0.9)
A3	(0.23, 0.39, 0.39, 0.48; 1, 1), (0.25, 0.36, 0.36, 0.43; 0.9, 0.9)	(0.27, 0.35, 0.35, 0.43; 1, 1), (0.30, 0.35, 0.35, 0.39; 0.9, 0.9)
A4	(0.45, 0.52, 0.52, 0.57; 1, 1), (0.49, 0.53, 0.53, 0.56; 0.9, 0.9)	(0.39, 0.46, 0.46, 0.50; 1, 1), (0.43, 0.47, 0.47, 0.49; 0.9, 0.9)
A5	(0.23, 0.39, 0.39, 0.48; 1, 1), (0.25, 0.36, 0.36, 0.43; 0.9, 0.9)	(0.13, 0.24, 0.24, 0.34; 1, 1), (0.16, 0.22, 0.22, 0.28; 0.9, 0.9)
A6	(0.21, 0.38, 0.38, 0.48; 1, 1), (0.23, 0.35, 0.35, 0.42; 0.9, 0.9)	(0.18, 0.27, 0.27, 0.37; 1, 1), (0.20, 0.26, 0.26, 0.31; 0.9, 0.9)

To achieve the final result, we should first calculate the ranking value of trapezoidal interval type-2 fuzzy sets. The following is obtained:

$$Rank(\tilde{\tilde{A}}_1^{\wedge} - \tilde{\tilde{L}}_1^{\wedge}) = 244; \ Rank(\tilde{\tilde{A}}_2^{\wedge} - \tilde{\tilde{L}}_2^{\wedge}) = 317; \ Rank(\tilde{\tilde{A}}_3^{\wedge} - \tilde{\tilde{L}}_3^{\wedge}) = 336;$$

$$Rank(\tilde{\tilde{A}}_4^{\wedge} - \tilde{\tilde{L}}_4^{\wedge}) = 340; \ Rank(\tilde{\tilde{A}}_5^{\wedge} - \tilde{\tilde{L}}_5^{\wedge}) = 291; \ Rank(\tilde{\tilde{A}}_6^{\wedge} - \tilde{\tilde{L}}_6^{\wedge}) = 314$$

Finally, the ranking of considered alternatives is shown in Table 11. As can be noticed, the alternative A4 achieved the best score. On the other hand, A1 is the postal branch with the lowest rank, which means that it should be reorganized first to optimize the postal network.

Table 11. Final ranking.

Alternatives	R_i
A1	11.52
A2	23.74
A3	28.92
A4	29.87
A5	18.28
A6	23.18

5. Discussion

The discussion section is related to three phenomena. The first relates to the sensitivity analysis based on different defuzzification approaches in the interval type-2 fuzzy AROMAN, the second to the calculation of computational complexity of the proposed algorithm, and the final to the possible approaches for postal network reorganization.

5.1. Sensitivity Analysis Based on Different Defuzzification Approaches

In the proposed methodology, we used the defuzzification approach proposed by Lee and Chen [57]. However, to examine the stability of the obtained results, we implement a different defuzzification approach in this subsection. It is based on the calculation of the centroid of a type-2 fuzzy set, as proposed by Karnik and Mendel [58]. The newly obtained results are shown in Table 12. It can be concluded that the obtained results are stable, meaning that the order of alternatives is not changed by using different defuzzification approaches.

Table 12. Final ranking based on the centroid defuzzification approaches.

	$\approx \hat{A_i} - \hat{\tilde{L_i}}$	The Centroid of Type-2 Fuzzy Number (μ_A, x)	New Ranking Values	Previous Ranking Values
A1	(−0.39, −0.20, −0.20, 0.00; 1, 1), (−0.33, −0.22, −0.22, −0.09; 0.9, 0.9)	−0.18, 0.37	0.93	11.52
A2	(−0.25, −0.08, −0.08, 0.08; 1, 1), (−0.18, −0.08, −0.08, 0.00; 0.9, 0.9)	−0.08, 0.37	0.97	23.74
A3	(−0.21, −0.03, −0.03, 0.20; 1, 1), (−0.13, −0.01, −0.01, 0.13; 0.9, 0.9)	−0.03, 0.38	0.98	28.92
A4	(−0.18, −0.05, −0.05, 0.05; 1, 1), (−0.13, −0.06, −0.06, 0.00; 0.9, 0.9)	−0.05, 0.37	0.98	29.87
A5	(−0.35, −0.14, −0.14, 0.12; 1, 1), (−0.27, −0.13, −0.13, 0.03; 0.9, 0.9)	−0.13, 0.38	0.95	18.28
A6	(−0.30, −0.11, −0.11, 0.15; 1, 1), (−0.22, −0.09, −0.09, 0.08; 0.9, 0.9)	−0.09, 0.38	0.96	23.18

5.2. Computational Complexity

The computational complexity of the MCDM methods can be evaluated by considering the time complexity—T [59]. The parameter T should be determined inside the calculations by considering the number of augmentations. Several examples are offered here to compare the complexity of the *AROMAN* approach to some other MCDM methods. Considering that there are c criteria and p alternatives, the complexity of the *AHP* approach can be calculated as follows [59]:

$$T_{AHP} = c(c+1) + p(c+1) + pc \quad (26)$$

The time complexity of the *TOPSIS* technique is computed by the following equation [59]:

$$T_{TOPSIS} = pc + pc + p(c+1) + p(c+1) + p = 4pc + 3p \quad (27)$$

Further, when it comes to the *VIKOR* approach, the time complexity is expressed through the following equation [59]:

$$T_{VIKOR} = 3c + 3p + 4 \quad (28)$$

Finally, the *AROMAN* method requires pc operations to compute normalization No. 1, and an additional pc for normalization No. 2. Further, pc operations are needed for aggregated normalization and the same number for weighted normalized matrix. For a summation of a weighted aggregated normalized matrix per the criteria type, there are c operations, while for raising the obtained values to the degree of λ, there are $2p$ more. To calculate the final ranking, there are additional p operations. The explained calculations can be expressed by Equation (29).

$$T_{AROMAN} = 4pc + c + 2p + p = 4pc + 3p + c \quad (29)$$

In the concrete case, we considered seven criteria and six alternatives; thus, the computational complexity per selected MCDM methods are the following: $T_{AHP} = 146$, $T_{TOPSIS} = 186$, $T_{VIKOR} = 43$ and $T_{AROMAN} = 193$. Figure 9 shows the computational complexity of four considered approaches.

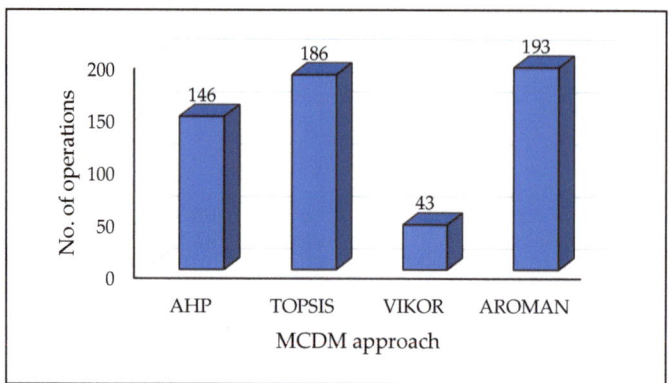

Figure 9. The computational complexity of selected MCDM techniques.

5.3. Possible Directions for Postal Network Reorganization

The options for the reorganization of the inefficient postal branches can be different. First, since the post office in a certain place can be considered to be of general interest to many stakeholders, people living in the community, business entities and state administration, then a possible solution to keep the postal branch is to provide additional funds for its functioning. These funds can be collected from postal service users or municipalities. Another option is to change the form of the postal branch. For example, it is possible to introduce a mobile post office (Figure 10), a vehicle transformed into a post office that spends a certain time parked in predefined points of interest. As can be concluded, the question of the reorganization of the inefficient postal branches can also be considered as an MCDM problem, and solving it may be a good possible direction for future research.

Figure 10. An example of a mobile post office [60].

6. Conclusions

The problem of the optimization of the postal network is very complex, keeping in mind that the interests of many stakeholders should be satisfied. The process of decision-making considering locations and the existence of the postal branch should be considered from multiple aspects, not just from the standpoint of achieved profit. Various criteria that are considered in this field are often described by uncertain or imprecise data. As a solution, we proposed an interval type-2 fuzzy AROMAN method to be implemented by policymakers and industry managers to optimize the postal network.

This study provides several contributions. Through an extensive literature review, we recognized the attributes that are important for the optimization of the postal network. Then, we grouped them into seven clusters by their similarity. The next step was to interview the experts to determine the relevance ranks of the set criteria, which was achieved using the FUCOM method. In the end, for the first time in the literature, we implemented the interval type-2 fuzzy AROMAN method. By solving a real-life numerical example, we confirmed the applicability of the proposed model. We demonstrated its implementation in the postal industry; however, it should be noted that the proposed model is general and can be used for various types of MCDM problems.

However, the model also has certain limitations. First, the procedure of the AROMAN model implies the existence of both criteria to be minimized and others to be maximized. This limitation is relatively easy to overcome in real-life problems, keeping in mind that complex phenomena are almost always described by both types of criteria. Further, the limitation of this case study can be related to a restricted group of interviewed experts that are from the postal industry. Further research can be directed toward interviewing different stakeholders, for example, people living in the community or representatives of local authorities. In addition, the proposed methodology can be expanded by using discrete type-2 fuzzy numbers or intuitionistic, Pythagorean or picture fuzzy numbers.

Author Contributions: Conceptualization, D.B. and M.D.; methodology, I.N. and M.D.; software, I.N. and D.B.; validation, I.N., D.B. and M.D.; formal analysis, I.N.; investigation, I.N. and J.M.; resources, I.N. and J.M.; data curation, I.N.; writing—original draft preparation, I.N. and J.M.; writing—review and editing, I.N.; visualization, I.N. and M.D.; supervision, D.B. and M.D.; project administration, I.N. All authors have read and agreed to the published version of the manuscript.

Funding: This research received no external funding.

Data Availability Statement: All research data are presented in the paper.

Conflicts of Interest: The authors declare no conflict of interest.

References

1. Puška, A.; Kozarević, S.; Okičić, J. Investigating and Analyzing the Supply Chain Practices and Performance in Agro-Food Industry. *Int. J. Manag. Sci. Eng. Manag.* **2019**, *15*, 9–16. [CrossRef]
2. Puška, A.; Nedeljković, M.; Zolfani, S.H.; Pamučar, D. Application of Interval Fuzzy Logic in Selecting a Sustainable Supplier on the Example of Agricultural Production. *Symmetry* **2021**, *13*, 774. [CrossRef]
3. Yang, Y.; Liu, Y.; Phang, C.W.; Wei, J. Using Microblog to Enhance Public Service Climate in the Rural Areas. *Gov. Inf. Q.* **2020**, *37*, 101402. [CrossRef]
4. Puška, A.; Štilić, A.; Stojanović, I. Approach for Multi-Criteria Ranking of Balkan Countries Based on the Index of Economic Freedom. *J. Decis. Anal. Intell. Comput.* **2023**, *3*, 1–14. [CrossRef]
5. Salemink, K.; Strijker, D.; Bosworth, G. Rural Development in the Digital Age: A Systematic Literature Review on Unequal ICT Availability, Adoption, and Use in Rural Areas. *J. Rural Stud.* **2017**, *54*, 360–371. [CrossRef]
6. Prus, P.; Sikora, M. The Impact of Transport Infrastructure on the Sustainable Development of the Region—Case Study. *Agriculture* **2021**, *11*, 279. [CrossRef]
7. Wieliczko, B.; Kurdyś-Kujawska, A.; Floriańczyk, Z. EU Rural Policy's Capacity to Facilitate a Just Sustainability Transition of the Rural Areas. *Energies* **2021**, *14*, 5050. [CrossRef]
8. Xue, E.; Li, J.; Li, X. Sustainable Development of Education in Rural Areas for Rural Revitalization in China: A Comprehensive Policy Circle Analysis. *Sustainability* **2021**, *13*, 13101. [CrossRef]
9. Tutak, M.; Brodny, J. Evaluating Differences in the Level of Working Conditions between the European Union Member States Using TOPSIS Method. *Decis. Mak. Appl. Manag. Eng.* **2022**, *5*, 1–29. [CrossRef]
10. EU Commission. *Poverty and Social Exclusion in Rural Areas*; Final Study Report; European Commission: Brussels, Belgium, 2008; 187p.
11. Puška, A.; Šadić, S.; Maksimović, A.; Stojanović, I. Decision Support Model in the Determination of Rural Touristic Destination Attractiveness in the Brčko District of Bosnia and Herzegovina. *Tour. Hosp. Res.* **2020**, *20*, 387–405. [CrossRef]
12. European Union. European Union Territorial Typologies Manual—Urban-Rural Typology—Statistics Explained. Available online: https://ec.europa.eu/eurostat/statistics-explained/index.php?title=Territorial_typologies_manual_-_urban-rural_typology#Results (accessed on 2 June 2023).

13. Abrhám, J. Rural Development and Regional Disparities of the New EU Member States. *Agric. Econ.* **2011**, *57*, 288–296. [CrossRef]
14. Murdoch, J. Networks—A New Paradigm of Rural Development? *J. Rural Stud.* **2000**, *16*, 407–419. [CrossRef]
15. Kovács, A.D.; Gulyás, P.; Farkas, J.Z. Tourism Perspectives in National Parks—A Hungarian Case Study from the Aspects of Rural Development. *Sustainability* **2021**, *13*, 12002. [CrossRef]
16. Oltean, F.D.; Gabor, M.R.; Oltean, F.D.; Gabor, M.R. Wine Tourism—A Sustainable Management Tool for Rural Development and Vineyards: Cross-Cultural Analysis of the Consumer Profile from Romania and Moldova. *Agriculture* **2022**, *12*, 1614. [CrossRef]
17. Camarero, L.; Oliva, J. Thinking in Rural Gap: Mobility and Social Inequalities. *Palgrave Commun. 2019 51* **2019**, *5*, 95. [CrossRef]
18. Ralević, P.; Dobrodolac, M.; Marković, D. Using a Nonparametric Technique to Measure the Cost Efficiency of Postal Delivery Branches. *Cent. Eur. J. Oper. Res.* **2016**, *24*, 637–657. [CrossRef]
19. Dobrodolac, M.; Ralević, P.; Švadlenka, L.; Radojičić, V. Impact of a New Concept of Universal Service Obligations on Revenue Increase in the Post of Serbia. *Promet Traffic Transp.* **2016**, *28*, 235–244. [CrossRef]
20. Dobrodolac, M.; Lazarević, D.; Švadlenka, L.; Živanović, M. A Study on the Competitive Strategy of the Universal Postal Service Provider. *Technol. Anal. Strateg. Manag.* **2016**, *28*, 935–949. [CrossRef]
21. Lazarević, D.; Dobrodolac, M.; Švadlenka, L.; Stanivuković, B. A Model for Business Performance Improvement: A Case of the Postal Company. *J. Bus. Econ. Manag.* **2020**, *21*, 564–592. [CrossRef]
22. Milutinović, J.; Marković, D.; Stanivuković, B.; Švadlenka, L.; Dobrodolac, M. A Model for Public Postal Network Reorganization Based on Dea and Fuzzy Approach. *Transport* **2020**, *35*, 401–418. [CrossRef]
23. Ralević, P.; Dobrodolac, M.; Švadlenka, L.; Šarac, D.; Đurić, D. Efficiency and Productivity Analysis of Universal Service Obligation: A Case of 29 Designated Operators in the European Countries. *Technol. Econ. Dev. Econ.* **2020**, *26*, 785–807. [CrossRef]
24. Sharma, H.K.; Majumder, S.; Biswas, A.; Prentkovskis, O.; Kar, S.; Skačkauskas, P. A Study on Decision-Making of the Indian Railways Reservation System during COVID-19. *J. Adv. Transp.* **2022**, *2022*, 7685375. [CrossRef]
25. Singh, A.; Singh, A.; Sharma, H.K.; Majumder, S. Criteria Selection of Housing Loan Based on Dominance-Based Rough Set Theory: An Indian Case. *J. Risk Financ. Manag.* **2023**, *16*, 309. [CrossRef]
26. Boskovic, S.; Svadlenka, L.; Jovcic, S.; Dobrodolac, M.; Simic, V.; Bacanin, N. An Alternative Ranking Order Method Accounting for Two-Step Normalization (AROMAN); A Case Study of the Electric Vehicle Selection Problem. *IEEE Access* **2023**, *11*, 39496–39507. [CrossRef]
27. Bošković, S.; Švadlenka, L.; Dobrodolac, M.; Jovčić, S.; Zanne, M. An Extended AROMAN Method for Cargo Bike Delivery Concept Selection. *Decis. Mak. Adv.* **2023**, *1*, 1–9. [CrossRef]
28. Čubranić-Dobrodolac, M.; Jovčić, S.; Bošković, S.; Babić, D. A Decision-Making Model for Professional Drivers Selection: A Hybridized Fuzzy–AROMAN–Fuller Approach. *Mathematics* **2023**, *11*, 2831. [CrossRef]
29. Hamilton, C. Changing Service Provision in Rural Areas and the Possible Impact on Older People: A Case Example of Compulsory Post Office Closures and Outreach Services in England. *Soc. Policy Soc.* **2016**, *15*, 387–401. [CrossRef]
30. Shergold, I.; Parkhurst, G. Transport-Related Social Exclusion amongst Older People in Rural Southwest England and Wales. *J. Rural Stud.* **2012**, *28*, 412–421. [CrossRef]
31. Cabras, I.; Lau, C.K.M. The Availability of Local Services and Its Impact on Community Cohesion in Rural Areas: Evidence from the English Countryside. *Local Econ.* **2019**, *34*, 248–270. [CrossRef]
32. Christiaanse, S.; Haartsen, T. The Influence of Symbolic and Emotional Meanings of Rural Facilities on Reactions to Closure: The Case of the Village Supermarket. *J. Rural Stud.* **2017**, *54*, 326–336. [CrossRef]
33. Ralevic, P.; Dobrodolac, M.; Markovic, D.; Mladenovic, S. The Measurement of Public Postal Operators' Profit Efficiency by Using Data Envelopment Analysis (DEA): A Case Study of the European Union Member States and Serbia. *Eng. Econ.* **2015**, *26*, 3360. [CrossRef]
34. Filippini, M.; Zola, M. Economies of Scale and Cost Efficiency in the Postal Services: Empirical Evidence from Switzerland. *Appl. Econ. Lett.* **2006**, *12*, 437–441. [CrossRef]
35. Dobrodolac, M.; Švadlenka, L.; Čubranić-Dobrodolac, M.; Čičević, S.; Stanivuković, B. A Model for the Comparison of Business Units. *Pers. Rev.* **2018**, *47*, 118–131. [CrossRef]
36. Klingenberg, J.P.; Bzhilyanskaya, L.Y.; Ravnitzky, M.J. Optimization of the United States Postal Retail Network by Applying GIS and Econometric Tools. In *Reforming the Postal Sector in the Face of Electronic Competition*; Edward Elgar Publishing Ltd.: Cheltenham, UK, 2013; pp. 118–131. [CrossRef]
37. Budziewicz-Guźlecka, A.; Drab-Kurowska, A. Problems of Infrastructure Markets with Particular Emphasis on the Postal Market in the Context of Digital Exclusion. *Sustainability* **2020**, *12*, 4719. [CrossRef]
38. Mizutani, F.; Uranishi, S. The Post Office vs. Parcel Delivery Companies: Competition Effects on Costs and Productivity. *J. Regul. Econ.* **2003**, *23*, 299–319. [CrossRef]
39. Matúšková, M.; Madleňáková, L. The Impact of the Electronic Services to the Universal Postal Services. *Procedia Eng.* **2017**, *178*, 258–266. [CrossRef]
40. Neupane, C.; Kyrönlahti, S.; Prakash, K.C.; Siukola, A.; Kosonen, H.; Lumme-Sandt, K.; Nikander, P.; Nygård, C.H. Indicators of Sustainable Employability among Older Finnish Postal Service Employees: A Longitudinal Study of Age and Time Effects. *Sustainability* **2022**, *14*, 5729. [CrossRef]
41. Drašković, D.; Průša, P.; Čičević, S.; Jovčić, S. The Implementation of Digital Ergonomics Modeling to Design a Human-Friendly Working Process in a Postal Branch. *Appl. Sci.* **2020**, *10*, 9124. [CrossRef]

42. Minami, K. Whole Life Appraisal of the Repair and Improvement Work Costs of Post Office Buildings in Japan. *Constr. Manag. Econ.* **2010**, *22*, 311–318. [CrossRef]
43. Neutens, T.; Delafontaine, M.; Schwanen, T.; van de Weghe, N. The Relationship between Opening Hours and Accessibility of Public Service Delivery. *J. Transp. Geogr.* **2012**, *25*, 128–140. [CrossRef]
44. Doble, M. Measuring and Improving Technical Efficiency in UK Post Office Counters Using Data Envelopment Analysis. *Ann. Public Coop. Econ.* **1995**, *66*, 31–64. [CrossRef]
45. Vaishar, A.; Šťastná, M.; Ilaria, M.; Kataishi, R.; Akhavan, M.; Senjyu, T. Accessibility of Services in Rural Areas: Southern Moravia Case Study. *Sustainability* **2021**, *13*, 9103. [CrossRef]
46. Mostarac, K.; Kavran, Z.; Rakić, E. Accessibility of Universal Postal Service According to Access Points Density Criteria: Case Study of Bjelovar-Bilogora County, Croatia. *Promet Traffic Transp.* **2019**, *31*, 173–183. [CrossRef]
47. Mostarac, K.; Mostarac, P.; Kavran, Z.; Šarac, D. Determining Optimal Locations of Postal Access Points Based on Simulated Annealing. *Sustainability* **2022**, *14*, 8635. [CrossRef]
48. Çakır, S.; Perçin, S.; Min, H. Evaluating the Comparative Efficiency of the Postal Services in Oecd Countries Using Context-Dependent and Measure-Specific Data Envelopment Analysis. *Benchmarking* **2015**, *22*, 839–856. [CrossRef]
49. Nebro, A.J.; García-Nieto, J.M.; Berlí, M.; Warchulski, E.; Kozdrowski, S. Applications of Metaheuristics Inspired by Nature in a Specific Optimisation Problem of a Postal Distribution Sector. *Appl. Sci.* **2022**, *12*, 9384. [CrossRef]
50. de Araújo, F.A.; Dos Reis, J.G.M.; da Silva, M.T.; Aktas, E. A Fuzzy Analytic Hierarchy Process Model to Evaluate Logistics Service Expectations and Delivery Methods in Last-Mile Delivery in Brazil. *Sustainability* **2022**, *14*, 5753. [CrossRef]
51. Pamučar, D.; Stević, Ž.; Sremac, S. A New Model for Determining Weight Coefficients of Criteria in MCDM Models: Full Consistency Method (FUCOM). *Symmetry* **2018**, *10*, 393. [CrossRef]
52. Mahmutagić, E.; Stević, Ž.; Nunić, Z.; Chatterjee, P.; Tanackov, I. An Integrated Decision-Making Model For Efficency Analysis of the Forklifts in Warehousing Systems. *Facta Univ. Ser. Mech. Eng.* **2021**, *19*, 537–553. [CrossRef]
53. Durmić, E.; Stević, Ž.; Chatterjee, P.; Vasiljević, M.; Tomašević, M. Sustainable Supplier Selection Using Combined FUCOM—Rough SAW Model. *Rep. Mech. Eng.* **2020**, *1*, 34–43. [CrossRef]
54. Chen, S.M.; Lee, L.W. Fuzzy Multiple Attributes Group Decision-Making Based on the Interval Type-2 TOPSIS Method. *Expert Syst. Appl.* **2010**, *37*, 2790–2798. [CrossRef]
55. Zadeh, L.A. The Concept of a Linguistic Variable and Its Application to Approximate Reasoning—I. *Inf. Sci.* **1975**, *8*, 199–249. [CrossRef]
56. Mendel, J.M. Uncertain Rule-Based Fuzzy Systems. In *Introduction and New Directions*, 2nd ed.; Springer: Berlin/Heidelberg, Germany, 2017; Volume 684. [CrossRef]
57. Lee, L.W.; Chen, S.M. Fuzzy Multiple Attributes Group Decision-Making Based on the Extension of TOPSIS Method and Interval Type-2 Fuzzy Sets. In Proceedings of the 7th International Conference on Machine Learning and Cybernetics, ICMLC, Kunming, China, 12–15 July 2008; Volume 6, pp. 3260–3265.
58. Karnik, N.N.; Mendel, J.M. Centroid of a Type-2 Fuzzy Set. *Inf. Sci.* **2001**, *132*, 195–220. [CrossRef]
59. Ghaleb, A.M.; Kaid, H.; Alsamhan, A.; Mian, S.H.; Hidri, L. Assessment and Comparison of Various MCDM Approaches in the Selection of Manufacturing Process. *Adv. Mater. Sci. Eng.* **2020**, *2020*, 4039253. [CrossRef]
60. Post Office—TheBythams.Org. UK. Available online: http://www.thebythams.org.uk/community/post-office-2/ (accessed on 30 June 2023).

Disclaimer/Publisher's Note: The statements, opinions and data contained in all publications are solely those of the individual author(s) and contributor(s) and not of MDPI and/or the editor(s). MDPI and/or the editor(s) disclaim responsibility for any injury to people or property resulting from any ideas, methods, instructions or products referred to in the content.

Article

Fuzzy Logic Model for Assessing Accident Proneness Based on Passenger Vehicle Speed in Real and Virtual Traffic Conditions

Nenad Marković [1], Tijana Ivanišević [2], Svetlana Čičević [1] and Aleksandar Trifunović [1,*]

[1] Faculty of Transport and Traffic Engineering, University of Belgrade, 11000 Belgrade, Serbia; n.markovic@sf.bg.ac.rs (N.M.); s.cicevic@sf.bg.ac.rs (S.Č.)
[2] Academy of Professional Studies Sumadija, 34000 Kragujevac, Serbia; tivanisevic@asss.edu.rs
* Correspondence: a.trifunovic@sf.bg.ac.rs

Citation: Marković, N.; Ivanišević, T.; Čičević, S.; Trifunović, A. Fuzzy Logic Model for Assessing Accident Proneness Based on Passenger Vehicle Speed in Real and Virtual Traffic Conditions. *Mathematics* **2024**, *12*, 421. https://doi.org/10.3390/math12030421

Academic Editor: Ben Niu

Received: 6 December 2023
Revised: 18 January 2024
Accepted: 22 January 2024
Published: 28 January 2024

Copyright: © 2024 by the authors. Licensee MDPI, Basel, Switzerland. This article is an open access article distributed under the terms and conditions of the Creative Commons Attribution (CC BY) license (https://creativecommons.org/licenses/by/4.0/).

Abstract: Inappropriate or unsafe speed is one of the main factors that affects the number of road crashes as well as the severity of the consequences. Research shows that speed is an influential factor in the occurrence of road crashes in more than 30% of road crashes with fatal outcomes and in over 12% of all road crashes. With an increase in speed, the risk of road crashes increases as well as the severity of the consequences. The perception of the vehicle speed in the traffic lane is one of the basic prerequisites for the safe functioning of traffic, that is, for the successful and timely interaction of all road users. Therefore, the challenge of this paper is to examine how the assessment of the speed of a passenger vehicle in different environments affects the prediction of the respondent's participation in road crashes. Bearing the above in mind, an experimental study was carried out, in real traffic conditions (RTC) as well as in a virtual environment using a driving simulator (DS), at different passenger vehicle speeds (30, 50 and 70 km/h), and at different perspectives of observing the oncoming vehicle (observing the vehicle from the front, from the back, from the side and from the driver's seat) by the respondents. The respondents had the task of evaluating the passenger vehicle speed, in all tested conditions and at all tested speeds. Standard statistical models and fuzzy logic were used to analyze the obtained results. The results show statistically significant differences for all tested situations and all tested speeds as well as statistically significant differences depending on the gender of the respondents, the driver's license category, the driver's experience, frequency of driving and depending on whether respondents wear glasses. Bearing in mind the results of the developed model, by applying fuzzy logic, it can be concluded that the proposed model can be used to assess the propensity of respondents to participate in road crashes, based on perception of vehicle speeds in two tested environments.

Keywords: passenger vehicle; speed; perception; fuzzy logic; road crash

MSC: 03B52; 62P30

1. Introduction

Speed is recognized as an important indicator of road safety [1]. Road crashes caused by speeding represent a major road safety problem [2]. Unsafe speed, i.e., inappropriate speed, is one of the main factors that affects the number of road crashes, but also the severity of the consequences of road crashes [3–6]. Research shows that unsafe or inappropriate speed is an influential factor in the occurrence of road crashes in more than 30% of road crashes with a fatal outcome and in over 12% of all road crashes [7].

It is estimated that around 50% of drivers commit a speeding offense at any time, with a third of road crashes resulting in fatalities occurring as a result of speeding [8]. Research shows that male drivers are more inclined to speeding, i.e., causing dangerous situations. Young drivers (up to two years of driving experience) as well as drivers of commercial vehicles, show a greater tendency to speed [2]. Research shows that as driving experience increases, the likelihood of speeding increases [9].

In the Republic of Serbia, the country where this research was conducted, "reckless action by the driver" is the most dominant group of influencing factors in road crashes with fatalities, while the most common influencing factors in the mentioned group are "speed not adapted to traffic and road conditions" and "driving over the speed limit" [10]. The average speed of passenger vehicles on the roads of the Republic of Serbia, in an inhabited place, during 2021 was 51.4 km/h (85th percentile = 61 km/h), the average speed of freight vehicles was 46.5 km/h (85th percentile = 55 km/h), the average speed of buses was 47.3 km/h (85th percentile = 55 km/h), while the average speed of motorcycles was 57.7 km/h (85th percentile = 70 km/h) [11]. During the attitudes survey of road users, it was observed that respondents consider "aggressive and careless driving" as well as "speeding" as the main factors in the occurrence of road crashes [12]. The survey of drivers' attitudes about speed indicated the alarming fact that the largest percentage of passenger vehicle drivers (46.7%) do not agree that driving over the speed limit, in an inhabited place, by 20 km/h increases the risk of a road crash. When it comes to motives for speeding, most drivers (32.6%) pointed out that it contributes to their experience of adapting to the driving of other drivers in traffic [13].

Many studies have shown that with an increase in speed, the risk of road crashes also increases. An average increase in average vehicle speed by 1 km/h contributes to an increase in the total number of road crashes by 3%, while when it comes to road crashes with fatalities, the total number of road crashes increases by 5% [14]. Research shows that reducing the average speed by 5 km/h results in a reduction in road crashes with fatalities by 22%, and a reduction in seriously injured by 16% and lightly injured by 10% [15]. Reducing the average speed by 1% contributes to reducing the number of people killed in road crashes by 4% and reducing the number of seriously injured by 3%, while with twice the number of drivers exceeding the speed limit, it leads to an increase in the risk of a road crash by 10% [16].

The perception of the motor vehicle's speed in traffic is one of the basic prerequisites for the safe functioning of traffic, i.e., for the successful and timely interaction of all road users [17,18]. In order to increase the safety of all road users, it is necessary to implement three measures: observing the oncoming vehicle, spotting the vehicle and correctly estimating the speed of the oncoming vehicle and the time required for the execution maneuver [18,19].

Research suggests that the contrast between the vehicle and the background has an important effect on the visibility of the vehicle (illumination contrast theory) [19]. In the research conducted by Pešić et al. [17], it was determined that respondents more accurately estimate lower speeds (30 km/h and 50 km/h) of passenger vehicles, without daytime running lights on, in contrast to the situation when respondents estimate lower speeds with daytime running lights on. At higher speeds (70 km/h and 90 km/h) of the passenger vehicle, the subjects estimate the speed more accurately with the daytime running lights on, in contrast to the situation when the subjects estimate a higher speed without the daytime running lights on [17]. In research conducted by the authors Ivanišević et al. [18] in which young drivers took part, it was found that the participants underestimated the speed at the analyzed motorcycle speeds of 50, km/h, 70 km/h and 90 km/h, with and without daytime running lights with halogen bulbs as well as when the daytime running lights were on light with LED bulbs, while overestimating the speed of 30 km/h in the situation when the daytime running lights with halogen bulbs are turned off on the motorcycle (M = 30.49; SD = 11.50) and when the daytime running lights with LED bulbs are turned on (M = 36.06; SD = 11.55), and they underestimate the speed of a motorcycle when the daytime running lights with halogen bulbs are on (M = 22.23; SD = 10.85). Bearing in mind the aforementioned research, the authors Ivanišević et al. [18] came to the conclusion that at speeds of 50 km/h, 70 km/h and 90 km/h, observed in all described conditions (with and without daytime running lights with halogen bulbs as well as when daytime running lights with LED bulbs are turned on), the respondents with the smallest error estimate the motorcycle speed when the daytime running lights with LED bulbs are on.

There is a limited number of studies that have dealt with the differences in vehicle speed estimation, taking into account the perspective from which the oncoming vehicle is viewed. Authors Čičević et al. [13] in their research, state that young road users cannot properly estimate the speed of the vehicle in front of them and the oncoming vehicle, which can cause problems when overtaking. The authors came to the conclusion that respondents perceive a speed of 30 km/h mainly as faster, while higher speeds are perceived as slower [13]. Obviously, the process of perceiving vehicle speed is very complex, and the research results have significant implications for the safety of different categories of road users [13].

Fuzzy logic models can be used to predict driver behavior [20–24], but also various aspects of the traffic profession [25–29]. A group of authors [29], in their work, analyzed the influence of the perception of speed and the spatial perception on the occurrence of road crashes and came to the conclusion that the spatial perception by the driver can better explain the tendency of the driver towards the occurrence of road crashes compared to the perception of speed.

Bearing the above in mind, this paper aims to examine the tendency of drivers to participate in road crashes, based on their perception of speed in real and virtual environments. In this study, potential research gaps can be identified, including a consistent stimulus paradigm (such as a single vehicle category, uniform vehicle color, and a specific viewing perspective, etc.), with the analysis limited to three distinct speeds of vehicles. Additionally, there is a limitation in the variety of traffic environments considered for speed assessments, as well as a singular focus on a specific age group (young drivers) of participants.

The paper comprises the "Introduction" section, which delineates the background of the road safety problem, provides a detailed literature review concerning vehicle speed perception, and shows the paper's objectives. Following this is the "Materials and Methods" section, which meticulously describes the experiment, stimuli, participants, the experimental procedure, and the method of data collection and processing, including the application of fuzzy logic. In the ensuing chapter, detailed results of statistical analyses and fuzzy logic are presented. The subsequent chapter involves a comprehensive discussion and comparison of the obtained results with other studies. The concluding chapter emphasizes the most crucial conclusions drawn from the study, along with guidelines for future research directions. For an easier understanding of the structure of the study, a flow chart diagram is shown in Figure 1.

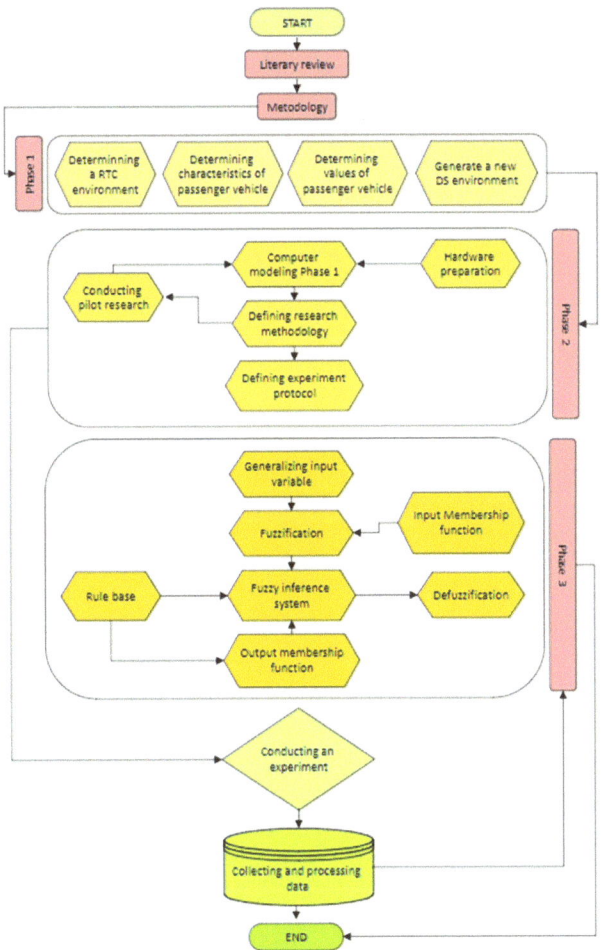

Figure 1. Overall research methodology flowchart.

2. Materials and Methods

This section is divided into two subsections. The first subsection refers to the description and method of conducting the experiment in order to collect empirical results, while the second subsection refers to the model development for determining the propensity for road crashes using fuzzy logic, and based on the speed perception of the passenger vehicle by the participants in real traffic conditions (RTC) and in a virtual environment (DS).

2.1. Data Collection

In order to collect empirical data for the purposes of this research, an experiment was conducted with the aim of examining differences in the speed perception of an oncoming passenger vehicle, in a situation where the subject observes the vehicle in front in real traffic conditions (RTC) and in a virtual environment using a driving simulator (DS). Respondents task was to estimate the speed of the passenger vehicle in all described conditions, at all tested speeds (30, 50 and 70 km/h). Also, respondents answered questions about demographic characteristics (gender and age), possession of a driver's license (category and years of possession), frequency of driving, whether respondents wear glasses or not [18,21,22] and participation in road crashes [20].

87 respondents participated in the experiment. One group of respondents consists of young drivers who have a driver's license, while the second group consists of respondents who are currently attending driver training programs in driving schools. Respondents did not receive any compensation for participation. Also, all ethical measures, rights and discretion of the respondents were respected during the research. Each respondent was tested individually and underwent preliminary trials.

2.1.1. Procedure

For the purposes of this experiment, the participants were presented with six different situations: three different situations of speed estimation in real traffic conditions (RTC environment) and three different situations of speed estimation in a virtual environment using a driving simulator (DS environment).

There was no horizontal or vertical signalization at the testing ground. The environment included common vegetation to avoid influencing participants' expectations about the motion of the visual targets and to prevent distraction [21]. The same conditions were simulated using a driving simulator. In the research, the participants had the task of estimating the passenger vehicle speed in all described situations, at all tested speeds. The respondents gave their answers orally, while the assistant in the experiment entered the spoken values into the online questionnaire [18,21,22]. The questionnaire also contained questions related to demographic characteristics (gender and age), possession of a driver's license (category and years of possession), frequency of driving [18,21,22] and data on the respondents' participation in road crashes [20].

2.1.2. Experimental Protocol

The experiment was conducted during August and September 2022. year. At the beginning of the experiment, each participant received his own combination of experimental stimulus order, which was chosen by using a random number generator. This procedure was carried out in order to neutralize the anchoring effect, by means of counterbalancing. Counterbalancing is accomplished by randomizing the order of presentation of the test stimuli [18,20–22].

The respondents estimated the passenger vehicle speed (at tested speeds of 30, 50 and 70 km/h) in real traffic conditions (RTC) and in a virtual environment using a driving simulator (DS), observing the oncoming vehicle from the front.

Each participant had a total of 6 tasks related to the passenger vehicle speed estimation (3 situations in real traffic conditions (RTC) and 3 situations in a virtual environment using a driving simulator (DS). The order of presentation of the situations was different for each participant [21]. The participants were not offered answers, but they estimated the speeds themselves. The estimated speeds were spoken by the subjects after each presented situation, while the assistant in the experiment entered the spoken values into the online questionnaire.

2.1.3. Participants

87 respondents, average age 21.54 (X_{min} = 19; X_{max} = 25), participated in the research. The share of male respondents in the sample is 50.6%, while the share of female respondents is 49.4%. The highest percentage of respondents, 70.1%, have a driver's license for a passenger car, while 20.7% of respondents have a driver's license for a motorcycle, passenger car or truck. More than a third of respondents, 34.5%, have had a driver's license for more than 5 years, 28.7% of respondents do not have a driver's license, 18.4% of respondents have a driver's license for a period of up to 3 years and 18.4% of respondents have a driver's license for 3 to 5 years. The largest percentage of respondents drive a motor vehicle almost every day (21.8%) as well as between 3 and 5 times a week (21.8%), while 20.7% of respondents participate in traffic less than 3 times a week. In total, 59.8% of respondents indicated that they do not use glasses, while 40.2% of respondents indicated that they use glasses while driving. In total, 82.8% of respondents participated in road crashes, whereby

70.1% of respondents experienced one road crash, 8% of respondents experienced two road crashes, and 4.6% of respondents experienced three road crashes.

Participants were recruited at the Faculty of Traffic and Transport Engineering—University of Belgrade. Potential participants were selected randomly, and they were not obliged to participate in the study. The study adhered to the Code of Ethics and Conduct of the Serbian Psychological Association. The participants did not receive any compensation for participation in the research.

2.1.4. Stimuli

Characteristics of Vehicle

For the purposes of this research, a "Skoda" type "Kamiq" passenger vehicle was used. Its dimensions are 4241 mm in length, 1793 mm in width and 1531 mm in height [21].

Passenger Vehicle Speeds

Three passenger vehicle speeds (30, 50 and 70 km/h) were selected for the research based on the legal regulations of the country where the research was conducted as well as on the basis of available studies that analyzed estimates of passenger vehicle speeds [17].

Characteristics of the Driving Simulator

The driving simulator was used to display the traffic situation in a virtual environment (RTC), and in order to examine the differences in the estimation of the vehicle speed. The driving simulator incorporates three 42″ plasma displays that give the respondents 180° horizontal and 50° vertical fields of view of the simulated environment. Each display has a resolution of 1360 × 768 pixels and a refresh rate of 60 Hz. It has previously been found that for the correct speed perception, a horizontal field of view of at least 120° is needed [22]. The traffic situation, which was defined on the testing ground, was also simulated in a virtual environment by means of a driving simulator. The characteristics of the passenger vehicle in real traffic conditions corresponded to the characteristics of the passenger vehicle in the virtual environment. In addition to the visual information, the respondents were also presented with sound information from the traffic surrounding them. Before starting the test, respondents were instructed about the use of the equipment inside the driving simulation [18].

Collecting and Processing Data

Demographic data of the participants in the experiment were collected through an online questionnaire and then imported into the software package MS Excel 2018 [21]. After importing, the data were examined and validated. Next, the statistical analysis of the obtained data was conducted in the software package IBM SPSS Statistics v.22 [17,18,22]. The normality of distribution was tested by inspection of histograms and the Kolmogorov–Smirnov test. Since the data for all the measured variable distributions were normally distributed, we used parametric methods [17,18,22]. To assess the significance of differences, the Independent Samples t-test, Paired-Samples t-test, One-way ANOVA and Post Hoc (Tukey) test were used [17,18,22].

The null hypothesis (H_0) was: There is no statistically significant difference in the perception of passenger vehicle speeds, for all speed tests and in all tested situations. An alternative hypothesis (H_a) is:

Hypothesis 1 (H_1). *There are statistically significant differences in the perception of passenger vehicle speeds, for all tested speeds, in all tested situations;*

Hypothesis 2 (H_2). *There are statistically significant differences in the perception of passenger vehicle speeds, depending on the gender of the respondents;*

Hypothesis 3 (H_3). *There are statistically significant differences in the perception of passenger vehicle speeds, depending on the driver's license category;*

Hypothesis 4 (H_4). *There are statistically significant differences in the perception of passenger vehicle speeds, depending on the driver's experience;*

Hypothesis 5 (H_5). *There are statistically significant differences in the perception of passenger vehicle speeds, depending on the frequency of driving.*

The threshold for the statistical significance (a) was set to 5%. Consequently, if probability (p) is smaller or equal to 0.05, H_0 is rejected, and H_a is accepted. On the contrary, if $p > 0.05$, H_0 is not rejected. The Bonferroni post hoc test was used for the additional comparison between groups [17,18,22].

2.2. Model Development for Determining Propensity for Road Crashes Using Fuzzy Logic

Because the answers of respondents related to the assessment of speed and space involve a certain level of imprecision and fuzziness, we assumed that the implementation of fuzzy inference systems would be a convenient tool for data processing. Fuzzy logic is widely used for explaining driver behaviour. The previous implementation can be segmented as follows: examination of the interaction between the driver and road infrastructure: examination of the interaction between the driver and in-vehicle systems, testing the psychophysical characteristics of drivers, and determining a driving style. The motivation to use fuzzy logic for modelling the tendency of drivers to participate in road crashes based on speed assessments and spatial abilities of drivers is actually the introduction of a new field of implementation. This new area can be called the perception of road traffic conditions and relations [20].

After collecting the empirical data necessary for this research, a model was developed for determining the tendency to participate in road crashes, using fuzzy logic, based on the speed perception of passenger vehicles by participants in real traffic conditions (RTC) and in a virtual environment (DS).

The input variables of the fuzzy logic system refer to the speed perception of the passenger vehicle in all described conditions (RTC and DS), at all tested speeds (30, 50 and 70 km/h), by each participant in the experiment, while the output variable refers on the number of crashes experienced by the respondent, i.e., determining propensity for road crashes. The minimum, mean, maximum values and standard deviation of each variable on the tested sample of 87 participants are shown in Table 1. Formulas for calculating the mean and standard deviation are as follows:

Table 1. Descriptive statistics of passenger vehicle speed in RTC and DS environments.

Environment	Vehicle Speed	Descriptive Statistics of the Sample			
		Minimum Speed Estimate	Mean Speed Estimate	Maximum Speed Estimate	Standard Deviation
RTC	30	5.00	25.57	40.00	7.68
RTC	50	7.00	36.18	50.00	10.17
RTC	70	20.00	49.77	60.00	9.91
DS	30	21.00	39.71	55.00	8.89
DS	50	24.00	52.44	68.00	10.40
DS	70	42.00	65.66	82.00	9.99

Mean (μ): The mean is calculated by summing up all the values in a dataset and then dividing by the total number of values (Formula (1)):

$$\mu = \frac{1}{N}\sum_{i=1}^{N} x_i \qquad (1)$$

where:
- μ is the mean,
- N is the total number of data points,
- x_i represents each individual data point.

Standard Deviation (σ): The standard deviation is a measure of the amount of variation or dispersion in a set of values. It is calculated as the square root of the variance (Formula (2)):

$$\sigma = \sqrt{\frac{1}{N}\sum_{i=1}^{N}(Xi-\mu)^2} \qquad (2)$$

where:
- σ is the standard deviation,
- N is the total number of data points,
- x_i represents each individual data point,
- μ is the mean of the dataset.

When defining the fuzzy sets and the corresponding fuzzy rules, a database was used that consisted of the speed perception by the respondents and the answers to the questions. The software used for the purpose of developing a model for determining the tendency to participate in road crashes using the fuzzy logic system is Matlab R2023b (Figure 2).

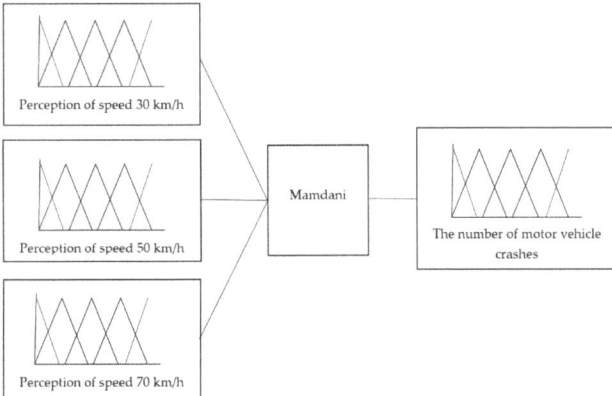

Figure 2. Fuzzy logic system for determining the tendency to participate in road crashes.

The input variables are represented by five fuzzy sets and their membership functions (Figure 3): VPLSE—very poor (low) speed perception, VLSE—very low-speed perception, GSE—good speed perception, HSE—high-speed perception and VHSE—very high-speed perception.

The output variable represents the number of crashes experienced by the respondent, i.e., determining the tendency to participate in road crashes. The output variable is displayed using five fuzzy sets and their membership functions (Figure 4): VSNTA—very small number of road crashes, SNTA—small number of road crashes, ANTA—average number of road crashes, LNTA—large number of road crashes and VLNTA—very large number of road crashes. Considering that the sample consists of young drivers, the number of road crashes is relatively small [20], with the possible empirical values of the number of crashes ranging from a minimum value of 0 to a maximum value of 4 (Figure 4).

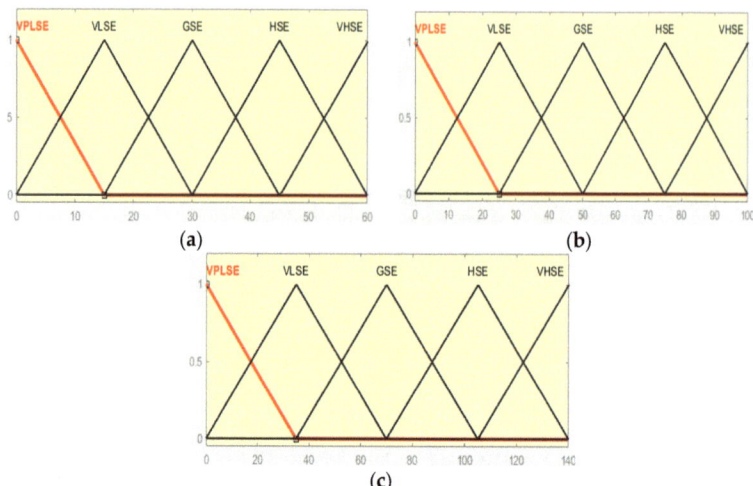

Figure 3. The input variable for speed perception of the passenger vehicle at speeds of 30 km/h (**a**), 50 km/h (**b**) and 70 km/h (**c**).

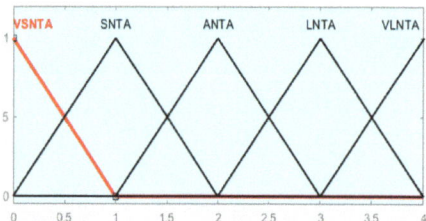

Figure 4. Output variable for the number of road crashes experienced.

After defining the fuzzy sets and corresponding membership functions, a regular database was generated based on the speed perception of the passenger vehicle by the respondents. When defining the model, an "and" connection was used to define the rules and a value of 1 for the rule weights. In accordance with the proposed model, rules were defined (Figure 5). Based on the created rules, it is possible to obtain the expected number of road crashes in which the participant will participate based on the speed perception of the passenger vehicle in the RTC and DS environment.

The null hypothesis (H_o) was: There is no statistically significant difference in determining the tendency for road crashes. An alternative hypothesis (Ha) is:

Hypothesis 6 (H_6). *There are statistically significant differences between the results related to the determining tendency for road crashes in the RTC environment and the empirical results on the participation of respondents in road crashes;*

Hypothesis 7 (H_7). *There are statistically significant differences between the results related to the determining tendency for road crashes in the DS environment and the empirical results on the participation of respondents in road crashes;*

Hypothesis 8 (H_8). *There are statistically significant differences between the results related to the determining tendency for road crashes in the RTC and DS environment.*

The threshold for the statistical significance (a) was set to 5%. Consequently, if probability (p) is smaller or equal to 0.05, H_0 is rejected, and H_a is accepted. On the contrary, if $p > 0.05$, H_0 is not rejected.

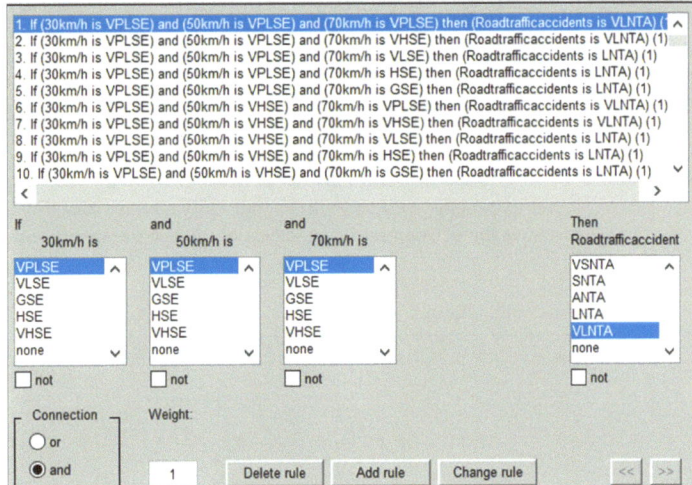

Figure 5. The rule base of the fuzzy logical system of tendency towards the occurrence of road crashes.

3. Results

In this chapter, the results of the research are presented with the aim of showing potential differences in the estimation of passenger vehicle speed, in situations where the respondents estimate the passenger vehicle speed by looking at the oncoming vehicle in real traffic conditions (RTC) as well as by looking at the oncoming vehicle in a virtual environment (DS), in situations where the examinee estimates the speed of the oncoming vehicle viewed from the front.

3.1. Descriptive Statistics—Estimation of the Passenger Vehicle Speed

Figure 6 shows the descriptive statistics of passenger vehicles' speed estimation in RTC and DS environments, in situations where the participant observes the oncoming vehicle from the front (Table 2).

Figure 6. Descriptive statistics of passenger vehicle speed in RTC and DS environments—mean.

Table 2. Descriptive statistics of passenger vehicle speed in RTC and DS environments—mean and standard deviation.

Speed	30 km/h	50 km/h	70 km/h
Mean (RTC)	25.57	36.18	49.88
Standard Deviation (RTC)	7.68	10.17	9.91
Mean (DS)	39.71	52.44	65.66
Standard Deviation (DS)	8.89	10.40	9.99

The arithmetic mean of the results shows that the respondent's speed perception of the passenger vehicle with higher values when observing the movement of the vehicle using the DS, compared to the estimation of the speed in the RTC (Figure 7).

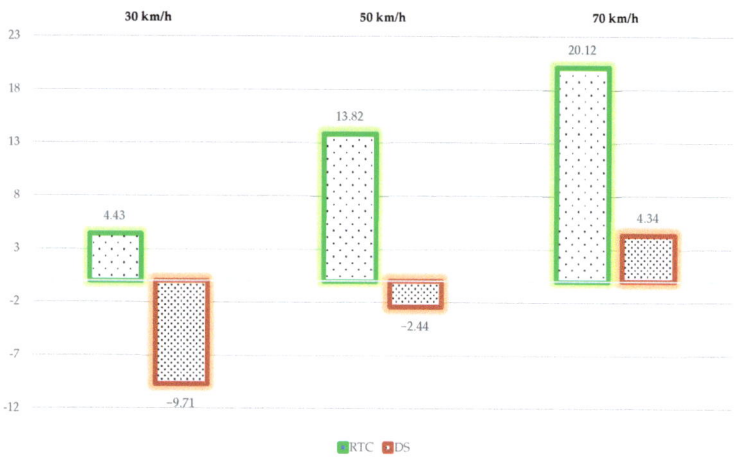

Figure 7. The mean error of passenger vehicle speed in RTC and DS environments.

Respondents using DS estimated the speed of a passenger vehicle at 50 km/h with the smallest error (M = 52.44; SD = 10.40), while with the highest error, they estimated the speed of 30 km/h (M = 39.71; SD = 8.89) (Figure 6). Respondents with the smallest error estimate the speed of a passenger vehicle at a speed of 30 km/h (M = 25.57; SD = 7.68), while with the largest error, they estimate the speed of 70 km/h (M = 49.88; SD = 9.91), when the vehicle's movement observed in the RTC (Figure 7).

The results of the One Sample test show a statistically significant difference for all the tested speeds and for all described conditions (RTC and DS). These results are presented in Table 3.

Table 3. Differences in the passenger vehicle speed estimation at all test speeds.

Speed	Conditions	Mean	Str. Deviation	t	p
30	RTC	25.575	7.679	31.064	<0.001
	DS	39.713	8.893	41.651	<0.001
50	RTC	36.184	10.167	33.197	<0.001
	DS	52.437	10.403	47.014	<0.001
70	RTC	49.770	9.910	46.845	<0.001
	DS	65.655	9.993	61.283	<0.001

3.2. The Relationship between Estimation of the Passenger Vehicle Speed

The results of the Paired Sample t-test show a statistically significant difference for all the tested speeds in all tested conditions. These results are presented in Table 4. Eta squares reveal significant differences in the estimation of a passenger vehicle's speed for all the tested speeds.

Table 4. Differences in the passenger vehicle speed estimation at all speeds.

Speed	Conditions	Mean	Str. Deviation	t	p	Eta Square	Magnitude of Impacts
30	RTC	−14.138	3.67952	−35.839	<0.001	0.94	Large
	DS						
50	RTC	−16.253	5.78132	−26.222	<0.001	0.89	Large
	DS						
70	RTC	−15.885	6.714	−22.068	<0.001	0.84	Large
	DS						

3.3. Gender Differences in the Estimation of the Passenger Vehicle Speed

The Independent Samples t-test was used to analyze the speed estimation of the passenger vehicle depending on the gender of the participants. The Independent Samples t-test results show statistically significant differences in men (M = 39.25; SD = 9.72) and women (M = 33.05; SD = 9.74) for speed estimation of a passenger vehicle at a speed of 50 km/h, in a situation where the respondent estimates speed by observing the oncoming vehicle in RTC environments (t = −2.972; p = 0.004). When estimating passenger vehicle speed in DS environments by the respondents, statistically significant differences were observed in men (M = 55.00; SD = 10.00) and women (M = 49.81; SD = 10.26) when estimating a speed of 50 km/h (t = −2.387; p = 0.019).

The vehicle speed of 30 km/h, in DS environments, is estimated by men with a larger error (M = 41.14; SD = 8.36), compared to the speed estimate by women (M = 38.26; SD = 9.28). Women estimate the speed of a passenger vehicle at 50 and 70 km/h with a higher error, compared to men, in RTC (Figure 8).

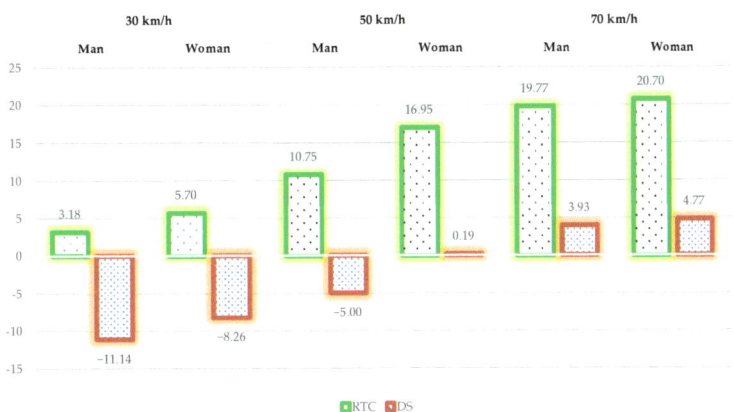

Figure 8. Mean error of estimation of the passenger vehicle speed, observed by gender.

3.4. Driving License Category and Estimation of the Passenger Vehicle Speed

The results of the one-way ANOVA show a significant statistical difference between drivers with different categories of driver's licenses in estimating the passenger vehicle speed in a situation where respondents estimate the passenger vehicle speed of 30 km/h, in RTC environments (F = 2.543; p = 0.026).

3.5. The Influence of Driver's Experience on the Estimation of the Passenger Vehicle Speed

The passenger vehicle speed was estimated by drivers with different driving experience (up to three years, between 3 and 5 years, more than 5 years and participants who do not have a driver's license).

The results of the one-way ANOVA show a significant statistical difference between drivers with different driving experiences for estimating the passenger vehicle speed at a speed of 30 (F = 5.383; p = 0.002), 50 (F = 7.695; p < 0.001) and 70 (F = 2.909; p = 0.039) km/h in RTC environments as well as when estimating the speed of 30 (F = 5.244; p = 0.002) and 50 (F = 7.140; p < 0.001) km/h in DS environments. Table 5 shows the results of Post Hoc Tests (Tukey) for different driver's experience on the estimation of the passenger vehicle speed—the influence of driver's experience.

Table 5. Results of Post Hoc Tests (Tukey) for different driver's experience on the estimation of the passenger vehicle speed—The influence of driver's experience.

Driver's Experience	Up to Three Years	Between 3 and 5 Years	More than 5 Years	I Do Not Have a Driver's License
Up to three years		* 50 km/h RTC	* 50 km/h RTC	* 50 km/h RTC
		50 km/h DS	50 km/h DS	50 km/h DS
I do not have a driver's license	* 30 km/h RTC			
	* 30 km/h DS			
	* 70 km/h RTC			

*—statistically significant differences.

3.6. The Influence of the Frequency of Driving and Estimation of the Passenger Vehicle Speed

Frequency of driving (less than 3 times a year, less than 3 times a month, less than 3 times a week, between 3 and 5 times a week, (almost every day, I do not have a driver's license) and estimation of the passenger vehicle speed was analyzed using a one-factor analysis of variance (one-way ANOVA).

The results show a statistically significant difference between drivers with different frequencies of driving for estimating the passenger vehicle speed at a speed of 30 (F = 4.109; p = 0.002) and 50 (F = 5.394; p < 0.001) km/h in RTC conditions as well as for a speed of 30 (F = 5.019; p < 0.001) and 50 (F = 4.842; p = 0.001) km/h in DS environments. Table 6 shows the results of Post Hoc Tests (Tukey) for different drivers' experiences on the estimation of the passenger vehicle speed—the influence of the frequency of driving.

Table 6. Results of Post Hoc Tests (Tukey) for different drivers' experience on the estimation of the passenger vehicle speed—The influence of the frequency of driving.

Frequencies of Driving	Less than 3 Times a Year	Less than 3 Times a Month	Less than 3 Times a Week	Between 3 and 5 Times a Week	Almost Every Day	I Do Not Have a Driver's License
Less than 3 times a year					* 50 km/h DS	
Less than 3 times a month				* 30 km/h DS	* 50 km/h DS	
Less than 3 times a week						* 50 km/h RTC
						* 30 km/h DS

Table 6. Cont.

Frequencies of Driving	Less than 3 Times a Year	Less than 3 Times a Month	Less than 3 Times a Week	Between 3 and 5 Times a Week	Almost Every Day	I Do Not Have a Driver's License
Between 3 and 5 times a week						* 30 km/h DS
Almost every day	* 50 km/h RTC	* 50 km/h RTC				* 50 km/h RTC
						* 50 km/h DS
I do not have a driver's license			* 30 km/h RTC	* 30 km/h RTC	* 30 km/h RTC	
					* 30 km/h DS	

*—statistically significant differences.

3.7. A Model for Determining Propensity for Road Crashes Using Fuzzy Logic

Defined Model Development for determining the tendency for road crashes using fuzzy logic needs to be tested. The deviation between the empirical data on the number of road crashes and the number of road crashes obtained by the application of the defined model is presented using the cumulative deviation (CD) [20].

$$CD = \sum_{i=1}^{87} |y_r - y_e| \qquad (3)$$

CD is a cumulative deviation [20]; y(r) is the number of road crashes experienced by the respondent (RTA); y(e) is the result of the number of road crashes of respondents using the model, and based on the assessment of faster vehicle movement.

The CD value for the difference between the empirical results on the number of road crashes experienced by the participants and the results related to determining the tendency for road crashes based on speed estimation in the RTC environment is equal to 45.744, while the CD value for the difference between the empirical results on the number of road crashes experienced by the participants and the results related to determining the tendency for road crashes based on the estimation of speed in the DS environment is equal to 48.123. A comparison of empirical results and results related to determining the tendency for road crashes is shown in Figures 9–11.

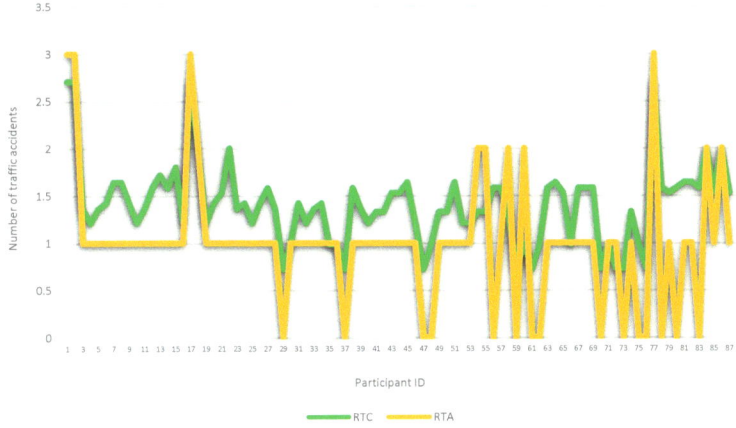

Figure 9. Comparison of empirical results on the number of road crashes experienced by the participants and results related to determining the tendency for road crashes based on speed estimation in the RTC environment.

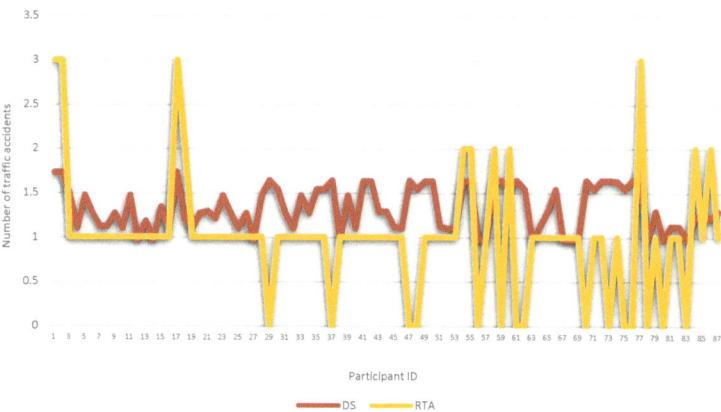

Figure 10. Comparison of empirical results on the number of road crashes experienced by the participants and results related to determining the tendency for road crashes based on speed estimation in the DS environment.

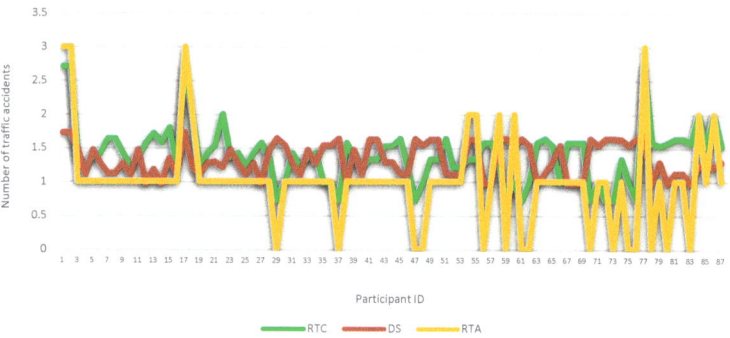

Figure 11. Comparison of empirical results on the number of road crashes experienced by the participants and results related to determining the tendency for road crashes based on speed estimation in RTC and DS environment.

The relationship between the results of the CD empirical results on the number of road crashes experienced by the participants and the results related to determining the tendency for road crashes based on the estimation of speed in the RTC environment as well as the empirical results on the number of road crashes experienced by the participants and the results related to determining the tendency for road crashes based on the estimation of speed in the DS environment was examined with a paired-samples t-test (Paired-Samples t-test). The results of the t-test of paired samples indicate that there are statistically significant differences (t = 7.643; $p < 0.001$).

The relationship between the results obtained by the application of the model and the empirical results was examined by the t-test of paired samples (Paired-Samples t-test). The results of the t-test of paired samples indicate that there are no statistically significant differences between the results related to determining the tendency for road crashes in the RTC and DS environment and the empirical results on the participation of respondents in road crashes. Therefore, there are no significant statistical differences between the results related to determining the tendency for road crashes in the RTC environment and the empirical results on the respondents' participation in road crashes (t = 1.231; p = 1.613) as well as between the results related to determining the tendency for road crashes in the DS environment and empirical results on the respondents' participation in road crashes (t = 1.183; p = 1.869). The results of the t-test of paired samples indicate that there are statistically significant differences between the results related to determining the tendency for road crashes in the RTC and DS environment (t = 7.643; $p < 0.001$) (Table 7).

Table 7. The relationship between the empirical results on the respondents' participation in road crashes (RTA) and the tendency to participate in road crashes in the RTC and DS environment (paired sample t-test results).

Conditions	Mean	Str. Deviation	t	p
RTC / RTA	0.410	0.463	1.231	1.613
DS / RTA	0.329	0.672	1.183	1.869
RTC / DS	0.081	0.537	7.643	<0.001

4. Discussion

The World Health Organization states that approximately 1.3 million people die each year as a result of road crashes, with 93% of fatalities occurring in low and middle-income countries [23]. Between 20 and 50 million people are injured in road crashes [23].

Inappropriate or unsafe speed is one of the main factors that affects the number of road crashes as well as the severity of the consequences. [3–6], where the World Health Organization states that with an increase in average speed, the likelihood of a road crash also increases [23].

Exceeding the speed limit is very common in all road categories [24]. It was determined that 40–50% of drivers drive faster than the defined speed limit [8]. In research conducted by Brake [25] 68% of drivers stated that they exceed the speed limit, while 85% of respondents admitted that they sometimes do not respect the speed limit [24]. Drivers often list exceeding the speed limit as an activity in which they participate [26]. Many studies have pointed to the fact that drivers will drive at the speed dictated by road and traffic conditions, while not paying attention to the defined speed limit [24].

Bearing the above in mind, it can be concluded that vehicle perception and vehicle speed are one of the basic prerequisites for safe traffic functioning. Therefore, the researchers believe that improvements in road safety occur as a result of the perception of the oncoming vehicle, the assessment of the speed and the correct assessment of the time required for the execution of the maneuver by other road users [17–19,22,30–32].

The number of studies that dealt with vehicle speed estimation is scarce, and it should be noted that in the studies that dealt with speed estimation, the participants conducted the experiments in real traffic conditions or in virtual traffic conditions.

The authors of this research, and bearing in mind the limited number of studies, decided to analyze the vehicle speed estimation by the respondents in real traffic conditions (RTC) and in virtual conditions using a driving simulator (DS), at a passenger vehicle speed of 30, 50 and 70 km/h, and which constitutes the first part of the research, all with the aim of collecting empirical results. In this paper, the authors have developed a model for determining the tendency for road crashes using fuzzy logic, based on the speed perception of the passenger vehicle by participants in real traffic conditions (RTC) and in a virtual environment (DS).

By analyzing the obtained results, it can be concluded that alternative hypotheses H_1, H_2, H_3, H_4, H_5 and H_8 are accepted, while alternative hypotheses were H_6 and H_7 rejected.

The conducted experiment and the results presented in the paper indicated that there are statistically significant differences in the passenger vehicle speed estimation by the respondents, for all conditions and all tested speeds.

Participants with the largest error estimate the speed of 30 km/h (M = 39.71; SD = 8.89), while with the smallest error, they estimate the passenger vehicle speed of 50 km/h

(M = 52.44; SD = 10.40), using DS. When it comes to speed estimation in RTC, the participants with the smallest error estimate the passenger vehicle speed at a speed of 30 km/h (M = 25.57; SD = 7.68), while with the largest error, they estimate the speed of 70 km/h (M = 49.88; SD = 9.91).

The results of the application of the developed model indicate that there are no significant statistical differences between the results related to determining the tendency for road crashes in the RTC environment and the empirical results on the respondents' participation in road crashes (t = 1.231; p = 1.613) as well as between the results which refer to determining the tendency for road crashes in the DS environment and empirical results on the participation of respondents in road crashes (t = 1.183; p = 1.869), where the results indicate that there are statistically significant differences between the results related to determining the tendency for road crashes in RTC and DS environment (t = 7.643; $p < 0.001$). Bearing the above results in mind, it can be concluded that the proposed model can be used to assess the respondents' tendency to participate in road crashes. The above results show another application of fuzzy logic, in addition to its already proven useful application in many areas [33–38], ordered recently.

5. Conclusions

Based on the data collected and analyzed in the conducted research, conclusions can be drawn:

- Participants with higher values estimate the speed of the vehicle when observing the vehicle using DS, compared to the speed estimate in the RTC environment;
- Participants using DS with the smallest error estimate the passenger vehicle speed of 50 km/h (M = 52.44; SD = 10.40), while with the largest error, they estimate the speed of 30 km/h (M = 39.71; SD = 8.89);
- Participants with the smallest error estimate the passenger vehicle speed at a speed of 30 km/h (M = 25.57; SD = 7.68), while with the largest error, they estimate the speed of 70 km/h (M = 49.88; SD = 9.91), when the vehicles are observed in the RTC;
- The results of the Paired Sample t-test show a statistically significant difference for all the tested speeds in all tested conditions;
- The vehicle speed of 30 km/h, in DS environments, is estimated by men with a larger error (M = 41.14; SD = 8.36), while women estimate the passenger vehicle speed at 50 and 70 km/h with a larger error;
- There are statistically significant differences in men (M = 39.25; SD = 9.72) and women (M = 33.05; SD = 9.74) for estimating the passenger vehicle speed of 50 km/h, in a situation where the participant estimates the speed by observing the oncoming vehicle in RTC environments (t = −2.972; p = 0.004). When estimating the passenger vehicle speed in DS environments by the participants, statistically significant differences were observed in men (M = 55.00; SD = 10.00) and women (M = 49.81; SD = 10.26) when estimating a speed of 50 km/h (t = −2.387; p = 0.019);
- The results show a significant statistical difference between drivers with different categories of driver's license in estimating the passenger vehicle speed in a situation where respondents estimate the passenger vehicle speed of 30 km/h, in RTC environments (F = 2.543; p = 0.026);
- There are statistically significant differences between drivers with different driving experience for estimating the passenger vehicle speed at speeds of 30 (F = 5.383; p = 0.002), 50 (F = 7.695; $p < 0.001$) and 70 (F = 2.909; p = 0.039) km/h in RTC environments as well as when estimating the speed of 30 (F = 5.244; p = 0.002) and 50 (F = 7.140; $p < 0.001$) km/h in DS environments;
- There are statistically significant differences between drivers with different frequencies of driving for estimating the passenger vehicle speed at a speed of 30 (F = 4.109; p = 0.002) and 50 (F = 5.394; $p < 0.001$) km/h in RTC conditions as well as for the speed of 30 (F = 5.019; $p < 0.001$) and 50 (F = 4.842; p = 0.001) km/h in DS environments;

- There are no significant statistical differences between the results related to determining the tendency for road crashes in the RTC environment and the empirical results on the respondents' participation in road crashes (t = 1.231; p = 1.613);
- There are no statistically significant differences between the results related to determining the tendency for road crashes in the DS environment and the empirical results on the participation of respondents in road crashes (t = 1.183; p = 1.869);
- There are statistically significant differences between the results related to determining the tendency for road crashes in RTC and DS environments (t = 7.643; p < 0.001).

The obtained results indicate significant differences in the estimation of vehicle speed in the driving simulator and the real environment. Subjects in the real environment, for higher speeds, more accurately estimated the vehicle speed in the driving simulator. This result warns of caution when educating young drivers through driving simulators. Also, it is a worrying fact that in real situations, the error increases by increasing the set speed of the vehicle, which should be paid special attention to when educating young drivers. Differences were observed in speed estimates depending on the gender of the subjects, driver's license category, driving experience, and driving frequency. The above results should be used for practical purposes, primarily for driving education in driving schools. A proposal for the practical application of these results includes improving the design of driving simulations with a focus on situations that cause greater uncertainty, adjusting driver training according to gender, experience, and frequency of driving, and adjusting the training area according to driver's license categories. This could contribute to improving the accuracy of vehicle speed estimation and increasing road safety.

Future research directions should involve an increase in the number of participants, encompassing a broader range of age groups, and obtaining more comprehensive demographic and psychophysical information about the participants. Additionally, there is a need to explore and assess various speeds and categories of vehicles as well as diverse traffic environments, such as roads with varying numbers of lanes in each direction (roads with one, two, three and more traffic lanes per direction, etc.). It is also necessary to include considerations of different vehicle colours and speeds, taking into account varying weather conditions and times of day, along with multiple perspectives for the perception of vehicle speed. On the analytical front, future investigations could incorporate the application of diverse fuzzy logic models, Artificial Neural Networks and the utilization of advanced statistical tools and analyses. The study's limitations include the need for further validation of the fuzzy logic model.

Author Contributions: Conceptualization, N.M. and A.T.; methodology, T.I.; software, S.Č.; validation, N.M., T.I. and A.T.; formal analysis, S.Č.; investigation, T.I.; resources, N.M.; data curation, A.T.; writing—original draft preparation, T.I.; writing—review and editing, N.M., T.I. and A.T; visualization, N.M.; supervision, S.Č. All authors have read and agreed to the published version of the manuscript.

Funding: This research received no external funding.

Data Availability Statement: Data sharing not applicable.

Conflicts of Interest: The authors declare no conflict of interest.

References

1. Van den Berghe, W.; Silverans, P.; Boudry, E.; Aarts, L.; Bijleveld, F.; Folla, K.; Yannis, G.A. Common Methodology for the Collection of Key Performance Indicators for Road Safety in the EU. In Proceedings of the 8th Technical Committee on Road Safety, Online, 6 October 2021.
2. Global Road Safety Partnership. *Drinking and Driving: A Road Safety Manual for Decision-Makers and Practitioners*; World Health Organization: Geneva, Switzerland, 2004.
3. Wu, Z.; Sharma, A.; Mannering, F.L.; Wang, S. Safety impacts of signal-warning flashers and speed control at high-speed signalized intersections. *Accid. Anal. Prev.* **2013**, *54*, 90–98. [CrossRef] [PubMed]
4. Elvik, R. A before–after study of the effects on safety of environmental speed limits in the city of Oslo, Norway. *Saf. Sci.* **2013**, *55*, 10–16. [CrossRef]

5. De Pauw, E.; Daniels, S.; Thierie, M.; Brijs, T. Safety effects of reducing the speed limit from 90 km/h to 70 km/h. *Accid. Anal. Prev.* **2013**, *62*, 426–431. [CrossRef] [PubMed]
6. Soole, D.W.; Watson, B.C.; Fleiter, J.J. Effects of average speed enforcement on speed compliance and crashes: A review of the literature. *Accid. Anal. Prev.* **2013**, *54*, 46–56. [CrossRef]
7. Hakkert, A.S.; Gitelman, V.; Vis, M.A. *Road Safety Performance Indicators: Theory*; European Commission: Brussels, Belgium, 2007.
8. OECD/ECMT. *Speed Management*; Organization for Economic Co-operation and Development OECD/European Conference of Ministers of Transport ECMT: Paris, France, 2006.
9. Zhang, G.; Yau, K.K.W.; Gong, X. Traffic violations in Guangdong Province of China: Speeding and drunk driving. *Accid. Anal. Prev.* **2014**, *64*, 30–40. [CrossRef] [PubMed]
10. Road Safety Agency. Statistical Reports on the State of Traffic Safety in the Republic of Serbia in 2021. 2022, Belgrade. Available online: https://www.abs.gov.rs/admin/upload/documents/20220915105252-statisticki_konacno_2021.pdf (accessed on 15 May 2023).
11. Road Safety Agency. Values of Traffic Safety Indicators Regarding the Use of Seat Belts, Child Protection Systems, Protective Helmets and Speeding (in the Period 2013–2021). 2022, Belgrade. Available online: https://www.abs.gov.rs/admin/upload/documents/20220324204026-master_tabela_ibs_2021.pdf (accessed on 15 May 2023).
12. Road Safety Agency. Attitudes of Traffic Participants about Dangers and Risks in Traffic in Serbia in 2017. 2017, Belgrade. Available online: https://www.abs.gov.rs/admin/upload/documents/20180514140701-brosura_stavovi_2017.pdf (accessed on 15 May 2023).
13. Fernandez Llorca, D.; Hernandez Martinez, A.; Garcia Daza, I. Vision-based vehicle speed estimation: A survey. *IET Intell. Transp. Syst.* **2021**, *15*, 987–1005. [CrossRef]
14. Finch, D.; Kompfner, P.; Lockwood, C.; Maycock, G. *Speed, Speed Limits and Accidents*; Transport Research Laboratory: Wokingham, UK, 1994.
15. ETSC. *Towards Safe and Sustainable Road Transport*; European Transport Safety Council: Brussels, Belgium, 1994.
16. Taylor, M.C.; Lynam, D.A.; Baruya, A. *The Effects of Drivers' Speed on the Frequency of Road Accidents*; Transport Research Laboratory: Wokingham, UK, 2000; p. 421.
17. McCartt, A.T.; Hu, W. Effects of vehicle power on passenger vehicle speeds. *Traffic Inj. Prev.* **2017**, *18*, 500–507. [CrossRef] [PubMed]
18. Ivanišević, T.; Ivković, I.; Čičević, S.; Trifunović, A.; Pešić, D.; Vukšić, V.; Simović, S. The impact of daytime running (LED) lights on motorcycles speed estimation: A driving simulator study. *Transp. Res. F Traffic Psychol.* **2022**, *90*, 47–57. [CrossRef]
19. Lee, Y.M.; Sheppard, E. The effect of lighting conditions and use of headlights on drivers' perception and appraisal of approaching vehicles at junctions. *Ergonomics* **2018**, *61*, 444–455. [CrossRef]
20. Mazandarani, M.; Xiu, L. Interval type-2 fractional fuzzy inference systems: Towards an evolution in fuzzy inference systems. *Expert Syst. Appl.* **2022**, *189*, 115947. [CrossRef]
21. Trifunović, A.; Ivanišević, T.; Čičević, S.; Simović, S.; Vukšić, V.; Slović, Ž. Do Statistics Show Differences between Distance Estimations of RTC Objects in the Traffic Environment Using Glances, Side View Mirrors, and Camera Display? *Mathematics* **2023**, *11*, 1258. [CrossRef]
22. Simović, S.; Ivanišević, T.; Trifunović, A.; Čičević, S.; Taranović, D. What affects the e-bicycle speed perception in the era of eco-sustainable mobility: A driving simulator study. *Sustainability* **2021**, *13*, 5252. [CrossRef]
23. World Health Organization. Available online: https://www.who.int/news-room/fact-sheets/detail/road-traffic-injuries (accessed on 12 May 2023).
24. Tubić, V.; Glavić, D.; Stepanović, N.; Milenković, M.; Vidas, M. Analysis of operating and exceeded speeds on state roads in municipality of Kraljevo. In Proceedings of the 13th International Conference Road Safety in Local Community, Kopaonik, Serbia, 18–21 April 2018; Available online: https://www.bslz-rs.org/Zbornici/2018.pdf (accessed on 15 May 2023).
25. Brake Road Safety Charity. The Green Flag Report on Safe Driving 2004 Part Two: Speed. *Brake*, 2004.
26. Department for Transport. Understanding Public Attitudes to Road user Safety—Literature Review: Final Report. *Road Saf. Annu. Rep.* **2010**, 112.
27. Bakhtari Aghdam, F.; Sadeghi-Bazargani, H.; Azami-Aghdash, S.; Esmaeili, A.; Panahi, H.; Khazaee-Pool, M.; Golestani, M. Developing a national road traffic safety education program in Iran. *BMC Public Health* **2020**, *20*, 1064. [CrossRef] [PubMed]
28. Kononen, D.W.; Flannagan, C.A.; Wang, S.C. Identification and validation of a logistic regression model for predicting serious injuries associated with motor vehicle crashes. *Accid. Anal. Prev.* **2011**, *43*, 112–122. [CrossRef] [PubMed]
29. Čubranić-Dobrodolac, M.; Švadlenka, L.; Čičević, S.; Trifunović, A.; Dobrodolac, M. A bee colony optimization (BCO) and type-2 fuzzy approach to measuring the impact of speed perception on motor vehicle crash involvement. *Soft. Comput.* **2022**, *26*, 4463–4486. [CrossRef]
30. Tang, X.; Li, B.; Du, H. A Study on Dynamic Motion Planning for Autonomous Vehicles Based on Nonlinear Vehicle Model. *Sensors* **2022**, *23*, 443. [CrossRef]
31. Wu, X.; Fu, S.; Guo, L. Study on Highway Alignment Optimization Considering Rollover Stability Based on Two-Dimensional Point Collision Dynamics. *Appl. Sci.* **2022**, *13*, 509. [CrossRef]
32. Zandi, K.; Tavakoli Kashani, A.; Okabe, A. Influence of traffic parameters on the spatial distribution of crashes on a freeway to increase safety. *Sustainability* **2022**, *15*, 493. [CrossRef]

33. Ghasemi, P.; Hemmaty, H.; Pourghader Chobar, A.; Heidari, M.R.; Keramati, M. A multi-objective and multi-level model for location-routing problem in the supply chain based on the customer's time window. *J. Appl. Res. Ind. Eng.* **2023**, *10*, 412–426.
34. Barreno, F.; Romana, M.G.; Santos, M. Fuzzy expert system for road type identification and risk assessment of conventional two-lane roads. *Expert Syst.* **2022**, *39*, e12837. [CrossRef]
35. Belay, G.F. Energy wastage on an automobile due to speed breakers: A case study on Woldia town. *Int. J. Res. Ind. Eng.* **2020**, *9*, 202–208.
36. Fu, X.; Meng, H.; Yang, H.; Wang, J. A hybrid deep learning method for distracted driving risk prediction based on spatio-temporal driving behavior data. *Transp. B Transp. Dyn.* **2024**, *12*, 2297144. [CrossRef]
37. Moslem, S.; Farooq, D.; Ghorbanzadeh, O.; Blaschke, T. Application of the AHP-BWM model for evaluating driver behavior factors related to road safety: A case study for Budapest. *Symmetry* **2020**, *12*, 243. [CrossRef]
38. Shaer, A.; Talebian, A.; Mishra, S. Informing the Work Zone Safety Policy Analysis: Reconciling Multivariate Prediction and Artificial Neural Network Modeling. *J. Transp. Eng. Part A Syst.* **2024**, *150*, 04023137. [CrossRef]

Disclaimer/Publisher's Note: The statements, opinions and data contained in all publications are solely those of the individual author(s) and contributor(s) and not of MDPI and/or the editor(s). MDPI and/or the editor(s) disclaim responsibility for any injury to people or property resulting from any ideas, methods, instructions or products referred to in the content.

Article

Strategic Warehouse Location Selection in Business Logistics: A Novel Approach Using IMF SWARA–MARCOS—A Case Study of a Serbian Logistics Service Provider

Vukašin Pajić *, Milan Andrejić, Marijana Jolović and Milorad Kilibarda

Faculty of Transport and Traffic Engineering, University of Belgrade, Vojvode Stepe 305, 11000 Belgrade, Serbia; m.andrejic@sf.bg.ac.rs (M.A.); jolovicmarijana@gmail.com (M.J.); m.kilibarda@sf.bg.ac.rs (M.K.)
* Correspondence: v.pajic@sf.bg.ac.rs

Abstract: Business logistics encompasses the intricate planning, seamless implementation, and precise control of the efficient and effective movement and storage of goods, services, and associated information from their origin to their final consumption point. The strategic placement of facilities is intricately intertwined with business logistics, exerting a direct influence on the efficiency and cost-effectiveness of supply chain operations. In the realm of business logistics, decisions regarding the location of facilities, including warehouses, distribution centers, and manufacturing plants, assume a pivotal role in shaping the overarching logistics strategy. Warehouses, serving as pivotal nodes in the supply chain network, establish crucial links at both local and global markets. They serve as the nexus connecting suppliers and customers across the entire supply chain, thus constituting indispensable elements that significantly impact the overall performance of the supply chain. The optimal location of warehouses is paramount for efficient supply chains, ensuring minimized costs and bigger profits. The decision on warehouse location exerts a profound influence on investment costs, operational expenses, and the distribution strategy of a company, thereby playing a substantial role in elevating customer service levels. Hence, the primary objective of this paper is to propose a novel methodology grounded in the application of the Improved Fuzzy Stepwise Weight Assessment Ratio Analysis (SWARA)-Measurement of Alternatives and Ranking according to Compromise Solution (MARCOS) methods for determining warehouse locations tailored to a logistics service provider (LSP) operating in the Serbian market. Through the definition of seven evaluation criteria based on a comprehensive literature review and expert insights, this study aims to assess five potential locations. The findings suggest that the proposed model offers great decision support for effectively addressing challenges akin to the one presented in this study.

Keywords: warehouse; location selection; supply chain; logistics; decision-making; IMF SWARA; MARCOS; logistics service provider

MSC: 90B06

1. Introduction

The issue of location selection is a widely debated phenomenon globally within the realms of transportation and logistics. This problem is inherently universal and can encompass the choice of various types of locations for facilities such as warehouses, distribution centers, transportation hubs, passenger and freight terminals, parking areas, and numerous others, taking into consideration the preferences of decision-makers and existing constraints [1,2]. In the context of transportation and logistics, this matter can be analyzed from various perspectives. For instance, when considering efficiency and costs, the selection of a location can profoundly impact the efficiency and costs of logistical operations—if a warehouse is strategically located near transportation networks or major roads, transportation time and costs will thus be diminished. Regarding proximity to clients and markets,

Citation: Pajić, V.; Andrejić, M.; Jolović, M.; Kilibarda, M. Strategic Warehouse Location Selection in Business Logistics: A Novel Approach Using IMF SWARA–MARCOS—A Case Study of a Serbian Logistics Service Provider. *Mathematics* 2024, 12, 776. https://doi.org/10.3390/math12050776

Academic Editor: Michael Voskoglou

Received: 31 January 2024
Revised: 29 February 2024
Accepted: 2 March 2024
Published: 5 March 2024

Copyright: © 2024 by the authors. Licensee MDPI, Basel, Switzerland. This article is an open access article distributed under the terms and conditions of the Creative Commons Attribution (CC BY) license (https:// creativecommons.org/licenses/by/ 4.0/).

opting for a location close to target clients or markets can expedite deliveries and reduce transportation costs. It is crucial to pay special attention to the availability of appropriate infrastructure supporting logistical operations to ensure swift and efficient distribution. The selection of a location is also heavily influenced by legal and regulatory obligations in the observed area, affecting logistical operations. Another noteworthy aspect is the potential for enhancing competitive advantage—a well-chosen location can give a company a competitive edge if the facility is strategically positioned in relation to competitors, leading to improved service, lower costs, and the attraction of more clients. In essence, effectively addressing the location selection problem in logistics contributes to more efficient supply chain management, heightened customer satisfaction, and reduced overall costs, rendering logistical operations more competitive and sustainable.

The primary objective of this paper is to propose a model for selecting an appropriate location for the establishment of a warehouse facility to meet the logistics service provider's (LSP) needs, employing relevant multi-criteria decision-making (MCDM) methods in accordance with specific criteria. Also, the aim is to fill the gap in the literature regarding the LSP warehouse location selection problem. This paper explores the feasibility of utilizing various multi-criteria decision-making methods in the warehouse location selection problem. To address the posed problem, a hybrid model has been employed, combining IMF SWARA and MARCOS methods. The SWARA method was implemented in a fuzzy form, considering the fact that experts found it more convenient to assess the significance of criteria using a linguistic scale. The advantages of employing the IMF SWARA method are evident in its ability to facilitate precise and high-quality determinations of criteria significance, requiring a reduced number of pairwise comparisons, and in it being user-friendly, especially for individuals unfamiliar with MCDM methods [3]. On the other hand, the MARCOS method was employed for alternative ranking due to its simplicity, capacity to deliver stable solutions, and precision [4]. The primary contribution of this paper lies in the development of an entirely new model for warehouse location selection, providing support to the decision-making process in choosing a suitable location. Additionally, the contribution extends to the fact that the developed model can be easily applied to other related problems in different industries and markets with minor adjustments to input parameters (criteria and alternatives). The application of the developed model enables the making of more informed decisions based on previously gathered data.

The paper is organized as follows. Following the introduction, Section 2 presents a problem description (highlighting the warehouse's pivotal role in supply chains, elucidating the essence and significance of the location selection problem in logistics, and discussing warehouse location within the supply chain) along with a literature review. Section 3 provides a more in-depth description of the proposed methodology model. In Section 4, a case study examined in this paper is outlined, along with the results obtained from applying the proposed methodology. In Section 5, a sensitivity analysis is conducted, and theoretical and managerial implications are discussed. Finally, Section 6 presents concluding remarks and limitations and proposes future research directions.

2. Problem Description and Literature Review

The concepts of supply chain (SC) and supply chain management (SCM) are increasingly attracting attention as essential tools for achieving or maintaining competitiveness in the globally challenging business environment. The network formed among various enterprises involved in producing, handling, and/or distributing a specific product is termed the supply chain. The SC can be described as a network of entities (suppliers, factories, distribution centers, warehouses, etc.) engaged in activities to acquire raw materials, transform them to add value, distribute these materials, and ultimately deliver them to the end-user. In simple terms, the SC is the link between a company and its suppliers and customers. It encompasses these three key components [5]:

- Sourcing: focusing on the raw materials supplied to production, including the delivery method, time, and location;

- Manufacturing: focusing on transforming these raw materials into finished products;
- Distribution: focusing on ensuring that products reach consumers through an organized network of distributors, warehouses, and retail outlets.

On the other side, SCM pertains to the coordination of activities essential for delivering the final product or service. These activities are initiated with raw material procurement and culminate in the delivery of the final product or service to the end-user. At the end of a product's lifecycle, supply chains are also accountable for coordinating recycling, reproduction (renewing the product to its original specifications using used parts), or the disposal of the final product. SCM can be described as the oversight of materials, information, and finances distributed from suppliers to consumers. It constitutes a set of approaches used to seamlessly integrate suppliers, manufacturers, warehouses, and sales outlets, ensuring that goods are produced and distributed in the correct quantities, at the right locations, and at the right time, thereby minimizing costs while maximizing satisfaction with service level requirements. SCM can be categorized into these three primary flows [5]:

- Product flow: encompassing the movement of products from suppliers to consumers;
- Information flow: involving information about orders and delivery status;
- Financial flow: covering payment schedules, credit terms, and additional arrangements.

Given that SC costs can represent up to 13% of the sales value, effective SCM has the potential to boost profitability through cost reduction. Studies have demonstrated that top-performing companies can decrease these costs to as little as 8% [6]. A substantial share of SC costs is attributed to product storage. Therefore, strategically configuring warehouses and distribution centers (DCs) can result in lower transportation costs. Proper warehouse placement can also facilitate more streamlined inventory management, consequently improving the service level. The establishment of DCs and warehouses is a pivotal factor in the redesign of the logistics system.

2.1. The Role of Warehouses in the Supply Chain

Warehouses play a vital role in the supply chain network, whether operating in local or global markets [7]. They serve as the crucial link connecting suppliers and customers throughout the entire SC and can be deemed as key elements influencing the overall performance of the SC [8]. Within the broader SC framework, storage stands out as a critical component in the distribution of goods—from raw materials and semi-finished products to finished goods. It operates as an integral part of the SC network, and its roles and objectives should align with the broader goals of the SC. Warehousing is not an isolated activity; rather, it must be a robust element within the overall SC network, avoiding weaknesses [9]. Warehousing directly contributes to ensuring the continuity of production and the distribution of products. Effective warehouse management enables companies to store and handle a wide range of products across the entire system [10]. Furthermore, it aids in reducing production, transportation, and distribution costs. Consequently, warehouses actively contribute to creating cost-effective shipments during production and distribution, resulting in a reduced average cost per unit and substantial savings in cargo loss management, along with the economical and efficient utilization of storage capacity. Warehousing supports the customer service process by ensuring the delivery of quality products in terms of quantity, quality, and delivery status, and it contributes to timely and specified deliveries [11]. The presence of warehouses in the SC yields various benefits [12], indicated as follows:

- Sustainable inventory management;
- Ensuring packaging that protects the product from unauthorized use;
- On-time delivery;
- Price stabilization;
- Operation optimization;
- Positive customer experience.

2.2. Facility Location Problem

Business logistics, often synonymous with SCM, involves the planning, implementation, and control of the efficient and effective movement and storage of goods, services, and related information from the point of origin to the point of consumption. It plays a pivotal role in ensuring that products and services are readily available to customers in the correct quantities, at the right time, and in optimal condition. Effective business logistics is an integral component of the overall company strategy, directly impacting its competitiveness, customer satisfaction, and overall business performance. The facility location problem is intricately connected to business logistics, as it directly influences the efficiency and cost-effectiveness of supply chain operations. In business logistics, decisions regarding the placement of facilities such as warehouses, distribution centers, and production plants are instrumental in shaping the overarching logistics strategy [13–16].

The term "facility location problem" (FLP) pertains to the modeling, formulation, and resolution of a class of problems best characterized as the positioning of facilities in specific spaces. The terms deployment, positioning, and location are often used interchangeably. The FLP represents a type of optimization problem where the primary objective is to determine the best or optimal location for placing a particular facility. The formal study of location theory commenced in 1909 when Alfred Weber considered how to locate a warehouse to minimize the overall distance between the warehouse and several customers [17]. FLP is a prevalent topic in the literature and often emerges in the context of logistics, manufacturing, or service delivery, where efficiently arranging facilities is crucial for minimizing costs or maximizing efficiency. Essentially, this type of problem involves selecting locations for placing facilities to meet specified criteria. Different variants of FLP include various conditions and constraints, making this research area challenging and significant, especially in the domains of business logistics. Researchers and experts employ various optimization methods and data analysis to solve these problems and find the most efficient solutions for facility placement in a given environment [1,2,18].

The choice of location is a longstanding and extensively debated decision-making domain related to determining specific sites for facilities such as factories, cargo and passenger terminals, distribution centers, warehouses, and similar entities. The number and placement of these facilities constitute fundamental decisions that form the foundation of designing a logistics system [19]. As selecting the most suitable location for a new organization is a critical strategic consideration in optimizing logistics systems, the ongoing development of global economies and market globalization demand continuous improvement in methods and research in this field [20]. Facility location decisions are pivotal elements in the strategic planning of a diverse range of private and public enterprises. The branches of facility location are extensive and enduring, influencing numerous operational and logistical decisions. The substantial costs associated with acquiring property and constructing a facility transform location projects into long-term investments. Decision-makers must choose locations that not only function well in the current state of the system but will also remain profitable throughout the lifecycle of the facility, even as surrounding factors change, populations shift, and market trends evolve [17].

The location of a facility represents a long-term decision and impacts numerous quantitative and qualitative factors, particularly costs and revenues [20]. It determines transport time, influences SC operational costs, and dictates the possible or minimum inventory quantity. These are crucial considerations in designing an efficient logistics system [21]. When addressing the problem itself, it is necessary to compare performance characteristics decisively when choosing among several alternative potential locations for a facility. Thus, due to the presence of multiple conflicting criteria, the decision on the optimal location becomes more complex, clearly indicating that it is a multifaceted MCDM problem, requiring the application of appropriate methods for effective resolution [22]. MCDM can be defined as the evaluation of alternatives for the purpose of selection or ranking, using a set of quantitative and/or qualitative criteria with different units of measurement [19]. Essentially, solving the facility location problem in the context of business logistics involves finding the optimal balance between costs, efficiency, and responsiveness. This is a strategic decision that shapes the entire supply chain network and impacts the overall competitiveness and success of the enterprise.

2.3. Literature Review Regarding Warehouse Location Selection in the SC

The efficiency and speed of a SC is largely determined by the location of warehouses. In today's competitive landscape, SCs vie for superiority, primarily focusing on delivery times and overall product costs. Storage processes contribute to accelerating material flow in SCs, with warehouses serving as significant facilities where raw materials or manufactured products are stored for a designated period before distribution for sales. Products are dispatched from production facilities to warehouses, from where they are distributed to various sellers based on market demand. To thrive in specific demand areas, companies must establish a presence in warehouse facilities. SCM, beyond managing the flow of goods, production decisions, and information sharing at various levels, also involves determining optimal storage levels at each stage of the process and, crucially, selecting warehouse locations—whether locally or globally [7]. Regardless of the success of other warehouse activities, if products dispatched from warehouses fail to meet customer needs promptly, companies risk losing customers [8].

Storage has become one of the pivotal facilitators in ensuring the efficiency of today's global SCNs. Each company endeavors to optimize its supply chain for specific objectives like market expansion, market penetration, and customer support, with warehouse-related factors playing a crucial role. Therefore, making various decisions regarding warehouse scheduling and location becomes paramount [7]. In the contemporary business landscape, the location of a warehouse can confer a substantial competitive advantage to companies. Indeed, the warehouse location stands as a key issue in SCM and a vital component of the overall logistics system. When determining where to situate a warehouse, companies aim to be in proximity to markets and facilities to minimize inventory and transportation costs. The challenge lies in deciding how many warehouses to establish, where to locate them, and how to efficiently serve retail outlets using these warehouse facilities [20]. For companies, it becomes imperative to focus on making decisions about the appropriate location from various alternatives for warehouse placement. Factors such as sufficient space, customer service, convenient transportation links with suppliers and key markets, access to highways, and proximity to railways, ports, and airports must be taken into account when selecting a location [7].

Optimal warehouse location ensures the success of the SC by minimizing costs and maximizing profits [7]. The decision on warehouse location significantly influences investment costs, operational expenses, and the company's distribution strategy, playing a critical role in enhancing customer service levels. The importance of choosing a suitable warehouse location is underscored by the fact that an incorrect location can disrupt SC activities. The primary goal of the SC is to enhance on-time delivery with minimal costs and increased efficiency [19]. The warehouse should be situated in an appropriate location to enhance the overall efficiency of the company's SC and avoid causing delays in the delivery process or increasing production costs. Choosing a warehouse location is a challenging task because once the decision is implemented, it cannot be changed, and any wrong decision can result in significant losses for the company [7].

The significance of the warehouse location selection problem is recognized in the literature as well. Thus, ref. [7] proposed a model based on a fuzzy AHP (analytical hierarchy process) for selecting the optimal warehouse location in a free-trade zone. The same method was applied by [23] for selecting the location for a sustainable warehouse. The authors assessed four potential locations using 11 evaluation criteria. Demonstrated in a case study by [24], the UTASTAR method facilitated the evaluation and ranking of alternative warehouse locations based on decision-makers' preferences and provided a valuable perspective for justifying the selection of the optimal warehouse location. The research by [8] introduced an integrated grey MCDM model, incorporating the grey preference selection index (GPSI) and grey proximity indexed value (GPIV), for evaluating the optimal location of a supermarket warehouse. This study contributes by introducing PSI and PIV methods with grey theory and combining GPSI and GPIV methods to determine the best warehouse location, evaluating the performance of five alternatives against twelve criteria. The study by [25] introduced three novel fuzzy MCDM methodologies designed to address both subjective and objective factors in the evaluation and selection of warehouse locations. Integrating fuzzy set theory with TOPSIS (technique for order of preference by similarity to ideal solution), SAW (simple additive weight), and MOORA (multi-objective optimization on the basis of ratio analysis) methods, these approaches considered subjective criteria through subjective factor measures, while objective criteria were assessed using a classical normalization technique. The Brown and Gibson model integrated subjective and objective factor measures to calculate the warehouse location selection index, demonstrating the applicability and effectiveness of the proposed methodologies in two examples of warehouse location selection within a supply chain context. A novel group decision-making model, based on the AHP method for warehouse location selection in a SC, was proposed by [26]. On the other hand, ref. [27] introduced a novel method employing fuzzy multi-criteria analysis (FMCA) for evaluating warehouse locations within a leagile SC. The algorithm, based on decision theory, calculates the benefit cost ratio (BCR) as the warehouse selection index, using the aggregate modified weighted value (MWV) of normalized scores for alternatives. A study by [28] aimed to employ several MCDM methods (SAW, AHP, TOPSIS) to select an appropriate warehouse location for businesses dealing with agricultural products, specifically grass flowers. The research explored seven key factors influencing warehouse selection, used to evaluate five alternatives. Cetinkaya and Akdas [19] used the best–worst method (BWM) for determining criteria weights for warehouse location selection. It was concluded, based on the results, that the criteria related to the market dominantly affect the selection process. Warehouse location selection was also addressed by [20]. The authors implemented a genetic algorithm (GA) in order to select an optimal location in Turkey. An examination of the sensitivity of the warehouse location problem was conducted by [21]. Namely, the authors used FLEXSIM software (FlexSim Software Products, Inc., Orem, UT, USA, https://www.flexsim.com/) to simulate several scenarios with different inputs and parameters of the model.

3. Methodology

The presence of conflicting criteria in solving the problem of selecting the optimal warehouse location eliminates the possibility of finding a singular solution that could satisfy all criteria simultaneously. Consequently, MCDM methods are employed to differentiate potential solutions based on the expressed preferences of decision-makers. The core of all MCDM methods is grounded in three essential steps: defining sets of alternatives and criteria for their evaluation, assigning weights to criteria through numerical values indicating their importance, and assigning numerical values to alternatives in relation to the considered criteria, aiming for the final ranking of alternatives and the selection of the best option from the pool of potentials. The concept of a proposed hybrid model in this paper is illustrated in Figure 1, where the IMF SWARA method is initially applied to determine criteria weights, followed by the MARCOS method to obtain evaluations of alternatives, the final ranking, and the selection of the most favorable alternative based on the considered criteria. The advantage of the proposed model over existing models in the literature lies in the application of the SWARA method in a fuzzy environment, enabling easier evaluation by experts through the use of linguistic scales. Additionally, the model employs the improved fuzzy SWARA method, which has been proven to yield superior results compared to the fuzzy SWARA method due to the application of a different linguistic scale [3]. On the other hand, the simplicity of application distinguishes the MARCOS method, which is particularly significant for practitioners who would implement the proposed model. Moreover, the MARCOS method is characterized by providing stable and precise solutions, adding further robustness to the model. The implementation steps of the proposed methodology are as follows:

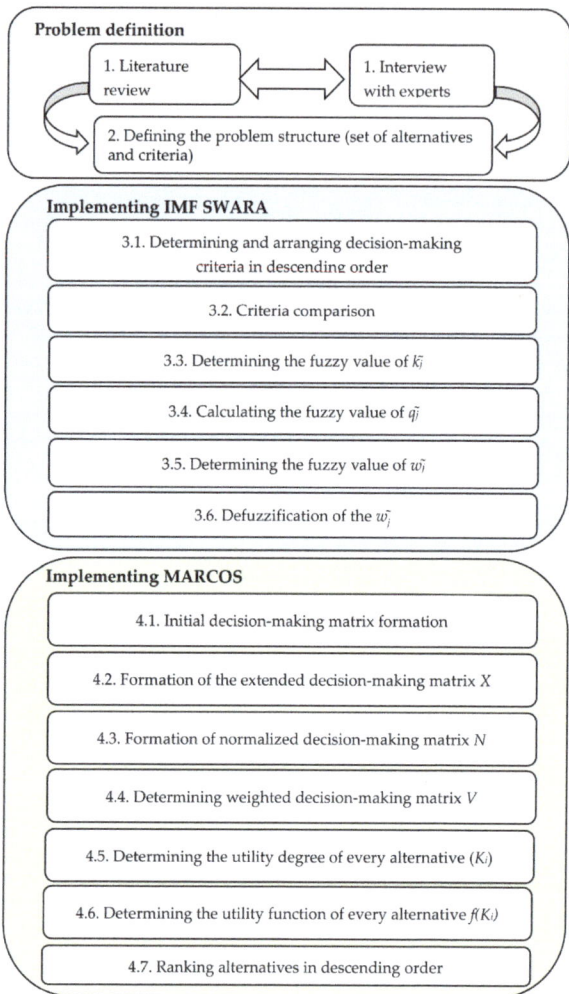

Figure 1. Methodology for warehouse location selection.

Step 1: Defining the problem is conducted in the first phase and also involves forming sets of alternatives and criteria for evaluating alternatives.

Step 2: Establishing a fuzzy scale for evaluating criteria and alternatives by decision-makers is undertaken. Linguistic expressions and corresponding triangular fuzzy values are provided in Table 1.

Step 3: Determining criteria weights are performed using the IMF SWARA method. The implementation steps of the method (3.1–3.6) are elaborated in more detail below.

Step 4: Assessing and ranking alternatives occurs by using the MARCOS method. The implementation steps of the method (4.1–4.7) are elaborated in more detail below.

Table 1. Linguistic and triangular fuzzy numbers (TFN) scale [3].

Linguistic Scale	Abbreviation	TFN Scale
Absolutely less significant	ALS	(1,1,1)
Dominantly less significant	DLS	(1/2,2/3,1)
Much less significant	MLS	(2/5,1/2,2/3)
Really less significant	RLS	(1/3,2/5,1/2)
Less significant	LS	(2/7,1/3,2/5)
Moderately less significant	MDLS	(1/4,2/7,1/3)
Weakly less significant	WLS	(2/9,1/4,2/7)
Equally significant	ES	(0,0,0)

3.1. Improved Fuzzy SWARA (IMF SWARA) Method

The fuzzy SWARA method used for assessing criteria weights efficiently addresses uncertainties in decision-makers' reasoning and the expression of preferences. This approach is utilized to determine criteria weights for the selection of warehouse locations based on the descending order of criterion importance (from most to least significant). What sets this method apart from other multi-criteria decision-making techniques is its numerous advantages. It boasts a simple application, with a straightforward problem-solving algorithm that is easily comprehensible even for less experienced users. It requires a minimal time investment for implementation and is equally effective for both group and individual decision-making. Moreover, the method stands out for its low demand for evaluations, exemption from consistency checks due to the predetermined descending order of criteria, high flexibility, and the absence of a need for a predefined scale to compare criteria. The application steps for this method are outlined in [3].

Step 1—Determining and arranging decision-making criteria $\{c_1, c_2, \ldots, c_n\}$ in descending order is undertaken with respect to their significance (from the most to the least significant).

Step 2—Criteria comparison. The significance of the criterion C_j is determined in relation to the previous one (C_{j-1}). The procedure is repeated for each subsequent criterion. A comparative significance of the average value ($\overline{s_j}$) is calculated based on this.

Step 3—Determining the fuzzy value of the coefficient $\overline{k_j}$ by applying Equation (1):

$$\overline{k_j} = \begin{cases} \overline{1} & j = 1 \\ \overline{s_j} & j > 1 \end{cases} \quad (1)$$

Step 4—Calculating the fuzzy value of the coefficient $\overline{q_j}$ by applying Equation (2):

$$\overline{q_j} = \begin{cases} \overline{1} & j = 1 \\ \frac{\overline{q_{j-1}}}{\overline{k_j}} & j > 1 \end{cases} \quad (2)$$

Step 5—Determining the fuzzy value of the criteria weights by applying Equation (3):

$$\overline{w_j} = \frac{\overline{q_j}}{\sum_{j=1}^{m} \overline{q_j}} \quad (3)$$

Step 6—Defuzzification of the $\overline{w_j}$ to obtain crisp values by applying Equation (4):

$$w_j = \frac{w_j^l + 4w_j^m + w_j^u}{6}, j = 1, 2, \ldots, n \quad (4)$$

3.2. MARCOS Method

The MARCOS method relies on establishing relationships between alternatives and reference values (ideal and anti-ideal alternatives). Utility functions for alternatives are determined based on these relationships, and a compromise ranking is established in relation to both ideal and anti-ideal solutions. Decision preferences are defined by utility functions that indicate the position of each alternative relative to the ideal and anti-ideal solutions. The best alternative is identified as the one closest to the ideal solution while simultaneously being farthest from the anti-ideal reference point. This method is characterized by considering ideal and anti-ideal solutions right from the initial formation of the initial decision-making matrix, providing a more precise determination of the degree of utility in relation to both solutions. It introduces a novel approach to determining utility functions and their aggregation, enabling the consideration of a large set of alternatives and criteria while maintaining the stability of the method. The MARCOS method is implemented through the following series of steps [4,29]:

Step 1—Defining the initial decision-making matrix consisting of n criteria and m alternatives.

Step 2—Determining ideal (AI) and anti-ideal (AAI) solutions to extend the initial decision-making matrix, via Equation (5):

$$\begin{array}{c} \\ AAI \\ A_1 \\ A_2 \\ \ldots \\ A_m \\ AI \end{array} \begin{bmatrix} C_1 & C_2 & \ldots & C_n \\ x_{aa1} & x_{aa2} & \ldots & x_{aan} \\ x_{11} & x_{12} & \ldots & x_{1n} \\ x_{21} & x_{22} & \ldots & x_{2n} \\ \ldots & \ldots & \ldots & \ldots \\ x_{m1} & x_{m2} & \ldots & x_{mn} \\ x_{ai1} & x_{ai2} & \ldots & x_{ain} \end{bmatrix} \quad (5)$$

The anti-ideal solution (AAI) represents the alternative that is the worst, while the ideal solution (AI) represents the best alternative. AAI and AI are obtained by applying Equations (6) and (7):

$$AAI = \min_i x_{ij} \text{ if } j \in B \text{ and } \max_i x_{ij} \text{ if } j \in C \quad (6)$$

$$AI = \max_i x_{ij} \text{ if } j \in B \text{ and } \min_i x_{ij} \text{ if } j \in C \quad (7)$$

where B stands for beneficial criteria, while C stands for cost criteria.

Step 3—Conducting the normalization of the extended initial decision-making matrix using Equations (8) and (9):

$$n_{ij} = \frac{x_{ai}}{x_{ij}} \text{ if } j \in C \quad (8)$$

$$n_{ij} = \frac{x_{ij}}{x_{ai}} \text{ if } j \in B \quad (9)$$

Step 4—Determining the weighted decision-making matrix $V = [v_{ij}]_{mxn}$ by applying Equation (10):

$$v_{ij} = n_{ij} \times w_j \quad (10)$$

Step 5—Determining the utility degree of every alternative (K_i) using Equations (11) and (12) with respect to AAI and AI:

$$K_i^- = \frac{S_i}{S_{aai}} \quad (11)$$

$$K_i^+ = \frac{S_i}{S_{ai}} \quad (12)$$

where S_i ($i = 1, 2, \ldots, n$) is the sum of the elements of the weighted matrix V and is obtained using Equation (13).

$$S_i = \sum_{i=1}^{n} V_{ij} \tag{13}$$

Step 6—Calculating the utility function of every alternative $f(K_i)$. This value represents the compromise of the observed alternative in relation to the AI and AAI solutions, obtained by using Equation (14):

$$f(K_i) = \frac{K_i^+ + K_i^-}{1 + \frac{1 - f(K_i^+)}{f(K_i^+)} + \frac{1 - f(K_i^-)}{f(K_i^-)}} \tag{14}$$

where $f(K_i^-)$ is the utility function in relation to the AAI, while $f(K_i^+)$ is the utility function in relation to the AI solution and are obtained using Equations (15) and (16):

$$f(K_i^-) = \frac{K_i^+}{K_i^+ + K_i^-} \tag{15}$$

$$f(K_i^+) = \frac{K_i^-}{K_i^+ + K_i^-} \tag{16}$$

Step 7—In the final step, the alternatives are ranked in descending order based on the value of the utility functions $f(K_i)$.

4. Warehouse Location Selection—Case Study
4.1. Case Study Description

In this section of the paper, the focus is on establishing the groundwork for addressing the warehouse location selection problem. The initial foundation of the problem involves identifying and forming a list of alternatives for consideration, as well as a list of criteria by which the alternatives are assessed using appropriate methods. The primary challenge in implementing the proposed methodology lies in gathering information during interviews, as well as in defining criteria, alternatives, and their evaluations. Consequently, it would be most beneficial to conduct interviews with all experts simultaneously, facilitating the exchange of thoughts and perspectives, contributing to more robust information. For practitioners, a challenge may arise in the application of the model, particularly for those unfamiliar with MCDM methods. This challenge can be easily addressed by using the proposed model through Excel or by developing an application with a user-friendly interface. The model's limitation is evident in its challenging application to problems with extremely large dimensions (given the large number of alternatives that need evaluation in accordance with criteria), although such situations are rare, especially in solving FLP where the number of potential alternatives is not typically substantial. The list of alternatives essentially comprises potential solutions, among which the optimal one must be chosen—the one that will most effectively satisfy the specified criteria. Potential locations were determined based on interviews with experts from the observed company who considered them for the establishment of a new warehouse. The preliminary foundation for selecting the warehouse location included the general urban plan of the city of Belgrade, illustrated in Figure 2. Areas designated for facility locations such as warehouses are highlighted in purple (industrial zones) and red (commercial facilities). Accordingly, locations with such designated areas were taken into consideration.

Figure 2. General urban plan of Belgrade [30].

The following locations were selected as potential alternatives for establishing the warehouse:

A1—Borča—The land price per square meter at this location is estimated at EUR 24.19 [31]. In terms of infrastructure access, Borča is intersected by Zrenjaninski Put, providing a connection to the E70 highway and the Pančevački Most. A crucial road link is facilitated by Pupinov Most, spanning the Danube River and linking Borča to central areas of Belgrade (Figure 3). This location is situated 26.7 km away from Belgrade, with a required driving time of 35 min [32]. Borča offers substantial site capacities, although they are smaller compared to Surčin and Dobanovci. This location does not have significant competitors, indicating that there is not a high demand for skilled labor, and a considerable number of qualified workers are available.

A2—Surčin—The estimated land price per square meter at this location is EUR 22.76 [31]. In terms of infrastructure, this location boasts access to the state road, linking Leštane–Grocka–Petrijevo–Ralja, serving as a connection to the A1 state road. Surčin is well connected to the E70 and E75 highways. The E70, running east–west, connects Surčin to Belgrade and further west to the Serbian border. The E75, spanning north–south, links Surčin to Belgrade and extends south through Serbia. These highway connections position Surčin as a significant transportation hub, facilitating the movement of goods between Belgrade and other parts of Serbia, as well as neighboring countries. Surčin is renowned for the "Nikola Tesla" airport, a crucial air traffic hub in Serbia that plays a vital role in connecting Belgrade with other cities and countries. Located on the southern edge of the Pannonian Plain along the Sava River, it provides a navigable route connecting with the Danube River as European Corridor 7 [33]. Surčin is 31.5 km away from Belgrade, with a delivery time of 34 min [32]. Surčin is situated within an industrial zone, and its capacities are smaller compared to those present in Dobanovci. As it is an industrial zone with numerous competitors, there is a high demand for skilled labor (Figure 4).

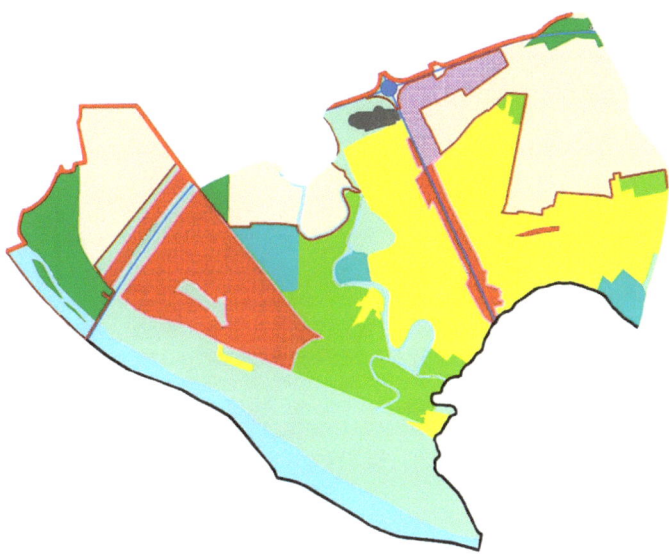

Figure 3. Urban plan of A1—Borča [30].

Figure 4. Urban plan of A2—Surčin [30].

A3—Batajnica—The estimated land price per square meter at this location is EUR 25.07 [31]. In terms of infrastructure access, Batajnica is connected to the state road, linking it to the A1 state road Batajnica–Ugrinovci–Surčin, and state road Horgoš–Subotica–Bačka Topola–Mali Iđoš–Srbobran–Novi Sad–Sremski Karlovci–Inđija–Stara Pazova–Belgrade. It is essential to mention the Batajnica loop, approximately 3.5 km in length, enhancing transportation connectivity and facilitating the flow of goods and services, connecting Batajnički Boulevard and the intermodal transport logistics center to the E-75 highway.

There is also good connectivity to the railway network via the mainline of railway 111 Belgrade "A"–Ostružnica–Batajnica [34]. The Batajnica intermodal terminal promotes the development of modern combined cargo transport by increasing the railway's share and creating a partnership with road transport. Batajnica is located 22.1 km from Belgrade, requiring a 32 min drive [32]. Batajnica has relatively smaller location capacities compared to other alternatives. Strong competitors are not present at this location, indicating a higher availability of skilled labor (Figure 5).

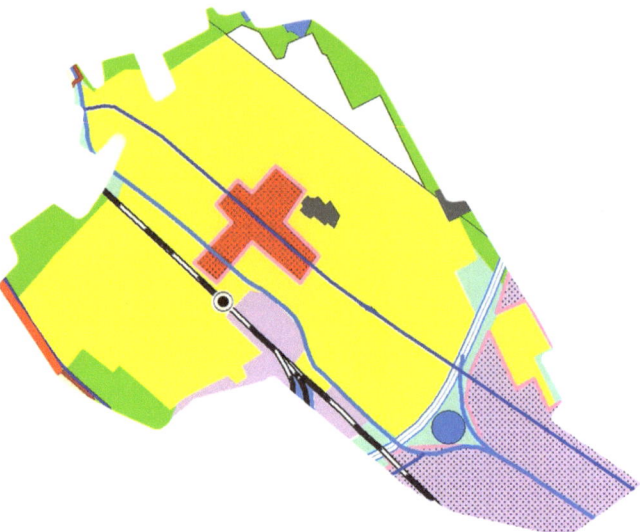

Figure 5. Urban plan of A3—Batajnica [30].

A4—Krnjača—The estimated land price per square meter at this location is EUR 25.5 [31]. Krnjača is connected to the state road Horgoš–Kanjiža–Novi Kneževac–Čoka–Kikinda–Zrenjanin–Čenta–Belgrade. Additionally, it is crucial to note that Krnjača is situated near the E70 highway, alongside which Zrenjaninski put stretches, and has a direct connection to Belgrade via the Pančevački Most. There is also connectivity to railway traffic through the Krnjača railway station located on the left bank of the Danube River. The railway continues towards Krnjača in one direction and Pančevački Most in the other. The distance on the Krnjača–Belgrade route is 10.7 km, requiring approximately 19 min of travel time [32]. The capacity of the Krnjača location is larger than Batajnica but smaller than other locations. There are competitors present, but not to a significant extent. As mentioned for Batajnica, the same applies to Krnjača; namely, due to a lack of competitors, there is a higher availability of qualified labor (Figure 6).

A5—Dobanovci—The estimated land price per square meter at this location is EUR 20.18 [31]. Dobanovci is characterized by excellent traffic connectivity with major road networks, including the E70 and E75 highways, as well as the M2 Miloš Veliki highway. Notably, there is an intermodal terminal situated within the central distribution-logistics center in Dobanovci, connected by rail to all major European ports and land terminals. The Dobanovci railway station serves as a crucial hub in the railway system, offering transportation services for both passengers and goods and facilitating substantial connectivity to the railway network. The distance from Belgrade is 22.8 km, covering a journey time of approximately 23 min [32]. A distinctive feature of Dobanovci is that it boasts the largest capacities for expansion and future warehouse development. Concerning the presence of a large number of competitors in this area, challenges may arise in attracting and retaining qualified labor due to increased demand, indicating a shortage of available skilled workforce (Figure 7).

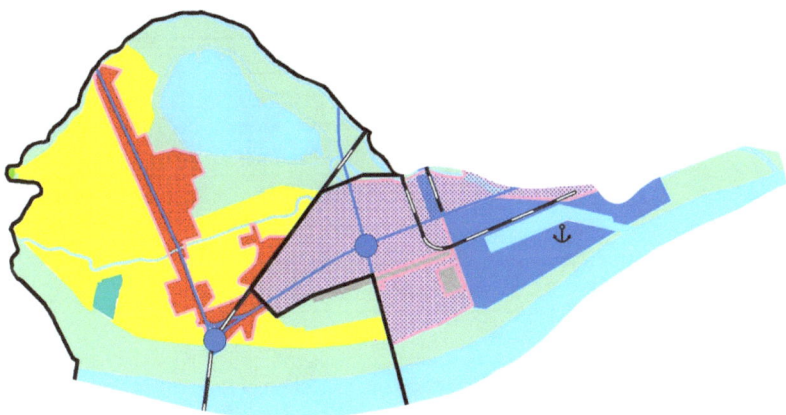

Figure 6. Urban plan of A4—Krnjača [30].

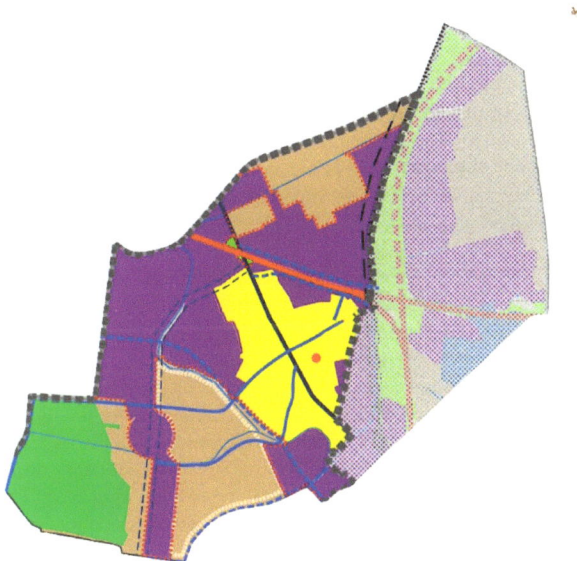

Figure 7. Urban plan of A5—Dobanovci [30].

Once the list of potential alternatives was formulated, the next step involved identifying criteria to facilitate the final decision-making process, specifically the selection of the optimal location from the available options. The identification and definition of criteria, which would vary among alternatives, needed to align with desired objectives, as they represent the preferred characteristics of potential solutions. Following the establishment of the final list of criteria with distinct variations, acknowledging that not every criterion holds equal importance, the subsequent task was to determine their respective weights. The quantitative expression of these weights signifies their significance and influence on the ranking of alternatives, culminating in the ultimate decision. Through these weights, the priorities and preferences of the decision-maker are reflected. For the evaluation of the specified alternatives or potential locations, the following criteria were applied (Table 2) [26,27,35,36]:

Table 2. Criteria used for evaluation.

Criteria	Reference
C1—Land Cost	[24–27,35,36]
C2—Infrastructure Access	[22,26,35]
C3—Workforce Availability	[22,27]
C4—Delivery Time	[22,24,25,27,35,36]
C5—Area Competitiveness	[35]
C6—Location Capacity	[24–27]
C7—Presence of Various Transportation Modes	[24]

C1—Land Cost. This criterion serves as a crucial factor in warehouse construction and directly impacts the escalation of investment costs. Beyond the required land area for the warehouse, there must also be sufficient additional surrounding space available for future development and expansion.

C2—Infrastructure Access. Transportation facilitates the movement of goods from producers to warehouses, between various warehouses, and from warehouses to retail or end customers. A warehouse must have excellent connectivity with transportation networks, including highways, railways, river ports, and airports to facilitate this transportation.

C3—Workforce Availability. Warehouse facilities require a qualified workforce to perform various tasks, ranging from handling inventory and order picking to managing warehouse operations. A qualified workforce in the warehouse includes employees who are trained and experienced in executing diverse warehouse tasks. This criterion is closely tied to C5, as increased competitiveness in the environment implies a higher demand for a skilled workforce.

C4—Delivery Time. This is directly linked to criterion C2 but also depends on the destination. For this study, the central location of Belgrade has been selected as the destination. It is of paramount importance since a short delivery time contributes to customer satisfaction, enhances adaptability to market changes, facilitates gaining a competitive advantage, and more.

C5—Area Competitiveness. This refers to the level of competition in the environment. The less competitive the environment, the better the location's result.

C6—Location Capacity. This relates to the location's ability to support the necessary warehouse capacities, including space for storing goods, handling cargo, parking for delivery vehicles, space for installing specific equipment and technology, and other required resources. This criterion also pertains to the location's availability for future expansions and warehouse development.

C7—Presence of Various Transportation Modes. The ability to utilize multiple transportation modes is crucial for adapting to diverse transport requirements and optimizing transportation costs.

4.2. Results

As previously outlined, the initial step involves the application of the IMF SWARA method to derive criteria weights. Determining the weights begins with ranking the criteria based on their significance, from the most significant to the least. Subsequently, experts utilize linguistic scales, which are then converted into fuzzy numbers (Table 3). Five experts from the observed company (LSP) participated in the evaluation. Among the overall pool of experts, two are engaged as logistics managers, another two hold positions as warehouse managers, and one assumes the role of a supply chain manager. All of the experts have more than 10 years of working experience. In the assessment process involving multiple experts, the chosen unified value corresponds to the one that occurs most frequently during the evaluation process.

Table 3. Criteria significance using a linguistic scale.

Criterion	Significance
C1	-
C2	MDLS
C7	WLS
C4	WLS
C6	LS
C5	LS
C3	WLS

Based on Table 3, it can be inferred that the most significant criterion is C1—land cost, given its direct impact on overall investments in establishing a warehouse and its potential decisive significance. Land price constitutes a portion of the total costs associated with facility setup. Companies often face financial constraints, and the cost of land is a pivotal factor in determining whether a specific location is viable within budget constraints. Following this, a slightly less significant criterion is C2—infrastructure access, representing a crucial element for timely and cost-effective deliveries. Well-developed infrastructure helps minimize transportation costs. Efficient connectivity leads to shorter distances, reduced fuel consumption, and lower overall logistics costs. Proximity to major infrastructure nodes like highways, railways, and ports ensures efficient transportation of goods to and from the warehouse. Additionally, good transportation connectivity allows for quick adaptation in case one mode of transport encounters challenges such as road closures, strikes, roadworks, traffic congestion, etc., enabling the swift utilization of alternative routes or transport modes. Criterion C7—the presence of various transport modes—represents the ability to access multiple transport modes, thus providing flexibility in choosing the most efficient and economical transportation method based on specific needs and requirements. A slightly less significant criterion is C4—delivery time, impacting customer satisfaction, logistical chain efficiency, the fulfillment of requirements, and overall costs. Criterion C6—location capacity, relating to capacity for current and future needs, is essential for adapting to business operations and accommodating growing demand. A bit less significant is C5—area competitiveness, which may limit access to resources like qualified labor, infrastructure, or land availability. Moreover, intense competition may exert pressure to reduce service prices to attract clients. The last-ranked criterion is C3—workforce availability, contributing to improved warehouse operations management but is not of paramount importance, as companies can provide various training programs to employees, aiding in enhancing overall operational efficiency and performing various operations (Table 4).

Following the determination of criteria weights, the MARCOS method was employed to rank potential locations. The initial decision-making matrix (Table 5) was formed as the first step in implementing the MARCOS method. For quantitative criteria, precise values were utilized, while values for qualitative criteria were derived from expert assessments, where experts evaluated criteria using a scale of 1–5.

The presented values were then normalized using Equations (8) and (9), depending on the type of criteria. The normalized values are shown in Table 6.

The normalized values were then multiplied by the corresponding criterion weights obtained after applying the IMF SWARA method. This way, the weighted decision-making matrix was formed (Table 7).

Table 4. IMF SWARA application.

	$\overline{s_j}$			$\overline{k_j}$			$\overline{q_j}$			$\overline{w_j}$		w_j (crisp)
C1				1.000	1.000	1.000	1.000	1.000	1.000	0.250	0.265	0.284	0.266
C2	0.25	0.286	0.333	1.250	1.286	1.333	0.750	0.778	0.800	0.188	0.206	0.227	0.206
C3	0.222	0.250	0.286	1.222	1.250	1.286	0.583	0.622	0.655	0.146	0.165	0.186	0.165
C4	0.222	0.250	0.286	1.222	1.250	1.286	0.454	0.498	0.536	0.114	0.132	0.152	0.132
C5	0.286	0.333	0.400	1.286	1.333	1.400	0.324	0.373	0.417	0.081	0.099	0.118	0.099
C6	0.286	0.333	0.400	1.286	1.333	1.400	0.231	0.280	0.324	0.058	0.074	0.092	0.074
C7	0.222	0.250	0.286	1.222	1.250	1.286	0.180	0.224	0.265	0.045	0.059	0.075	0.060
						SUM	3.523	3.775	3.996				

Table 5. Initial decision-making matrix.

Alternative	C1	C2	C3	C4	C5	C6	C7
type	min	max	max	min	min	max	max
AAI	25.5	3	1	35	5	2	1
A1	24.19	3	5	35	1	4	1
A2	22.76	5	2	34	4	2	5
A3	25.07	4	5	32	1	2	4
A4	25.5	3	4	19	2	3	3
A5	20.18	5	1	23	5	5	3
AI	20.18	5	5	19	1	5	5

Table 6. Normalized decision-making matrix.

Alternative	C1	C2	C3	C4	C5	C6	C7
AAI	0.79	0.60	0.20	0.54	0.20	0.40	0.20
A1	0.83	0.60	1.00	0.54	1.00	0.80	0.20
A2	0.89	1.00	0.40	0.56	0.25	0.40	1.00
A3	0.80	0.80	1.00	0.59	1.00	0.40	0.80
A4	0.79	0.60	0.80	1.00	0.50	0.60	0.60
A5	1.00	1.00	0.20	0.83	0.20	1.00	0.60
AI	1.00	1.00	1.00	1.00	1.00	1.00	1.00
w_j	0.266	0.206	0.059	0.132	0.073	0.099	0.165

Table 7. Weighted decision-making matrix.

Alternative	C1	C2	C3	C4	C5	C6	C7
AAI	0.21	0.12	0.01	0.07	0.01	0.04	0.03
A1	0.22	0.12	0.06	0.07	0.07	0.08	0.03
A2	0.24	0.21	0.02	0.07	0.02	0.04	0.17
A3	0.21	0.17	0.06	0.08	0.07	0.04	0.13
A4	0.21	0.12	0.05	0.13	0.04	0.06	0.10
A5	0.27	0.21	0.01	0.11	0.01	0.10	0.10
AI	0.27	0.21	0.06	0.13	0.07	0.10	0.17

To perform the final ranking, Equations (11)–(16) were applied. After applying the described equations, a utility function value for every alternative was obtained, based on which the alternatives were ranked (Table 8).

Table 8. Final ranking of the alternatives.

Alternatives	S_i 0.50	K_i^-	K_i^+	$f(K_i^-)$	$f(K_i^+)$	$f(K_i)$	Rank
A1	0.66	1.31	0.66	0.34	0.66	0.57	4
A2	0.76	1.51	0.76	0.34	0.66	0.65	2
A3	0.76	1.51	0.76	0.34	0.66	0.65	2
A4	0.71	1.40	0.71	0.34	0.66	0.61	3
A5	0.81	1.60	0.81	0.34	0.66	0.69	1
	1.000						

Based on the results in Table 8, it can be concluded that the best-ranked alternative (potential location) is A5—Dobanovci, followed by A2 and A3 sharing the same position, and then A4 and A1. The alternative ranking can also be represented as A5 > A2 = A3 > A4 > A1. Based on the results, it can be inferred that criteria with higher weights (for example C1 and C2) exert a greater influence on the final ranking of alternatives, whereas, on the other hand, criteria with lower weights (for example C6 and C7) have a smaller impact. For this reason, sensitivity analysis was conducted in this study to assess whether there would be any changes in the ranking of alternatives.

5. Discussion

5.1. Sensitivity Analysis and Model Validation

After applying the proposed methodology, a sensitivity analysis was conducted to test the proposed model against changes in input values. For this reason, five scenarios were defined, each involving different weights assigned to the criteria. In the first scenario, labeled "performance-related", higher weights (and therefore significance) were assigned to criteria that could significantly impact performance, leading to an increased weight for criteria C2, C4, and C7 (Table 9). In the second scenario, named "cost-related", weights were increased for criteria related to costs, specifically C1, C5, and C6. In the third scenario, all criteria were considered equally important, thus receiving equal weights. In the fourth scenario, weights for the first three criteria were decreased by 5% (while the weights for the remaining criteria were proportionally increased). In the last (fifth) scenario, weights for criteria C4, C5, C6, and C7 were decreased by 5% (with the weights for the remaining criteria proportionally increased to maintain a sum equal to 1).

Table 9. Criteria weights in different scenarios.

Criterion	Scenario 1	Scenario 2	Scenario 3	Scenario 4	Scenario 5
C1	0.107	0.29	0.143	0.2527	0.272
C2	0.266	0.13	0.143	0.1957	0.215
C3	0.059	0.059	0.143	0.05605	0.067
C4	0.206	0.09	0.143	0.142	0.1254
C5	0.073	0.15	0.143	0.088	0.06935
C6	0.099	0.18	0.143	0.101	0.09405
C7	0.19	0.101	0.143	0.165	0.15675

The weights obtained in this way were subsequently used to create weighted decision-making matrices in the MARCOS method, with the goal of calculating the utility function for each alternative to determine their rankings (Table 10).

Table 10. Alternative ranking in different scenarios.

Alternatives	Scenario 1		Scenario 2		Scenario 3		Scenario 4		Scenario 5	
	$f(K_i)$	Rank	$f(K_i)$	Rank	$f(K_i)$	Rank	$f(K_i)$	Rank	$f(K_i)$	Rank
A1	0.53	4	0.64	3	0.63	2	0.57	5	0.57	4
A2	0.65	2	0.58	5	0.57	5	0.64	3	0.65	2
A3	0.65	2	0.65	2	0.69	1	0.65	2	0.65	2
A4	0.62	3	0.59	4	0.62	3	0.61	4	0.61	3
A5	0.68	1	0.67	1	0.61	4	0.68	1	0.69	1

Based on the results of the conducted sensitivity analysis, it can be inferred that the proposed model is quite stable, considering that alternative 5 is not ranked the highest in only one scenario (the third), while it is in all others. In the second, third, and fourth scenarios with changes in the criteria weights, alterations in the ranking of alternatives are observed. Conversely, in the first and fifth scenarios, the ranking remains unchanged. Additionally, it was determined that reducing the weights of the most significant criteria results in a change in the final ranking. On the other hand, reducing the weights of the least significant criteria does not lead to a change in the ranking. Furthermore, it is evident that the rankings of other alternatives vary considerably across scenarios, depending on the decision-maker's preferences (weights assigned to specific criteria).

In addition to the sensitivity analysis, model validation was conducted to assess whether there would be a change in ranking if other MCDM methods were applied instead of the MARCOS method. For this purpose, the presented case study was solved using the ADAM (axial-distance-based aggregated measurement), TOPSIS, MOOSRA (multi-objective optimization on the basis of simple ratio analysis), and MABAC (multi-attributive border approximation area comparison) methods [37–39]. The rankings obtained from these methods are illustrated in Figure 8. Based on the figure, it can be concluded that the ranking of alternatives changed only when the TOPSIS method was applied, where alternative 2 was ranked the highest. In all other cases, alternative 5 consistently held the best rank.

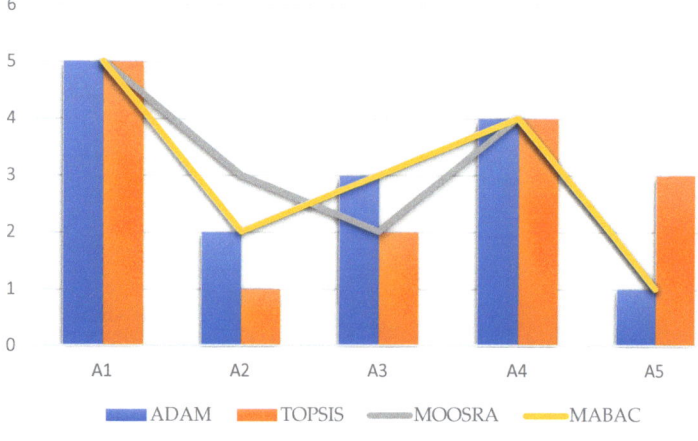

Figure 8. Alternative ranking using different MCDM methods.

5.2. Contributions and Theoretical and Managerial Implications

The literature review has revealed a significant gap in research concerning the warehouse location selection problem. This research contributes to the theoretical landscape by delving into this critical issue and providing a systematic exploration of the relevant methodologies. The proposed model, rooted in innovative methods, introduces a novel approach to solving the warehouse location selection problem. By employing techniques not previously utilized for this purpose, we contribute to the theoretical advancement of location-based decision-making models.

This paper systematizes the most significant criteria for warehouse location, enhancing the theoretical foundation of logistics and supply chain management. The systematic identification and prioritization of these criteria contribute to a more comprehensive understanding of the complexities involved in location-based decision-making.

In practical terms, the proposed model serves as an excellent decision-making tool for industry professionals. Through user-friendly Excel tables, practitioners can efficiently utilize the model to address a variety of location-related challenges, including the placement of distribution centers and terminals. With minimal adjustments, this model can extend its utility to solve location-related issues in diverse logistics systems. Its flexibility makes it applicable to a broad spectrum of challenges, showcasing its practical relevance in addressing real-world logistical complexities.

In the practical realm, this paper fills a significant gap in the literature by offering a tangible tool to support decision-making processes. Practitioners can rely on this model to streamline and enhance their warehouse location selection processes, thereby improving overall operational efficiency. The reliability of the proposed model has been rigorously validated through sensitivity analysis, unequivocally confirming its quality and the dependability of the results obtained. This further solidifies the practical applicability of the proposed model in aiding decision-makers in the field.

In summary, this research not only contributes to bridging the theoretical gap in the literature but also offers a practical and adaptable model that can be readily employed by industry professionals. The systematic approach to warehouse location selection criteria, coupled with the demonstrated reliability of the model, positions this research as a valuable asset for both academics and practitioners in the field of logistics and supply chain management.

6. Conclusions

The process of determining the optimal location for a warehouse involves a complex interplay of various factors, and the location selection significantly impacts the overall efficiency and effectiveness of the entire SCM system. This paper proposed a hybrid MCDM model that integrates the IMF SWARA and the MARCOS methods, demonstrated through the identification of the most suitable warehouse location in Belgrade. While the IMF SWARA method is employed to determine the criteria weights, the MARCOS method was used to assess the performance of alternatives and to rank them. The application of MCDM methodologies, as demonstrated in this paper, provides a structured and systematic approach to solving warehouse location problems. Additionally, this paper emphasizes the importance of including diverse criteria, such as land cost, infrastructure access, workforce availability, delivery time, area competitiveness, location capacity, and presence of various transportation modes. The applied IMF SWARA method represents a type of MCDM method that utilizes subjective determination of criteria weights. Integrating fuzzy logic into SWARA accounts for uncertainty and subjectivity in weight assessments, offering flexibility in modeling the real complexities of decision-making problems. Among the considered criteria, C1—land cost—is identified as the most significant criterion in the decision-making process. Potential locations, considered based on the general urban plan of Belgrade, include the following five: Borča, Surčin, Batajnica, Krnjača, and Dobanovci. Dobanovci, based on the evaluation, received the highest scores. Consequently, this alternative is expected to represent the optimal solution to the problem. Also, sensitivity analysis results as well as model validation confirmed that the A5—Dobanovci—is the best ranked alternative even in different scenarios (using different criteria weights) and even when combining different MCDM methods. The results of implementing the proposed model indicate that the warehouse should be constructed at the location of alternative A5 (Dobanovci), aligning with internal company data (obtained during the site selection research conducted by the company), obtained after interviews with company managers. After solving the FLP problem, it can be concluded that the proposed model serves as a suitable tool for MCDM, providing a simple and rapid solution to the defined problem. From the perspective of LSP, the developed model serves as a tool that facilitates decision-making regarding warehouse location selection. Furthermore, this tool lays the foundation for similar decisions that the company may encounter in the future. Essentially, the warehouse location selection problem is a dynamic and complex challenge, and this paper not only contributes to understanding location choices but also offers a practical framework that integrates qualitative investigation and MCDM evaluation for efficient and strategically positioned warehouses within the broader context of the supply chain.

A limitation of this study lies in the fact that only municipalities near Belgrade were considered as potential locations, excluding other parts of the country. Additionally, a relatively small-scale problem was addressed in this study (with only five alternatives). As far as future research directions are concerned, the following are highlighted: the application of the proposed methodology in combination with other MCDM methods, metaheuristics, and linear programming models for determining the optimal location. Furthermore, the development of a software application to assist decision-makers in such situations is also identified as a future research direction. The application of the proposed methodology to related location problems and larger-scale examples is emphasized as another future research direction. Finally, the implementation of the model in different industries and different geographical areas (markets) represents additional future research directions.

Author Contributions: Conceptualization, V.P., M.A., M.J. and M.K.; methodology, V.P., M.A., M.J. and M.K.; software, V.P., M.A. and M.J.; writing—original draft preparation, V.P., M.A., M.J. and M.K.; writing—review and editing, V.P., M.A., M.J. and M.K. All authors have read and agreed to the published version of the manuscript.

Funding: This research received no external funding.

Data Availability Statement: Data are contained within the article.

Conflicts of Interest: The authors declare no conflicts of interest.

References

1. Corberan, A.; Landete, M.; Peiro, J.; Saldanha-da-Gama, F. The facility location problem with capacity transfers. *Transp. Res. E Logist. Transp. Rev.* **2020**, *138*, 101943. [CrossRef]
2. Alenezy, E.J. Solving Capacitated Facility Location Problem Using Lagrangian Decomposition and Volume Algorithm. *Adv. Oper. Res.* **2020**, *2020*, 5239176. [CrossRef]
3. Vrtagić, S.; Softić, E.; Subotić, M.; Stević, Ž.; Dordevic, M.; Ponjavic, M. Ranking Road Sections Based on MCDM Model: New Improved Fuzzy SWARA (IMF SWARA). *Axioms* **2021**, *10*, 92. [CrossRef]
4. Pajić, V.; Andrejić, M.; Kilibarda, M. Sustainable transportation mode selection from the freight forwarder's perspective in trading with western EU countries. *Sustain. Futures* **2022**, *4*, 100090. [CrossRef]
5. Supply Chain Management. Available online: https://sjce.ac.in/wp-content/uploads/2021/10/jnu-Supply-Chain-Management.pdf (accessed on 8 January 2024).
6. O'byrne, R. Available online: https://www.logisticsbureau.com/reducing-supply-chain-costs (accessed on 13 January 2024).
7. Singh, R.K.; Chaudhary, N.; Saxena, N. Selection of warehouse location for a global supply chain: A case study. *IIMB Manag. Rev.* **2018**, *30*, 343–356. [CrossRef]
8. Ulutaş, A.; Balo, F.; Sua, L.; Demir, E.; Topal, A.; Jakovljević, V. A new integrated grey MCDM model: Case of warehouse location selection. *Facta Univ. Ser. Mech. Eng.* **2021**, *19*, 515–535. [CrossRef]
9. Kadwe, R.; Saha, A. The Study of Efficiency and Effectiveness of Warehouse Management in the Context of Supply Chain Management. *J. Emerg. Technol. Innov. Res.* **2018**, *5*, 129–135.
10. Pajić, V.; Andrejić, M. Risk Analysis in Internal Transport: An Evaluation of Occupational Health and Safety Using the Fine-Kinney Method. *J. Oper. Strateg. Anal.* **2023**, *1*, 147–159. [CrossRef]

11. Nguyen, M.H.; Nguyen, T.C.H. Importance of Warehousing in the Logistics System. *Int. J. Multidiscip. Res. Pub.* **2020**, *2*, 18–21.
12. Patil, A.L.; Rane, B.V.; Patil, L.P. Significance of Warehousing in Supply Chain Management. *J. Orient. Res.* **2021**, *92*, 230–235.
13. Puška, A.; Beganović, A.; Stojanović, I. Optimizing Logistics Center Location in Brčko District: A Fuzzy Approach Analysis. *J. Urban Dev. Manag.* **2023**, *2*, 160–171. [CrossRef]
14. Liu, C.J.; Wu, Z.; Zhang, Y.; Wang, Y.Y.; Guo, F.F.; Wang, Y.T. Optimizing Emergency Supply Location Selection in Urban Areas: A Multi-Objective Planning Model and Algorithm. *J. Urban Dev. Manag.* **2023**, *2*, 34–46. [CrossRef]
15. Huang, S.-W.; Liou, J.J.H.; Tang, W.; Tzeng, G.-H. Location Selection of a Manufacturing Facility from the Perspective of Supply Chain Sustainability. *Symmetry* **2020**, *12*, 1418. [CrossRef]
16. Zhang, X.; Mo, T.; Zhang, Y. Optimization of Storage Location Assignment for Non-Traditional Layout Warehouses Based on the Firework Algorithm. *Sustainability* **2023**, *15*, 10242. [CrossRef]
17. Farahani, R.Z.; Hekmatfar, M. *Facility Location Concepts, Models, Algorithms and Case Studies*, 1st ed.; Physica: Heidelberg/Berlin, Germany, 2009.
18. Kang, C.N.; Kung, L.C.; Chiang, P.H.; Yu, J.Y. A service facility location problem considering customer preference and facility capacity. *Comput. Ind. Eng.* **2023**, *177*, 109070. [CrossRef]
19. Çetinkaya, V.; Akdaş, O. Measuring The Importance Of Warehouse Location Selection Criteria Using Best-Worst Method. *Marit. Fac. J.* **2022**, *14*, 291–305. [CrossRef]
20. Eroglu, E.; Keskintürk, T. Warehouse location problem with genetic algorithm. In Proceedings of the 35th International Conference on Computers and Industrial Engineering, Istanbul, Turkey, 19–25 June 2005; pp. 655–660.
21. Szczepański, E.; Jachimowski, R.; Izdebski, M.; Jacyna-Gołda, I. Warehouse location problem in supply chain designing: A simulation analysis. *Arch. Transp.* **2019**, *50*, 101–110. [CrossRef]
22. Niyazi, M.; Tavakkoli-Moghaddam, R. Solving a facility location problem by three multi-criteria decision making methods. *Int. J. Res. Ind. Eng.* **2014**, *3*, 41–56.
23. Raut, R.D.; Narkhede, B.E.; Gardas, B.B.; Raut, V. Multi-criteria decision-making approach: A sustainable warehouse location selection problem. *Int. J. Manag. Conc. Philos.* **2017**, *10*, 260–281. [CrossRef]
24. Ehsanifar, M.; Wood, D.A.; Babaie, A. UTASTAR method and its application in multi-criteria warehouse location selection. *Oper. Manag. Res.* **2021**, *14*, 202–215. [CrossRef]
25. Dey, B.; Bairagi, B.; Sarkar, B.; Sanyal, S.K. Warehouse location selection by fuzzy multi-criteria decision making methodologies based on subjective and objective criteria. *Int. J. Manag. Sci. Eng. Manag.* **2016**, *11*, 262–278. [CrossRef]
26. Dey, B.; Bairagi, B.; Sarkar, B.; Sanyal, S.K. Group heterogeneity in multi member decision making model with an application to warehouse location selection in a supply chain. *Comput. Ind. Eng.* **2017**, *105*, 101–122. [CrossRef]
27. Bairagi, B. A novel MCDM model for warehouse location selection in supply chain management. *Decis. Mak. Appl. Manag. Eng.* **2022**, *5*, 194–207. [CrossRef]
28. Khaengkhan, M.; Hotrawisaya, C.; Kiranantawat, B.; Shaharudin, M.R. Comparative Analysis of Multiple Criteria Decision Making (MCDM) Approach in Warehouse Location Selection of Agricultural Products in Thailand. *Int. J. Supply Chain Manag.* **2019**, *8*, 168–175.
29. Stević, Ž.; Pamučar, D.; Puška, A.; Chatterjee, P. Sustainable supplier selection in healthcare industries using a new MCDM method: Measurement of alternatives and ranking according to COmpromise solution (MARCOS). *Comput. Ind. Eng.* **2019**, *140*, 106231. [CrossRef]
30. Beoland. Available online: https://www.beoland.com (accessed on 10 January 2024).
31. Katastar. Available online: https://katastar.rgz.gov.rs (accessed on 15 January 2024).
32. Moja Avantura. Available online: https://www.mojaavantura.com/rastojanje (accessed on 10 January 2024).
33. Surčin. Available online: https://surcin.rs (accessed on 12 January 2024).
34. Infrastruktura železnice Srbije. Available online: https://infrazs.rs (accessed on 12 January 2024).
35. Mihajlović, J.; Rajković, P.; Petrović, G.; Ćirić, D. The selection of the logistics distribution center location based on MCDM methodology in southern and eastern region in Serbia. *Oper. Res. Eng. Sci. Theory Appl.* **2019**, *2*, 72–85. [CrossRef]
36. Ozcan, T.; Celebi, N.; Esnaf, S. Comparative analysis of multi-criteria decision-making methodologies and implementation of a warehouse location selection problem. *Expert Syst. Appl.* **2011**, *38*, 9773–9779. [CrossRef]
37. Andrejić, M.; Pajić, V.; Kilibarda, M. Distribution Channel Selection Using FUCOM-ADAM: A Novel Approach. *Sustainability* **2023**, *15*, 14527. [CrossRef]
38. Petrović, N.; Živojinović, T.; Mihajlović, J. Evaluating the Annual Operational Efficiency of Passenger and Freight Road Transport in Serbia Through Entropy and TOPSIS Methods. *J. Eng. Manag. Syst. Eng.* **2023**, *2*, 204–211. [CrossRef]
39. Puška, A.; Stojanović, I. Fuzzy Multi-Criteria Analyses on Green Supplier Selection in an Agri-Food Company. *J. Intell. Manag. Decis.* **2022**, *1*, 2–16. [CrossRef]

Disclaimer/Publisher's Note: The statements, opinions and data contained in all publications are solely those of the individual author(s) and contributor(s) and not of MDPI and/or the editor(s). MDPI and/or the editor(s) disclaim responsibility for any injury to people or property resulting from any ideas, methods, instructions or products referred to in the content.

Article

Analysing the Hidden Relationship between Long-Distance Transport and Information and Communication Technology Use through a Fuzzy Clustering Eco-Extended Apostle Model

Panayotis Christidis [1], Juan Carlos Martín [2,*] and Concepción Román [2]

[1] Joint Research Centre, European Commission, 41092 Seville, Spain; panayotis.christidis@ec.europa.eu
[2] Institute of Tourism and Sustainable Economic Development, University of Las Palmas de Gran Canaria, 35017 Las Palmas, Spain; concepcion.roman@ulpgc.es
* Correspondence: jcarlos.martin@ulpgc.es

Abstract: The study analyses the hidden relationship between transport and ICT use for an extensive sample of 26,500 EU citizens. To that aim, a fuzzy clustering Eco-extended apostle model is applied to both latent variables: interurban transport trips and ICT use. The interurban long-distance trip (LDT) latent variable is measured by four different indicators (long- and medium-distance trips for work and leisure in the past twelve months), and the ICT use is based on a ten-item scale that provides information on different transport modes. The fuzzy Eco-extended apostle model is compared with the classical apostle model, translating the satisfaction and loyalty dimensions to our case. The fuzzy clustering model shows that most EU citizens are similar to the representative citizen who moved and used ICT at very low rates (56.5 and 50.4 per cent, respectively). The classical apostle model shows that the quadrants low LDT–high ICT and low LDT–low ICT are more represented by 38.5 and 35.2 per cent, respectively. However, the Eco-extended apostle model reinforces the results of the quadrant of low LDT–low ICT (40.22%) but softens those obtained in the quadrant of low LDT–high ICT (21.01%). Interesting insights of the effects of gender, age, education, and employment status are discussed.

Keywords: interurban transport; ICT use; fuzzy logic; fuzzy clustering; apostle model; fuzzy clustering Eco-extended apostle model

MSC: 62A86

Citation: Christidis, P.; Martín, J.C.; Román, C. Analysing the Hidden Relationship between Long-Distance Transport and Information and Communication Technology Use through a Fuzzy Clustering Eco-Extended Apostle Model. *Mathematics* **2024**, *12*, 791. https://doi.org/10.3390/math12060791

Academic Editors: Momcilo Dobrodolac, Stefan Jovcic and Marjana Čubranić-Dobrodolac

Received: 25 January 2024
Revised: 4 March 2024
Accepted: 6 March 2024
Published: 7 March 2024

Copyright: © 2024 by the authors. Licensee MDPI, Basel, Switzerland. This article is an open access article distributed under the terms and conditions of the Creative Commons Attribution (CC BY) license (https://creativecommons.org/licenses/by/4.0/).

1. Introduction

All transport systems, especially air transport, have developed more or less sophisticated tools based on the use of information and communication technologies (ICTs). Gössling [1] raised the question of whether ICT affects the transport sector's growth, structure, and sustainability. Salomon [2] was the first to observe that transport and telecommunication technology are interrelated. After a review, he concluded that many previous studies focused on the substitution relationship between transportation and telecommunications, a relationship that was often viewed as the most desirable one by transport planners. Nevertheless, the relationships are usually complex, and telecommunications modify the transport behaviour of individuals and organizations, impacting citizens' lifestyles.

Kwan et al. [3] contended that the interaction between ICT and human activity/travel behaviour has become a paramount issue in transportation research in recent years. Researchers have found that there was an ample set of mutual non-exclusive relationships between the use of ICT and activity and travel patterns in space–time dimensions. The authors found that the interaction between ICT and transport is highly complex, and describing it simply by substitution and/or generation is not enough. The earliest studies belonged mainly to the sphere of teleworking. For example, Saxena and Mokhtarian [4] found that there was an increase in the share of close-to-home activities performed by teleworkers on those days on which they did not travel to the office. The topic lately received an interest revival because of the COVID-19 pandemic, as the corona crisis changed habits from regular work to working from home. Kogus et al. [5] analyse the impact of the pandemic on telecommuting, trying to answer whether, at the end of the crisis, teleworking will become a reality for most citizens or whether working at offices will resume at the pre-pandemic figures.

Besides teleworking, the relationship between e-shopping and ICT use also captured the researchers' attention in the past. Farag et al. [6] found that online searching positively affects the frequency of shopping trips and online buying. E-shopping is task-oriented for some and leisure-oriented for others. Urban residents shop online more often than suburban residents due to better internet connection. In-store shopping is more frequent for those with more shopping opportunities within 10 min by bike.

Thomopoulos et al. [7] evaluated the potential synergies between ICT use and transport on the grounds that accurate and timely information is highly valued in transport. Transport apps and infrastructure in hubs like railway stations, airports, car parks, bus stations, and stops have increased ICT use. A significant number of passengers are using these travel apps in the majority of transport systems and transport modes, either for getting on-time information or booking and paying for some transport sharing systems. The authors concluded that ICT use and transport will be essential in the near future due to the technological developments foreseen in the so-called Internet of Things.

Considering the boomed interest in studying the relationship between ICT use and long-distance transport (LDT), this study aims to gain deeper insights and clarity into the complex relationship between ICT use and long-distance transport (LDT). To that aim, this study employs an alternative and novel research method that analyses the relationship between ICT use and LDT. Thus, it is possible to provide deeper insights into how ICT use influences LDT patterns beyond traditional quantitative methods, offering a framework for analysing subjective or loosely defined concepts in transport research.

Our study intentionally avoids formulating a prior hypothesis about the relationship between ICT use and LDT due to three reasons: (1) The relationship between these variables at the EU level is relatively unexplored, lacking robust empirical evidence to support a pre-defined hypothesis. Speculating without such grounding could introduce bias and limit the scope of discovery. (2) The study is primarily exploratory, aiming to uncover the hidden and complex relationship between these variables. By avoiding a pre-existing hypothesis, we remain open to various potential relationships and unexpected patterns that might emerge from the analysis. (3) Both ICT use and LDT are complex and multifaceted concepts, requiring a careful consideration of their underlying components. Analysing them as latent variables allows us to capture the nuances and variations within each, leading to a more comprehensive understanding of the hidden interaction between them which is unknown and complex.

The methodology employs fuzzy sets and fuzzy clustering methods to develop a fuzzy Eco-extended apostle model to analyse the LDT and ICT dimensions across the following four quadrants: (1) low LDT–low ICT use; (2) high LDT–low ICT use; (3) low LDT–high ICT use; and (4) high LDT–high ICT use. Then, conditional probabilities are obtained using a bootstrap method to analyse positive and negative associations with individual sociodemographic traits. The analysis conducted has led to the discovery of insightful results that can be used to build a sturdy framework for future studies. The framework will be useful in analysing the intricate relationship between LDT and ICT use to test new hypotheses. The dataset provides valuable insights that can be used to improve our understanding of how LDT and ICT use are interrelated. The results will help researchers in designing better experiments and studies that can shed more light on the topic.

The remainder of the paper is organised as follows: Section 2, Theoretical Framework and Literature Review; Section 3, Research and Analysis Methodology; Section 4, Results; Section 5, Discussion; and Section 6, Conclusions.

2. Theoretical Framework and Literature Review

2.1. Long- and Medium-Distance Trips

Magdolen et al. [8] contended that LDT trips are less studied than regular and everyday commuting travel, where the number of studies is more abundant. The authors concluded that the knowledge of LDT trips is still low and the lack of studies is mainly based on the existing difficulty of collecting data, as LDT trips are characterized by their irregular nature. The authors investigated the discrepancies between LDT and people's everyday mobility in major German cities. They analysed how German citizens compensated for the LDT climate impact with sustainable behaviour in their everyday mobility.

Nevertheless, there is no consensus defining LDT trips, and the definition basically depends on the context and the type of information that is available. Dargay and Clark [9] defined LDT trips in Great Britain using 150 miles (one way) as a threshold that separated two categories of LDT trips. The dataset based on the British NTS constrained the definition of LDT trips to those whose distance is 50 miles or more (one way). The authors estimated different models taking into account transport mode (car, rail, coach, and air), travel purpose (business, commuting, leisure, holiday, and VFR) and trip length (<150 miles and 150+ miles one way). Magdolen et al. [8] defined LDT as trips with a one-way distance exceeding 100 km. On other occasions, as in [10], LDT trips are based on the interurban travel demand obtained for a particular year of the trips made at the domestic level between the capital provinces of the country.

Kuhnimhof et al. [11] discussed available national household survey data on long-distance travel (LDT), concluding that mobility diary surveys capture journeys up to 200 km, while LDT surveys capture travel beyond 400 km. LDT data are needed for multiple stakeholders such as policymakers, transportation planners, airline and railway managers, and, in general, all the transport service suppliers. However, LDT data availability is often insufficient and unsatisfactory because of the limited financial budgets of public administrations.

The EU launched several projects to correct the drawback of the lack of available LDT data. Ahern et al. [12] examined the National Travel Surveys (NTSs) in different countries of the EU, identifying some general differences among the methods, the scope, the geographical coverage, and the additional information included in the survey. The authors concluded that the comparison of travel patterns across the EU is limited by the variety of methods and the type and format of the data. In addition, there were a significant number of countries which did not administer any NTS during the past 10 years, and some others did not share the datasets with third parties.

Despite the fact that NTS do not always provide comparable data referring to individual LDT, they usually suffer less than other approaches such as mobile phone tracking or credit card payments to generate a piece of more homogenous information that can be used to analyse intra-zone mobility, origins, destinations, and trip purpose. Thus, it is possible to model individual LDT choices at the national or supra-national level. Kuhnimhof et al. [11] provided a synthesis of the characteristics of five common NTSs implemented in Europe: France, Germany, Switzerland, Sweden, and the UK. The authors concluded that as LDT trips exceeding a certain distance range are usually associated with staying a number of days away from home, the reporting days to minimize the non-response answers should include a long period of time such as the past year or the past summer, or as they worded this issue "Tell me about your long-distance travel in the last x weeks. (p. 19)" The authors found that there is some variability in the definition of LDT (80, 100, or 300 km) and the reporting period (two weeks to one year).

Stopher and Greaves [13] contended that NTS inaccuracies are common because some of the non-respondent households are mainly characterized by travelling more than the average household. In fact, the households do not respond to the survey because either they are difficult to contact as they are absent from the home or because they see the survey task as being significantly time-consuming for the number of trips that need to be reported. The authors added that the estimation of more sophisticated travel demand models will procure more difficulties in the area of data collection in NTSs, concluding that diary survey datasets are rapidly becoming a thing of the past, and proposing as new alternatives the use of GPS datasets, panel surveys, continuous measurement surveys, and dataset fusion.

Fekih et al. [14] found that mobile phone networks can be used to track individual travel behaviour at a low cost. Interestingly, it is possible to accurately determine the spatial and temporal dimensions of the individuals' whereabouts. Thus, big data based on the mobile phone passive information provide a promising and low-cost source for acquiring information that can be used in travel demand models.

NTSs suffered from other different problematic areas like underrepresented trips such as those related to special events. For example, trips related to the Summer Olympic Games in which spectators travel long distances to the major venues located in the main city where the events are held are usually not covered by the NTS [15]. The associated problems could be resolved by specific data collection methodologies that take into account the diversity of the events, in which special event surveys need to be complemented by a combination of attendance and gate counts by time periods. Special event categories are obtained according to seven salient characteristics: (1) predicted attendance; (2) event frequency; (3) venue type; (4) start and end time; (5) one or multiple days; (6) day(s) of the week; and (7) event market area that determines to what extent the event is local, regional, national, or international. The survey should include the following questions: (1) origin of the trip and destination when the event is over; (2) mode choice; (3) party size; (4) length of stay; (5) household size; (6) household income; and (7) vehicle availability.

Breyer et al. [16] contended that classification methods applicable to mobile phone data are not easily adapted from the existing methods applied to GPS-datasets, as the datasets based on the mobile phone information are typically noisier and of lower resolution in space and time than that based on GPS information. Therefore, the authors compared different classification methods applied to mobile phone information, using a labelled dataset containing 255 trips in only two OD pairs to train and evaluate the classification correction methods. They found that two of the geometric-based methods provide less reliable results than those obtained by the supervised methods.

Andersson et al. [17] did recognize that NTSs suffered from low response rates that could compromise the validity of travel demand models, as data collection based on GPS tracking systems is not absent from low response rates. For this reason, the authors contended that mobile phone datasets in travel demand modelling are gaining the researchers' attention. However, mobile phone data often lack relevant information about socio-economic and demographic characteristics of travellers. Thus, the characteristics and the type of information included in mobile phone datasets differ greatly from those obtained in NTS or GPS survey administrations. Andersson and her colleagues were the first to estimate a mode choice model based only on a mobile phone dataset where the nature of the dataset did not provide information about the travel mode used in an LDT trip. The authors extended the identification model proposed by Breyer et al. [16], estimating with a probability the transport mode chosen (air, road, or railways) by passengers in a set of long-distance trips.

2.2. ICT Use

Gössling [1] reviewed the relationship between ICT applications and transport behaviour, finding that the first studies discussing comprehensively the relationship were Wagner et al. [18] and Banister and Stead [19]. Nevertheless, since then, ICT applications have increasingly evolved with the evolution of smartphones, which are nowadays a regular tool passengers use for different purposes such as navigation in road transport, ticketing purchases in urban and interurban transport modes, or for online live information about the expected waiting time at bus stops.

According to Wagner et al. [18] and Banister and Stead [19], the relationship between ICT and transport behaviour is unclear as two opposite effects could arise. Firstly, ICT could stimulate travel as new transport opportunities become available. Secondly, it could also lead to the substitution of travel as more and more tasks can be carried out from remote locations. Van Wee [20] highlighted the substitution pattern, especially for young generations, in which the decrease in car use, also known as peak car or peak travel, can be partly explained due to a transition towards more ICT-based activity patterns and accessibility.

According to the analysis conducted by Mokhtarian [21], the impact of travel generation effects appears to be as significant as the substitution effects. In other words, the factors that encourage travel, such as personal preferences and social norms, are just as crucial as the factors that discourage it, such as the cost of transportation or limited resources. This finding highlights the complexity of travel behaviour and the need for a comprehensive approach to understanding and managing it. A number of reasons for that are that 'not all activities have an ICT counterpart'; 'even when an ICT alternative exists in theory, it may not be practically feasible or desirable'; 'Travel carries a positive utility'; 'Not all uses of ICT constitute a travel replacement'; 'ICT saves time and/or money for other activities associated to transport'; 'ICT permits travel to be sold more cheaply'; 'ICT increases the efficiency of the transportation system, making travel more attractive'; 'Personal ICT use can increase the productivity and/or enjoyment of travel time'; 'ICT directly stimulates additional travel'; 'ICT is an engine driving the increasing globalisation of commerce that is facilitated by the reverse logistics'; and 'ICT facilitates shifts to more decentralised and lower-density land use patterns'.

Lyons [22] contended that the relationship between ICT use and transport behaviour is more complex than the simple dichotomy between substitution and generation effects. It is true that ICT-based activities such as e-working, e-retailing, e-learning, e-physician, and e-exercising will reduce the travel to offices, shops, schools, academies, universities, medical centres, hospitals, gyms, and sports facilities. Thus, the travel time saved from these trips can be used for additional activities that can incur other travel needs and use, so the net effects are unclear. In our study, we will explore how ICT use is associated with interurban trips for work and leisure, clustering the individuals into four different categories.

E-activities were not commonly available until the appearance of the smartphone in 2007, so the older generations are not as used to participating in them as the digital natives in their twenties. For that reason, we expect that young generations will display high ICT use in comparison with the older generations. Van Wee [20] discussed how this same fact could speculatively explain the decreasing levels of car use of the less car-oriented young generations. He speculated on how much ICT-based activities could reduce average travel time, breaking the theory of constant travel time budgets. It is difficult to predict the net result, but, in our opinion, the constant travel time budget may still be valid if calculated annually.

Gössling [1] found the following dimensions in the analysis of ICT use and transport behaviour: (1) travel information, planning, and routing; (2) sharing; (3) e-work; (4) payment and price comparisons; (5) safety; (6) convenience; (7) space and distribution; (8) health; and (9) mobility. The latent variable used to measure ICT use in our study is more related to the first, fourth, and sixth dimensions. Car drivers do often use navigation systems such as the popular portable Garmin or TomTom devices, smartphone apps like Google or Waze, or integrated vehicle systems. Most of the systems are nowadays provided with live information that recalculates the best route alternative in the case of severe congestion or disruptions.

This section ends with a topic that would explain the complementarity between ICT use and travel demand, namely, that 'ICT increases the efficiency of the transportation system, making travel more attractive'. Bak and Borkowski [23] analysed public transport (PT) systems, concluding that a key driver for improving the service resided in implementing smartphone e-ticketing. Smart ticketing facilitates passengers' travelling without a paper ticket, and this technology is also common in railways and metros worldwide. Graham [24] analysed the main transport payment systems, discussing payment technologies ranging from smartphone applications to electronic toll collectors. Some payment systems can be implemented in all the transport modes that coexist in a region, enabling the passengers' payment for tolls, PT, and shared rides. Martín-Domingo and Martín [25] analysed the adoption of mobile internet by airports, finding that most of the studied airports offered flight status notifications, and four airports really were innovators by providing dedicated smartphone apps. Airlines also offer many e-services to current and potential passengers through the internet or smartphone apps, the most popular being ticket purchases and online boarding passes [26].

3. Research and Analysis Methodology

3.1. Data Collection

The dataset was collected from a survey administered by TRT Trasporti e Territorio and IPSOS Italy for the Joint Research Centre–Institute for Perspective and Technological Studies (JRC-IPTS). The survey aimed to explore various aspects related to transportation in Europe. It focused on two key areas: (1) everyday mobility; and (2) long-distance trips covering distances of over 300 km and up to 1000 km, and over 1000 km, categorised by purpose and mode of transportation used within the previous 12 months. The overall objective was to collect comparable information on transport mobility at the EU level, overcoming the limitations in various national surveys regarding scope and definitions.

The survey also focused on ICT use and other policy-relevant issues, such as whether the passengers have substituted some trips to their workplaces or to their preferred shops with e-working or e-shopping. The type of information needed did not exist at the EU level. In order to gather valuable insights, a comprehensive survey instrument was meticulously developed and administered using the Computer Aided Web Interview (CAWI) methodology in June 2018.

The survey was conducted in all 28 European countries, with a sample size of 1000 individuals in each country. Cyprus, Luxembourg, and Malta had a sample size of 500 each, totalling 26,500 respondents. The sample selection process for the surveys involved the random selection of participants from the IPSOS panels in each country. These panels are maintained and monitored on a consistent basis to ensure that the participants are representative of the general population and are willing to participate in the survey. The sample quotas for each survey were established based on various socio-economic characteristics, including age, gender, employment status, and educational level. These quotas aimed to ensure that the sample was representative of the population being studied. By taking these factors into account, the surveys were able to provide accurate and reliable data on the attitudes and opinions of the population being surveyed.

Table 1 shows that the sample was more represented by women (51.00%) than by men (49.00%). Regarding age groups, respondents aged 75 years or older form the smallest category, representing only 0.46%. The next least represented age group are those between 66 and 75 years, accounting for 4.10% of the respondents, followed by those between 56 and 65 years, representing 12.57%. The remaining age groups have more balanced representation, with each group accounting for more than 20% of the respondents. Our sample consists primarily of educated individuals, as over 84% hold a high school degree or higher. It can be observed that the majority of the sample is composed of full-time employed individuals (60.20%) along with those who work part-time (10.74%). Retirees account for 9.40% of the sample.

Table 1. Survey socio-demographic characteristics (n and %).

Variable	n	% *	Variable	n	% *
Gender			Education		
Male	12,986	49.00	Primary	738	2.78
Female	13,514	51.00	Secondary	3167	11.95
Age			High School	11,365	42.89
26–35	6449	24.34	University	11,230	42.38
36–45	6453	24.35	Employment Status		
46–55	5467	20.63	Full-time employed	15,954	60.20
56–65	3330	12.57	Part-time employed	2845	10.74
66–75	1087	4.10	Unemployed	1696	6.40
75 years or older	123	0.46	Studying	1933	7.29
			Retired	2490	9.40
			Other	1319	4.98

* Some categories do not add to 100 because the variable contains some missing values.

3.2. Interurban Trips and ICT Use Latent Variables

The latent variable of interurban trips was analysed based on four different indicators that measure the number of trips taken for work or leisure purposes over long distances (more than 1000 km) or medium distances (more than 300 km but less than 1000 km) in the previous twelve months. To ensure the accuracy of the responses, a map link was provided to respondents who were unsure about the exact distance of their trips. Moreover, a confirmation check was included for responses that exceeded five trips, which helped to prevent any potential errors or exaggerations. The answer format for each of the indicators was based on the number of trips taken in each category during the previous twelve months. This detailed analysis will provide valuable insights for measuring the latent variable that proxies the interurban travel patterns of the respondents at the EU level.

Regarding the ICT use latent variable, the following ten items were included in the questionnaire: (1) in-vehicle navigation system; (2) mobile phone map and/or navigation application; (3) online flight ticket purchasing; (4) online flight check-in; (5) flight ticket purchasing application; (6) flight check-in application; (7) online public transport ticket purchasing; (8) public transport ticket purchasing application; (9) online/mobile access to live public transport schedule information; and (10) interoperable onboard device to pay road tolls.

A first screen of the ICT module was presented to respondents, explaining to them the meaning of each of the categories. For example, in the case of the 'mobile phone map and/or navigation application', the following explanation was provided in the questionnaire: application for smartphones that allows route planning for travelling by foot, car, bike or with public transportation and may receive a live update on traffic conditions. The answer format for all the items was based on a full four-point semantic scale, as follows: 1. Never; 2. Sometimes; 3. Often; and 4. Always.

3.3. TOPSIS and Fuzzy Hybrid Analysis

Figure 1 contains the flowchart that condenses the relative information of the proposed methodology. It can be seen that the methodology starts from the input matrices obtained from the dataset for the latent variables LDT and ICT use. This section provides the basic information needed for the methods employed in the first part of the figure that appears as the fuzzy hybrid analysis which will provide the synthetic indicators of both latent variables.

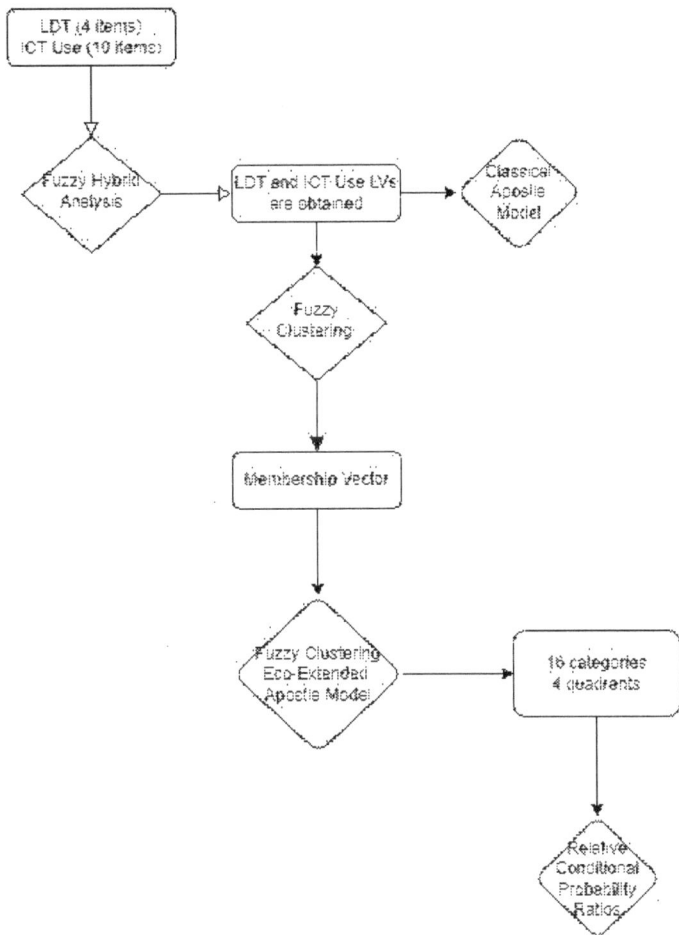

Figure 1. Flowchart for visualising the research methodology.

We first apply the Technique for Order Preference by Similarity to Ideal Solution (TOPSIS) [27,28], which is still one of the most employed multi-criteria decision-making (MCDM) techniques, to the four-component vector that provides the information of the interurban transport trips.

Then, we obtain the ideal solutions that are going to be based on the respondents who travel the most and the least of the whole sample. The ideal solutions can be obtained as follows:

$$A^+ = \{(\max V_{ij} | j \in J), \ i = 1, 2, \ldots, m\} \\ A^- = \{(\min V_{ij} | j \in J), \ i = 1, 2, \ldots, m\} \quad , \tag{1}$$

where the matrix V represents the number of interurban long-distance and medium-distance trips that each respondent made for work and leisure in the previous twelve months, i goes from 1 to the sample total (26,500), and j stands for each four-component of the set of interurban trips.

Thus, a TOPSIS synthetic interurban transport trip indicator (*LDT-TOPSIS* index) is obtained for each respondent taking a second step, which now calculates the Euclidean distance between each four-component observation and the ideal solutions ($A+$ and $A-$), and then compares the relative distances, as follows:

$$D_i^+ = dist(V_i, A^+) = \sqrt{\sum_{j=1}^{n}\left(V_{ij} - A_j^+\right)^2} \; i = 1, 2, \ldots, m$$

$$D_i^- = dist(V_i, A^-) = \sqrt{\sum_{j=1}^{n}\left(V_{ij} - A_j^-\right)^2} \; i = 1, 2, \ldots, m \, , \quad (2)$$

$$LDT-TOPSIS_i = \frac{D_i^-}{D_i^+ + D_i^-} \; i = 1, 2, \ldots, m$$

Similarly, the ICT use latent variable synthetic indicator is obtained but now using a fuzzy hybrid approach that adequately handles the vagueness of the information provided by the responses given to the ICT use module. First, the semantic ordinal scales are converted into triangular fuzzy numbers (TFNs), as the information provided by answers such as sometimes and often is intrinsically vague.

The triangular fuzzy numbers $\tilde{A}$ are parameterized using a triplet (a_1, a_2, a_3) with the following membership function $\mu_A(x)$:

$$\mu_A(x) = \begin{cases} \frac{x-a_1}{a_2-a_1}, & a_1 \leq x \leq a_2, \\ \frac{x-a_3}{a_2-a_3}, & a_2 \leq x \leq a_3, \\ 0, & \text{otherwise}. \end{cases} \quad (3)$$

In this study, we transform the four-point semantic scale provided by the respondents in TFNs into the universe of discourse within the interval (0, 100) as follows: (1) never (0, 0, 50); (2) sometimes (30, 50, 70); (3) often (50, 70, 90); and (4) always (70, 100, 100). In each of the categories, it can be seen that the intersection of two consecutive TFNs is not empty which is the essence of the application of the fuzzy set theory. The same type of conversion has already been applied in [29,30]. The TOPSIS method can be adapted to the case of TFNs to obtain a synthetic index indicator for the ICT use latent variable as in [29,31].

3.4. The Fuzzy Clustering Method

The fuzzy clustering Eco-extended apostle model has already been applied by Indelicato and Martín [30] to study national identity, and by Martín et al. [31] to study the impartiality of public service provision. The method is based on the application of a fuzzy clustering technique that obtains the three-cluster solution for which the representative respondents are usually interpreted as the positive, negative, and intermediate profiles. The profiles are derived from the synthetic indicators that were obtained in the previous steps. For example, in analysing interurban trips, the three-cluster solution can be interpreted as high-frequent, low-frequent, and intermediate-frequent travellers, and the respective profiles are those who have the highest, lowest, and median values of the LDT-TOPSIS indicator.

The fuzzy clustering analysis is applied to study both latent variables LDT and ICT use. Therefore, for each latent variable and respondent, a membership function that determines the degree of similarity between each respondent and the specific representative respondent discussed above is obtained [32]. The fuzzy clustering algorithm is an extension of the bag grouping algorithm introduced by Leisch [33], and interested readers can consult [34–36] to get more insights from the method. The C-means fuzzy algorithm for fuzzy data is expressed as follows (Fuzzy Clustering in Figure 1):

$$\begin{cases} \min : \sum\limits_{i=1}^{n} \sum\limits_{c=1}^{C} u_{ic}^m d_F^2(\tilde{x}_i, \tilde{p}_c) = \sum\limits_{i=1}^{n} \sum\limits_{c=1}^{C} u_{ic}^m [w_2^2 \| a_2^i - p_2^c \|^2 + \\ \qquad\qquad + w_1^2 (\| a_1^i - p_1^c \|^2 + \| a_3^i - p_3^c \|^2)] \\ s.t. \begin{cases} m > 1, \ u_{ic} \geq 0, \ \sum\limits_{c=1}^{C} u_{ic} = 1, \\ w_1 \geq w_2 \geq 0, \ w_1 + w_2 = 1 \end{cases} \end{cases} \qquad (4)$$

We follow the same notation as Martín, Moreira and Román [37], where $d_F^2(\tilde{x}_i, \tilde{p}_c)$ represents the fuzzy distance squared between the ith respondent i, $\tilde{x}_i \equiv \{(a_{1ik} a_{2ik} a_{3ik}) : k = 1 \ldots K\}$, where the vector represents the TFN assigned to the information provided by the ith respondent. On the other hand, $\tilde{p}_c \equiv \{(p_{1ck}, p_{2ck}, p_{3ck}) : k = 1 \ldots K\}$ represents the TFN provided by the representative respondent of the cth cluster; $\| a_2^i - p_2^c \|^2$ is the square Euclidean distance between the centres of the TFN vectors of the ith respondent and the representative respondent of the c_{th} cluster; $\| a_1^i - p_1^c \|^2$ and $\| a_3^i - p_3^c \|^2$ are the Euclidean squared distances between the extreme left and right components of the TFN vectors of the ith respondent and the representative respondent of the cth cluster, respectively; $w_1 \geq w_2 \geq 0$ are suitable weights for the centre and extreme components for the blurred distance considered; $m > 1$ is a weighted exponent that controls the blur of the partition obtained; and u_{ic} gives the degree of membership of the ith resident in the cth cluster. The parameterization of the method is based on the following selection $m = 1.5$, and $w_1 = w_2 = 0.5$. The Lagrangian minimization problem is solved to obtain the membership function for each respondent given by the solution u_{ic}. The membership function vector synthesizes the resemblance degree of each respondent with respect to the selected representative for each cluster (Membership Vector in Figure 1). The discussion of cluster validation and cluster profiles is omitted, and interested readers are referred again to [34–36].

3.5. The Fuzzy Clustering Eco-Extended Apostle Model

Jones and Sasser [38], from the Harvard Business School, introduced the classical apostle model. The model assumed that customer satisfaction was an antecedent of loyalty. Schaefer [39] transferred the "classical apostle model" into biology by transforming the classical axes of satisfaction and loyalty into habitats and species. Thus, the original categories labelled as deserters, mercenaries, hostages, and apostles were more appropriately reclassified using ecological terms. (Classical Apostle Model in Figure 1). More recently, a similar approach has been used to analyse national identity using as main axes the ethnic and civic latent variables [30].

This approach can be used to analyse the relationship between any two latent variables. Researchers only need to transfer the logic of the old clients' pair of latent variables, such as loyalty–satisfaction, into the new two axes of interest. Indelicato and Martin [30] also extended the classical apostle model using synthetic indicators that measure each latent variable through the membership function obtained by applying the fuzzy clustering technique, amplifying the four categories into sixteen.

Similarly to previous studies, the original axes of satisfaction and loyalty are transformed as follows: LDT and ICT use take the role of satisfaction and loyalty, respectively. Thus, the model will classify different LDT–ICT use patterns: (1) low LDT–low ICT use; (2) high LDT–low ICT use; (3) low LDT–high ICT use; and (4) high LDT–high ICT use.

Figure 2 shows the classical four quadrants explained above through the latent variable synthetic indicators *LDT-TOPSIS* and ICT use. Thus, the deserters quadrant (south-west) can be seen now as the group of citizens who do not travel very much and do not use ICT frequently. Similarly, the northeast quadrant (apostles) is characterised by those citizens who travel and use ICT very much. According to the literature review, these two quadrants can be seen as examples of a complementary use of ICT and transport. However, the southeast (high LDT and low ICT use) and northwest quadrants (low LDT and high ICT use) are characterised by those citizens who do not seem to use ICT as a complement when they are travelling.

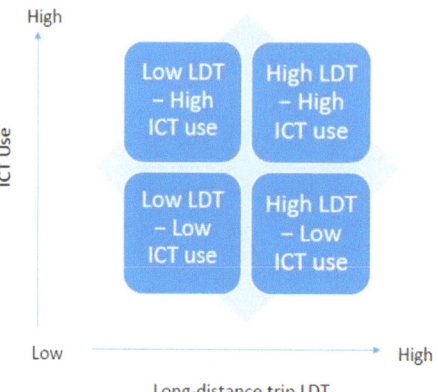

Figure 2. Apostle model applied to interurban transport trips and ICT use.

As explained in Indelicato and Martín [30], a limitation of the classical apostle method is that the taxonomy of the citizens near the average latent variable values for both dimensions is unclear. Researchers would expect to have a clear distinction between each of the quadrants, and in some cases, the distances between the observed data are certainly low. Therefore, the authors propose a new method which is based on the membership function obtained for each latent variable after applying the fuzzy clustering algorithm. This new method is named the alpha fuzzy clustering Eco-extended apostle method, and it aims to reduce the potential blur area that exists around the average values area.

Let us assume that $m_i = (m_{1i}, m_{2i}, m_{3i})$ is a vector that contains the membership function for the citizen i obtained with the three-cluster fuzzy clustering method explained above. We define the following function for each vector m:

$$f(m) = \begin{cases} 1 \text{ if } m_2 > \alpha \\ 3 \text{ if } m_3 > \alpha \\ 4 \text{ if } m_1 > \alpha \\ 2 \text{ otherwise} \end{cases}, \quad (5)$$

Without loss of generality, the function can be applied to any membership function to provide four categories for each citizen. Let us assume that the vector coordinates represent the similarity to the positive, negative, and intermediate clusters representative of the latent variable under study. In the case of the LDT latent variable, this would correspond to the following profiles: the citizen that travels the most, the citizen that travels the least, and the citizen that travels an intermediate number of trips. The original model with the four classical categories has been expanded to a model with sixteen categories, where the pure categories are now located in the corner quadrant positions [(1, 1), (4, 1), (1, 4), and (4, 4)]. The alpha selection depends on the research interest, but it has to be greater than 0.5. However, if researchers want to analyse some of the corner categories, the alpha value can be between 0.6 and 0.8, but if researchers want to analyse the behaviour of all citizens, the 0.5 value is highly recommended (Fuzzy Clustering Eco-Extended Apostle Model in Figure 1).

3.6. Relative Conditional Probability Ratios

This section on methodology ends with the presentation of the relative conditional probability ratio approach. The analysis of whether two events are independent is empirically tested by the estimation of the confidence intervals of the mentioned ratios. Thus, it would be possible to analyse to what extent, for example, some covariates such as gender, age, employment status, or education have a positive (driver) or negative (barrier) effect on the probability of belonging with more or less intensity to some of the categories obtained by the fuzzy clustering Eco-extended apostle model.

From a theoretical point of view, it is known that two events A and B are independent if and only if:

$$P(A \cap B) = P(A)P(B) \Leftrightarrow P(A/B) = P(A) \Leftrightarrow P(B/A) = P(B) \qquad (6)$$

Thus, the conditional probability ratios can be calculated for each pair (category, covariate) of the categories and covariates of research interest. Thus, the method is based on the calculus of the following ratios:

$$R_{AB} = \frac{P(A \cap B)}{P(A)P(B)}, \qquad (7)$$

When the ratios denoted by A and B are significantly greater than one, it indicates a positive association between A and B, showing that they are not independent. Similarly, when the ratios are lower than one, A and B are negatively associated. The relationship between the LDT and ICT use categories and other sociodemographic categories of citizens can be analysed with this approach.

The ratios of Equation (7) are obtained for 1000 bootstrap subsamples obtained with replacement (Relative Conditional Probability Ratios in Figure 1). Bootstrap is a statistical tool that is widely used for statistical inference. The concept behind this method is that we can estimate the accuracy of a statistic of interest by calculating subsamples from a sample that closely represents the population from which it was derived [40]. When there is doubt regarding the validity and accuracy of the usual distributive assumptions and asymptotic results, bootstrapping is a useful technique. Bootstrap is a non-parametric method that allows us to calculate estimated standard errors, confidence intervals, and hypothesis tests [41].

4. Results

4.1. Interurban Transport Trips and ICT Use

The fuzzy clustering method is based on the respondents' representative profiles obtained from the latent variable synthetic indicators for the highest, lowest, and median values. Table 2 displays three profiles in these cases, each named after the degree of interurban travelling and ICT use indicated by the corresponding indicators: (1) high, (2) low, and (3) intermediate. Respondents who answered the highest figures on the scale correspond to the citizen with the highest synthetic indicator for both latent variables. Thus, the profile of the representative citizen is characterised by those who travel the most and use ICT very frequently. On the other hand, the "low" profile represents those citizens who travel the least and use ICT infrequently. Finally, the intermediate profile is represented by the citizen who has the median position with respect to both latent variables and can be considered a representative of the average citizen in the EU.

Analysing the profiles of the interurban trip latent variable, it can be seen that the profiles for the three clusters show remarkably different behaviour for each of them. There is a citizen who has travelled more than 40 times in each of the four categories of interurban transport trips. The profile for those who travelled the least is found for citizens who do not travel any trip in any of the four categories. The intermediate profile is characterised by a traveller who made two trips between 300 and 1000 km for leisure or personal motives.

Regarding ICT use, it can be seen that the profile of the citizen who represents the high cluster is characterised by always using all the options of ICT use in transportation. The low cluster is represented by a citizen who never uses any ICT option. The intermediate cluster is represented by a citizen who always uses smartphones for navigation aid on the roads and for buying tickets and check-in processes in air transport, as well as interoperable on-board devices to pay road tolls. At the same time, this citizen does not frequently use online services and never uses any option for PT.

Table 2. Fuzzy cluster profiles.

Interurban Transport Trips	High	Low	Intermediate	ICT Use	High	Low	Intermediate
LDT1	40	0	0	ICT1	4	1	1
LDT2	45	0	0	ICT2	4	1	4
LDT3	46	0	0	ICT3	4	1	2
LDT4	47	0	2	ICT4	4	1	2
				ICT5	4	1	4
				ICT6	4	1	4
				ICT7	4	1	1
				ICT8	4	1	1
				ICT9	4	1	1
				ICT10	4	1	4

LDT1: Trips above 1000 km for work, business, or study motives; LDT2: Trips above 1000 km for leisure or personal motives; LDT3: Trips between 300 and 1000 km for work, business, or study motives; LDT4: Trips between 300 and 1000 km for leisure or personal motives. ICT1: In-vehicle navigation system; ICT2: Mobile phone map and/or navigation application; ICT3: Online flight ticket purchasing; ICT4: Online flight check-in; ICT5: Flight ticket purchasing application; ICT6: Flight check-in application; ICT7: Online public transport ticket purchasing; ICT8: Public transport ticket purchasing application; ICT9: Online/mobile access to live public transport schedule information; ICT10: Interoperable on-board device to pay road tolls.

Figure 3 displays two ternary figures representing the distribution of respondents' use of ICT for transport and travel frequency. The analysis of the figures reveals that the transport and ICT use behaviours are very different. It can be seen that the interurban transport trips (Figure 3a) show less heterogeneity than the ICT use (Figure 3b). The spread of the points in the first figure seems to be in a line that goes from the highest LDT to the midpoint of the side of the triangle, joining the vertices of the one that makes the least number of trips and the one that makes an average number of trips. The aggregate of the membership function shows that only 0.6% of citizens are similar to the citizen who has the highest LDT, 56.5% are similar to the one who does not make any interurban trip longer than 300 km, and 42.9% are similar to the citizen who makes two trips between 300 and 1000 km for leisure or personal motives.

Figure 3b, on the other hand, represents the ICT use latent variable. It can be seen now that the membership function is more widespread than in the previous LDT case. High, low, and intermediate transport ICT users are now represented by 19.8%, 50.4%, and 29.8%, respectively. Thus, to our surprise, it can be concluded that only 20 per cent of the EU population uses ICT for transport on most occasions.

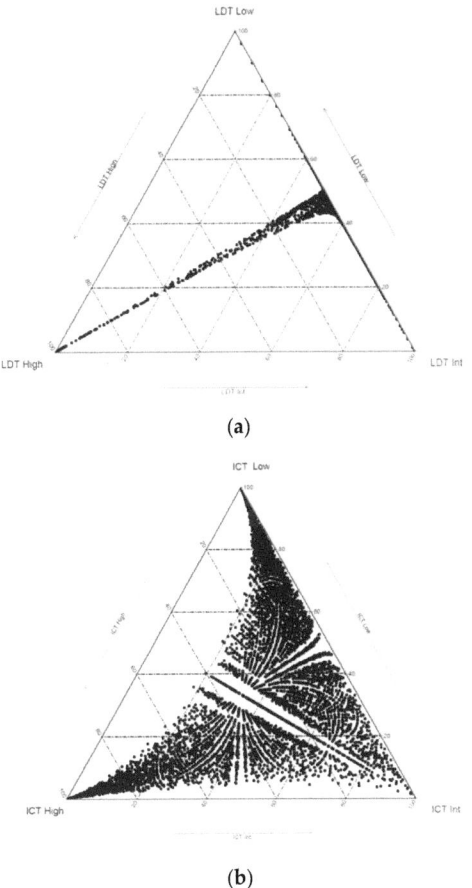

Figure 3. Fuzzy clustering ternary graphs. (**a**) Interurban transport trips (LDT); (**b**) ICT use.

4.2. The Classical vs. the Fuzzy Clustering Eco-Extended Apostle Model

In this study, the apostles would be those who travel more and use ICT for transport more frequently, and the deserters would be those who neither travel nor use ICT frequently. In addition, the other two categories—hostages and mercenaries—are represented by "low LDT and high ICT use" and "high LDT and low ICT use".

As seen in Figure 2, travel patterns and ICT adoption for transportation vary significantly among different citizens. The classical and the extended apostle models will categorise different travellers according to the two latent variables studied. The subjacent hypothesis that can be assessed is whether (in)frequent travellers are also (less)more tech-savvy and utilise ICT tools like the options considered in the study (less)more frequently. The models will also permit the analysis of those travellers who do not adopt ICT for transport purposes or those who use ICT but are not frequent travellers.

Applying the classical apostle model using the TOPSIS and the fuzzy hybrid methods, we obtain that the most represented category is that of low LDT and high ICT use with 38.5 per cent of the sample, followed by low LDT and low ICT use with 35.2 per cent, and by high LDT and high ICT use with 16.8 per cent. The group with the least representation is that of high LDT and low ICT use, which is only represented by 9.5 per cent of the sample (Figure 4).

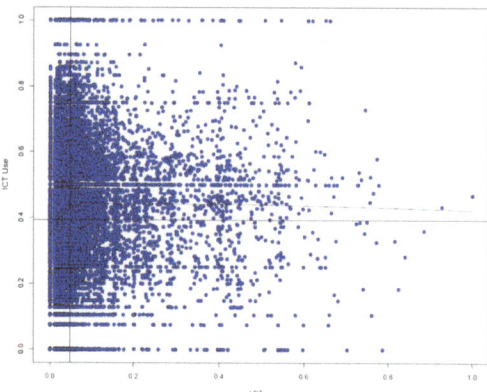

Figure 4. Classical apostle model for interurban transport trips (LDT) and ICT use.

Nevertheless, results change substantially when applying the fuzzy clustering Eco-extended apostle model, as the most represented group is now low LDT and low ICT use with 40.2 per cent of the sample, followed by high LDT and low ICT use with 24.8 per cent of the sample, and by low LDT and high ICT use with 21.0 per cent of the sample. The least represented group is now that of high LDT and high ICT use with 14 per cent of the sample.

Overall, 39.7 per cent of the sample changed category when the extended apostle model was applied. The analysis of the correspondence function determines that a large group of citizens is classified by the classical apostle model as low LDT and high ICT users that the extended apostle model better classifies as low LDT and low ICT users. Regarding the pure categories, the extended model shows that the most represented group is that of low LDT and low ICT use with 18.1 per cent of the sample.

4.3. The Analysis of Gender, Age, Education, and Employment Status on the Relationship between Interurban Transport LDT and ICT Use

The results section ends with the analysis of relative conditional probability ratios of each of the categories found by the fuzzy clustering Eco-extended apostle model and the covariates studied, namely, gender, age, education, and employment status. The ninety-five per cent confidence interval is calculated for each pair of events, for example, male and low LDT and low ICT use, resampling the whole sample one thousand times, and dropping 50 individuals in each draw. Table 3 shows the confidence intervals for all the categories of the covariates and Eco-extended apostle quadrants.

The interpretation of the table is straightforward. For example, the confidence interval of the conditional probability ratio for males and low LDT and low ICT use is obtained from the percentiles 2.5 and 97.5 of the distribution of the ratios obtained with the bootstrap method shown in the table (0.976, 0.977). These values represent the lower and upper bound of the 95 per cent confidence interval. Thus, it can be concluded that there is a negative association between being male and belonging to the category of low LDT and low ICT use. Following the same reasoning, results also show a negative association between males belonging to the category of low LDT and high ICT use. In addition, the positive association of males is found for belonging to the categories of high LDT for both types of ICT use, high and low. For females, we obtain the symmetric results that show a negative association for belonging to the high LDT categories, and a positive relationship for belonging to the low LDT categories.

Table 3. Conditional probability ratios (95 per cent confidence intervals).

Name	Q1 (2.5)	Q1 (97.5)	Q2 (2.5)	Q2 (97.5)	Q3 (2.5)	Q3 (97.5)	Q4 (2.5)	Q4 (97.5)
Male	0.976	0.977	1.038	1.039	0.970	0.972	1.042	1.044
Female	1.022	1.023	0.962	0.964	1.027	1.028	0.958	0.960
Age. ≤25	0.927	0.930	0.997	1.001	1.051	1.055	1.123	1.129
Age. 26–35	0.956	0.958	1.019	1.022	0.964	0.967	1.136	1.140
Age. 36–45	1.004	1.006	0.992	0.995	1.014	1.017	0.970	0.974
Age. 46–55	1.021	1.023	1.026	1.029	0.992	0.995	0.896	0.900
Age. 56–65	1.068	1.071	0.944	0.948	1.002	1.007	0.886	0.890
Age. 66–75	1.098	1.103	0.995	1.001	0.924	0.931	0.816	0.824
Age. >75	1.304	1.325	0.525	0.529	1.171	1.210	0.638	0.645
Primary	1.065	1.071	0.766	0.773	1.310	1.319	0.727	0.739
Secondary	1.144	1.147	0.802	0.805	1.164	1.168	0.676	0.681
High School	1.046	1.048	0.950	0.952	1.030	1.031	0.904	0.907
University	0.906	0.908	1.119	1.120	0.900	0.902	1.202	1.205
Full-time employed	0.944	0.944	1.066	1.067	0.944	0.946	1.125	1.127
Part-time employed	1.101	1.104	0.931	0.935	0.986	0.991	0.838	0.843
Unemployed	1.166	1.170	0.749	0.754	1.214	1.221	0.624	0.630
Studying	0.958	0.961	1.005	1.010	1.053	1.059	1.012	1.019
Retired	1.103	1.106	0.960	0.964	1.001	1.005	0.757	0.762
Other	1.093	1.097	0.740	0.746	1.262	1.270	0.775	0.783

Q1. Low LDT and low ICT use; Q2. High LDT and low ICT use; Q3. Low LDT and high ICT use; Q4. High LDT and high ICT use.

Analysing the age covariate, the results show that the most positive relationship is seen in the oldest generation (those whose age is greater than 75) for belonging to the category low LDT and low ICT use, and also to the category low LDT and high ICT use. In addition, the most negative associations are seen again for the oldest generation and their belonging to the category of high LDT. Other remarkable negative associations are also found for those whose ages are between 66 and 75 and between 56 and 65 for belonging to the category of high LDT and high ICT use.

Regarding the educational level and employment status, the results show that the most negative associations are found for being in the category of high LDT and high ICT use for unemployed citizens and for those with primary and secondary educational levels. In contrast, the most positive associations are found for the citizens with university studies who belong with more probability to the high LDT and high ICT use, and for those who are unemployed and have only primary studies who belong with more probability to the category of low LDT and high ICT use.

In some cases, it can be seen that one is contained in the confidence interval, and it can be concluded that events A and B are independent. This is the case for the youngest generation (25 years old or younger) and those whose age is between 66 and 75, and their belonging to the category of high LDT and low ICT use. These are the only two exceptions in all the events under analysis. For the rest of the cases, it can be concluded that there exists a positive or negative association between the categories of the covariates analysed and each category of the quadrants determined by the Eco-extended apostle model. Thus, the results show that gender, age, education, and employment status significantly affect the categories determined by LDT and ICT use.

5. Discussion

To our knowledge, this is the first study analysing the relationship between interurban transport trips and ICT use in the EU. For this reason, it is difficult to compare the results obtained in the study with previous research. Nevertheless, some of the results will be partly compared, at least by analysing LDT or ICT use patterns.

In the sample, there was a citizen who travelled more than 40 times in each of the four categories used to analyse interurban transport trips, which is evidently a rare case that can only be explained by the LDT of particular professions such as salesmen, ambassadors, or Euro parliamentarians. This outlier profile causes the aggregate average values of the membership function of the fuzzy clustering analysis for the latent variable to be only represented by 0.6% of citizens for the high LDT cluster. However, the sample population is more similar to those who do not make any trip longer than 300 km during a year, as it is represented by 56.5 per cent of the population.

This unbalanced behaviour between a minority, who travel a lot, and a majority, who do not make any trips, has also been found in previous studies. Aultman-Hall [42] found that the definition of long-distance travel is particularly blurred because there are many different distance thresholds that have been used in the past such as the 50-, 75-, or 100-miles threshold. This fact has created even more confusion than the verbatim definition based on the intercity "out-of-town" trips, which can involve overnight stays or not. Long-distance travel trips usually have large standard deviations, i.e., long-distance travel is highly variable. Frei et al. [43] concluded that the long-distance travel thresholds should be chosen between 75 and 100 km. Our study includes long-distance trips using two more distant categories than the thresholds mentioned above. The only comparable figures are shown in [11], where the authors summarised the number of long-distance trips above 400 km per person per year in 16 European countries, finding the highest and lowest figures in Sweden (1.4) and Portugal (0.2), respectively.

We find that the intermediate profile is characterised by a traveller who made two trips between 300 and 1000 km for leisure or personal motives. LaMondia et al. [44] defined purpose-based long-distance travel using the main purpose of the trip, such as work travel, leisure, and personal travel. Dargay and Clark [9] proposed other categories such as business, commuting, holiday, leisure, and visiting friends and relatives. Analysing travellers who occasionally travel long distances by coach, Van Acker et al. [45] found that 68 per cent of the sample were travelling for leisure or to visit friends or family, so it can be inferred that the intermediate profile concurs with these results.

The ICT use profiles also differ substantially according to each of the clusters. We find that high, low, and intermediate transport ICT users are now represented by 19.8%, 50.4%, and 29.8%, respectively. It is surprising that almost fifty per cent of the sample never uses any ICT option and that the intermediate profile was mainly characterised by not using any ICT option for public transport. It is beyond the scope of the current study, but the last result could be explained by the spatial heterogeneity of the sample in which some of the respondents might not even use public transport for their commuting daily needs. In addition, Bak and Borkowski [23] also found a similar result of a large group of non-ICT users. Aultman-Hall [42] concluded that future modelling would be based on two separate datasets that split travel into daily trips from the regular residence and a series of long-distance trips performed in the previous year.

As discussed in the literature review, ICT use was first perceived as a potential driver to reduce long-distance travel, but this has also been largely disputed [46]. Senbil and Kitamura [47] contended that the impact of ICT on long-distance travel suffers from complex interactions where four potential outcomes such as substitution, complementarity, modification, and neutrality could be observed. However, to our knowledge, the relationship between long-distance travel and ICT use has not been previously analysed in the literature.

However, in a daily context, Jamal and Habib [48] found a limited impact (neutrality) of ICT use on the number of travel trips performed but a significant impact on deciding the departure times.

The fuzzy clustering Eco-extended apostle model finds that the most represented group is low LDT and low ICT use with 40.2 per cent of the sample, and interestingly, the least represented group is that of high LDT and high ICT use with 14 per cent of the sample. Thus, it seems that a majority group travel long-distance trips and use ICT transport options very scarcely in comparison with a minority group of citizens who travel and use ICT very frequently. The other two quadrants (low LDT and high ICT use vs. high LDT and low ICT use) are represented by a lower number of citizens. Speculatively, we can think of some respondents who very frequently use ICT options such as navigation systems or PT apps for their daily needs and who do not travel on long-distance trips.

Regarding the relationship of the socio-demographic characteristics such as gender, age, education, and employment status, we have already mentioned that comparison is made on each different latent variable under study: interurban transport trips and ICT use. Aultman-Hall [42] reported similar results to those obtained here for the LDT latent variable. Thus, older individuals tend to travel less, while men's travel for work exceeds that of women, and, additionally, travel frequency increases with higher income and education levels. Jamal and Habib [48] found that age is negatively associated with ICT use for trip planning, concurring with our results.

New ICT alternatives are improving the options to travel long-distance in the EU, and this is particularly suitable for the younger generation, who have more opportunities to make new trips that were not so available in the past. Dargay and Clark [9] described long-distance travel in Great Britain, finding that income is one of the most important drivers, i.e., more wealthy citizens travel more than less affluent citizens. Kuhnimhof et al. [11] analysed the number of annual trips in some European countries, finding that the number of trips above 400 km varied significantly from country to country: 1.4 trips per year (Sweden), 1 (Germany and France), 0.9 (Great Britain, Switzerland, Finland, and Denmark), 0.8 (Ireland, Netherlands, Belgium, and Luxembourg), 0.6 (Spain and Austria), 0.3 (Greece), and 0.2 (Portugal). The results are aligned with the previous comment on the dependence on income, and can also be used to explain the obtained results on education, income, and employment status in our study.

6. Conclusions

This study analysed the hidden relationship between interurban transport and ICT use by a representative sample of EU citizens. We used sophisticated methods based on the fuzzy set theory to better handle the vague information provided in the answer format of the survey employed for the analysis. Two methods, the classical apostle model and the fuzzy clustering Eco-extended apostle model, were used to analyse the relationship between the two latent variables under study. Both methods appear to be suitable for the analysis of the categorical, Likert-scale variables used in the survey. The fuzzy approach handles the underlying uncertainty successfully and reduces the dimensionality of the dataset in an efficient manner.

This study breaks new ground by offering the first-ever analysis of its kind, paving the way for exciting future research. Its unique contributions lie in two key areas. First, this study employs a thoughtful dataset at the EU level, analysing two important latent variables, namely, LDT and ICT use. Second, the study utilizes cutting-edge methods (fuzzy hybrid analysis, fuzzy clustering, fuzzy clustering Eco-extended apostle model, and relative conditional probabilities) to analyse the relationship between both latent variables. This novel approach provides deeper insights than traditional methods and sets a precedent for future studies to adopt and adapt these techniques for further exploration.

The fuzzy clustering methods found that a minority group were responsible for the highly frequent long-distance travel in the EU, that a majority group do not make any type of these trips, and, in addition, that an important large group represents moderate long-distance travel characterised by a low figure of trips between 300 and 1000 km for leisure and personal motives. Aultman-Hall [42] named this minority group of citizens the "global mobile elite". Ten items were analysed to study transport ICT adoption for navigation aid, PT, air transport, and toll collection. The cluster similarities were more spread than for the LDT case, but extreme values for the high and low ICT use were also found.

Our results showed that the low LDT and low ICT use category was more represented by females, older generations, low educational levels, and unemployed, part-time employed, or retired citizens. This category can be named digital-phobic settlers. Czepkiewicz et al. [49] studied five different explanation factors that determine long-distance travel ranging from socio-economic and demographic characteristics to lifestyles and social networks, and found that all the aspects affect travel activity. However, long-distance international travel was mainly determined by a cosmopolitan attitude and adequate language skills. Moreover, the high LDT and high ICT use category was positively associated with males, younger generations, higher educational levels, and full-time employed citizens. These results were partly found for each individual latent variable by other previous studies.

Besides being a first attempt to study the relationship between long-distance interurban transport and ICT transport adoption, this study is not exempt from a number of limitations that need to be addressed in future research. Firstly, the analysis might be partly determined by the existing outliers, probably due to the peculiar observations of ambassadors, EU parliamentarians, or salesmen in the survey of long-distance interurban transport. This analysis could be better addressed by making the distribution discrete by joining the numeric observation in a fixed number of categories such as 5- or 7-point scales. Secondly, another point to consider is that the Eco-extended apostle model, which uses fuzzy clustering, is based on an alpha coefficient of 0.5. However, exploring the adoption of other alpha parameters can help in analysing the robustness of the results, and it can also provide a deeper understanding of the pure categories. Thirdly, in light of the COVID-19 pandemic, the prevalence of ICT use has significantly grown, dominating daily activities such as e-commerce, e-work, and e-entertainment. This considerable surge in ICT usage may also impact other non-routine activities, such as the long-distance interurban transport (LDT). Consequently, the potential effects of this increased reliance on ICT on LDT and other non-routine activities could prove to be a fascinating research topic worthy of further investigation. Finally, this study only considered four socioeconomic variables, and it would be interesting to examine how other factors, like the country and city size of citizens, as well as their attitudes towards climate change, could also impact the relationship between LDT and ICT use.

Author Contributions: Conceptualisation, P.C., J.C.M. and C.R.; methodology, J.C.M.; software, J.C.M. and C.R.; validation, P.C., J.C.M. and C.R.; investigation, P.C., J.C.M. and C.R.; data curation, P.C., J.C.M. and C.R.; writing—original draft preparation, P.C., J.C.M. and C.R.; writing—review and editing, P.C., J.C.M. and C.R. All authors have read and agreed to the published version of the manuscript.

Funding: This research received no external funding.

Data Availability Statement: The data presented in this study are available on request from the corresponding author.

Conflicts of Interest: The authors declare no conflicts of interest.

References

1. Gössling, S. ICT and Transport Behavior: A Conceptual Review. *Int. J. Sustain. Transp.* **2018**, *12*, 153–164. [CrossRef]
2. Salomon, I. Telecommunications and Travel Relationships: A Review. *Transp. Res. Part A Gen.* **1986**, *20*, 223–238. [CrossRef]
3. Kwan, M.P.; Dijst, M.; Schwanen, T. The Interaction between ICT and Human Activity-Travel Behavior. *Transp. Res. Part A Policy Pract.* **2007**, *41*, 121–124. [CrossRef]
4. Saxena, S.; Mokhtarian, P.L. The Impact of Telecommuting on the Activity Spaces of Participants. *Geogr. Anal.* **1997**, *29*, 124–144. [CrossRef]

5. Kogus, A.; Brůhová Foltýnová, H.; Gal-Tzur, A.; Shiftan, Y.; Vejchodská, E.; Shiftan, Y. Will COVID-19 Accelerate Telecommuting? A Cross-Country Evaluation for Israel and Czechia. *Transp. Res. Part A Policy Pract.* **2022**, *164*, 291–309. [CrossRef] [PubMed]
6. Farag, S.; Schwanen, T.; Dijst, M.; Faber, J. Shopping Online and/or in-Store? A Structural Equation Model of the Relationships between e-Shopping and in-Store Shopping. *Transp. Res. Part A Policy Pract.* **2007**, *41*, 125–141. [CrossRef]
7. Thomopoulos, N.; Givoni, M.; Rietveld, P. ICT for Transport: Opportunities and Threats. In *ICT for Transport: Opportunities and Threats*; Edward Elgar Publishing: Cheltenham, UK, 2015; pp. 1–316. ISBN 9781783471294.
8. Magdolen, M.; von Behren, S.; Chlond, B.; Vortisch, P. Long-Distance Travel in Tension with Everyday Mobility of Urbanites—A Classification of Leisure Travellers. *Travel Behav. Soc.* **2022**, *26*, 290–300. [CrossRef]
9. Dargay, J.M.; Clark, S. The Determinants of Long Distance Travel in Great Britain. *Transp. Res. Part A Policy Pract.* **2012**, *46*, 576–587. [CrossRef]
10. Martín, J.C.; Nombela, G. Microeconomic Impacts of Investments in High Speed Trains in Spain. *Ann. Reg. Sci.* **2007**, *41*, 715–733. [CrossRef]
11. Kuhnimhof, T.; Collet, R.; Armoogum, J.; Madre, J.L. Generating Internationally Comparable Figures on Long-Distance Travel for Europe. *Transp. Res. Rec.* **2009**, *2105*, 18–27. [CrossRef]
12. Ahern, A.; Weyman, G.; Redelbach, M.; Schulz, A.; Akkermans, L.; Vannacci, L. *OPTIMISM Deliverable 2.1: Gather and Analyze National Travel Statistics*; European Commission FP7 Project: FP7-284892-OPTIMISM; European Commission: Brussels, Belgium, 2012.
13. Stopher, P.R.; Greaves, S.P. Household Travel Surveys: Where are We Going? *Transp. Res. Part A Policy Pract.* **2007**, *41*, 367–381. [CrossRef]
14. Fekih, M.; Bonnetain, L.; Furno, A.; Bonnel, P.; Smoreda, Z.; Galland, S.; Bellemans, T. Potential of Cellular Signaling Data for Time-of-Day Estimation and Spatial Classification of Travel Demand: A Large-Scale Comparative Study with Travel Survey and Land Use Data. *Transp. Lett.* **2022**, *14*, 787–805. [CrossRef]
15. Kuppam, A.; Copperman, R.; Lemp, J.; Rossi, T.; Livshits, V.; Vallabhaneni, L.; Jeon, K.; Brown, E. Special Events Travel Surveys and Model Development. *Transp. Lett.* **2013**, *5*, 67–82. [CrossRef]
16. Breyer, N.; Gundlegard, D.; Rydergren, C. Travel Mode Classification of Intercity Trips Using Cellular Network Data. *Transp. Res. Procedia* **2021**, *52*, 211–218. [CrossRef]
17. Andersson, A.; Engelson, L.; Börjesson, M.; Daly, A.; Kristoffersson, I. Long-Distance Mode Choice Model Estimation Using Mobile Phone Network Data. *J. Choice Model.* **2022**, *42*, 1–11. [CrossRef]
18. Wagner, P.; Banister, D.; Dreborg, K.; Eriksson, A.; Stead, D.; Weber, K.M.; Zoche, P.; Beckert, B.; Joisten, M.; Hommels, A.; et al. Impacts of ICTs on Transport and Mobility (ICTRANS). In *(ICTRANS) Technical Report EUR 21058 EN*; European Commission, Joint Research Centre: Brussels, Belgium, 2003.
19. Banister, D.; Stead, D. Impact of Information and Communications Technology on Transport. *Transp. Rev.* **2004**, *24*, 611–632. [CrossRef]
20. Wee, B. van Peak Car: The First Signs of a Shift towards ICT-Based Activities Replacing Travel? A Discussion Paper. *Transp. Policy* **2015**, *42*, 1–3. [CrossRef]
21. Mokhtarian, P.L. If Telecommunication Is Such a Good Substitute for Travel, Why Does Congestion Continue to Get Worse? *Transp. Lett.* **2009**, *1*, 1–17. [CrossRef]
22. Lyons, G. Viewpoint: Transport's Digital Age Transition. *J. Transp. Land Use* **2014**, *8*, 1–19. [CrossRef]
23. Bak, M.; Borkowski, P. Young Transport Users' Perception of ICT Solutions Change. *Soc. Sci.* **2019**, *8*, 222. [CrossRef]
24. Graham, D. Electronic Toll Collections and Smart City Payments. In *Integrated Electronic Payment Technologies for Smart Cities*; Springer International Publishing: Cham, Switzerland, 2023; pp. 25–45.
25. Martin-Domingo, L.; Martín, J.C. Airport Mobile Internet an Innovation. *J. Air Transp. Manag.* **2016**, *55*, 102–112. [CrossRef]
26. Díaz, E.; Martín-Consuegra, D. A Latent Class Segmentation Analysis of Airlines Based on Website Evaluation. *J. Air Transp. Manag.* **2016**, *55*, 20–40. [CrossRef]
27. Tzeng, G.H.; Huang, J.J. *Multiple Attribute Decision Making: Methods and Applications*; Springer: New York, NY, USA, 2011; ISBN 9781439861585.
28. Masud, A.S.M.; Ravi Ravindran, A. *Multiple Criteria Decision Making*; McGraw-Hill: New York, NY, USA, 2008; ISBN 9781420091830.
29. Leon, S.; Martín, J.C. A Fuzzy Segmentation Analysis of Airline Passengers in the U.S. Based on Service Satisfaction. *Res. Transp. Bus. Manag.* **2020**, *37*, 100550. [CrossRef]
30. Indelicato, A.; Martín, J.C. Are Citizens Credentialist or Post-Nationalists? A Fuzzy-Eco Apostle Model Applied to National Identity. *Mathematics* **2022**, *10*, 1978. [CrossRef]
31. Martín, J.C.; Moreira, P.; Román, C. The Unstudied Effects of Wording and Answer Formats in the Analysis of Impartiality in Public Service Provision. *PLoS ONE* **2023**, *18*, e0288977. [CrossRef] [PubMed]
32. Kruse, R.; Döring, C.; Lesot, M. Fundamentals of Fuzzy Clustering. In *Advances in Fuzzy Clustering and its Applications*; Wiley: Hoboken, NJ, USA, 2007; pp. 1–30. ISBN 9780470027608.
33. Leisch, F. *Bagged Clustering. Working Paper 51. SFB Adaptive Information Systems and Modelling in Economics and Management Science*; WU Vienna University of Economics and Business: Vienna, Austria, 1999.
34. D'Urso, P.; De Giovanni, L.; Disegna, M.; Massari, R. Bagged Clustering and Its Application to Tourism Market Segmentation. *Expert Syst. Appl.* **2013**, *40*, 4944–4956. [CrossRef]

35. D'Urso, P.; Disegna, M.; Massari, R.; Osti, L. Fuzzy Segmentation of Postmodern Tourists. *Tour. Manag.* **2016**, *55*, 297–308. [CrossRef]
36. D'Urso, P.; Disegna, M.; Massari, R.; Prayag, G. Bagged Fuzzy Clustering for Fuzzy Data: An Application to a Tourism Market. *Knowledge-Based Syst.* **2015**, *73*, 335–346. [CrossRef]
37. Martín, J.C.; Moreira, P.; Román, C. A Hybrid-Fuzzy Segmentation Analysis of Residents' Perception towards Tourism in Gran Canaria. *Tour. Econ.* **2020**, *26*, 1282–1304. [CrossRef]
38. Jones, T.O.; Sasser, W.E. Why Satisfied Customers Defect. *IEEE Eng. Manag. Rev.* **1998**, *26*, 16–26. [CrossRef]
39. Schaefer, V. Nature's Apostles: A Model for Using Ecological Restoration to Teach Ecology. *Am. Biol. Teach.* **2013**, *75*, 417–419. [CrossRef]
40. Davison, A.C.; Hinkley, D.V.; Young, G.A. Recent Developments in Bootstrap Methodology. *Stat. Sci.* **2003**, *18*, 141–157. [CrossRef]
41. Hesterberg, T. Bootstrap. *Wiley Interdiscip. Rev. Comput. Stat.* **2011**, *3*, 497–526. [CrossRef]
42. Aultman-Hall, L. *Incorporating Long-Distance Travel into Transportation Planning in the United States*; National Center for Sustainable Transportation: Davis, CA, USA, 2018.
43. Frei, A.; Kuhnimhof, T.; Axhausen, K.W. *Long-Distance Travel in Europe Today: Experiences with a New Survey*; Arbeitsberichte Verkehrs-und Raumplanung: Zürich, Switzerland, 2010.
44. LaMondia, J.J.; Aultman-Hall, L.; Greene, E. Long-Distance Work and Leisure Travel Frequencies Ordered Probit Analysis across Non-Distance-Based Definitions. *Transp. Res. Rec.* **2014**, *2413*, 1–12. [CrossRef]
45. Van Acker, V.; Kessels, R.; Palhazi Cuervo, D.; Lannoo, S.; Witlox, F. Preferences for Long-Distance Coach Transport: Evidence from a Discrete Choice Experiment. *Transp. Res. Part A Policy Pract.* **2020**, *132*, 759–779. [CrossRef]
46. Dal Fiore, F.; Mokhtarian, P.L.; Salomon, I.; Singer, M.E. "Nomads at Last"? A Set of Perspectives on How Mobile Technology May Affect Travel. *J. Transp. Geogr.* **2014**, *41*, 97–106. [CrossRef]
47. Senbil, M.; Kitamura, R. The Use of Telecommunications Devices and Individual Activities Relationships. In Proceedings of the Transportation Research Board 82nd Annual Meeting, Washington, DC, USA, 12–16 January 2003; pp. 1–38.
48. Jamal, S.; Habib, M.A. Investigation of the Use of Smartphone Applications for Trip Planning and Travel Outcomes. *Transp. Plan. Technol.* **2019**, *42*, 227–243. [CrossRef]
49. Czepkiewicz, M.; Heinonen, J.; Næss, P.; Stefansdóttir, H. Who Travels More, and Why? A Mixed-Method Study of Urban Dwellers' Leisure Travel. *Travel Behav. Soc.* **2020**, *19*, 67–81. [CrossRef]

Disclaimer/Publisher's Note: The statements, opinions and data contained in all publications are solely those of the individual author(s) and contributor(s) and not of MDPI and/or the editor(s). MDPI and/or the editor(s) disclaim responsibility for any injury to people or property resulting from any ideas, methods, instructions or products referred to in the content.

Article

A Novel Data-Envelopment Analysis Interval-Valued Fuzzy-Rough-Number Multi-Criteria Decision-Making (DEA-IFRN MCDM) Model for Determining the Efficiency of Road Sections Based on Headway Analysis

Dejan Andjelković [1], Gordan Stojić [2], Nikola Nikolić [3], Dillip Kumar Das [4], Marko Subotić [5] and Željko Stević [6,*]

1. Faculty of Applied Sciences Niš, University Business Academy in Novi Sad, Dušana Popovića 22a, 18000 Niš, Serbia; dejan.andjelkovic@fpn.rs
2. Faculty of Technical Sciences, University of Novi Sad, Trg Dositeja Obradovića 6, 21000 Novi Sad, Serbia; gordan@uns.ac.rs
3. Faculty of Technical Sciences "Mihajlo Pupin" Zrenjanin, University of Novi Sad, Djure Djakovica bb, 23101 Zrenjanin, Serbia; kontakt@nikola-nikolic.com
4. Sustainable Transportation Research Group, Civil Engineering, School of Engineering, University of Kwazulu Natal, Durban 4041, South Africa; dasd@ukzn.ac.za
5. Faculty of Transport and Traffic Engineering, University of East Sarajevo, Vojvode Mišića 52, 74000 Doboj, Bosnia and Herzegovina; marko.subotic@sf.ues.rs.ba
6. College of Engineering, Korea University, 145 Anam-Ro, Seongbuk-gu, Seoul 02841, Republic of Korea
* Correspondence: zeljkostevic88@yahoo.com

Abstract: The capacity of transport infrastructure is one of the very important tasks in transport engineering, which depends mostly on the geometric characteristics of road and headway analysis. In this paper, we have considered 14 road sections and determined their efficiency based on headway analysis. We have developed a novel interval fuzzy-rough-number decision-making model consisting of DEA (data envelopment analysis), IFRN SWARA (interval-valued fuzzy-rough-number stepwise weight-assessment-ratio analysis), and IFRN WASPAS (interval-valued fuzzy-rough-number weighted-aggregate sum–product assessment) methods. The main contribution of this study is a new extension of WASPAS method with interval fuzzy rough numbers. Firstly, the DEA model was applied to determine the efficiency of 14 road sections according to seven input–output parameters. Seven out of the fourteen alternatives showed full efficiency and were implemented further in the model. After that, the IFRN SWARA method was used for the calculation of the final weights, while IFRN WASPAS was applied for ranking seven of the road sections. The results show that two sections are very similar and have almost equal efficiency, while the other results are very stable. According to the results obtained, the best-ranked is a measuring segment of the Ivanjska–Šargovac section, with a road gradient = −5.5%, which has low deviating values of headways according to the measurement classes from PC-PC to AT-PC, which shows balanced and continuous traffic flow. Finally, verification tests such as changing the criteria weights, comparative analysis, changing the λ parameter, and reverse rank analysis have been performed.

Keywords: road traffic; headway; DEA; IFRN SWARA; IFRN WASPAS

MSC: 90B50; 90B20; 90C08

1. Introduction

Traffic congestion is one of the leading problems [1] around the world that affects the economy and productivity of countries in the world. Traffic jams are the result of traffic demands at different periods of time. Under congested conditions, drivers usually reduce the time headway (Th), which usually leads to deviations in the stochastic representation of these traffic parameters. This parameter depends not only on traffic conditions, but also on the drivers' behavior during different traffic scenarios. The headway of vehicles represents an important microscopic traffic-flow parameter that can be defined as the time difference between the passage of the fronts of any two consecutive vehicles on an observed road section [2]. This parameter is used in various research areas applied to traffic, starting with road capacity, road safety, traffic efficiency, as well as many other indicators based on stochastic traffic phenomena. That is why modeling and an analytical description of headway play a key role in obtaining traffic analyses and making relevant decisions related to road infrastructure. A large number of studies applied different probability models, machine learning algorithms, as well as neural networks for the short-term prediction of headways. Nevertheless, headway is characterized as a random variable, varying from case to case, and is especially functionally dependent on road and traffic characteristics, as well as characteristics of the environment, climate, altitude, and other influences.

Headway as a traffic-flow parameter particularly affects traffic safety, the level of service, and road capacity. This parameter, when observing the following between two vehicles, depends on the type of the leading vehicle and on its vehicle dynamic characteristics. The influence of the leading vehicle is especially evident on two-lane two-way roads with a heterogeneous flow structure where there are a large number of different types of vehicles.

The contributions and novelty of the paper are reflected in the following facts:

- In accordance with the previously defined importance of headways for the entire area of road transport, a total of 14 sections of road infrastructure were considered and a new model to determine their efficiency was created. In addition to five headway classifications, AADT (annual average daily traffic) and road gradient were taken as influential parameters.
- A new multiphase efficiency model, which includes the DEA model, SWARA, and WASPAS methods in the form of interval fuzzy rough numbers, was created. IFRNs were used due to their ability to treat uncertainty in the decision-making process adequately. The greatest contribution of the paper can be seen from the aspect of a new algorithm of the IFRN WASPAS method, which, according to the authors' knowledge, is presented for the first time in the literature. So far, certain comparative analyses have been presented, but without the algorithm of this method.
- Another aspect of the contribution is reflected through the sustainable management of road infrastructure based on the results obtained and future recommendations. From a practical aspect, the study provides valuable insights for infrastructure managers and traffic experts, helping them make informed decisions to optimize road section efficiency.

Research gaps are described in the following sections. The paper thoroughly analyzes road-section efficiency by considering multiple input–output parameters, determining criteria weights by applying the IFRN SWARA method, sorting road sections with the IFRN WASPAS method, and performing verification tests. This comprehensive model enhances the credibility and reliability of the research findings.

Further in the paper, Section 2 provides a review of the literature that considers headway as a basis for defining input parameters. In Section 3, an overall procedure using the applied methods is presented with an emphasis on a new algorithm of the IFRN WASPAS method. Section 4 presents the formulation of the multiphase model with subsections that refer individually to the application of each method. It is important to emphasize that the procedure for applying the model is explained in detail by phases. Section 5 includes verification tests through four extensive analyses, while the paper ends with a conclusion in Section 6.

2. Literature Review

Vehicles that move in conditions of free traffic flow are vehicles that move individually or follow other vehicles. When the traffic flow reaches the saturation value, headway tends to the minimum value. Based on these traffic conditions, a large number of researchers analyzed headway with the aim of obtaining representative values. Based on research conducted in Pakistan [3] on two-lane roads with heterogeneous traffic, which included traffic flow, headway, and traffic density, the moving method (MM) was compared with the most commonly used stationary method (SM). A linear model was used to obtain headways by applying the moving method. Also, in the research on two-lane two-way roads in northern Italy [4], a set of headway distribution models was tested by the statistical analysis of data obtained from radar sensors and inductive loops. Research on four measurement sections has shown that an inverse Weibull distribution is the most suitable for representing headways for most flow-rate ranges. A study conducted in Iran [5] on the Shahid Kharrazi six-lane highway investigated the influence of lane position on the time-headway distribution under a high level of traffic flow. The appropriate model of headway distribution is based on the χ^2 test for each traffic lane, where the results of the study confirm the assumption that the appropriate model for the passing lane is different from the model for the middle lane. By following cars in the passing lane, a large number of drivers adopt unsafe headways leading to significant differences in the capacity and statistical models of headway distribution for different lanes. Also, a significant number of studies [3,6–8], in addition to headway, use other traffic-flow parameters (free speed, density, flow rate, etc.) to assess traffic conditions on road sections, where the 85th percentile values are often analyzed. In the research described in [6], it was concluded that headway cannot be used to identify free-flow speed on multi-lane roads, because this interval depends on the length of vehicles. Also, in this research, credibility values of speeds (−7 km/h to +15 km/h) were analyzed, where a gap of 10 s was identified, and this was used to identify the next vehicle on four highway lanes under heterogeneous traffic conditions. Also, research in India [9] on two-lane roads showed headway values distributed according to the log-logistic distribution in conditions of moderate flow-rate values, and Pearson-5 distribution was used in conditions of congestion. This was selected out of four considered distributions.

Veng et al. [10] proved that the type of vehicle has a significant influence on headway distribution, and the scenarios of car–car, car–truck, truck–truck and truck–car rarely appear in real traffic conditions, so the headway distribution model is analyzed separately for different types of vehicles. Also, by analyzing headway in the conditions of heterogeneous traffic flow, the truck–car ratio is included as one of specific variables for determining functional parameters [11]. Based on the research carried out in Iraq [12] on over 8000 headways, in order to determine the critical headway, it was found that the range of the critical interval was from 2.5 to 4 s, with a corresponding critical headway of 3.2 s on 10 measuring sections of the two-lane highways. The best model for headway distribution in free-flow conditions is with a negative exponential distribution, while in conditions with vehicle restrictions, it is a lognormal distribution model. By analyzing seven probability headway distributions on two rural two-lane two-way roads in Egypt [13], one-hour videotaped data were collected, and they showed that gamma and shifted exponential distributions are appropriate distributions for modeling headways in the Dakahliya province.

The headway research [14] was conducted by considering the influence of lateral distances between vehicles moving on the roadway in different lanes. In this study, driving behavior, speed/headway relationship, and the following threshold were investigated, with headways being segmented into five classes: unsafe (0–0.7 s), non-lane-based car following (0.9 s), lane-based car following (1.0 s), overtaking (1.3 s) and free driving (over 2.5 s). A linear relationship was found between time headway and lateral distances in non- lane-based car-following conditions. Also, when observing the behavior of vehicles in two different lanes, an insignificant lateral distance between the following and preceding vehicles was shown for the lowest headway value.

Research [15] based on deep learning showed that there is no suitable model for the long-term prediction of traffic headways, since current models do not use a large data set and do not solve the problem of a longitudinal gradient. The obtained headway values are not of constant size in the same ambient conditions, so they mainly depend on the drivers' perceptive ability, processing of the received data, actions taken, and heterogeneous vehicle performance [16]. In the research [11] based on the use of two sets of experimental data for the calculation of headway values, 18 commonly used value distribution models were applied in order to select the best model. The study demonstrated a distribution model with adaptive parameters, and its performance and applicability were verified. The performance of the model was improved by 62.7% compared with the model with fixed parameters. Also, on the basis of sixteen pairs of vehicles identified in the field, the movement of specific types of vehicles in a heterogeneous flow on a national road in Northeast India was analyzed [17]. The observations in that study showed that car drivers have a conservative attitude and usually keep a safe distance from the leading vehicle. In addition, a comparison of computed headway probabilities was made with the values obtained from more or less homogeneous traffic. The values obtained in the current study were found to be high in most cases, indicating risk-taking driver behavior. Also, to determine headway in the study [4] on Italian two-lane roads, an exponential moving model was introduced in order to identify a criterion above which vehicle movements could be considered unconditional. However, by applying this model, it was possible to identify vehicles that still have a certain autonomy in their speed and maneuvering, so an additional criterion was introduced to distinguish apparently and truly conditioned vehicles by analyzing the differences in the speeds of vehicles following each other.

In order to improve the quality of two-lane roads and model prediction, the effects of vehicle driving variables on road-performance measures were evaluated, and then critical headways were identified with the aim of accepting optimal gaps between vehicles. In order to achieve the research objective, multiple linear-regression and Bayesian linear-regression models were developed, which showed a headway threshold of 2.4 s based on vehicular platooning [18]. Also, a platoon is defined as a series of vehicles where the time interval between the leading and following vehicles is 3 s [19,20]. Additionally, it should be noted that in the past, the time headway limit was 5 s [21], while more recent recommendations indicate a value of 3 s [19,22]. The research conducted on 50 different sections of rural two-lane roads classified into two classes in Serbia shows that there is a difference in headway-limit values for two classes of roads in free-flow conditions. For class I, headway was 6.3 s, and for class II, it was 8.4 s [23]. A capacity survey conducted on the Benin—Lagos road section in Edo State, Nigeria, showed an average space headway of 0.025 km (25 m) and an average time headway of 2.26 s, indicating a moderate traffic flow. The values obtained in this way show a low probability of traffic accidents [7].

A study based on determining time gaps between vehicles (the rear part of a vehicle and the front part of its follower) was conducted on 13 km of the airport access road in Washington, using a sample of 168,053 time gaps. The study showed significant variations in the values of the time gaps. Also, at speeds above 108 km/h, the minimum time gaps made by some drivers could be 1.6 times longer compared with the minimum values made by other drivers [24].

3. Methods

3.1. Preliminaries

This approach provides three rough sets expressed as an interval. The expression obtained is called the interval fuzzy rough number "A".

$$A = \left[A_q^L, A_q^U\right] = \left[\left(a_{1q}^L, a_{1q}^U\right), \left(a_{2q}^L, a_{2q}^U\right), \left(a_{3q}^L, a_{3q}^U\right)\right] \quad (1)$$

where $a_{jq}^L = \underline{Lim}\left(I * (a_j)_{lq}\right)$ and $a_{jq}^U = \overline{Lim}\left(I * (a_j)_{uq}\right); (j = 1, 2, 3; 1 \leq q \leq k)$

The interval fuzzy rough number A defined in the interval $(-\infty, +\infty)$ can be shown by Equations (2) and (3) [25,26].

$$A = \left\{x, \left[\mu_{A_q^L}(x), \mu_{A_q^U}(x)\right]\right\}, x \in (-\infty, +\infty), \mu_{A_q^L}(x), \mu_{A_q^U}(x) : (-\infty, +\infty) \to [0, 1] \quad (2)$$

$$\mu_A(x) = \left[\mu_{A_q^L}(x), \mu_{A_q^U}(x)\right], \mu_{A_q^L}(x) \leq \mu_{A_q^U}(x), \forall x \in (-\infty, +\infty) \tag{3}$$

The values $\mu_{A_q^L}(x)$ and $\mu_{A_q^U}(x)$ are the degree of membership to the lower and upper functions, respectively, of the interval fuzzy rough number A.

When manipulating with two interval fuzzy rough numbers A and B, different mathematical operations between them can be performed.

Addition of two interval fuzzy rough numbers:

$$\begin{aligned} A + B &= \left[(a_1^L, a_1^U), (a_2^L, a_2^U), (a_3^L, a_3^U)\right] + \left[(b_1^L, b_1^U), (b_2^L, b_2^U), (b_3^L, b_3^U)\right] \\ &= \left[(a_1^L + b_1^L, a_1^U + b_1^U), (a_2^L + b_2^L, a_2^U + b_2^U), (a_3^L + b_3^L, a_3^U + b_3^U)\right] \end{aligned} \tag{4}$$

Subtraction of two interval fuzzy rough numbers:

$$\begin{aligned} A - B &= \left[(a_1^L, a_1^U), (a_2^L, a_2^U), (a_3^L, a_3^U)\right] - \left[(b_1^L, b_1^U), (b_2^L, b_2^U), (b_3^L, b_3^U)\right] \\ &= \left[(a_1^L - b_3^U, a_1^U - b_1^L), (a_2^L - b_2^U, a_2^U - b_2^L), (a_3^L - b_1^U, a_3^U - b_1^L)\right] \end{aligned} \tag{5}$$

Multiplication of two interval fuzzy rough numbers:

$$\begin{aligned} A \times B &= \left[(a_1^L, a_1^U), (a_2^L, a_2^U), (a_3^L, a_3^U)\right] \times \left[(b_1^L, b_1^U), (b_2^L, b_2^U), (b_3^L, b_3^U)\right] \\ &= \left[(a_1^L \times b_1^L, a_1^U \times b_1^U), (a_2^L \times b_2^L, a_2^U \times b_2^U), (a_3^L \times b_3^L, a_3^U \times b_3^U)\right] \end{aligned} \tag{6}$$

Division of two interval fuzzy rough numbers:

$$\begin{aligned} A \div B &= \left[(a_1^L, a_1^U), (a_2^L, a_2^U), (a_3^L, a_3^U)\right] \div \left[(b_1^L, b_1^U), (b_2^L, b_2^U), (b_3^L, b_3^U)\right] \\ &= \left[(a_1^L \div b_3^U, a_1^U \div b_1^L), (a_2^L \div b_2^U, a_2^U \div b_2^L), (a_3^L \div b_1^U, a_3^U \div b_1^L)\right] \end{aligned} \tag{7}$$

3.2. Interval Fuzzy-Rough-Number SWARA Method

We have used this subjective method for calculating criteria weights because this case study needs the adequate expertise of DMs and their preferences based on skills and knowledge. This method is extended with numerous theories [27–30] and, finally, with the IFRN [31].

Step 1: Formation of a group of m criteria.

Step 2: Definition of a team of e experts to evaluate the criteria. Experts can use any of the given scales to determine the significance of the criteria.

Step 3: Transformation of individual experts' estimates into a group fuzzy rough matrix x_j.

$$IFRN(X_j) = \left[\left(x_j^{L1}, x_j^{U1}\right), \left(x_j^{L2}, x_j^{U2}\right), \left(x_j^{L3}, x_j^{U3}\right)\right]_{1 \times n} \tag{8}$$

Step 4. Ranking of criteria by their significance obtained using the fuzzy rough matrix from Step 3.

Step 5: Normalization of the matrix $IFRN(X_j)$ in order to gain the matrix $IFRN(N_j)$

$$IFRN(N_j) = \left[\left(n_j^{L1}, n_j^{U1}\right), \left(n_j^{L2}, n_j^{U2}\right), \left(n_j^{L3}, n_j^{U3}\right)\right]_{1 \times n} \tag{9}$$

The elements of the matrix $IFRN(N_j)$ are calculated as follows:

$$IFRN(N_j) = \frac{IFRN(X_j)}{IFRN(Z_j)} \tag{10}$$

where $IFRN(Z_j) = \left[\left(z_j^{L1}, z_j^{U1}\right), \left(z_j^{L2}, z_j^{U2}\right), \left(z_j^{L3}, z_j^{U3}\right)\right] = \max IFRN(X_j)$.

The first element of $IFRN(N_j)$, i.e.,

$\left[\left(n_j^{L1}, n_j^{U1}\right), \left(n_j^{L2}, n_j^{U2}\right), \left(n_j^{L3}, n_j^{U3}\right)\right] = [(1.00, 1.00), (1.00, 1.00), (1.00, 1.00)]$, because $j = 1$. For other elements where $j > 1$, Equation (11) should be applied:

$$IFRN(N_j) = \left[\left(\frac{n_j^{L1}}{z_j^{U3}}, \frac{n_j^{U1}}{z_j^{L3}}\right), \left(\frac{n_j^{L2}}{z_j^{U2}}, \frac{n_j^{U2}}{z_j^{L2}}\right), \left(\frac{n_j^{L3}}{z_j^{U1}}, \frac{n_j^{U3}}{z_j^{L1}}\right)\right]_{1 \times n} \quad j = 2, 3, \dots, n \qquad (11)$$

In the case where there are two most significant criteria, the second element is a fuzzy rough number $[(1.00, 1.00), (1.00, 1.00), (1.00, 1.00)]$.

Step 6: Computation of the matrix $IFRN(\Im_j)$:

$$IFRN(\Im_j) = \left[\left(\Im_j^{L1}, \Im_j^{U1}\right), \left(\Im_j^{L2}, \Im_j^{U2}\right), \left(\Im_j^{L3}, \Im_j^{U3}\right)\right]_{1 \times n} \qquad (12)$$

by Equation (13):

$$IFRN(\Im_j) = \left[\left(n_j^{L1} + 1, n_j^{U1} + 1\right), \left(n_j^{L2} + 1, n_j^{U2} + 1\right), \left(n_j^{L3} + 1, n_j^{U3} + 1\right)\right]_{1 \times n} j = 2, 3, \dots, n \qquad (13)$$

In the case where there are two most significant criteria, the second element is a fuzzy rough number $[(1.00, 1.00), (1.00, 1.00), (1.00, 1.00)]$.

Step 7: Computation of the matrix of recalculated weights $IFRN(\Re_j)$:

$$IFRN(\Re_j) = \left[\left(\Re_j^{L1}, \Re_j^{U1}\right), \left(\Re_j^{L2}, \Re_j^{U2}\right), \left(\Re_j^{L3}, \Re_j^{U3}\right)\right]_{1 \times n} \qquad (14)$$

The elements of the matrix $IFRN(\Re_j)$ are obtained as follows:

$$IFRN(\Re_j)\begin{bmatrix} \Re_j^{L1} = \begin{pmatrix} 1.00 \ j=1 \\ \frac{\Re_{j-1}^{L1}}{\Im_j^{U3}} \ j>1 \end{pmatrix}, & \Re_j^{U1} = \begin{pmatrix} 1.00 \ j=1 \\ \frac{\Re_{j-1}^{U1}}{\Im_j^{L3}} \ j>1 \end{pmatrix}, \\ \Re_j^{L2} = \begin{pmatrix} 1.00 \ j=1 \\ \frac{\Re_{j-1}^{L2}}{\Im_j^{U2}} \ j>1 \end{pmatrix}, & \Re_j^{U2} = \begin{pmatrix} 1.00 \ j=1 \\ \frac{\Re_{j-1}^{U2}}{\Im_j^{L2}} \ j>1 \end{pmatrix}, \\ \Re_j^{L3} = \begin{pmatrix} 1.00 \ j=1 \\ \frac{\Re_{j-1}^{L3}}{\Im_j^{U1}} \ j>1 \end{pmatrix}, & \Re_j^{U3} = \begin{pmatrix} 1.00 \ j=1 \\ \frac{\Re_{j-1}^{U3}}{\Im_j^{L1}} \ j>1 \end{pmatrix}, \end{bmatrix} \qquad (15)$$

In the case where any two of n criteria have equal importance, then the following equation should be used:

$$IFRN(\Re_j) = IFRN(\Re_{j-1}) \qquad (16)$$

Step 8: Calculation of final weight values $IFRN(W_j)$:

$$IFRN(W_j) = \left[\left(w_j^{L1}, w_j^{U1}\right), \left(w_j^{L2}, w_j^{U2}\right), \left(w_j^{L3}, w_j^{U3}\right)\right]_{1 \times n} \qquad (17)$$

Individual weight values of the criteria are obtained as follows:

$$IFRN(W_j) = \left[\frac{IFRN(\Re_j)}{IFRN(\aleph_j)}\right] \qquad (18)$$

where $IFRN(\aleph_j) = \sum_{j=1}^{n} IFRN(\Re_j)$. Finally,

$$IFRN(W_j) = \left[\left(\frac{\Re_j^{L1}}{\aleph_j^{U3}}, \frac{\Re_j^{U1}}{\aleph_j^{L3}}\right), \left(\frac{\Re_j^{L2}}{\aleph_j^{U2}}, \frac{\Re_j^{U2}}{\aleph_j^{L2}}\right), \left(\frac{\Re_j^{L3}}{\aleph_j^{U1}}, \frac{\Re_j^{U3}}{\aleph_j^{L1}}\right)\right]_{1 \times n} \quad j = 2, 3, \dots, n \qquad (19)$$

3.3. A Novel Interval Fuzzy-Rough-Number WASPAS Method

This section of the paper is devoted to the development of the interval fuzzy-rough-number WASPAS method, which, in its various forms [32,33], was applied to solve different problem structures. A new algorithm, which includes the extension of the WASPAS method with the IFRN, is presented below.

Step 1. Form a set of alternatives and influential criteria.

Step 2. Since group decision-making is assumed, it is necessary to define a set of DMs that will evaluate potential alternatives.

Step 3. Transform linguistic variables into interval fuzzy rough numbers and form an initial decision matrix as shown:

$$IFRN(A_{ij}) = \begin{bmatrix} (a_{11}^{L1}, a_{11}^{U1}), (a_{11}^{L2}, a_{11}^{U2}), (a_{11}^{L3}, a_{11}^{U3}) & \cdots & (a_{1n}^{L1}, a_{1n}^{U1}), (a_{1n}^{L2}, a_{1n}^{U2}), (a_{1n}^{L3}, a_{1n}^{U3}) \\ (a_{21}^{L1}, a_{21}^{U1}), (a_{21}^{L2}, a_{21}^{U2}), (a_{21}^{L3}, a_{21}^{U3}) & \cdots & (a_{2n}^{L1}, a_{2n}^{U1}), (a_{2n}^{L2}, a_{2n}^{U2}), (a_{2n}^{L3}, a_{2n}^{U3}) \\ \cdots & \vdots & \cdots \\ (a_{m1}^{L1}, a_{m1}^{U1}), (a_{m1}^{L2}, a_{m1}^{U2}), (a_{m1}^{L3}, a_{m1}^{U3}) & \cdots & (a_{mn}^{L1}, a_{mn}^{U1}), (a_{mn}^{L2}, a_{mn}^{U2}), (a_{mn}^{L3}, a_{mn}^{U3}) \end{bmatrix} \quad (20)$$

Step 4: Determine the normalized values that make up the matrix $IFRN(D_{ij})$, which is obtained as follows:

$$d_{ij} = \left[\left(\frac{a_{ij}^{L1}}{\max a_{ij}^{U3}}, \frac{a_{ij}^{U1}}{\max a_{ij}^{L3}} \right), \left(\frac{a_{ij}^{L2}}{\max a_{ij}^{U2}}, \frac{a_{ij}^{U2}}{\max a_{ij}^{L2}} \right), \left(\frac{a_{ij}^{L3}}{\max a_{ij}^{U1}}, \frac{a_{ij}^{U3}}{\max a_{ij}^{L1}} \right) \right] \text{ for } B \quad (21)$$

$$d_{ij} = \left[\left(\frac{\min a_{ij}^{L1}}{a_{ij}^{U3}}, \frac{\min a_{ij}^{U1}}{a_{ij}^{L3}} \right), \left(\frac{\min a_{ij}^{L2}}{a_{ij}^{U2}}, \frac{\min a_{ij}^{U2}}{a_{ij}^{L2}} \right), \left(\frac{\min a_{ij}^{L3}}{a_{ij}^{U1}}, \frac{\min a_{ij}^{U3}}{a_{ij}^{L1}} \right) \right] \text{ for } C \quad (22)$$

Step 5. Integrate normalized matrix values $IFRN(D_{ij})$ with criteria weights $IFRN(W_j)$.

$$v_{ij} = \left[\left(a_{ij}^{L1} \times w_j^{L1}, a_{ij}^{U1} \times w_j^{U1} \right), \left(a_{ij}^{L2} \times w_j^{L2}, a_{ij}^{U2} \times w_j^{U2} \right), \left(a_{ij}^{L3} \times w_j^{L3}, a_{ij}^{U3} \times w_j^{U3} \right) \right] \quad (23)$$

Step 6. Summarize the IFRN values by rows in order to determine the sum-weighted model $IFRN(S_{ij})$.

$$IFRN(S_{ij}) = \sum_{j=1}^{n} IFRN(v_{ij}) \quad (24)$$

Step 7. Determine the product-weighted function $IFRN(Q_{ij})$ as follows:

$$IFRN(Q_{ij}) = \prod_{j=1}^{n} (d_{ij})^{w_j} \quad (25)$$

Step 8. Rank the alternatives in descending order based on the calculated final values:

$$IFRN(T_{ij}) = \lambda \times IFRN(S_{ij}) + (1 - \lambda) \times IFRN(Q_{ij}), \lambda = 0 - 1 \quad (26)$$

4. Efficiency of Road Sections Based on Headway Analysis

4.1. Collection and Processing of Data

In order to determine the road-section efficiency based on headways, data was collected for a total of 14 sections with the following characteristics: The length of a measuring segment along which the measurements were made is at least 1000 m long, the road gradient ranges from -5.50 to 7.50%, the section length is from 7.45 km to 38.55 km, while the size of the measurement sample varies from 713 to 1011. Also, it is important to note that headway was measured for all types of vehicles. The characteristics of the measuring sections are presented in Table 1.

Table 1. Characteristics of road sections and average headways.

	Section Symbol	Measuring-Segment Length	Road Gradient	Section Length (km)	Measurement Sample Size (No. of Measurements)	Th [s] (PC-PC)	Th [s] (LDV-PC)	Th [s] (HDV-PC)	Th [s] (BUS-PC)	Th [s] (AT-PC)
DMU1	M-I-108	min 1000 m	−5.50%	14.967	1000	5.349	7.714	7.577	8.633	10.136
DMU2	M-I-103	min 1000 m	−5.00%	14.073	1000	19.269	25.272	40.269	29.491	44.767
DMU3	M-I-108	min 1000 m	−3.00%	14.967	1000	5.331	9.406	9.107	4.979	7.934
DMU4	M-I-108	min 1000 m	1.50%	14.967	1000	12.553	21.713	19.393	23.681	12.926
DMU5	M-I-103	min 1000 m	−1.00%	14.073	1010	18.174	21.102	36.395	26.04	33.222
DMU6	M-I-105	min 1000 m	0%	7.405	1011	3.6	8.609	11.969	10.162	16.488
DMU7	M-I-106	min 1000 m	1.00%	38.553	912	9.794	25.096	18.537	26.949	16.669
DMU8	M-I-108	min 1000 m	2.00%	16.734	775	24.22	65.23	66.46	64.88	97.99
DMU9	M-I-106	min 1000 m	3.00%	38.553	908	12.43	31.124	24.458	21.191	64.944
DMU10	M-I-106	min 1000 m	4.00%	38.553	1007	8.48	31.271	31.253	34.794	63.897
DMU11	M-I-103	min 1000 m	5.00%	14.073	918	4.79	32.367	36.991	36.362	82.858
DMU12	M-I-108	min 1000 m	6.00%	20.134	736	12.907	82.888	126.711	118.67	189.593
DMU13	M-I-108	min 1000 m	7.00%	20.134	713	14.739	90.027	132.791	135.949	236.574
DMU14	M-I-108	min 1000 m	7.50%	20.134	811	16.559	97.84	141.196	146.706	264.434

DMU (Decision-making unit); PC (Passenger car); LDV (Light-Duty Vehicle); HDV (Heavy-Duty Vehicle); AT (Auto train).

After the collection, processing, and sorting of data, a DEA model [34] was applied based on a total of seven parameters, which later represent criteria in the MCDM model. In addition to the given parameters related to the headway and road gradient, AADT was in-cluded as an additional parameter. C1—AADT; C2—road gradient; C3—Th [s] (PC-PC); C4—Th [s] (LDV-PC); C5—Th [s] (HDV-PC); C6—Th [s] (BUS-PC); C7—Th [s] (AT-PC).

4.2. Application of DEA Model

The results after applying the DEA model are as follows:

$DMU1 = 1.000$, $DMU2 = 0.119$, $DMU3 = 1.000$, $DMU4 = 1.000$, $DMU5 = 0.153$, $DMU6 = 1.000$, $DMU7 = 0.667$
$DMU8 = 0.315$, $DMU9 = 1.000$, $DM10 = 1.000$, $DMU11 = 1.000$, $DMU12 = 0.519$, $DMU13 = 0.503$, $DMU14 = 0.496$

This means that half of the road sections are efficient in terms of the observed parameters, namely DMU1, DMU3, DMU4, DMU6, DMU9, DMU10, and DMU11. Since the discriminatory power in the DEA model is only 50% in this case, the IFRN MCDM model is defined in order to finally determine the efficiency for each road section.

4.3. Determining the Importance of Parameters Using the IFRN SWARA Method

In this section of the paper, it is first necessary to define the mutual relationship between the criteria, which was carried out by three decision-makers (DMs), and this is shown in Table 2.

Table 2. DM assessment of criteria significance.

	Criterion	DM1	DM2	DM3
C1	AADT	(3,4,5)	(4,5,6)	(4,5,6)
C2	Road gradient	(4,5,6)	(4,5,6)	(5,6,7)
C3	Th [s] (PC-PC)	(3,4,5)	(3,4,5)	(3,4,5)
C4	Th [s] (LDV-PC)	(2,3,4)	(3,4,5)	(3,4,5)
C5	Th [s] (HDV-PC)	(2,3,4)	(2,3,4)	(1,2,3)
C6	Th [s] (BUS-PC)	(1,2,3)	(2,3,4)	(0,1,2)
C7	Th [s] (AT-PC)	(0,1,2)	(1,2,3)	(1,2,3)

In order to be able to apply the steps of the IFRN SWARA method, it is necessary to convert the DMs' estimates into interval fuzzy rough numbers.

A rough matrix for C7 is obtained as follows:

According to the DMs' estimates given in Table 2, three classes of objects are selected, i.e., l, m, and u, where $l = (0;1;1)$, $m = (1;2;2)$, and $u = (2;3;3)$.

For *l*:

$$Lim(0) = 0, \overline{Lim}(0) = \frac{1}{3}(0+1+1) = 0.667; \underline{Lim}(1) = \frac{1}{3}(0+1+1) = 0.667, \overline{Lim}(1) = 1$$

For *m*:

$$\underline{Lim}(1) = 1, \overline{Lim}(1) = \frac{1}{3}(1+2+2) = 1.667; \underline{Lim}(2) = \frac{1}{3}(1+2+2) = 1.667, \overline{Lim}(2) = 2$$

For *u*:

$$\underline{Lim}(2) = 2, \overline{Lim}(2) = \frac{1}{3}(2+3+3) = 2.667; \underline{Lim}(3) = \frac{1}{3}(2+3+3) = 2.667, \overline{Lim}(3) = 3$$

Thus, IFRNs are obtained as follows:

$$IFRN(DM_1) = [(0.00, 0.67), (1.00, 1.67), (2.00, 2.67)]$$

$$IFRN(DM_2) = [(0.67, 1.00), (1.67, 2.00), (2.67, 3.00)]$$

$$IFRN(DM_3) = [(0.67, 1.00), (1.67, 2.00), (2.67, 3.00)].$$

Using an aggregation equation, the final fuzzy rough number for C7 is computed:

$$IFRN(C_7) = [(0.45, 0.89), (1.45, 1.89), (2.45, 2.89)]$$

and the final interval fuzzy rough matrix $IFRN(X_j)$ is obtained (Table 3).

Table 3. Initial fuzzy rough matrix in the IFRN SWARA method.

	Xj
C7	[(0.447,0.890),(1.447,1.890),(2.447,2.890)]
C6	[(0.500,1.500),(1.500,2.500),(2.500,3.500)]
C5	[(1.447,1.890),(2.447,2.890),(3.447,3.890)]
C4	[(2.447,2.890),(3.447,3.890),(4.447,4.890)]
C3	[(3.000,3.000),(4.000,4.000),(5.000,5.000)]
C1	[(3.447,3.890),(4.447,4.890),(5.447,5.890)]
C2	[(4.110,4.553),(5.110,5.553),(6.110,6.553)]

The normalized matrix $IFRN(X_j)$ given below is obtained in the following way: The first element of the matrix $IFRN(N_j)$, i.e.,

$[(n_7^{L1}, n_7^{U1}), (n_7^{L2}, n_7^{U2}), (n_7^{L3}, n_7^{U3})] = [(1.000, 1.000), (1.000, 1.000), (1.000, 1.000)]$, represents a rule, and it is required in each decision-making process.

$$IFRN(N_j) = \begin{bmatrix} (1.000, 1.000), (1.000, 1.000), (1.000, 1.000) \\ (0.076, 0.245), (0.270, 0.489), (0.549, 0.852) \\ (0.221, 0.309), (0.441, 0.556), (0.757, 0.946) \\ (0.373, 0.473), (0.621, 0.761), (0.977, 1.190) \\ (0.458, 0.491), (0.720, 0.783), (1.098, 1.217) \\ (0.526, 0.637), (0.801, 0.957), (1.196, 1.433) \\ (0.627, 0.745), (0.920, 1.087), (1.342, 1.594) \end{bmatrix}$$

$$IFRN(Z_j) = [(4.11, 4.55), (5.11, 5.55), (6.11, 6.55)]$$

$[(n_6^{L1}, n_6^{U1}), (n_6^{L2}, n_6^{U2}), (n_6^{L3}, n_6^{U3})] = \left[\left(\frac{0.50}{6.55}, \frac{1.50}{6.11}\right), \left(\frac{1.50}{5.55}, \frac{2.50}{5.11}\right), \left(\frac{2.50}{4.55}, \frac{3.50}{4.11}\right)\right] = [(0.076, 0.245), (0.270, 0.489), (0.549, 0.852)]$

The next step is to compute the following interval fuzzy rough matrix:

$IFRN(\Im_6) = [(0.076 + 1.00, 0.245 + 1), (0.270 + 1.00, 0.489 + 1.00), (0.549 + 1.00, 0.852 + 1.00)] = [(1.076, 1.245), (1.270, 1.489), (1.549, 1.852)]$

$$IFRN(\Im_j) = \begin{bmatrix} (1.000, 1.000), (1.000, 1.000), (1.000, 1.000) \\ (1.076, 1.245), (1.270, 1.489), (1.549, 1.852) \\ (1.221, 1.309), (1.441, 1.566), (1.757, 1.946) \\ (1.373, 1.473), (1.621, 1.761), (1.977, 2.190) \\ (1.458, 1.491), (1.720, 1.783), (2.098, 2.217) \\ (1.526, 1.637), (1.801, 1.957), (2.196, 2.433) \\ (1.627, 1.745), (1.920, 2.087), (2.342, 2.594) \end{bmatrix}$$

Then, the matrix $IFRN(\Re_j)$ is calculated as follows:

$$IFRN(\Re_6) \begin{bmatrix} \Re_6^{L1} = \left(\frac{\Re_7^{L1}}{\Im_6^{U3}}\right) = \left(\frac{1}{1.852}\right), & \Re_6^{U1} = \left(\frac{\Re_7^{U1}}{\Im_6^{L3}}\right) = \left(\frac{1}{1.549}\right) = (0.540, 0.646) \\ \Re_6^{L2} = \left(\frac{\Re_7^{L2}}{\Im_6^{U2}}\right) = \left(\frac{1}{1.489}\right), & \Re_6^{U2} = \left(\frac{\Re_7^{U2}}{\Im_6^{L2}}\right) = \left(\frac{1}{1.270}\right) = (0.671, 0.787) \\ \Re_6^{L3} = \left(\frac{\Re_7^{L3}}{\Im_6^{U1}}\right) = \left(\frac{1}{1.245}\right), & \Re_6^{U3} = \left(\frac{\Re_7^{U3}}{\Im_6^{L1}}\right) = \left(\frac{1}{1.076}\right) = (0.803, 0.929) \end{bmatrix}$$

The total matrix is as follows:

$$IFRN(\Re_j) = \begin{bmatrix} (1.000, 1.000), (1.000, 1.000), (1.000, 1.000) \\ (0.540, 0.646), (0.671, 0.787), (0.803, 0.929) \\ (0.277, 0.367), (0.429, 0.547), (0.613, 0.761) \\ (0.127, 0.186), (0.244, 0.337), (0.416, 0.554) \\ (0.057, 0.089), (0.137, 0.196), (0.279, 0.380) \\ (0.023, 0.040), (0.070, 0.109), (0.171, 0.249) \\ (0.009, 0.017), (0.033, 0.057), (0.098, 0.153) \end{bmatrix}$$

The sum of the matrix is computed and
$IFRN(\aleph_j) = [(2.034, 2.345), (2.584, 3.033), (3.380, 4.027)]$ is obtained.
Finally,

$$IFRN(W_7) = \left[\left(\frac{1}{4.027}, \frac{1}{3.380}\right), \left(\frac{1}{3.033}, \frac{1}{2.584}\right), \left(\frac{1}{2.345}, \frac{1}{2.034}\right)\right] = [(0.248, 0.296), (0.330, 0.387), (0.426, 0.492)]$$

The final criteria values are shown in Table 4.

Table 4. Results of the IFRN SWARA method.

	wj		wj
C7	[(0.248,0.296),(0.330,0.387),(0.426,0.492)]	C1	[(0.006,0.012),(0.023,0.042),(0.073,0.122)]
C6	[(0.134,0.191),(0.221,0.305),(0.342,0.457)]	C2	[(0.002,0.005),(0.011,0.022),(0.042,0.075)]
C5	[(0.069,0.109),(0.141,0.212),(0.261,0.374)]	C3	[(0.014,0.026),(0.045,0.076),(0.119,0.187)]
C4	[(0.031,0.055),(0.080,0.131),(0.178,0.272)]	C4	[(0.031,0.055),(0.080,0.131),(0.178,0.272)]
C3	[(0.014,0.026),(0.045,0.076),(0.119,0.187)]	C5	[(0.069,0.109),(0.141,0.212),(0.261,0.374)]
C1	[(0.006,0.012),(0.023,0.042),(0.073,0.122)]	C6	[(0.134,0.191),(0.221,0.305),(0.342,0.457)]
C2	[(0.002,0.005),(0.011,0.022),(0.042,0.075)]	C7	[(0.248,0.296),(0.330,0.387),(0.426,0.492)]

Based on the analysis by experts in this field, using the presented seven criteria (C1–C7), the least significant criterion refers to the ascent/descent (C2) on the measuring segments that are not shorter than 1000 m before an imagined cross-section and to the volume of traffic (C1), which is expressed as the AADT (*veh/day*). The other five criteria (C3–C7) represent the arithmetic means (AM) of headways based on the measured values of a total of 12,801 measurements according to vehicle classes from PC-PC to PC-AT. The importance of these five criteria is C7 > C6 > C5 > C4 > C3.

4.4. Determining Overall Efficiency Using the IFRN WASPAS Method

In this section of the paper, the final efficiency of the observed road sections is determined based on headways. Table 5 shows a group assessment for the first road section.

Table 5. The values of the fuzzy numbers for the first road section.

	DM1	DM2	DM3	DM1	DM2	DM3	DM1	DM2	DM3
		l			m			u	
C1	5	5	5	7	7	7	9	9	9
C2	7	7	5	7	9	7	9	9	9
C3	5	7	5	7	9	7	9	9	9
C4	7	7	7	9	9	9	9	9	9
C5	7	9	7	9	9	9	9	9	9
C6	7	7	7	7	7	7	9	7	7
C7	7	7	7	7	9	7	9	9	9

Then, the rough set values are calculated. The following calculation is based on criterion C2:

For l:

$$\underline{Lim}(5) = 5,\ \overline{Lim}(5) = \frac{1}{3}(7+7+5) = 6.33;\ \underline{Lim}(7) = \frac{1}{3}(7+7+5) = 6.33,\ \overline{Lim}(7) = 7$$

For m:

$$\underline{Lim}(7) = 7,\ \overline{Lim}(7) = \frac{1}{3}(7+9+7) = 7.67;\ \underline{Lim}(9) = \frac{1}{3}(7+9+7) = 7.67,\ \overline{Lim}(9) = 9$$

For u:

$$\underline{Lim}(9) = 9,\ \overline{Lim}(9) = 9$$

The first road section is assigned the following interval fuzzy rough numbers for criterion C2:

$$IFRN\ (DM_1) = [(6.33, 7.00), (7.00, 7.67), (9.00, 9.00)]$$

$$IFRN\ (DM_2) = [(6.33, 7.00), (7.67, 9.00), (9.00, 9.00)]$$

$$IFRN\ (DM_3) = [(5.00, 6.33), (7.00, 7.67), (9.00, 9.00)]$$

The final value of the interval fuzzy rough numbers is obtained by computing the average values for all DMs. By this approach, an interval fuzzy rough decision matrix is created (Table 6).

Table 6. Interval fuzzy rough decision matrix.

	C1	C2	...	C7
DMU1	[(5.00,5.00),(7.00,7.00),(9.00,9.00)]	[(5.89,6.78),(7.22,8.11),(9.00,9.00)]	...	[(7.00,7.00),(7.22,8.11),(9.00,9.00)]
DMU3	[(5.00,5.00),(7.00,7.00),(9.00,9.00)]	[(5.00,5.00),(7.00,7.00),(7.22,8.11)]	...	[(7.00,7.00),(9.00,9.00),(9.00,9.00)]
DMU4	[(5.00,5.00),(7.00,7.00),(9.00,9.00)]	[(5.00,5.00),(7.00,7.00),(7.00,7.00)]	...	[(7.00,7.00),(7.00,7.00),(7.22,8.11)]
DMU6	[(7.22,8.11),(9.00,9.00),(9.00,9.00)]	[(3.00,3.00),(3.89,4.78),(7.00,7.00)]	...	[(5.00,5.00),(7.00,7.00),(7.00,7.00)]
DMU9	[(3.00,3.00),(3.89,4.78),(5.89,6.78)]	[(5.22,6.11),(7.00,7.00),(9.00,9.00)]	...	[(3.00,3.00),(5.00,5.00),(5.00,5.00)]
DMU10	[(3.00,3.00),(5.00,5.00),(7.00,7.00)]	[(7.00,7.00),(7.00,7.00),(9.00,9.00)]	...	[(3.00,3.00),(3.00,3.00),(5.00,5.00)]
DMU11	[(5.00,5.00),(7.00,7.00),(9.00,9.00)]	[(5.89,6.78),(7.22,8.11),(9.00,9.00)]	...	[(7.00,7.00),(7.22,8.11),(9.00,9.00)]
Max	[(7.22,8.11),(9.00,9.00),(9.00,9.00)]	[(7.00,7.00),(7.22,8.11),(9.00,9.00)]	...	[(7.00,7.00),(9.00,9.00),(9.00,9.00)]

The normalization of the initial IFRN matrix is performed by applying Equation (21) since all criteria have been modeled as a benefit, and it is shown in Table 7. For DMU1, according to the first criterion, it is as follows:

$$d_{DMU1} = \left[\left(\frac{5.00}{9.00}, \frac{5.00}{9.00}\right), \left(\frac{7.00}{9.00}, \frac{7.00}{9.00}\right), \left(\frac{9.00}{8.10}, \frac{9.00}{7.20}\right)\right] = [(0.56, 0.56), (0.78, 0.78), (1.11, 1.25)]$$

Table 7. Normalized interval fuzzy rough decision matrix.

	C1	C2	...	C7
DMU1	[(0.56,0.56),(0.78,0.78),(1.11,1.25)]	[(0.65,0.75),(0.89,1.12),(1.29,1.29)]	...	[(0.78,0.78),(0.80,0.90),(1.29,1.29)]
DMU3	[(0.56,0.56),(0.78,0.78),(1.11,1.25)]	[(0.56,0.56),(0.86,0.97),(1.03,1.16)]	...	[(0.78,0.78),(1.00,1.00),(1.29,1.29)]
DMU4	[(0.56,0.56),(0.78,0.78),(1.11,1.25)]	[(0.56,0.56),(0.86,0.97),(1.00,1.00)]	...	[(0.78,0.78),(0.78,0.78),(1.03,1.16)]
DMU6	[(0.80,0.90),(1.00,1.00),(1.11,1.25)]	[(0.33,0.33),(0.48,0.66),(1.00,1.00)]	...	[(0.56,0.56),(0.78,0.78),(1.00,1.00)]
DMU9	[(0.33,0.33),(0.43,0.53),(0.73,0.94)]	[(0.58,0.68),(0.86,0.97),(1.29,1.29)]	...	[(0.33,0.33),(0.56,0.56),(0.71,0.71)]
DMU10	[(0.33,0.33),(0.56,0.56),(0.86,0.97)]	[(0.78,0.78),(0.86,0.97),(1.29,1.29)]	...	[(0.33,0.33),(0.33,0.33),(0.71,0.71)]
DMU11	[(0.56,0.56),(0.78,0.78),(1.11,1.25)]	[(0.65,0.75),(0.89,1.12),(1.29,1.29)]	...	[(0.78,0.78),(0.80,0.90),(1.29,1.29)]

After that, the weighting of the normalized decision matrix is completed, multiplying the normalized data by corresponding weights. For the previous examples, the computation procedure is as follows:

$$v_{DMU1} = [(0.56 \times 0.006, 0.56 \times 0.012), (0.78 \times 0.023, 0.78 \times 0.042), (1.11 \times 0.073, 1.25 \times 0.122)]$$
$$= [(0.003, 0.07), (0.018, 0.033), (0.081, 0.153)]$$

Then, the function $IFRN(S_{ij})$ is computed as follows:

$$IFRN(S_{DMU1}) = \begin{bmatrix} (0.00 + 0.00 + 0.01 + 0.02 + 0.06 + 0.10 + 0.19), (0.01 + 0.00 + 0.02 + 0.04 + 0.10 + 0.15 + 0.23), \\ (0.02 + 0.01 + 0.04 + 0.08 + 0.14 + 0.18 + 0.26), (0.03 + 0.02 + 0.08 + 0.13 + 0.21 + 0.27 + 0.35), \\ (0.08 + 0.05 + 0.15 + 0.23 + 0.29 + 0.35 + 0.55), (0.15 + 0.10 + 0.24 + 0.35 + 0.47 + 0.53 + 0.63) \end{bmatrix} =$$
$$[(0.39, 0.55), (0.73, 1.10), (1.71, 2.47)]$$

and after that, the function $IFRN(Q_{ij})$ is as follows:

$$IFRN(Q_{DMU1}) = \begin{bmatrix} (0.56)^{0.122} \times (0.65)^{0.075} \times (0.58)^{0.187} \times (0.78)^{0.272} \times (0.80)^{0.374} \times (0.78)^{0.457} \times (0.78)^{0.492} \\ (0.56)^{0.073} \times (0.75)^{0.042} \times (0.68)^{0.119} \times (0.78)^{0.178} \times (0.90)^{0.261} \times (0.78)^{0.342} \times (0.78)^{0.426} \\ (0.78)^{0.042} \times (0.89)^{0.022} \times (0.82)^{0.076} \times (1.00)^{0.131} \times (1.00)^{0.212} \times (0.80)^{0.305} \times (0.80)^{0.387} \\ (0.78)^{0.023} \times (1.12)^{0.011} \times (1.03)^{0.045} \times (1.00)^{0.080} \times (1.00)^{0.141} \times (0.89)^{0.221} \times (0.90)^{0.330} \\ (1.11)^{0.012} \times (1.29)^{0.005} \times (1.29)^{0.026} \times (1.29)^{0.055} \times (1.11)^{0.109} \times (1.03)^{0.191} \times (1.29)^{0.296} \\ (1.25)^{0.006} \times (1.29)^{0.002} \times (1.29)^{0.014} \times (1.29)^{0.031} \times (1.25)^{0.069} \times (1.16)^{0.134} \times (1.29)^{0.248} \end{bmatrix} = [(0.74, 0.86), (0.96, 0.99), (1.01, 1.06)]$$

Finally, the alternatives are ranked in descending order based on the obtained final values:

$$IFRN(T_{DMU1}) = \begin{bmatrix} (0.50 \times 0.39 + 0.50 \times 0.74), (0.50 \times 0.55 + 0.50 \times 0.86), (0.50 \times 0.73 + 0.50 \times 0.96) \\ (0.50 \times 1.10 + 0.50 \times 0.99), (0.50 \times 1.71 + 0.50 \times 1.01), (0.50 \times 2.47 + 0.50 \times 1.06) \end{bmatrix} = [(0.57, 0.71), (0.85, 1.05), (1.36, 1.76)]$$

The final results after applying the integrated DEA-IFRN SWARA-IFRN WASPAS model are given in Table 8.

Table 8. Results of applying the DEA-IFRN SWARA-IFRN WASPAS model.

	$IFRN(S_{ij})$	$IFRN(Q_{ij})$	$IFRN(T_{ij})$	Rank
DMU1	[(0.39,0.548),(0.728,1.097),(1.707,2.468)]	[(0.743,0.864),(0.962,0.994),(1.013,1.057)]	1.05	1
DMU3	[(0.384,0.529),(0.768,1.14),(1.733,2.438)]	[(0.706,0.822),(0.951,0.985),(1.01,1.069)]	1.04	2
DMU4	[(0.297,0.401),(0.52,0.794),(1.295,1.893)]	[(0.538,0.717),(0.874,0.949),(0.992,0.976)]	0.85	4
DMU6	[(0.292,0.406),(0.682,1.004),(1.563,2.233)]	[(0.664,0.791),(0.935,0.981),(1.009,1.006)]	0.96	3
DMU9	[(0.163,0.228),(0.462,0.677),(1.093,1.58)]	[(0.395,0.607),(0.843,0.928),(0.984,0.918)]	0.74	5
DMU10	[(0.122,0.174),(0.279,0.443),(1.014,1.501)]	[(0.333,0.542),(0.789,0.894),(0.979,0.917)]	0.67	6
DMU11	[(0.07,0.124),(0.324,0.517),(0.902,1.309)]	[(0.314,0.529),(0.819,0.912),(0.976,0.86)]	0.64	7

By analyzing the ranking of efficiency, and applying the DEA-IFRN SWARA-IFRN WASPAS model, the ranking of alternatives for the observed sections of two-lane roads was performed. According to the results obtained, the best-ranked is a measuring segment of the Ivanjska–Šargovac section, with a road gradient = −5.5%, which has low deviating values of headways according to the measurement classes from PC-PC to AT-PC, which shows balanced and continuous traffic flows. The Vrhovi–Šešlije section, with a road gradient = 5%, stands out as the worst-ranked of the given sections, where the headway values from PC-PC to AT-PC differ by up to 20 times. It is obvious that the measure of efficiency, which refers to continuous traffic flows on this section, was significantly lost by applying the given model.

5. Verification Tests

5.1. Sensitivity Analysis (SA)

In order to be able to determine the stability of the obtained results and the influence of criterion values on the final ranks of the alternatives, a sensitivity analysis is often performed, which has been confirmed by a number of studies [35–38]. In this section, 70 new cases have been formed with new values of seven criteria, whereby their values have been reduced to within a range of 5–95%. The values of all criteria are shown in Figure 1.

The next step entails the creation of 70 new IFRN SWARA-IFRN WASPAS models by implementing new simulated criteria values in each scenario. The results of changing the criteria values are given in Figure 2.

The ranks obtained through the 70 scenarios show the stability of the model and confirm the initial results, regardless of the change to the best alternative. In general, as previously noted, DMU1 and DMU3 represent road sections that are almost identical in terms of final efficiency. Therefore, it is not surprising that they exchanged their positions in certain scenarios, primarily due to the drastic drop in the value of the first, fourth, and fifth criteria. There were a total of 17 such cases, which is 24.29%.

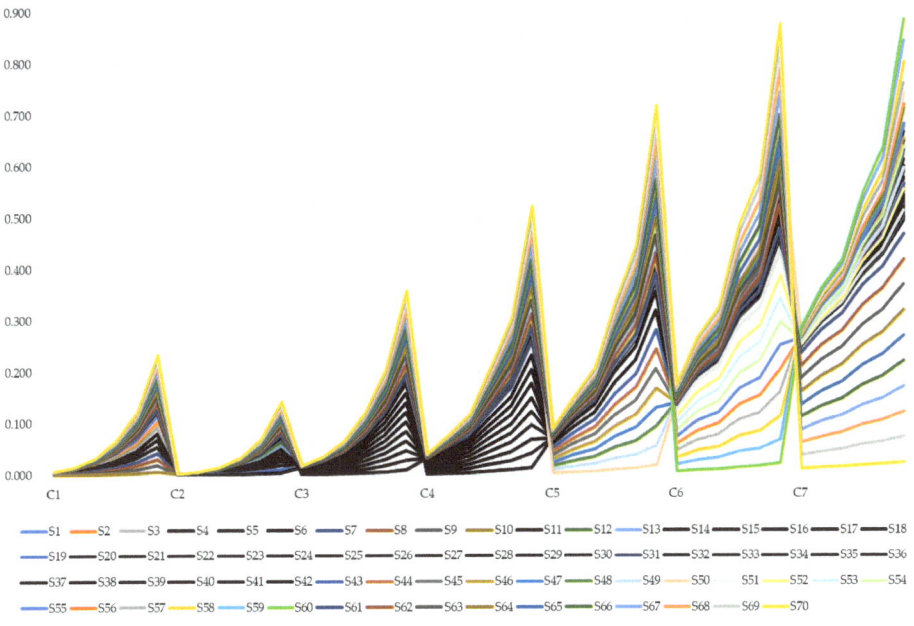

Figure 1. New criteria weights in 70 cases.

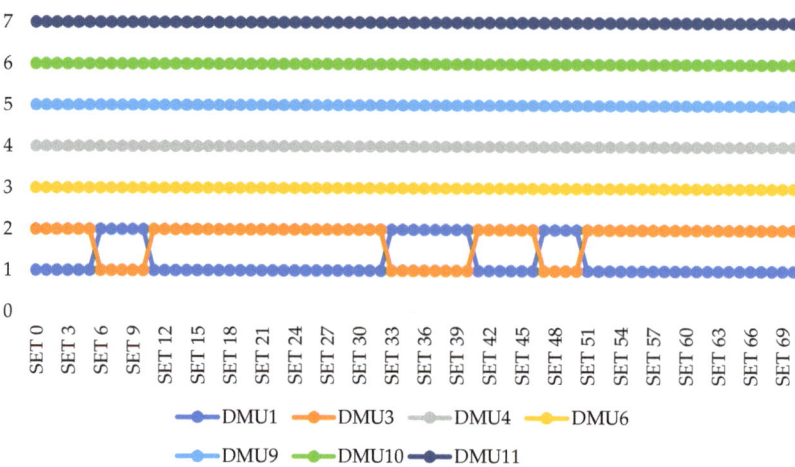

Figure 2. Results of the SA.

5.2. Comparative Analysis (CA)

This section refers to the application of four other MCDM methods—MARCOS: measurement of alternatives and ranking according to the compromise solution [39]; MABAC: multi-attributive border-approximation area comparison [35]; GRADIS: compromise ranking of alternatives from distance to ideal solution [40]; and ARAS: additive ratio assessment [41]—in the IFRN environment in order to confirm the new results (Figure 3) and compliance with the initial ranks of the IFRN SWARA-IFRN WASPAS model.

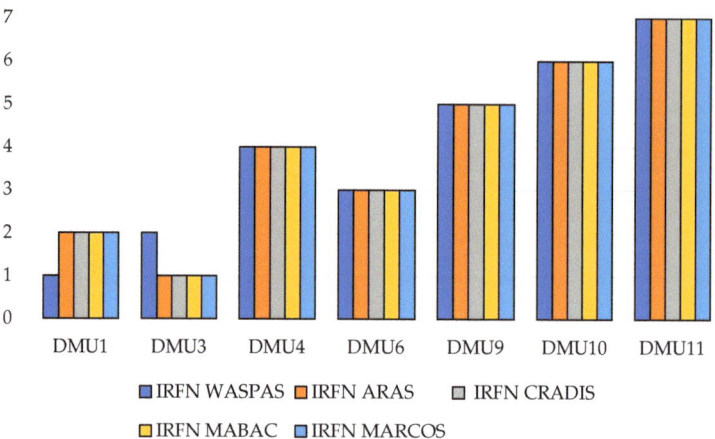

Figure 3. Ranks in the CA.

The CA results confirm what has been presented in the SA, i.e., DMU3 has the highest efficiency and is ranked first. This is also the case with the IFRN WASPAS method at a higher value of the λ parameter, which is verified in the next section.

5.3. Changing the λ Parameter

An integral part of the IFRN WASPAS method is the coefficient λ, with a range of 0–1, where its mean value, i.e., 0.50, is most often taken. In this section of the paper, the influence of this coefficient on the ranks of road sections has been determined, which is shown in Figure 4.

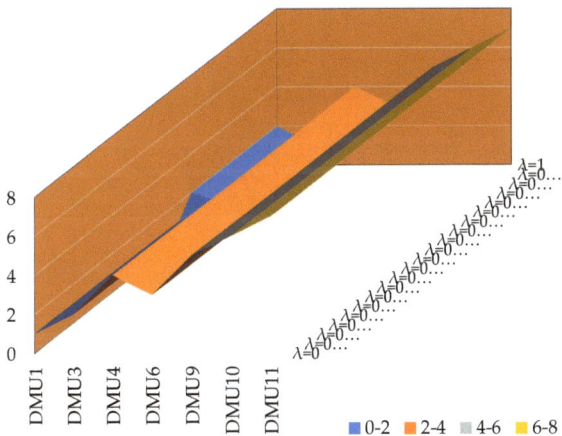

Figure 4. Ranking of road sections in accordance to changing the λ parameter.

The parameter λ was modeled in its established interval of 0–1 with a sequence of 0.05, which means that a total of 21 scenarios were formed, including the value of 0.50. The results show that at a value of this parameter of up to 0.60, DMUs keep their original positions, while at a value of 0.65–1.00, DMU3 becomes the most efficient section, which is also the case in the CA.

5.4. Reverse Rank (RR) Analysis

In order to ensure the credibility of the proposed IFRN SWARA-IFRN WASPAS model, a reverse-rank analysis [42] with different variations was performed. First, different scenarios were formed, implying that the worst road section was eliminated. After that, the worst alternative was added to the existing structure of the initial interval fuzzy-rough-number matrix. The next scenario implied that the worst alternative was replaced with the second worst, and in the last scenario, the two most significant criteria (C7 and C6) were removed from the model. The results from the aspect of reverse rank analysis with the values of road sections are shown in Figure 5, i.e., from the aspect of ranks in Figure 6.

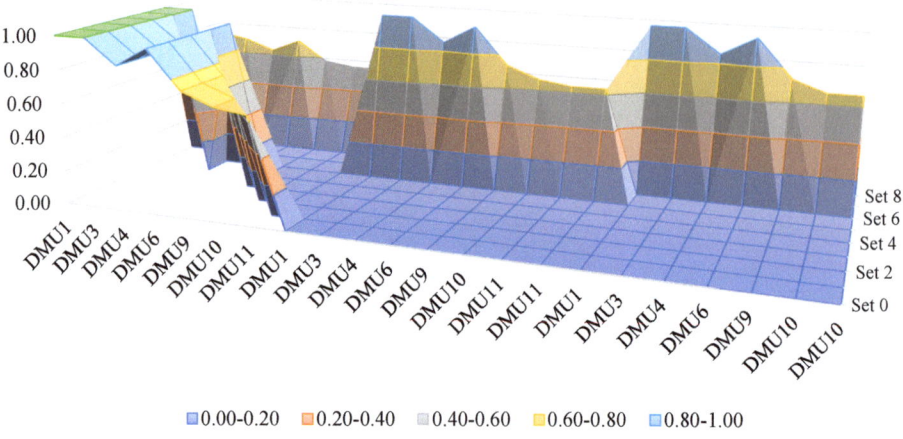

Figure 5. Values of road sections after the RR analysis.

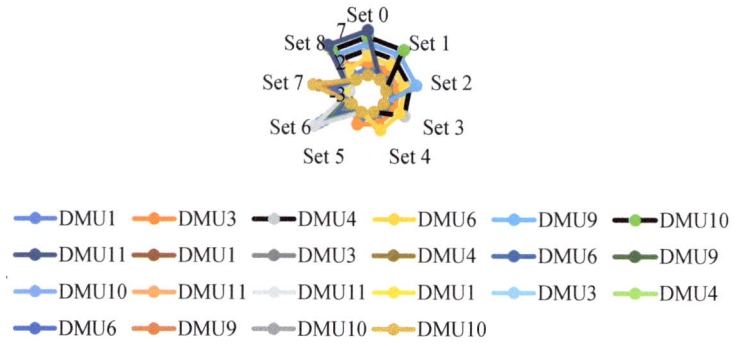

Figure 6. Ranks of road sections after the RR analysis.

In general, the results concerning the change in the final values of the alternatives in the RR analysis do not show large deviations compared to the original values.

When it comes to ranks, DMU1 remains the most efficient road section in the overall RR analysis. In addition, the other DMUs keep their original positions, except in the last scenario, where the two most influential criteria are deleted. Then, DMU3 and DMU6 exchange their positions.

6. Conclusions

Based on the development of the model and its application in a specific case study of 14 initial measuring segments of the given sections, ranking from the aspect of the efficiency of traffic flows on the sections was conducted. By generalizing and modeling the applied criteria of AADT, gradients, and AM headways, it was shown that the rank of efficiency is achieved with a lower deviation of headways according to the specified vehicle class. Also, the measure of efficiency implies an optimal flow, balanced and continuous, which is especially noticeable for the measuring segment of the Ivanjska–Šargovac section on a descent of -5.5%, where there is a low headway deviation. Too-high headway deviations imply an unbalanced flow, and these are often noticeable on an ascent, which caused some of those sections to be ranked significantly worse in terms of efficiency measures. Using a specific real case study that contains 14 road sections gives practical relevance to the research. By analyzing real data and using the proposed model to evaluate efficiency based on headway analysis, the research provides actionable insights for improving traffic flow and infrastructure management.

In this paper, a novel integrated DEA-IFRN SWARA-IFRN WASPAS model has been developed to determine the efficiency of 14 road infrastructure sections. The contribution of the research can be viewed in two ways, from a scientific–methodological and professional aspect. From the scientific aspect, it is certainly a dominant contribution, which is reflected in the development of the IFRN WASPAS method, while from the professional aspect, it represents support for the infrastructure manager and traffic experts in order to define certain measures. Also, the proposed innovative model has the potential to advance the field of transportation engineering by providing a more comprehensive analysis of infrastructure efficiency.

On the other hand, the findings of the study may have limited generalizability due to the focus on a specific set of road sections and the relatively small sample size. This restricts the broader applicability of the developed model to different geographical contexts or transportation systems, potentially limiting its usefulness to practitioners in diverse settings. Limitations related to this research can be manifested through the relatively short measuring segments (with a length of 1000 m) and the small number of DMs who participated in the group decision-making. Also, one of the limitations may be the lack of new data related to the AADT or the fact that integration of multiple decision-making methods and the use of interval fuzzy rough numbers may introduce methodological complexity, making it challenging for readers to grasp the intricacies of the approach. This complexity could hinder understanding and replication by other researchers or practitioners, potentially limiting the adoption of the developed model. These limitations can be mitigated if the reproduction of the model is made soon with more parameters and if the model is applied under the advice of experts in the field of methodology.

Future research refers to the collection of data and the determination of the efficiency of new sections of road infrastructure, as well as the definition of additional parameters and the inclusion of DMs for different structures. The developed model can be applied in any other case study that contains multiple variants and criteria. Also, from a methodological aspect, future research can be related to extension methods in other forms like quasirung fuzzy sets [43], polytopic fuzzy sets [44], integration with machine learning [45,46], multi-objective optimization [47], etc.

Author Contributions: Conceptualization, M.S. and D.A.; methodology, Ž.S. and G.S.; validation, D.K.D. and M.S.; formal analysis, N.N. and M.S.; investigation, D.A. and Ž.S.; writing—original draft preparation, Ž.S., D.A. and G.S.; writing—review and editing, D.K.D., N.N. and M.S.; visualization, N.N. All authors have read and agreed to the published version of the manuscript.

Funding: This research has been supported by the Ministry of Science, Technological Development and Innovation (Contract No. 451-03-65/2024-03/200156) and the Faculty of Technical Sciences, University of Novi Sad through project "Scientific and Artistic Research Work of Researchers in Teaching and Associate Positions at the Faculty of Technical Sciences, University of Novi Sad" (No. 01-3394/1).

Data Availability Statement: The data presented in this study are available on request from the corresponding author.

Acknowledgments: The paper is part of the research conducted within Project No. 19.032/961-39/23 "Investigation of time headway in models of efficiency and safety analysis of two-lane roads" supported by the Ministry of Scientific and Technological Development and Higher Education of the Republic of Srpska.

Conflicts of Interest: The authors declare no conflicts of interest.

References

1. Khan, A.B.F.; Ivan, P. Integrating Machine Learning and Deep Learning in Smart Cities for Enhanced Traffic Congestion Management: An Empirical Review. *J. Urban Dev. Manag.* **2023**, *2*, 211–221. [CrossRef]

2. Biswas, R.K.; Friswell, R.; Olivier, J.; Williamson, A.; Senserrick, T. A systematic review of definitions of motor vehicle headways in driver behaviour and performance studies. *Transp. Res. Part F Traffic Psychol. Behav.* **2021**, *77*, 38–54. [CrossRef]
3. Khan, J.A.; Shah, A.U. Comparison of Headway Measurement Methods for Heterogeneous Traffic Conditions. *Int. J. Res. Appl. Sci. Eng. Technol.* **2023**, *11*, 1362–1367. [CrossRef]
4. Cantisani, G.; Del Serrone, G.; Mauro, R.; Peluso, P.; Pompigna, A. Traffic Stream Analysis by Radar Sensors on Two-Lane Roads for Free-Moving and Constrained Vehicles Identification. *Sensors* **2023**, *23*, 6922. [CrossRef] [PubMed]
5. Abtahi, S.M.; Tamannaei, M.; Haghshenash, H. Analysis and modeling time headway distributions under heavy traffic flow conditions in the urban highways: Case of Isfahan. *Transport* **2011**, *26*, 375–382. [CrossRef]
6. Boora, A.; Ghosh, I.; Chandra, S.; Rani, K. Measurement of free-flow conditions on multilane intercity highways under heterogeneous traffic conditions. *J. South Afr. Inst. Civ. Eng.* **2018**, *60*, 2–9. [CrossRef]
7. Oghoyafedo, K.N.; Enunwa, B.T.; Nwankwo, E. Capacity Evaluation Along Benin-Lagos Expressway by Traffic Flow and Time Headway Approach. *NIPES J. Sci. Technol. Res.* **2022**, *4*, 322–328. [CrossRef]
8. Samadi, H.; Aghayan, I.; Nasiri, A.S.A.; Rahmani, O.; Hasanvand, M. Platoon-Based Assessment of Two-Way Two-Lane Roads Performance Measure: A Classification Method. *J. Adv. Transp.* **2023**, *2023*, 5054427. [CrossRef]
9. Roy, R.; Saha, P. Headway distribution models of two-lane roads under mixed traffic conditions: A case study from India. *Eur. Transp. Res. Rev.* **2017**, *10*, 3. [CrossRef]
10. Weng, J.; Meng, Q.; Fwa, T.F. Vehicle headway distribution in work zones. *Transp. A Transp. Sci.* **2013**, *10*, 285–303. [CrossRef]
11. Yu, R.; Zhang, Y.; Wang, L.; Du, X. Time headway distribution analysis of naturalistic road users based on aerial datasets. *J. Intell. Connect. Veh.* **2022**, *5*, 149–156. [CrossRef]
12. Abdul Mawjoud, A.A. Headway Modeling in Northern Iraqi Two-Lane Highways. *Acad. J. Nawroz Univ.* **2018**, *7*, 1–8. [CrossRef]
13. Shoaeb, A.; El-Badawy, S.; Shawly, S.; Shahdah, U.E. Time headway distributions for two-lane two-way roads: Case study from Dakahliya Governorate, Egypt. *Innov. Infrastruct. Solut.* **2021**, *6*, 165. [CrossRef]
14. Khansari, E.R.; Tabibi, M.; Nejad, F.M. A study on following behavior based on the time headway. *J. Kejuruter.* **2020**, *32*, 187–195. [CrossRef] [PubMed]
15. Masud, S.S.B. Traffic Time Headway Prediction and Analysis: A Deep Learning Approach. Ph.D. Thesis, The University of Texas Rio Grande Valley, Edinburg, TX, USA.
16. Li, L.; Chen, X. Vehicle headway modeling and its inferences in macroscopic/microscopic traffic flow theory: A survey. *Transp. Res. Part C Emerg. Technol.* **2017**, *76*, 170–188. [CrossRef]
17. Roy, R.; Saha, P. Analysis of vehicle-type-specific headways on two-lane roads with mixed traffic. *Transport* **2020**, *35*, 588–604. [CrossRef]
18. Samadi, H.; Aghayan, I.; Shaaban, K.; Hadadi, F. Development of Performance Measurement Models for Two-Lane Roads under Vehicular Platooning Using Conjugate Bayesian Analysis. *Sustainability* **2023**, *15*, 4037. [CrossRef]
19. HCM. Highway Capacity Manual. In *Transportation Research Board*; National Research Council: Washington, DC, USA, 2016.
20. Luttinen, R.T. Percent time-spent-following as performance measure for two-lane highways. *Transp. Res. Rec.* **2001**, *1776*, 52–59. [CrossRef]
21. HCM. *Highway Capacity Manual*, 3rd ed.; Transportation Research Board, National Research Council: Washington, DC, USA, 1985.
22. HCM. *Highway Capacity Manual*, 5th ed.; Transportation Research Board, National Research Council: Washington, DC, USA, 2010.
23. Stepanović, N.; Tubić, V.; Zdravković, S. Determining Free-Flow Speed on Different Classes of Rural Two-Lane Highways. *Promet–Traffic Transp.* **2023**, *35*, 315–330. [CrossRef]
24. Loulizi, A.; Bichiou, Y.; Rakha, H. Steady-State Car-Following Time Gaps: An Empirical Study Using Naturalistic Driving Data. *J. Adv. Transp.* **2019**, *2019*, 7659496. [CrossRef]
25. Pamučar, D.; Petrović, I.; Ćirović, G. Modification of the Best–Worst and MABAC methods: A novel approach based on interval-valued fuzzy-rough numbers. *Expert Syst. Appl.* **2018**, *91*, 89–106. [CrossRef]
26. Wang, N.; Xu, Y.; Puška, A.; Stević, A.; Alrasheedi, A.F. Multi-Criteria Selection of Electric Delivery Vehicles Using Fuzzy–Rough Methods. *Sustainability* **2023**, *15*, 15541. [CrossRef]
27. Korucuk, S.; Aytekin, A. Evaluating logistics flexibility in Istanbul-based companies using Interval-Valued Fermatean Fuzzy SWARA. *J. Intell Manag. Decis.* **2023**, *2*, 192–201. [CrossRef]
28. Badi, I.; Bouraima, M.B. Development of MCDM-Based Frameworks for proactively managing the most critical risk factors for transport accidents: A case study in Libya. *Spectr. Eng. Manag. Sci.* **2023**, *1*, 38–47. [CrossRef]
29. Qiu, Y.; Bouraima, M.B.; Kiptum, C.K.; Ayyildiz, E.; Stević, E.; Badi, I.; Ndiema, K.M. Strategies for Enhancing Industry 4.0 Adoption in East Africa: An Integrated Spherical Fuzzy SWARA-WASPAS Approach. *J. Ind. Intell.* **2023**, *1*, 87–100. [CrossRef]
30. Seikh, M.R.; Chatterjee, P. Determination of best renewable energy sources in India using SWARA-ARAS in confidence level based interval-valued Fermatean fuzzy environment. *Appl. Soft Comput.* **2024**, *155*, 111495. [CrossRef]
31. Chen, X.; Zhou, B.; Štilić, A.; Stević, E.; Puška, A. A Fuzzy–Rough MCDM Approach for Selecting Green Suppliers in the Furniture Manufacturing Industry: A Case Study of Eco-Friendly Material Production. *Sustainability* **2023**, *15*, 10745. [CrossRef]
32. Khan, A.A.; Mashat, D.S.; Dong, K. Evaluating Sustainable Urban Development Strategies through Spherical CRITIC-WASPAS Analysis. *J. Urban Dev. Manag.* **2024**, *3*, 1–17. [CrossRef]
33. Pamučar, D.; Sremac, S.; Stević, Ž.; Ćirović, G.; Tomić, D. New multi-criteria LNN WASPAS model for evaluating the work of advisors in the transport of hazardous goods. *Neural Comput. Appl.* **2019**, *31*, 5045–5068. [CrossRef]

34. Damjanović, M.; Stević, M.; Stanimirović, D.; Tanackov, I.; Marinković, D. Impact of the number of vehicles on traffic safety: Multiphase modeling. *Facta Univ. Series Mech. Eng.* **2022**, *20*, 177–197. [CrossRef]
35. Božanić, D.; Epler, I.; Puška, A.; Biswas, S.; Marinković, D.; Koprivica, S. Application of the DIBR II–rough MABAC decision-making model for ranking methods and techniques of lean organization systems management in the process of technical maintenance. *Facta Univ. Ser. Mech. Eng.* **2023**. [CrossRef]
36. Więckowski, J.; Kizielewicz, B.; Shekhovtsov, A.; Sałabun, W. How do the criteria affect sustainable supplier evaluation?—A case study using multi-criteria decision analysis methods in a fuzzy environment. *J. Eng. Manag. Syst. Eng.* **2023**, *2*, 37–52. [CrossRef]
37. Tešić, D.; Božanić, D.; Radovanović, M.; Petrovski, A. Optimising assault boat selection for military operations: An application of the DIBR II-BM-CoCoSo MCDM model. *J. Intell. Manag. Decis.* **2023**, *2*, 160–171. [CrossRef]
38. Albahri, O.; Alamoodi, A.; Deveci, M.; Albahri, A.; Mahmoud, M.A.; Al-Quraishi, T.; Moslem, S.; Sharaf, I.M. Evaluation of organizational culture in companies for fostering a digital innovation using q-rung picture fuzzy based decision-making model. *Adv. Eng. Inform.* **2023**, *58*, 102191. [CrossRef]
39. Stević, Ž.; Pamučar, D.; Puška, A.; Chatterjee, P. Sustainable supplier selection in healthcare industries using a new MCDM method: Measurement of alternatives and ranking according to COmpromise solution (MAR-COS). *Comput. Ind. Eng.* **2020**, *140*, 106231. [CrossRef]
40. Chakraborty, S.; Chatterjee, P.; Das, P.P. Compromise Ranking of Alternatives from Distance to Ideal Solution (CRADIS) Method. In *Multi-Criteria Decision-Making Methods in Manufacturing Environments*; Apple Academic Press: New York, NY, USA, 2024; pp. 343–347.
41. Zavadskas, E.K.; Turskis, Z. A new additive ratio assessment (ARAS) method in multicriteria decision-making. *Technol. Econ. Dev. Econ.* **2010**, *16*, 159–172. [CrossRef]
42. Zolfani, S.H.; Bazrafshan, R.; Ecer, F.; Karamaşa, F. The suitability-feasibility-acceptability strategy integrated with Bayesian BWM-MARCOS methods to determine the optimal lithium battery plant located in South America. *Mathematics* **2022**, *10*, 2401. [CrossRef]
43. Seikh, M.R.; Mandal, U. Multiple attribute decision-making based on 3, 4-quasirung fuzzy sets. *Granul. Comput.* **2022**, *7*, 965–978. [CrossRef]
44. Beg, I.; Abbas, M.; Asghar, M.W. Polytopic fuzzy sets and their applications to multiple-attribute decision-making problems. *Int. J. Fuzzy Syst.* **2022**, *24*, 2969–2981. [CrossRef]
45. Das, K.; Kumar, R. A Comprehensive Review of Categorization and Perspectives on State-of-Charge Estimation Using Deep Learning Methods for Electric Transportation. *Wirel. Pers. Commun.* **2023**, *133*, 1599–1618. [CrossRef]
46. Das, K.; Kumar, R. Electric vehicle battery capacity degradation and health estimation using machine-learning techniques: A review. *Clean Energy* **2023**, *7*, 1268–1281. [CrossRef]
47. Das, K.; Kumar, R. Assessment of Electric Two-Wheeler Ecosystem Using Novel Pareto Optimality and TOPSIS Methods for an Ideal Design Solution. *World Electr. Veh. J.* **2023**, *14*, 215. [CrossRef]

Disclaimer/Publisher's Note: The statements, opinions and data contained in all publications are solely those of the individual author(s) and contributor(s) and not of MDPI and/or the editor(s). MDPI and/or the editor(s) disclaim responsibility for any injury to people or property resulting from any ideas, methods, instructions or products referred to in the content.

Article

Transferability of Multi-Objective Neuro-Fuzzy Motion Controllers: Towards Cautious and Courageous Motion Behaviors in Rugged Terrains

Adham Salih [1], Joseph Gabbay [2] and Amiram Moshaiov [2,3,*]

[1] Mechanical Engineering Department, Braude College of Engineering, Karmiel 2161002, Israel; adhamsalih@braude.ac.il
[2] School of Mechanical Engineering, Tel-Aviv University, Tel-Aviv 6997801, Israel; josephgabbay@mail.tau.ac.il
[3] Sagol School of Neuroscience, Tel-Aviv University, Tel-Aviv 6997801, Israel
* Correspondence: moshaiov@tauex.tau.ac.il

Abstract: This study is motivated by the need to develop generic neuro-fuzzy motion controllers for autonomous vehicles that may traverse rugged terrains. Three types of target problems are investigated. These problems differ in terms of the expected motion behavior, including cautious, intermediate, and courageous behaviors. The target problems are defined as evolutionary multi-objective problems aiming to evolve near optimal neuro-fuzzy controllers that can operate in a variety of scenarios. To enhance the evolution, sequential transfer optimization is considered, where each of the source problems is defined and solved as a bi-objective problem. The performed experimental study demonstrates the ability of the proposed search approach to find neuro-fuzzy controllers that produce the required motion behaviors when operating in various environments with different motion difficulties. Moreover, the results of this study substantiate the hypothesis that solutions with performances near the edges of the obtained approximated bi-objective Pareto fronts of the source problems provide better transferability as compared with those that are associated with performances near the center of the obtained fronts.

Keywords: multi-objective optimization; Pareto-optimization; fuzzy-inference system; evolutionary transfer optimization; fuzzy control; non-specialized controllers

MSC: 93C42; 68W50

Citation: Salih, A.; Gabbay, J.; Moshaiov, A. Transferability of Multi-Objective Neuro-Fuzzy Motion Controllers: Towards Cautious and Courageous Motion Behaviors in Rugged Terrains. *Mathematics* 2024, 12, 992. https://doi.org/10.3390/math12070992

Academic Editors: Momcilo Dobrodolac, Stefan Jovcic and Marjana Čubranić-Dobrodolac

Received: 11 March 2024
Revised: 24 March 2024
Accepted: 26 March 2024
Published: 27 March 2024

Copyright: © 2024 by the authors. Licensee MDPI, Basel, Switzerland. This article is an open access article distributed under the terms and conditions of the Creative Commons Attribution (CC BY) license (https://creativecommons.org/licenses/by/4.0/).

1. Introduction

Increasing interest from the car industry in autonomous driving and the availability of new technologies have given rise to vast research efforts on the control of autonomous vehicles (e.g., [1,2]). However, such studies have hardly dealt with off-road autonomous driving. This study is motivated by the expected difficulties that a motion control system of an autonomous vehicle will face when traversing rugged terrains. For such off-road situations, it is envisioned that a range of motion behaviors might be of interest, spanning from a cautious behavior to a courageous one. As a first step towards the development of such control systems, this study considers an academic problem that applies a dynamic model of a cart that interacts with various environments. These environments differ by their motion difficulties, which are expressed by various friction functions and varying speed limitations. An attractive approach to address the development challenges of such controllers is to use a multi-objective evolutionary neuro-fuzzy optimization approach (e.g., [3,4]). The use of such an evolutionary approach, as compared with a traditional neuro-fuzzy approach, e.g., ANFIS [5], has three main advantages. First, it avoids the need to rely on an expert to determine the relevant fuzzy rules. Second, it avoids the need to create data sets for the tuning of the parameters of the membership functions. In addition, the use of an evolutionary search is most suited for solving multi-objective optimization problems, i.e., to find a set of Pareto-optimal solutions [6]. In this kind of optimization problem, no prior articulation of the objective preferences is provided. As described in the following, this study utilizes the above three advantages while focusing on the use of multi-objective optimization in conjunction with transfer optimization.

This study deals with a Sequential Transfer Optimization (STO) approach [7,8]. Namely, it assumes the existence of relevant knowledge from solving multi-objective source problems to the solution of multi-objective target problem(s). Moreover, this study involves an evolutionary STO in which a genetic transfer is employed. Namely, the knowledge is transferred via the use of individual solutions of the source problems to serve as an initial population for solving the target problems [9,10].

When defining the target optimization problem for the development of robot motion controllers, it is important to realize the difference between specialized and non-specialized controllers [11]. Specialized controllers are optimized for a particular environment, whereas non-specialized controllers are optimized for a set of environments. For the current motivation, it appears that the development of controllers for rugged terrains should focus on non-specialized controllers that may cope with a variety of terrains. According to [11], defining the problem as a meta-problem, which aims at performance optimization for a set of environments, produces both specialized and non-specialized neuro-controllers.

Following [11], this study considers the target problem as a meta-problem, i.e., the problem is a multi-objective optimization problem in which each objective is associated with a different environment. In this study, we define three types of behavior-based meta-problems. These problems differ by the desired behavior, including cautious, courageous, and intermediate behaviors. For example, we aim at non-specialized controllers that produce courageous behaviors in each one of the environments.

We seek to extract knowledge from a set of source problems to support solving the three types of target problems considered. The source problems are defined as optimization problems that differ by the source environment. Each of these problems is defined as a bi-objective Pareto-optimization problem in which one of the objectives corresponds to a cautious behavior and the other one corresponds to a courageous behavior. Each of these bi-objective source problems is solved using Pareto-optimization. Solving a set of source problems, which differ by the considered environment, results in a set of Pareto-optimal sets. The union of these sets is expected to hold relevant knowledge to support solving the target problems. Namely, it is expected to hold controllers of different behaviors that are relevant to different environments. While the diverse solutions of the union set are considered an advantage, they raise the following difficulty.

In general, a union set of Pareto-optimal sets of solutions from several source problems has a large cardinality. This cardinality is expected to be much beyond the size of the population that is needed to solve the target meta-problem. This study aims to answer a major question that results from the large cardinality of the union set. Namely, what subset of the individual solutions of the bi-objective source problems is more suited to serve as the initial populations for solving the target meta-problem? To provide an answer to this research question, two types of knowledge extraction techniques are suggested and investigated. The first type involves an initial population of edge controllers, i.e., controllers with performance vectors that are located close to the edges of the obtained fronts. The second type of knowledge extraction is based on an initial population of center controllers, i.e., controllers whose performance vectors are located close to the center of the obtained fronts. In addition, these types of knowledge extraction are compared with random initialization. We compare the three types of initial populations with respect to the three behavior-based target meta-problems considered here. We aim to substantiate the hypothesis that the use of edge controllers is a preferred approach regardless of the considered target problem.

Given the state-of-the-art, as presented in Section 2.3, the main contributions of this paper are:

(a) It is the first study that defines target meta-problems that aim to find non-specialized Neuro-Fuzzy Controllers (NFCs) that produce various motion behaviors.
(b) It is the first study that applies knowledge extraction from solving multi-objective source problems to support finding non-specialized NFCs that produce various motion behaviors for environments that are different due to their motion difficulties.
(c) It is the first study that raises the hypothesis that the genetic transfer of edge solutions of multi-objective source problems is preferred over that of the center solutions. Furthermore, it is the first study to substantiate the hypothesis with respect to the considered type of evolutionary neuro-fuzzy control problem.

The rest of this paper is organized as follows. Section 2 describes the background for this study and locates this study with respect to the state-of-the-art. Section 3 introduces the problem formulation and the proposed solution approach. Next, in Section 4, details are provided on the experimental study. Finally, Section 5 summarizes and concludes this study.

2. Background

This section provides the background for this study and a state-of-the-art analysis related to the contributions of this study. First, Section 2.1 presents the basic principles of evolutionary multi-objective optimization. Then, Section 2.2 describes the use of such optimization in the design of NFCs. Finally, Section 2.3 provides the positioning of this research with respect to the state-of-the-art.

2.1. Multi-Objective Optimization

Engineering design commonly involves decisions under conflicting objectives. In such situations, improving performance in one objective may deteriorate the performance in the other objectives. To make decisions based on the understanding of the performance trade-offs, more than two decades ago, engineers started to apply Pareto-based optimization [6]. This type of optimization results in a set of Pareto-optimal solutions and their associated Pareto-front in the objective space. This allows a posteriori solution selection based on assessable performance tradeoffs that are exposed by the obtained front. The following highlights the fundamentals of Pareto optimization.

Pareto-based multi-objective optimization is commonly described as a vector optimization problem with M objectives to be optimized. Without the loss of generality, the problem can be defined as a minimization problem as follows:

$$\min_{x \in X} F(x) \qquad (1)$$

where X is the set of feasible solutions and $F = [F_1(x), F_2(x), \ldots, F_M(x)]^T$ is the performance vector.

Let two solutions of (1), a and b, be associated with $F(a) = [F_1(a), \ldots, F_M(a)]^T$ and $F(b) = [F_1(b), \ldots, F_M(b)]^T$, respectively. Then, a is said to dominate b, denoted by $a \preccurlyeq b$, if the following condition is satisfied:

$$\forall i \in \{1, \ldots, M\}, F_i(a) \leq F_i(b) \text{ and } \exists j \in \{1, \ldots, M\} \text{ such that } F_j(a) < F_j(b) \qquad (2)$$

Without loss of generality, for a given minimization problem, the Pareto-optimal-Set (PS) is the set of all Non-Dominated Solutions (NDS) of the feasible set X. Namely, a solution $a \in X$ is called Pareto-optimal if and only if there is no solution $b \in X$ for which $b \preccurlyeq a$. The set of performance vectors corresponding to the aforementioned set is known as the Pareto-Front (PF). Solving (1) means finding the PS and the associated PF.

Usually, there is no analytical solution to real-life Multi-objective Optimization Problems (MOPs) [12]. Therefore, computational techniques are commonly employed to obtain at least good approximations of the PS and PF. Dedicated evolutionary algorithms for solving MOPs are termed Multi-Objective Evolutionary Algorithms (MOEAs). MOEAs, including NSGA-II [13], which is used in this study, follow the ideas of natural evolution, such as selection, recombination, and mutation, aiming to evolve a population of solutions towards the Pareto-optimal solutions. With over two decades of proven success, MOEAs are the leading algorithms for solving MOPs. This is evident from reviews such as in [12,14,15].

2.2. Neuro-Fuzzy Systems and Control

Fuzzy Inference Systems (FISs) are computational frameworks that implement fuzzy reasoning to make decisions. The mathematical basis, which was founded by L. Zadeh (1965), defines linguistic variables, fuzzy sets, and logical operators extending crisp set theory [16]. Fuzzy sets are defined using Membership Functions (MFs), while Fuzzy Rules (FRs) express relationships between such sets. The structure and parameters of FRs and MFs determine the mapping of given inputs to outputs. There are at least two main differences between mapping by an FIS as compared with mapping by a Neural Network (NN). First, an FIS can be formed based on expert knowledge, while an NN commonly requires data. Second, an FIS is interpretable, while an NN is considered to be a black box. The main advantage of using an NN is that the mapping can be learned and adapted. A Neuro-Fuzzy (NF) approach synergistically combines the main features of FISs and NNs. The advantages of the NF approach over the FIS approach have created new research and application opportunities [3,17–19]. As evident from the literature, over the years, both FISs and NF systems have been applied to control design [20–22]. The common approach to tuning NF controllers is supervised learning based on some data (e.g., [23,24]). However, the design of NFCs can be based on evolutionary techniques [25] to reach the desired optimum/optima without adhering to any data (e.g., [26]).

Using the concept of Pareto optimization for the design of controllers is not new (see review [27]). However, applying Pareto-based optimization/adaptation to the design of neuro-fuzzy systems is rare (e.g., [4,28,29]). Several studies tried to find Pareto-optimal fuzzy controllers with static structure, e.g., [30–32], whereas in [26], such studies were extended to also include the rule structure.

2.3. Positioning of This Research

The idea of defining and solving meta-problems for obtaining specialized and non-specialized controllers has been recently suggested in [11]. The current study is the first study to use this idea in the context of evolutionary neuro-fuzzy control.

Applying STO to solving neuro-fuzzy control problems is not new [33–40]. However, in this study, several uncommon/unique aspects concerning the use of STO for such problems should be noted. First, commonly in STO studies on solving neuro-fuzzy control problems, the knowledge that is transferred is data, which is used in the context of supervised learning (e.g., [33–35]). In contrast, the current study applies a different type of knowledge that is transferred, namely, a genetic type. Second, the majority of STO studies on solving neuro-fuzzy control problems are based on using just one source problem (e.g., [37]), while the current study is based on the use of multiple source problems. Moreover, in contrast to the current study, to the best of our knowledge, no study on NF systems concerns source problems that are defined as MOPs. To substantiate this claim, we conducted the following Scopus search:

(TITLE-ABS-KEY ((neuro-fuzzy OR "neuro fuzzy"))) AND ("source problem" OR "source task" OR sequential) AND ("transfer learning" OR "transfer optimization"). A manual check of all the resulting documents revealed no study that deals with source problems that are defined as MOPs.

While the above positioning is restricted to STO studies that are concerned with neuro-fuzzy problems, to the best of our knowledge, this study contains a major difference with respect to any STO study. We claim that this study is the first to raise and investigate the hypothesis that the use of edge solutions of multi-objective source problems for genetic transfer is preferred over the use of the center solutions. To substantiate this novelty assertion, we conducted the following Scopus search:

(TITLE-ABS-KEY ((Pareto OR multi-objective OR "multi objective") AND transfer)) AND ("transfer learning" OR "transfer optimization") AND (sequential OR "source problem" OR "source task"). A manual check of all the resulting documents revealed no study that concerns the suggested hypothesis.

For convenience, Table 1 summarizes the positioning results according to the main research attributes as well as the application focus of the related studies. In the table, X/V refers to non-existing/existing features, respectively.

Table 1. Positioning Table with respect to STO Neuro-Fuzzy studies.

Related Study	Evolutionary Driven	Pareto-Based Source	Application
Aouf et al., 2018 [33]	X	X	Indoor robotics
Juang & Bui 2019 [34]	X	X	Indoor robotics
Sell & Coupland 2015 [35]	X	X	Classification
Fouladvand et al., 2015 [36]	X	X	Indoor robotics
Chou & Juang 2018 [37]	V	X	Indoor robotics
Ferdaus et al., 2019a [38]	V	X	Aerial vehicles
Ferdaus et al., 2019b [39]	X	X	Aerial vehicles
Ferdaus et al., 2018 [40]	V	X	Aerial vehicles
Current study	V	V	Offroad robotics

3. Problem Description and Solution Approach

This paper deals with using transfer optimization to solve a target problem, which is defined as a set of SOPs in Section 3.1. In addition to the target problem definition, this section describes the proposed research methodology. The main steps of the methodology are described in Figure 1. First, starting from the left side of the figure, several MOPs are generated, which serve as source problems. Next, each source MOP is solved separately using MOEA, as described in Section 3.2. Solving each of the source problems results in a set of non-dominated solutions. Then, the obtained solutions are used to form an initial population, which is to be used for solving the target problem. This step, which is the knowledge extraction step, is detailed in Section 3.3. In this study, we examine two alternatives for generating the initial population. Finally, each of the extracted populations is used as an initial population to solve the target problem. To evaluate the obtained results, the target problem is also solved using an initial random population. In this study, the well-known NSGA-II [13] is used to solve both source and target problems. However, it should be noted that many alternative MOEAs can be used. In case the considered MOPs would involve a large number of objectives, then it is recommended to use an algorithm that was designed to cope with more than three objectives (see [41]).

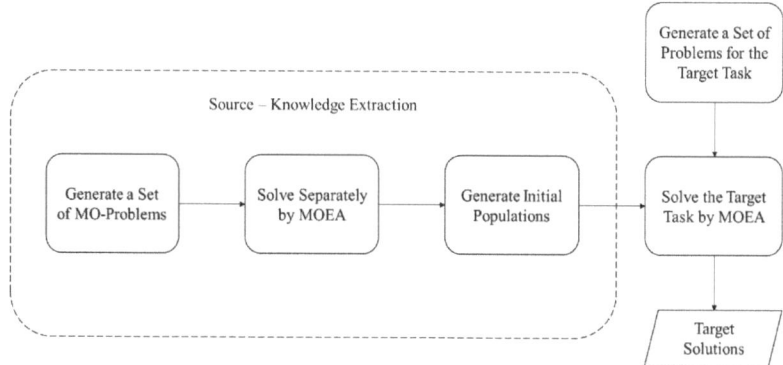

Figure 1. Proposed transfer optimization methodology.

3.1. Target Meta-Problem

The considered target problem is a multi-objective fuzzy control meta-problem in which each objective is associated with finding an optimal controller for a specific task. This meta-problem is defined as follows. Let $P_T = \{P_T^1, P_T^2, \ldots, P_T^{N_T}\}$ be a given set of N_T fuzzy control problems. Then, the target meta-problem is formulated as follows:

$$\min_{a \in X_T} \left[f(P_T^1; a), f(P_T^2; a), \ldots, f(P_T^{N_T}; a) \right] \quad (3)$$

where X_T is the feasible set of fuzzy controllers for the target meta-problem, and f is a scalar objective function that is used to evaluate the controllers' performance. The main goal is to search for a set of non-specialized controllers, i.e., controllers that evolved to provide a successful behavior in all of the given set of control problems, following the approach in [11].

3.2. Source Problems and Their Solutions

In this study, each source problem is formulated as a MOP. Let $P_s = \{P_s^1, P_s^2, \ldots, P_s^{N_s}\}$ be a given set of N_s source fuzzy control problems. Each of these problems is formulated as follows:

$$\min_{a \in X_{si}} \left[f_1(P_s^i; a), f_2(P_s^i; a), \ldots, f_M(P_s^i; a) \right] \quad (4)$$

where X_{si} is the set of feasible fuzzy controllers of the ith source problem. Each fuzzy controller is evaluated using scalar objective functions, $f_1, \ldots, f_M$. Assuming no prior objective preferences, the solution of (4) results in a set of non-dominated solutions for each of the source problems.

3.3. Knowledge Extraction and Research Hypothesis

This study deals with the STO of NFCs. As mentioned in the introduction section, two types of knowledge extraction techniques are proposed and studied here. The first type involves an initial population of edge controllers, i.e., controllers whose performance vectors are located close to the edges of the obtained fronts. The second type of knowledge extraction is based on an initial population of center controllers, i.e., controllers whose performance vectors are located close to the line connecting the ideal and the nadir points. For a given front, the ideal point is a vector of the best objective values, whereas the nadir point is a vector of the worst objective values of the considered front.

This study deals with bi-objective source problems. Hence, the following presents a step-by-step procedure of the knowledge extraction approach as implemented in this study. Given a non-dominated set (NDS) of solutions and their performance vectors (PVs) of a source problem, then:

1. Define the number of transferred edge-controllers ($2n_{ec}$), such that $2n_{ec} \ll |NDS|$.
2. For each edge:
   a. Find the edge PV and store the associated solutions in a set of extracted edge controllers (EEC).
   b. Select the $n_{ec} - 1$ controllers that their PVs are the closest to the edge PV and add them to EEC.
3. Define the number of transferred center controllers (n_{cc}), such that $n_{cc} \ll |NDS|$.
4. Find the line connecting the ideal and the nadir points.
5. Select the n_{cc} controllers for which their PVs are the closest to the line found in 4 and store them in a set of extracted center controllers (ECC).

Repeat this process for all source problems and create the union of the EECs (UEECs) and the union of the ECCs (UECCs). Each of these unions contains extracted knowledge as needed to investigate the suggested hypotheses, as presented below.

Figure 2 illustrates these two types of controllers. In the figure, an example of normalized PVs is shown and marked as dots. Assuming that $2n_{ec} = n_{cc} = 4$, the PVs of the EECs are marked by circles, whereas squares mark the PVs of ECCs.

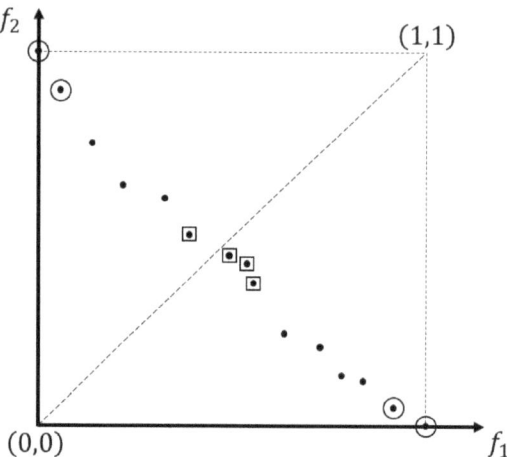

Figure 2. Knowledge extraction illustration.

The main research question that this study aims to solve is which of the proposed two types of knowledge extraction techniques is preferred from a transferability viewpoint. It is hypothesized that the edge controllers are preferred over the center ones. This hypothesis is intuitively justified by the expected higher diversity of the edge controllers. In addition, a secondary hypothesis is examined, which suggests that each of the proposed types of knowledge extraction techniques is better than the case of using random initial population, i.e., the case of no knowledge transfer.

4. Numerical Study

This section is organized as follows. First, Section 4.1 provides a detailed description of the source and target problems. Section 4.2 describes the applied NFC. Then, the comparison methods are given in Section 4.3. Next, in Section 4.4, the experimental setup is described. Finally, the obtained results and their analysis are provided in Section 4.5.

4.1. Source and Target Problems

The considered numerical study is based on simulations of a theoretical cart and environment interaction model. The study involves a set of constrained motion source control problems of a point-mass cart, and an additional set of target scenarios, as presented in the following. In this study, the cart is assumed to travel horizontally along a linear path. The linear path is defined by start and goal points. Each path is characterized by a friction function and a speed limitation function. These functions could be viewed as representing various types of motion difficulties as expected in rugged terrains. The equation of motion of the considered cart model and the involved constraints are:

$$\begin{cases} \ddot{x}(t) = -\frac{c(x)}{m}\dot{x}(t) + \frac{1}{m}U(t) \\ \text{s.t.} \quad |\dot{x}(t)| \leq V_O(x(t)) \leq V_{max} \\ \quad\quad |U(t)| \leq U_{max} \end{cases} \quad (5)$$

where $x(t)$ is the position of the cart, m is the mass of the cart, $0 \leq c(x) \leq 1$ is a damping coefficient as a function of the position $x(t)$, $U(t)$ is the control force, V_{max} is the speed limit of the cart, and U_{max} is the saturation value of the control force. In addition, the path imposes a speed constraint function $V_O(x)$. An interaction between the cart and a given path is termed here as a scenario.

Both the target and the source optimization problems, which are defined in Equations (6) and (7), use the following two cost functions. The first function reflects a desire to find NFCs that bring the cart from the initial position x_0 to the goal point x_g as fast as possible, whereas the second one corresponds to the case of safe motion behavior. These are defined as follows:

$$J_{fast} = 1 - \frac{T_{min}}{T_g} \text{ where } T_{min} = \frac{|x_g - x_0|}{V_{max}} \tag{6}$$

$$J_{safe} = \int_0^{T_g} |c(x(t)) \cdot \dot{x}(t)| dt \tag{7}$$

where T_g is the time it takes to reach the goal point, using the considered NFC, and T_{min} is the time it would take to reach the goal if the entire motion involves the maximal speed limit. During the evolutionary process, a controller is considered numerically feasible if the following constraints are met, where T_{max} is the simulation time limit.

$$\begin{array}{c} \exists T_g < T_{max} \text{ s.t } x(T_g) = x_g \\ |\dot{x}(t)| < V_O(x(t)) \forall t < T_{max} \end{array} \tag{8}$$

Figure 3 presents the $c(x)$ and $V_O(x)$ functions that are used in the source problems scenarios, whereas Figures 4 and 5 present them for the first and the second set of the target problems, respectively. In these figures, the solid and the dashed curves present $c(x)$ and $V_O(x)$, respectively. It should be noted that the functions used in the source and target problems were randomly created. In particular, for each $c(x)$, a random number of Gaussian functions was selected, and their parameters were also randomly selected. Any Gaussian that exceeded the value of 0.8 was truncated. The $V_O(x)$ functions were created as a function of the resulting $c(x)$ functions.

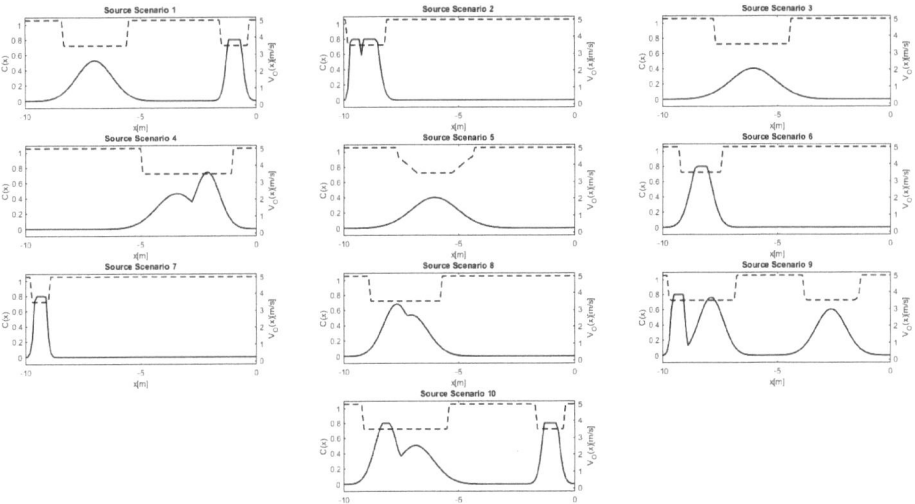

Figure 3. Source control problems.

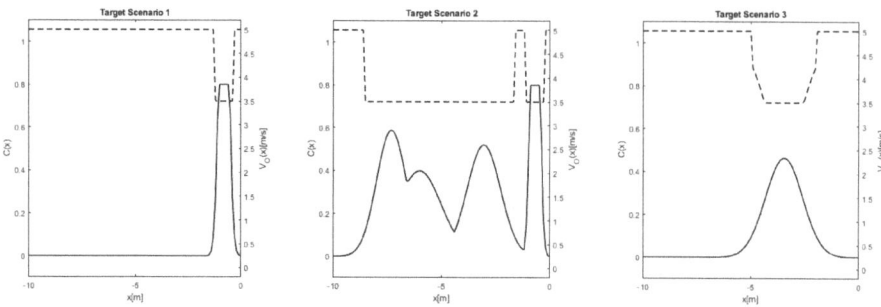

Figure 4. Target set 1.

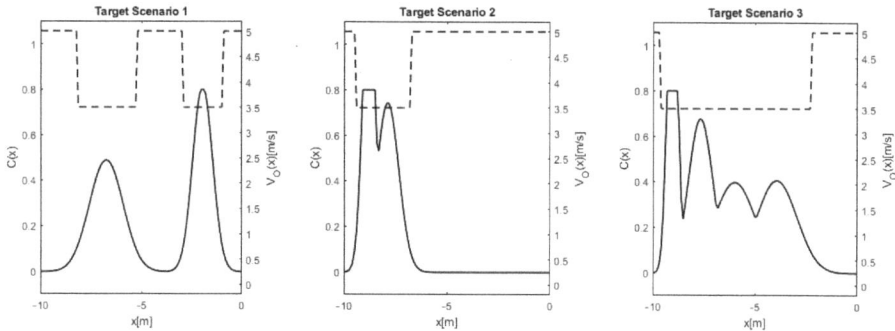

Figure 5. Target set 2.

In this study, each of the target sets is composed of three different scenarios, as given in Figures 4 and 5. For each target set, three alternative MOPs are examined. These are defined as follows:

$$MOP_1 : \min_{a \in X_T} \left[J_{fast}(P_T^1; a) + J_{safe}(P_T^1; a), J_{fast}(P_T^2; a) + J_{safe}(P_T^2; a), J_{fast}(P_T^3; a) + J_{safe}(P_T^3; a) \right]$$

$$MOP_2 : \min_{a \in X_T} \left[J_{fast}(P_T^1; a), J_{fast}(P_T^2; a), J_{fast}(P_T^3; a) \right] \quad (9)$$

$$MOP_3 : \min_{a \in X_T} \left[J_{safe}(P_T^1; a), J_{safe}(P_T^2; a), J_{safe}(P_T^3; a) \right]$$

The three alternative MOPs are defined in accordance with the knowledge extraction techniques (see Section 3.3). MOP_1 corresponds to the center controllers, whereas MOP_2 and MOP_3 correspond to the edge controllers, i.e., to the fast and safe controllers, respectively. In total, we examine six target problems, i.e., three alternative MOPs, each with two target sets. These three MOP definitions are expected to encourage three types of behaviors. Namely, MOP_2 and MOP_3 are expected to encourage courageous behavior and cautious behavior, respectively, whereas MOP_1 is expected to encourage intermediate behavior. In the context of this study, it should be noted that these terminologies correspond not only to the speed but also to the level of motion difficulty as presented in $c(x)$.

The ith bi-objective source problem is given by:

$$\min_{a \in X_S^i} \left[J_{fast}(P_S^i; a), J_{safe}(P_S^i; a) \right] \quad (10)$$

where X_S^i is the feasible set of fuzzy controllers, as described in Equation (8).

4.2. Fuzzy Controllers

The cart is controlled by a neuro-fuzzy inference system. The controller receives three inputs, including the relative location of the goal point $e(t)$, the normalized velocity of the cart $v(t)$, and an effective damping coefficient $c_{eff}(t)$. Each of these inputs is mapped into the range of $[-1, 1]$, as given in Equations (11)–(13), respectively. The NFC maps these inputs into a force $U(t)$ to be applied to the cart, as described in Equation (5).

$$e(t) = \begin{cases} 1 & \frac{x_g - x(t)}{x_g - x_0} > 1 \\ -1 & \frac{x_g - x(t)}{x_g - x_0} < -1 \\ \frac{x_g - x(t)}{x_g - x_0} & \text{otherwise} \end{cases} \quad (11)$$

$$v(t) = \frac{\dot{x}(t)}{V_{max}} \quad (12)$$

$$c_{eff}(t) = -1 + c(x(t)) + c(x(t) + dx) \quad (13)$$

where dx is a pre-defined number, which has been set as 0.1 m.

In the current implementation, the NFC is based on zero-order Takagi-Sugeno (TS) rules [42]. The main reason for choosing TS rules, in which the rules result in crisp outputs, is that it avoids the need for defuzzification. Selecting zero-order TS rules reduces the number of search parameters for the evolutionary search; hence, it results in a major reduction in the required computational resources. Each input belongs to one of three fuzzy sets. These fuzzy sets are based on the general Gaussian membership function. This results in 27 combinations of the TS rules, where each rule is considered as follows:

$$\text{If } e(t) \text{ is } A_i \text{ and } v(t) \text{ is } B_j \text{ and } c_{eff}(t) \text{ is } C_k \text{ then } U(t) = U_f \quad (14)$$

where $i, j, k \in \{1, 2, 3\}$ are the indices of the inputs' fuzzy sets A_i, B_j, C_k, respectively. $f \in \{1, \ldots, 27\}$ is the index of the output $|U_f| \leq U_{max}$. The final crisp conclusion is calculated as the average of the rule conclusions.

The decision variables of the optimization problem include the parameters of A_i, B_j, C_k, and U_f. Given that each general Gaussian function has two parameters, and the total number of rules is 27, then the total number of decision variables results in 9 (input sets) · 2 (parameters) + 27 (rules) = 45 variables.

4.3. Comparison Methods

In this study, the substantiations of the research hypotheses are achieved by comparing the results of solving the target meta-problems as obtained by each of the knowledge extraction techniques and by the random initialization technique (see Section 3). In particular, two indicators are used to evaluate the transfer capabilities of the compared techniques based on the Hyper-Volume (HV) metric [43]. The first indicator, which is inspired by the Asymptotic Performance (AP) measure [44], calculates the final value of the HV for each of the compared approaches. The second indicator, which is based on the Time-to-Threshold (ToT) measure [44], is calculated as the number of generations it took HV to reach a threshold. In addition, the obtained best performance in each scenario of the target meta-problem is also compared.

Given the stochastic nature of the applied MOEA, 31 runs were conducted for each approach to make statistical inferences. As commonly done when comparing MOEAs, the medians and Inter-Quartile Ranges (IQRs) are used rather than the means and the standard deviations. For the statistical comparisons, the Wilcoxon rank-sum test was applied for each pair of compared techniques.

4.4. Experimental Setup

Here, NSGA-II [13], which is a well-known MOEA, is applied to solving the optimization problems presented in Equations (9) and (10). The run parameters that were applied for solving each of the source MOPs and the target MOPs are summarized in Table 2. In this study, the applied stopping criterion of NSGA-II is the total number of generations. It should be noted that the run parameters for the source problems were selected to ensure convergence in all source problems. To deal with the constraint problem, a penalty approach is applied. Here, a non-feasible controller is penalized by adding a high penalty value, which practically serves as a death penalty. It should be noted that the population size for the target meta-problem is a result of the applied knowledge extraction technique (see Section 4.5.1).

Table 2. Run parameters.

Parameter	Signal Source	Target
Number of generations	300	200
Population size	100	60
Penalty value	100	
Weight Mutation (WM) mechanism	Polynomial	
WM parameters (probability, distribution index)	(0.2, 15)	
Weight Crossover (WC) mechanism	SBX	
WC parameters (probability, distribution index)	(0.8, 20)	
Simulation time limit T_{max}	20 [s]	
Cart mass m	1 [kg]	
Force saturation value U_{max}	50 [N]	
Starting point x_0	-10 [m]	
Starting Velocity $\dot{x}(0)$	0 [m/s]	
Goal point x_g	0 [m]	
Speed limit V_{max}	5 [m/s]	

4.5. Experimental Results and Analyses

This section, in which the results are presented, is organized as follows. First, in Section 4.5.1, typical results obtained by solving one of the ten source control problems are presented, including the knowledge extraction from the presented results. Then, the results of the target meta-problems are presented and analyzed in Section 4.5.2.

4.5.1. Demonstration of Knowledge Extraction

In this section, typical results are presented based on solving a randomly selected source control problem. Figure 6 shows the approximated Pareto front as obtained by solving the problem in Equation (10).

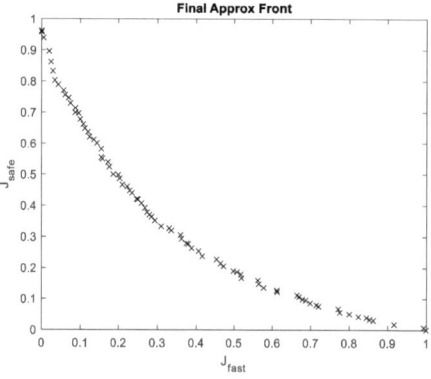

Figure 6. Approximated front for the selected source problem.

In the figure, each point represents the performance vector of a non-dominated NFC. As expected, the tradeoff between the objectives is evident. This tradeoff is further shown in Figure 7. In Figure 7, the behaviors of the edge controllers are presented. The left solid curves show the position and the velocity versus time for the fastest NFC, and the right solid curves show these behaviors for the safest one. The dashed curves show the corresponding damping coefficient and speed limit. It is evident from Figure 7 that the velocity, as obtained by applying the fastest NFC, quickly reaches the vicinity of the speed limit. In this case, the goal point is reached in less than 2.5 s. In contrast, the application of the safest NFC results in a much lower velocity, and the goal-point is reached after about twenty seconds.

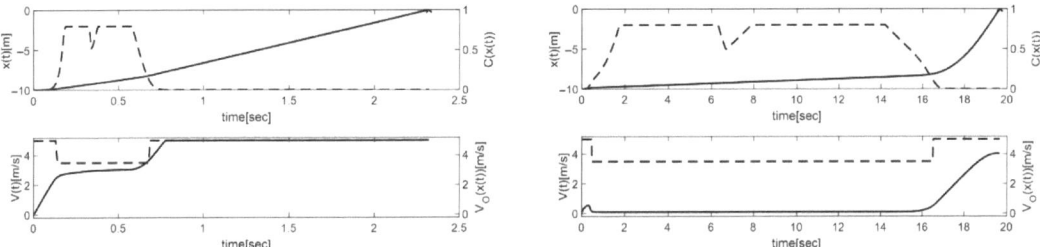

Figure 7. Controller behavior: fastest controller (**left**), safest controller (**right**).

The convergence curve of the run of the presented case is shown in Figure 8. This figure shows the HV measure at each generation. It is suggested from the figure that convergence is reached.

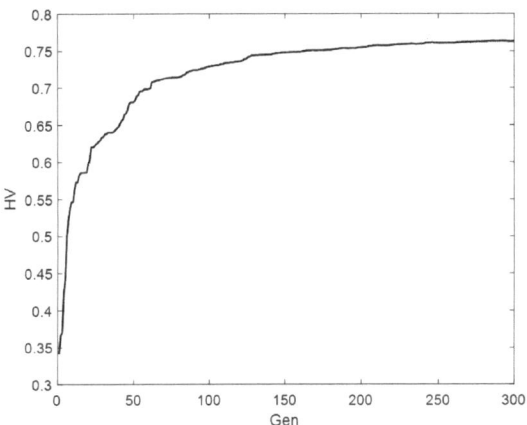

Figure 8. Convergence curve for the presented source problem.

Following the method presented in Section 3.3, the knowledge extraction from the results of solving the presented source problem is presented in Figure 9. In the left plot, the extraction of center controllers, which are marked as squares, is presented. The circles in the right plot present the selected edge-controllers. It should be noted that for this demonstration, six controllers were selected from each source problem for each of the controller types.

Given that ten source problems are used in this study, and that each of these problems provides six edge controllers and six center controllers, then the population size is sixty for solving each of the corresponding meta-problems.

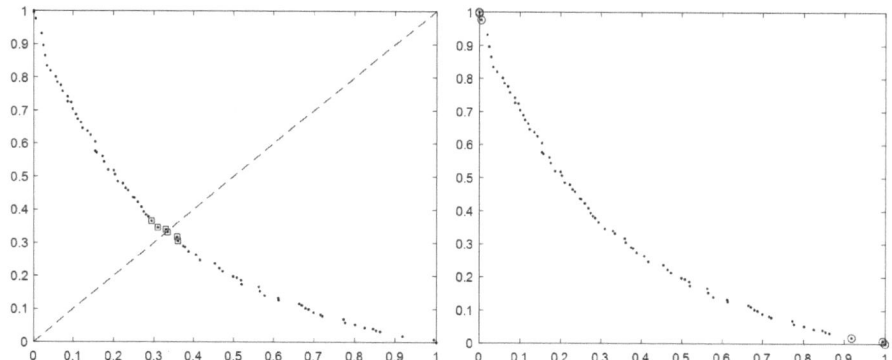

Figure 9. Knowledge extraction: (**left**) center controllers, (**right**) edge controllers.

4.5.2. Results and Analysis of the Target Meta-Problems

Tables 3 and 4 summarize the results of the ToT, AP, and the best performances in each of the objectives for target sets 1 and 2, respectively. For each method, the tables outline the medians and IQRs of the indicators. In the tables, the superior values are marked in bold numbers. In general, better medians are obtained when using the edge controller for the initialization as compared to either using the center controllers or the random controllers. In addition, better results were obtained by the center-controllers than with the random ones.

Table 3. Transfer capabilities comparison—target set 1.

Problem	Indicator	Random	Center	Edge
MOP_1 Target set 1	ToT	33 (±20)	12 (±7.5)	**3 (±2)**
	AP	0.88124 (±0.0601)	0.91951 (±0.0314)	**0.93812 (±0.0107)**
	Best-F1	0.00829 (±0.0079)	**0.00230 (±0.0018)**	0.00355 (±0.0011)
	Best-F2	0.01216 (±0.0098)	0.00258 (±0.0012)	**0.00127 (±0.0001)**
	Best-F3	0.00546 (±0.0022)	0.00493 (±0.0020)	**0.00375 (±0.0010)**
MOP_2 Target set 1	ToT	24 (±197)	**2 (±2)**	2 (±149)
	AP	0.90159 (±0.944)	0.95214 (±0.094)	**0.96308 (±0.730)**
	Best-F1	0.03682 (±1.071)	**0.02305 (±0.023)**	0.01784 (±0.816)
	Best-F2	0.01970 (±1.094)	0.00620 (±0.037)	**0.00387 (±0.825)**
	Best-F3	0.02136 (±1.087)	0.01029 (±0.018)	**0.00849 (±0.820)**
MOP_3 Target set 1	ToT	43 (±150)	8 (±148)	**5 (±149)**
	AP	0.75407 (±0.589)	0.79441 (±0.640)	**0.85067 (±0.643)**
	Best-F1	0.00830 (±0.063)	**0.00425 (±0.183)**	0.00596 (±0.085)
	Best-F2	0.01917 (±0.067)	0.00570 (±0.210)	**0.00183 (±0.096)**
	Best-F3	0.00492 (±0.032)	0.01093 (±0.466)	**0.00799 (±0.048)**

Table 4. Transfer capabilities comparison—target set 2.

Problem	Indicator	Random	Center	Edge
MOP_1 Target set 2	ToT	24 (±197)	**2 (±2)**	2 (±149)
	AP	0.21958 (±0.387)	0.67058 (±0.236)	**0.70545 (±0.116)**
	Best-F1	0.00568 (±0.007)	0.00258 (±0.003)	**0.00081 (±0.001)**
	Best-F2	0.00480 (±0.003)	**0.00135 (±0.001)**	0.00151 (±0.001)
	Best-F3	0.00369 (±0.005)	0.00220 (±0.002)	**0.00082 (±0.001)**
MOP_2 Target set 2	ToT	4 (±163)	**1 (±1)**	2 (±150)
	AP	0.95268 (±0.780)	0.96454 (±0.077)	**0.97688 (±0.770)**
	Best-F1	0.00818 (±0.836)	0.00625 (±0.020)	**0.00398 (±0.831)**
	Best-F2	0.01925 (±0.828)	**0.01686 (±0.014)**	0.01099 (±0.831)
	Best-F3	0.00772 (±0.836)	0.00648 (±0.0236)	**0.00475 (±0.830)**
MOP_3 Target set 2	ToT	129 (±122)	15 (±9)	**13 (±9)**
	AP	0.61719 (±0.178)	**0.73587 (±0.080)**	0.73441 (±0.057)
	Best-F1	0.00525 (±0.003)	0.00293 (±0.002)	**0.00093 (±0.001)**
	Best-F2	0.00571 (±0.003)	**0.00374 (±0.002)**	0.00462 (±0.001)
	Best-F3	0.00445 (±0.004)	0.00246 (±0.001)	**0.00145 (±0.001)**

The results of the rank-sum Wilcoxon test are presented in Table 5, which allows statistical inference. In the table, + is assigned for comparison in which the statement is statistically correct, − is assigned for cases where the opposite statement is statically correct, and ≈ is assigned for cases where the obtained p-values are larger than the significance level, i.e., the compared cases are statistically equivalent. For example, the entry 3/1/2 in the 1st row and column of the table means that the statement that using the edge controllers was better than using the center ones was found to be correct in three out of the six meta problems, etc. The last row of the table provides the accumulated numbers with respect to all the indicators.

Table 5. Statistical comparisons.

Indicator	Edge Better Than Center	Edge Better Than Random	Center Better Than Random
ToT (+/−/≈)	3/1/2	5/0/1	6/0/0
AP (+/−/≈)	5/0/1	5/0/1	4/1/1
Best-F1 (+/−/≈)	4/2/0	6/0/0	5/0/1
Best-F2 (+/−/≈)	3/1/2	5/0/1	5/0/1
Best-F3 (+/−/≈)	5/0/1	5/0/1	5/0/1
Total (+/−/≈)	20/4/6	26/0/4	25/1/4

As shown in the table, when comparing initialization using the edge controllers, as opposed to using the center controllers, there are 20 comparisons in which using the edge controllers was better than using the center controllers. The opposite statement was found to be correct in 4 comparisons and no statistical superiority was found in 6 of the 30 comparisons. These observations suggest that, in general, edge controllers are better than the center-controllers for the considered meta-problems in terms of the obtained values of most indicators. These findings substantiate the first hypothesis of this study.

When comparing initialization by the edge controllers with that of the random controllers, the accumulated results show that there was no comparison in which the latter controllers were superior. When comparing initialization by the center controllers with that of the random controllers, there was only one case out of the 30 in which the random ones were superior. These findings substantiate the second hypothesis of this study.

4.5.3. Detailed Demonstration of the Transferability Results

The following presents some details of the results and analysis for the case of MOP_1 with the first target set. The boxplots in Figure 10 show the statistical results of the HV metric, as obtained by each initialization. The left plot in the figure presents the results achieved by the edge controller initialization, the results of center controller initialization are presented in the center plot, and the right plot shows the result of the random initialization. The results of this demonstration suggest that the best results are achieved by the edge controller initialization. It can be observed that the edge results are better in terms of higher median values as well as lower variance and outliers. It is also evident that the center controller initialization is superior to those achieved when a random initialization is used.

To make statistical inferences, the rank-sum test, with a significance level of 0.05, is applied for each comparison. Table 6 outlines p-values as obtained by the test. Bold results represent comparisons where initialization by the edge controllers is statistically superior, whereas underlined results are for comparisons where initialization by the center controllers is superior.

The obtained results show that edge controllers are better than the center controllers for the considered meta-problem in terms of the obtained values of most indicators. In addition, the results indicate that both the center and edge controllers are better than the random ones for the considered problem. These findings substantiate the two hypotheses of this study (see Section 3.3).

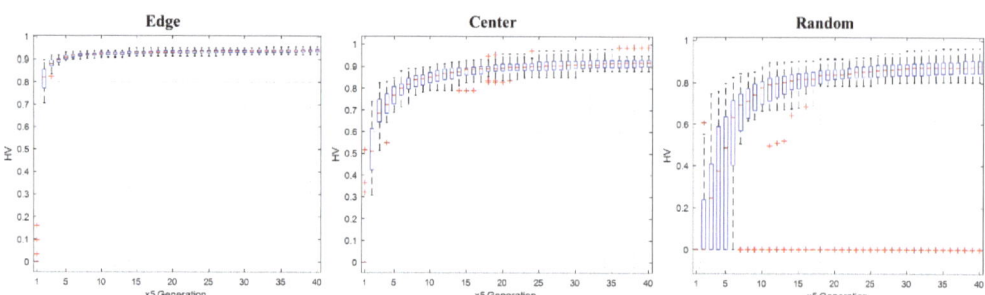

Figure 10. Statistical results: HV versus generations. Initialization by the edge-, center- and random-controllers, in the (**left**), (**center**), and (**right**) panels, respectively.

Table 6. Statistical tests (*p*-values).

Indicator	Center vs. Edge	Random vs. Edge	Random vs. Center
ToT	2×10^{-11}	1×10^{-11}	5×10^{-9}
AP	8×10^{-5}	3×10^{-10}	4×10^{-6}
Best-F1	7×10^{-4}	7×10^{-9}	4×10^{-9}
Best-F2	1×10^{-7}	1×10^{-11}	9×10^{-11}
Best-F3	7×10^{-5}	2×10^{-4}	4×10^{-1}

4.5.4. Demonstration of the Obtained Behaviors

This section provides discussion and analysis regarding the obtained behaviors by solving each of the target meta-problems, as defined in Section 4.1. Figures 11 and 12 present the behaviors of randomly selected NFCs as obtained by solving the three MOPs for target set 1 and target set 2, respectively. Each row of the figures provides the results for a specific scenario of the target sets as obtained by the three MOPs. The solid curve in each of the figures shows the velocity versus time, whereas the dashed curves show the corresponding speed limit.

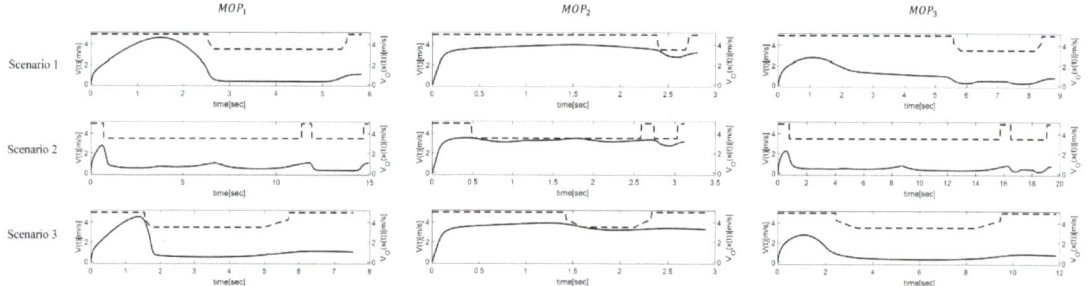

Figure 11. Motion Behavior—Target Set 1.

Considering the results of MOP_2 (in the middle panels), as compared with those of solving MOP_1 and MOP_3, it is observed that the obtained NFCs provide higher velocities without any violation of the speed limits. As expected from the definition of MOP_2, its solutions exhibit safe yet courageous behaviors. Furthermore, when comparing the results of solving MOP_1 and MOP_3, it can be observed that the solutions of MOP_3 resulted in slower motions. As expected from the definitions of these two problems, MOP_3 exhibits the most cautious behaviors, while MOP_1 exhibits intermediate behaviors.

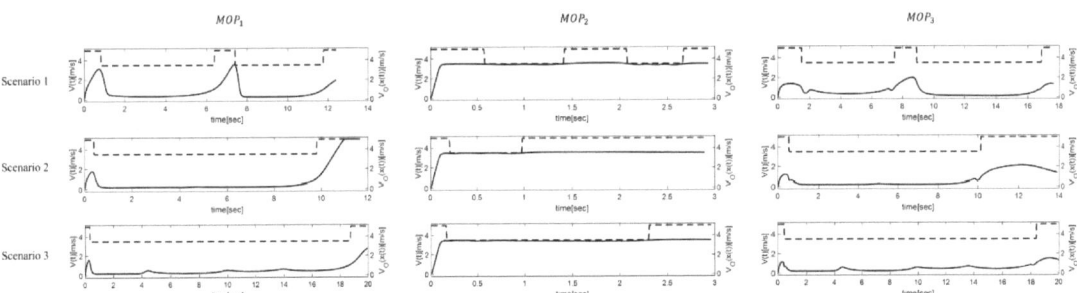

Figure 12. Motion Behavior—Target set 2.

The following provides a statistical comparison between the NFCs of MOP_2 and those of MOP_3, which aims to highlight the clear difference between cautious and courageous behaviors. In particular, the presented statistics are obtained for the case of using initialization by the edge NFCs, using 31 runs per each of the MOPs as applied per each scenario of each of the target sets. The statistics are provided with respect to an average-time to reach the goal point at each of the presented scenarios. Table 7 summarizes the medians and IQRs of the average times. Each of these averages is calculated as follows. For each of the runs, the average is taken over the entire set of the obtained approximated Pareto optimal NFCs (of each MOP and target set). To obtain this average time, first, each of these NFCs of the run is applied to the considered scenario to find its resulting time to reach the goal point. Next, these times are used to find the average time for the run of the considered scenario. In addition, the last row of Table 7 provides the accumulated results of the Wilcoxon rank-sum tests over the six scenarios. As expected, these results clearly show that the average times as obtained using the definition of MOP_2 are statistically shorter than those obtained by MOP_3.

Table 7. Behavior comparison of time to goal point.

Target Set	Scenario	Edge Initialization	
		MOP_2	MOP_3
1	1	8.140 (±0.66)	15.73 (±4.70)
	2	18.70 (±1.09)	19.97 (±2.40)
	3	9.650 (±0.80)	16.70 (±4.28)
2	1	17.45 (±0.52)	19.02 (±0.32)
	2	15.35 (±0.35)	17.30 (±0.60)
	3	19.95 (±0.06)	19.99 (±0.02)
$(+/-/\approx)$			(6/0/0)

In summary, the time-to-goal results in Table 7 further emphasize the differences between the outcomes of courageous and cautious behaviors. While not presented here, similar conclusions about the time to the goal point were obtained not just for the initialization by the edge controllers but also by the other two types, including initialization by center controllers and by random controllers. Namely, each of the initialization types resulted in the expected behavior as associated with the considered MOP.

5. Summary and Conclusions

This study concerns the evolutionary search for generic neuro-fuzzy motion controllers in conjunction with the use of sequential transfer optimization. The search aims to evolve near optimal neuro-fuzzy controllers that can operate in a variety of scenarios. Three types of target meta-problems are defined, which differ by the expected motion behavior, including cautious, intermediate, and courageous behaviors. Each of these meta-problems is defined as a multi-objective problem, where each objective is associated with optimizing the performance in a particular scenario.

A unique kind of sequential transfer optimization is proposed that involves multiple source problems, where each of the source problems is defined and solved as a bi-objective problem. The use of multiple source problems aims to diversify the source solutions with respect to scenarios, whereas the use of the two objectives aims to diversify the source solutions with respect to the obtained behaviors. This kind of multiple-source problem raises the dilemma of which of the source solutions should be transferred to solve the target problems. The main research hypothesis is that solutions with performances near the edges of the obtained approximated bi-objective Pareto fronts provide better transferability as compared with those that are associated with performances near the center of the obtained fronts.

Given the stochastic nature of the applied search technique, a statistical numerical study was conducted. First, ten source problems were defined and solved. Next, a total of six target meta-problems were defined. Each of these target problems was solved using three types of initializations including random initializations and two additional types in accordance with the aforementioned hypothesis.

The main contribution of this study is that it substantiates the hypothesis that edge controllers should be preferred over the center ones. This has a pragmatic impact on applying sequential transfer optimization to the development of neuro-fuzzy controllers for the considered motion control type of problems. This is because the proposed approach produces useful information out of the large and diverse knowledge that is created by solving many Pareto-based source problems. As shown in this study, and similar studies, using selected solutions from source problems to serve as an initial population to solve a target problem is much more efficient as compared with the traditional use of a random initial population. In addition, this study shows that the proposed approach is useful for finding neuro-fuzzy controllers that produce different motion behaviors when operating in various environments with different motion difficulties.

This study assumed that experts select the source problems based on their cognitive abilities to choose relevant problems to the considered target problems. It is suggested to investigate in the future the influence of restricting the transferred solutions based on similarity measures among tasks (e.g., [8]). It should be noted that the current study defines and substantiates the considered hypotheses for bi-objective source problems. Future work should also deal with extending the hypotheses to source problems with more than two objectives. In particular, the definition of edge controller should be revised and investigated.

Author Contributions: Conceptualization, A.M.; methodology, A.S. and A.M.; software, A.S.; validation, J.G. and A.M.; formal analysis, A.S.; investigation, A.S. and A.M.; writing—original draft preparation, J.G. and A.S.; writing—review and editing, A.M.; visualization, A.S.; supervision, A.M.; project administration, A.M.; funding acquisition, A.M. All authors have read and agreed to the published version of the manuscript.

Funding: This research was funded by the Israeli Ministry of Innovation, Science and Technology, grant number: 3-17388.

Data Availability Statement: All code programs will be provided on request.

Acknowledgments: The authors would like to thank the Israeli Ministry of Innovation, Science, and Technology for supporting this research.

Conflicts of Interest: The authors declare no conflict of interest. The funders had no role in the design of the study; in the collection, analyses, or interpretation of data; in the writing of the manuscript; or in the decision to publish the results.

References

1. Kuutti, S.; Bowden, R.; Jin, Y.; Barber, P.; Fallah, S. A Survey of Deep Learning Applications to Autonomous Vehicle Control. *IEEE Trans. Intell. Transp. Syst.* **2020**, *22*, 712–733. [CrossRef]
2. Yao, Q.; Tian, Y.; Wang, Q.; Wang, S. Control Strategies on Path Tracking for Autonomous Vehicle: State of the Art and Future Challenges. *IEEE Access* **2020**, *8*, 161211–161222. [CrossRef]
3. De Campos Souza, P.V. Fuzzy Neural Networks and Neuro-Fuzzy Networks: A Review the Main Techniques and Applications Used in the Literature. *Appl. Soft Comput.* **2020**, *92*, 106275. [CrossRef]
4. Fazzolari, M.; Alcala, R.; Nojima, Y.; Ishibuchi, H.; Herrera, F. A Review of the Application of Multiobjective Evolutionary Fuzzy Systems: Current Status and Further Directions. *IEEE Trans. Fuzzy Syst.* **2013**, *21*, 45–65. [CrossRef]
5. Jang, J.-S.R. ANFIS: Adaptive-Network-Based Fuzzy Inference System. *IEEE Trans. Syst. Man. Cybern.* **1993**, *23*, 665–685. [CrossRef]
6. Deb, K. Multi-Objective Optimisation Using Evolutionary Algorithms: An Introduction. In *Multi-Objective Evolutionary Optimisation for Product Design and Manufacturing*; Wang, L., Ng, A.H.C., Deb, K., Eds.; Springer: London, UK, 2011; pp. 3–34. ISBN 978-0-85729-652-8.
7. Gupta, A.; Ong, Y.S.; Feng, L. Insights on Transfer Optimization: Because Experience Is the Best Teacher. *IEEE Trans. Emerg. Top. Comput. Intell.* **2018**, *2*, 51–64. [CrossRef]
8. Tan, K.C.; Feng, L.; Jiang, M. Evolutionary Transfer Optimization—A New Frontier in Evolutionary Computation Research. *IEEE Comput. Intell. Mag.* **2021**, *16*, 22–33. [CrossRef]
9. Koçer, B.; Arslan, A. Genetic Transfer Learning. *Expert. Syst. Appl.* **2010**, *37*, 6997–7002. [CrossRef]
10. Moshaiov, A.; Tal, A. Family Bootstrapping: A Genetic Transfer Learning Approach for Onsetting the Evolution for a Set of Related Robotic Tasks. In Proceedings of the 2014 IEEE Congress on Evolutionary Computation, CEC, Beijing, China, 6–11 July 2014; pp. 2801–2808.
11. Salih, A.; Moshaiov, A. Evolving Topology and Weights of Specialized and Non-Specialized Neuro-Controllers for Robot Motion in Various Environments. *Neural Comput. Appl.* **2022**, *34*, 17071–17086. [CrossRef]
12. Pereira, J.L.J.; Oliver, G.A.; Francisco, M.B.; Cunha, S.S.; Gomes, G.F. A Review of Multi-Objective Optimization: Methods and Algorithms in Mechanical Engineering Problems. *Arch. Comput. Methods Eng.* **2022**, *29*, 2285–2308. [CrossRef]
13. Deb, K.; Pratap, A.; Agarwal, S.; Meyarivan, T. A Fast and Elitist Multiobjective Genetic Algorithm: NSGA-II. *IEEE Trans. Evol. Comput.* **2002**, *6*, 182–197. [CrossRef]
14. Li, K.; Wang, R.; Zhang, T.; Ishibuchi, H. Evolutionary Many-Objective Optimization: A Comparative Study of the State-of-the-Art. *IEEE Access* **2018**, *6*, 26194–26214. [CrossRef]
15. Cho, J.-H.; Wang, Y.; Chen, R.; Chan, K.S.; Swami, A. A Survey on Modeling and Optimizing Multi-Objective Systems. *IEEE Commun. Surv. Tutor.* **2017**, *19*, 1867–1901. [CrossRef]
16. Jang, J.-S.R.; Sun, C.-T.; Mizutani, E. *Neuro-Fuzzy and Soft Computing*; Prentice Hall: Upper Saddle River, NJ, USA, 1997; ISBN 0-13-261066-3.
17. Vieira, J.; Mota, A.; Morgado Dias, F. *Neuro-Fuzzy Systems: A Survey Artificial Neural Networks Fault Tolerance View Project Vision. 3D View Project Neuro-Fuzzy Systems: A Survey*; Springer Science & Business Media: Berlin/Heidelberg, Germany, 2004.
18. Shihabudheen, K.V.; Pillai, G.N. Recent Advances in Neuro-Fuzzy System: A Survey. *Knowl. Based Syst.* **2018**, *152*, 136–162. [CrossRef]
19. Kar, S.; Das, S.; Ghosh, P.K. Applications of Neuro Fuzzy Systems: A Brief Review and Future Outline. *Appl. Soft Comput.* **2014**, *15*, 243–259. [CrossRef]
20. Sugeno, M. An Introductory Survey of Fuzzy Control. *Inf. Sci.* **1985**, *36*, 59–83. [CrossRef]
21. Feng, G. A Survey on Analysis and Design of Model-Based Fuzzy Control Systems. *IEEE Trans. Fuzzy Syst.* **2006**, *14*, 676–697. [CrossRef]
22. Precup, R.-E.; Hellendoorn, H. A Survey on Industrial Applications of Fuzzy Control. *Comput. Ind.* **2011**, *62*, 213–226. [CrossRef]
23. Masood, M.K.; Hew, W.P.; Rahim, N.A. Review of ANFIS-Based Control of Induction Motors. *J. Intell. Fuzzy Syst.* **2012**, *23*, 143–158. [CrossRef]
24. Kabini, K. Review of ANFIS and Its Application in Control of Machining Processes. *Sustain. Res. Innov. Proc.* **2011**, *3*, 1–9.
25. Lughofer, E. Evolving Fuzzy and Neuro-Fuzzy Systems: Fundamentals, Stability, Explainability, Useability, and Applications. In *Handbook on Computer Learning and Intelligence: Volume 2: Deep Learning, Intelligent Control and Evolutionary Computation*; World Scientific: Hackensack, NJ, USA, 2022; pp. 133–234.
26. Moshaiov, A.; Salih, A. Multi-Objective Structure and Parameter Evolution of Neuro-Fuzzy Systems. In Proceedings of the 2021 IEEE Symposium Series on Computational Intelligence, SSCI 2021—Proceedings, Orlando, FL, USA, 5–7 December 2021; pp. 1–7.
27. Fleming, P.J.; Purshouse, R.C. Evolutionary Algorithms in Control Systems Engineering: A Survey. *Control Eng. Pract.* **2002**, *10*, 1223–1241. [CrossRef]
28. Bejarano, L.A.; Espitia, H.E.; Montenegro, C.E. Clustering Analysis for the Pareto Optimal Front in Multi-Objective Optimization. *Computation* **2022**, *10*, 37. [CrossRef]
29. Li, W.; Li, D.; Feng, Y.; Zou, D. Fuzzy Weighted Pareto–Nash Equilibria of Multi-Objective Bi-Matrix Games with Fuzzy Payoffs and Their Applications. *Mathematics* **2023**, *11*, 4266. [CrossRef]
30. Silva, F.L.; da Silva, S.F.; Mazzariol Santiciolli, F.; Eckert, J.J.; Silva, L.C.A.; Dedini, F.G. *Multi-Objective Optimization of the Steering System and Fuzzy Logic Control Applied to a Car-Like Robot BT—Multibody Mechatronic Systems*; Pucheta, M., Cardona, A., Preidikman, S., Hecker, R., Eds.; Springer: Cham, Switzerland, 2021; pp. 195–202.

31. Kubota, N.; Nojima, Y.; Kojima, F.; Fukuda, T. Multi-Objective Behavior Coordinate for a Mobile Robot with Fuzzy Neural Networks. In Proceedings of the IEEE-INNS-ENNS International Joint Conference on Neural Networks. IJCNN 2000. Neural Computing: New Challenges and Perspectives for the New Millennium, Como, Italy, 27 July 2000; Volume 6, pp. 311–316.
32. Van Nguyen, T.T.; Phung, M.D.; Tran, Q.V. Behavior-Based Navigation of Mobile Robot in Unknown Environments Using Fuzzy Logic and Multi-Objective Optimization. *arXiv* **2017**, arXiv:1703.03161. [CrossRef]
33. Aouf, A.; Boussaid, L.; Sakly, A. TLBO-Based Adaptive Neurofuzzy Controller for Mobile Robot Navigation in a Strange Environment. *Comput. Intell. Neurosci.* **2018**, *2018*, 4. [CrossRef] [PubMed]
34. Juang, C.-F.; Bui, T.B. Reinforcement Neural Fuzzy Surrogate-Assisted Multiobjective Evolutionary Fuzzy Systems with Robot Learning Control Application. *IEEE Trans. Fuzzy Syst.* **2019**, *28*, 434–446. [CrossRef]
35. Shell, J.; Coupland, S. Fuzzy Transfer Learning: Methodology and Application. *Inf. Sci.* **2015**, *293*, 59–79. [CrossRef]
36. Fouladvand, S.; Salavati, S.; Masajedi, P.; Ghanbarzadeh, A. A Modified Neuro-Evolutionary Algorithm for Mobile Robot Navigation: Using Fuzzy Systems and Combination of Artificial Neural Networks. *Int. J. Knowl.-Based Intell. Eng. Syst.* **2015**, *19*, 125–133. [CrossRef]
37. Chou, C.-Y.; Juang, C.-F. Navigation of an Autonomous Wheeled Robot in Unknown Environments Based on Evolutionary Fuzzy Control. *Inventions* **2018**, *3*, 3. [CrossRef]
38. Ferdaus, M.M.; Pratama, M.; Anavatti, S.G.; Garratt, M.A.; Pan, Y. Generic Evolving Self-Organizing Neuro-Fuzzy Control of Bio-Inspired Unmanned Aerial Vehicles. *IEEE Trans. Fuzzy Syst.* **2019**, *28*, 1542–1556. [CrossRef]
39. Ferdaus, M.M.; Hady, M.A.; Pratama, M.; Kandath, H.; Anavatti, S.G. Redpac: A Simple Evolving Neuro-Fuzzy-Based Intelligent Control Framework for Quadcopter. In Proceedings of the 2019 IEEE International Conference on Fuzzy Systems (FUZZ-IEEE), New Orleans, LA, USA, 23–26 June 2019; pp. 1–7.
40. Ferdaus, M.M.; Pratama, M.; Anavatti, S.G.; Garratt, M. A Generic Self-Evolving Neuro-Fuzzy Controller Based High-Performance Hexacopter Altitude Control System. In Proceedings of the 2018 IEEE International Conference on Systems, Man, and Cybernetics (SMC), Miyazaki, Japan, 7–10 October 2018; pp. 2784–2791.
41. Li, B.; Li, J.; Tang, K.; Yao, X. Many-Objective Evolutionary Algorithms: A Survey. *ACM Comput. Surv. (CSUR)* **2015**, *48*, 13. [CrossRef]
42. Takagi, T.; Sugeno, M. Fuzzy Identification of Systems and Its Applications to Modeling and Control. *IEEE Trans. Syst. Man. Cybern.* **1985**, *SMC-15*, 116–132. [CrossRef]
43. Zitzler, E.; Thiele, L. Multiobjective Evolutionary Algorithms: A Comparative Case Study and the Strength Pareto Approach. *IEEE Trans. Evol. Comput.* **1999**, *3*, 257–271. [CrossRef]
44. Taylor, M.E.; Stone, P. Transfer Learning for Reinforcement Learning Domains: A Survey. *J. Mach. Learn. Res.* **2009**, *10*, 257–271.

Disclaimer/Publisher's Note: The statements, opinions and data contained in all publications are solely those of the individual author(s) and contributor(s) and not of MDPI and/or the editor(s). MDPI and/or the editor(s) disclaim responsibility for any injury to people or property resulting from any ideas, methods, instructions or products referred to in the content.

Article

Risk Analysis of the Use of Drones in City Logistics

Snežana Tadić [1], Mladen Krstić [1,2,*], Miloš Veljović [1], Olja Čokorilo [3] and Milica Milovanović [3]

[1] Logistics Department, Faculty of Transport and Traffic Engineering, University of Belgrade, Vojvode Stepe 305, 11000 Belgrade, Serbia; s.tadic@sf.bg.ac.rs (S.T.); m.veljovic@sf.bg.ac.rs (M.V.)
[2] Department of Economic Sciences, University of Salento, 73100 Lecce, Italy
[3] Air Transport Department, Faculty of Transport and Traffic Engineering, University of Belgrade, Vojvode Stepe 305, 11000 Belgrade, Serbia; oljav@sf.bg.ac.rs (O.Č.); m.milovanovic.22d004@sf.bg.ac.rs (M.M.)
* Correspondence: m.krstic@sf.bg.ac.rs or mladen.krstic@unisalento.it

Abstract: Drone delivery in city logistics is gaining attention due to road congestion, environmental threats, etc. However, there are risks associated with using drones which can result in hazardous events, such as conflicts in the air, loss of control, and system failures. It is crucial to assess the risks involved in using different types of drones and choose the option with the lowest risk. The existence of different criteria important for this decision imposes the need to apply the multi-criteria decision-making (MCDM) method(s). This paper proposes a new hybrid model that combines the fuzzy Factor Relationship (FARE) method for obtaining the criteria weights and the Axial Distance-based Aggregated Measurement (ADAM) method for obtaining the final ranking of the alternatives. A single-rotor microdrone weighing up to 4.4 lb was chosen as the optimal solution, and after that, the most favorable are also the drones of this size (multi-rotor and fixed-wing microdrones). The establishment of a novel hybrid MCDM model, the identified risks, the set of criteria for evaluating the least risky drones, and the framework for prioritizing the drones are the main novelties and contributions of the paper.

Keywords: city logistics; delivery; drones; risk; ADAM method; fuzzy FARE

MSC: 90B06; 90B50

1. Introduction

The central area of the city has the biggest logistics problems. Although it takes up a relatively small space, a significant portion of the population lives here, and there are many jobs. The majority of logistics flows come from small businesses in the trade, service, and catering industries. The historical parts of the city present an additional challenge due to their inherited infrastructure. Streets are often narrow and meant for specific types of traffic, such as pedestrian zones, making it difficult for urban facilities to function efficiently. The transport infrastructure is overloaded and expansion possibilities are limited by a lack of space. To improve the quality of service and create efficient, safe, and environmentally friendly logistics systems, various city logistics initiatives have been introduced. These initiatives aim to improve the city's attractiveness and quality of life. One such initiative is the use of drones [1].

Drones for delivering packages have become increasingly popular due to the rise of e-commerce and home delivery services. It is estimated that the number of packages delivered by drones worldwide will increase from 220 to 262 billion by 2026 [2].

Considering drones, deliveries to users in various market niches are of the highest interest for city logistics. Retail and e-commerce companies, the fresh food/meal industry, and the hospitality industry are beginning to implement drones for product delivery [3]. Additionally, courier, express, package, or postal services use drones for delivery to customers. Finally, drones are also used to deliver medical supplies to hospitals or patients' homes [3], and even to patients' beds [4], which is of particular importance considering the necessity of providing these services promptly.

Three characteristics (strengths) that make drone delivery most suitable for city logistics are the capability to fly over traffic, environmental impact, and the ability to access various areas in various (e.g., emergency) situations [5]. By transporting goods through the air, drones can help reduce road traffic. The drones increase the speed of delivery, reduce the number of drivers and costs, and improve customer satisfaction, especially in combination with rider delivery [6]. They also require only an operator and can be equipped with devices for loading and unloading goods. This makes them ideal for delivering packages in busy urban areas, resulting in shorter delivery times, greater flexibility, and reduced environmental impact. However, there are concerns about noise pollution and underdeveloped regulations [1], as well as the safety of goods, people, and environment, and various risks. For this reason, among other aspects, the probability, consequences, and risk costs of the application of drones for delivery in urban areas are evaluated, concerning the geographical coverage [7], the use of services [8], type of risk [9], etc.

However, according to the best of the authors' knowledge, risk assessments of the different types of drone applications in city logistics, comprehensively considering significant, diverse criteria, have not been performed so far. The heterogeneity of logistical requirements and risks generated by urban areas, the perspective of application, market development, the ever-growing offering of drones with different characteristics, and the number and variety of criteria that should be taken into account when choosing the optimal type of drone create a research gap, the bridging of which is a complex and significant undertaking. This can be undertaken most effectively by applying multi-criteria decision-making (MCDM) methods. Moreover, their applicability and effectiveness have been demonstrated in related fields, for the assessment and evaluation of concepts [10] and barriers to the application of drones in city logistics [11], strategies for overcoming these barriers [12], etc.

This paper aims to choose the least risky drone for use in city logistics from among the types of drones that differ in size and configuration. To solve the problem, a combination of fuzzy FARE and ADAM methods is used. Considering its numerous advantages (simplicity, ease of understanding, adapted nature, resistance to increasing criteria number, high intuitiveness, minimal risk of ranking changes, etc.), the ADAM [13] MCDM method is adequate for the mentioned problem. Its quality and applicability have been proven through the initial application in logistics, supply chains, and economy. Considering that the method is relatively new, its applicability, flexibility, and quality are additionally tested and validated by its applications in some other areas, by combining it with other MCDM methods, with new sets of input data, and comparing its results with the results of the other MCDM methods. Since the ADAM method requires direct entry of criteria weights, another method must be used to determine them. One of the most suitable is FARE because, compared to other methods, it has a higher accuracy of calculations and requires less expert engagement [14]. Moreover, considering that it is not easy to give precise assessments of the criteria weights, i.e., their importance for the drone use risks, it is suitable to apply the method in a fuzzy environment—fuzzy FARE.

The main novelty of the paper is the development and application of a new hybrid multi-criteria decision-making (MCDM) model that combines fuzzy FARE and ADAM methods for the first time, thus contributing to the MCDM theory. Integration of these methods offers a more robust and adaptable decision-making framework, particularly suited for complex and uncertain environments. Furthermore, the study introduces a comprehensive framework for assessing and selecting drones optimized for city logistics applications, emphasizing risk mitigation as a central goal. This framework lays the groundwork for evaluating drones within urban contexts and delineates actionable criteria for assessing their suitability, thereby fostering safer and more efficient logistics operations.

The paper is composed of seven sections. Following the introduction, the Section 2 offers an overview of the literature. The Section 3 describes the structure of the problem, different drone variants, and the criteria for their evaluation. In the Section 4, the methodology is presented, which includes a description of the methods and application steps. The Section 5 evaluates and ranks alternatives, selects the best option, and performs a sensitivity analysis of the obtained solution. The Section 6 is dedicated to discussion, whereas the Section 7 presents concluding remarks.

2. Literature Review

Whereas MCDM, city logistics, and the use of drones for delivery are popular topics in the literature, relatively few studies have utilized MCDM methods to assess delivery options using various types of drones. A thorough review of the relevant literature on these topics is crucial for successful research in this area.

2.1. Methods Applied in the Model

MCDM aids decisionmakers in assessing alternatives based on various criteria. Every month or two a new method appears, but not all of them find widespread use among researchers or practitioners [15]. Over the past few decades, a large number of MCDM methods have been developed. They are often upgraded, modified, and/or combined with other methods or approaches to optimize the decisionmaking depending on the type of problem. Usually, the goal is to exploit the advantages and suppress the disadvantages of individual methods. A model that combines the fuzzy FARE and ADAM methods for the evaluation, ranking, and selection of drones with the lowest risk for application in city logistics was developed in this study.

The FARE method was developed by Ginevicius [16]. This method establishes the connections and associations among all the elements involved in the decision-making process, including criteria and sub-criteria. The data to be examined are entered into comparison matrices. The consistency check of the comparison matrices ensures that the results will be more reliable and stable, which is a great advantage of this method [17]. FARE belongs to the group of outranking methods [16]. It is characterized by various advantages against other methods from this group (ELECTRE, PROMETHEE, KEMIRA, MABAC, and ITARA) and other groups of MCDM methods. It represents one of the most accurate MCDM methods [14]. Compared to methods that are based on pairwise comparisons (e.g., AHP), the relationships between criteria are formalized and integrated [16] and require fewer evaluations [18]. This method is based on the often subjective and uncertain decision-makers' opinions. Therefore, a shortcoming of the method can be the reliance on the individuals' evaluations that do not have a realistic picture of the connections between the criteria. This can be overcome by a fuzzy extension of the FARE method [19]. This modification of the method has found application mostly in combination with other methods, e.g., for the selection of optimal cold chain logistics service providers [20], candidate selection in e-voting [21], selection of logistics service providers [19], production materials [22], machine processes [23], assessment of the impact of technology transfer on the created value [24], and evaluation of cargo vehicles visibility [25].

To overcome the shortcomings of the existing methods, the ADAM method was developed as a pioneer of a new group of so-called geometric MCDM methods [13]. It is an aggregated measurement method based on axial distances. The primary strengths of the ADAM against other methods lie in its simplicity, ease of comprehension, user-friendly nature, resilience to an expanding number of criteria, high intuitiveness, and minimal risk of ranking alterations [13]. The method was applied in an unmodified form or a fuzzy environment, independently or in combination with other methods for evaluating business models based on the circular economy in supply chains [13], the evaluation of strategic alternatives for support to decisionmakers in achieving circularity goals [26], determining the drivers of e-traceability in supply chains [27], the selection of the starting point of delivery of electronically ordered goods [28], the ranking of countries based on the entrepreneurship conditions [29], evaluating Industry 4.0 technologies [30], and transshipment technologies in intermodal terminals [31]. Due to its advantages and proven applicability, it is selected in this study for solving the defined problem.

2.2. Application of Drones in City Logistics

Drones were initially used for military purposes [32,33]. Today, they are applied or tested in various operations, from recording with cameras, through functions provided by a wide range of advanced sensors, to performing physically intensive jobs. They are used indoors or outdoors, underwater, on water, on land, or in the air [33]. Most of the systems of commercial application of drones are still in an early stage, but their development opens up significant potential and opportunities for more massive applications in various fields. Some of them are [3,34] conservation, archaeology, a survey of power facilities, health care, surveillance and monitoring, retail and e-commerce, postal services and package delivery, food and hospitality industry, humanitarian logistics and emergency services, security/disaster management, and agriculture. In logistics, drones are applied for regional transport and deliveries to users, which are the main application areas, but also rescue (emergency logistics) and storage management (inventory, inspection, etc.) [35]. The growing difficulties of logistics in urban areas have fueled an increase in interest in scientific research of the drone application in CL, i.e., various challenges, solutions, initiatives, concepts, and approaches of using drones in CL [36].

Some studies examine drones as supplementary tools for ground delivery vehicles (GDVs). Referred to in papers as a tandem vehicle–drone system, this concept involves employing drones for deliveries to specific locations while GDVs simultaneously handle others [10]. Wang and Sheu [37] proposed a model for the operational planning of ground vehicle–drone tandem delivery, allowing for the interchange of drones between GDVs. Most studies have focused on drone-based delivery, but there are also studies dealing with both drone pickup and delivery [10].

In the literature, there is a distinct drone delivery approach that involves integrating drones with larger vehicles, functioning as mobile depots. Mobile depots play a crucial role in bringing goods and drones closer to the delivery zone, with the final leg of delivery exclusively handled by drones. Within the literature, these variations primarily differ based on the type of vehicle used as mobile depots, encompassing GDVs and means of public transportation like trams, barges, and even unconventional options such as balloons or dirigibles (a type of aerostat) [10].

Whereas the current literature extensively discusses diverse drone delivery models, certain aspects remain relatively unexplored. Specifically, those relying on micro-consolidation and alternative transportation modes are not thoroughly investigated. There are only a few articles that analyze different drone-based delivery variants within the framework of city logistics concepts and select the most favorable among them. One notable article [36] demonstrates that various forms of flow consolidation on the outskirts of urban areas and near flow generators, combined with drones for the final stage of delivery, present a sustainable city logistics solution [10,38,39]. The use of drones in city logistics has many advantages: reducing city road traffic and the number of vehicles on the streets, supporting humanitarian logistics, reducing delivery time, costs, carbon dioxide, and noise emissions, and increasing the flexibility and sustainability of city logistics [40,41]. In addition to the above benefits, there are also negative effects. Regulatory challenges, along with concerns related to privacy and security, emerge as critical barriers to the widespread implementation of drones in city logistics. Additionally, public perception and considerations regarding psychology, environment, technology, and economics are identified as other substantial barriers [42].

2.3. Risk Analysis in Drone Delivery Logistics

Risk analysis can be broken down into several stages [43]: risk management, determining the likelihood of risk occurrence, assessing the severity of risk consequences, determining whether the risk is acceptable, and implementing risk control/mitigation measures. Risk analysis is used to solve many problems, in different fields, for example, meta-analysis of the risk of hypertension in living kidney donors [44], analysis of the impact of lightning strikes on flight safety [45], and risk analysis in engineering and economics [46].

Logistic systems occasionally face disruptions that represent a significant challenge for normal operations. These disruptions were particularly evident during the COVID-19 virus pandemic when the need to deliver products directly to consumers (food, masks, vaccines, etc.) was additionally created [47]. Therefore, in recent years, many studies have indicated the importance of risk management in logistics [48] and focus on creating strategies to improve reliability and risk management in logistics [49].

The reliability of logistics systems, i.e., the creation of risks, is influenced by numerous external (production, demand, globalization, terrorist attacks, thefts, natural disasters, etc.) and internal factors (human: decisions and behavior of employees, character, professional approach, etc.; and technical factors) [48,50,51].

Businesses involved in supply chains and logistics are anticipated to recognize, evaluate, mitigate, and effectively address risks [52]. It is important to carry out risk categorization. According to [53], risk categorization in logistics can be undertaken based on three perspectives: risk sources, risk amplifiers/absorbers, and risk releasers.

Growing apprehension surrounds the risks associated with natural disasters, such as tsunamis, fires, earthquakes, floods, and snowfalls; the threats posed by man-made accidents; and terrorism. Whereas these risks should be acknowledged and evaluated within the realm of city logistics, their full consideration is lacking in both the modeling of city logistics [54] and the implementation of city logistics schemes in urban areas.

Risks stemming from natural and anthropogenic hazards within the city logistics system vary in terms of frequency of occurrence, complexity, uncertainty, and ambiguity [55]. Typically, the focus lies on daily risks, such as potential delays in reaching customers for delivery or goods collection due to common occurrences like traffic jams, accidents, or events like sports gatherings. However, it is necessary to include rare but serious effects caused by cyclones, earthquakes, floods, etc. [55].

The main sources of risk in the application of delivery drones work at low altitudes (danger of collision, fall, injury, etc.), propeller work (noise, the anxiety of people, etc.), and cameras (possibility of endangering privacy) [56]. Risks can relate to three parties: people and property directly related to drone operations, people and property that have nothing to do with drone operations but directly benefit from them, and people and property that are not involved in drone operations and do not directly benefit from them.

The identification of the main risks in drone operations is based on the following categories [43]: conflict in the air (risk of a collision between a drone and another aircraft and similar events, as well as loss of connection with the air traffic control service provider); loss of control (risk of injury to people on the ground depending on the flight plan and maneuvering of the drone itself after a technical malfunction); system failures (engine, control system, software, electrical system failures, etc.); and conflicts with third parties and property damage (accidental impact of the drone on a person or property damage). Barr et al. [57] successfully leveraged information gleaned from numerous drone accident reports to provide an initial risk assessment for small drones.

3. Problem Description

Drones can be classified based on wingspan, wing load, maximum height, speed, configuration, flight-enabling technology, engine type, level of autonomy, size, weight, range and endurance, applications, manufacturing costs, etc. [33]. The classification criteria that will be considered in this paper are size and configuration.

There are drones of various sizes, spanning from dimensions comparable to that of an insect to those matching a commercial aircraft [58]. Drones of smaller dimensions are of particular importance for deliveries (Table 1), which will also be discussed in this paper.

Table 1. Smaller drone characteristics [57].

Drone Class	Weight, Max [lb]	Velocity, Max [knots]	Kinetic Energy, Max [ft-lb]
A: Microdrone	4.4	60	704
B: Minidrone	20	87	6727
C: Small drone	55	87	18,498

According to the configuration, there are three types of drones, which will be described below: fixed-wing drones, and multi-rotor and single-rotor drones. Multirotor drones are the simplest form of drones. They usually use at least four rotors, do not need a landing strip, are not noisy, and can hover in the air [58]. The disadvantage of such drones is lower endurance (shorter flight time and low payload) and speed [59].

The disadvantage of such drones is lower endurance (shorter flight time and low payload) and speed [59]. Fixed, static-wing drones use a wing-like structure (similar to airplanes) for their operation, and the way they take off is different than in the case of other drones [59]. They have greater endurance (they are more suitable for longer distances and can carry up to 110.2 lb) and speed than multi-rotor drones, but they require more space for take-off and balancing, proper training of the operator, high costs, and cannot hover in place [33]. Unlike multi-rotor drones where a sudden loss of power can cause them to stop working, fixed-wing drones can recover in such situations and continue flying [33]. In such drones, fixed wings can be combined with one or more rotors. Single-rotor drones are provided with greater durability by a throttle control system, and larger rotor blades provide greater system efficiency, but as with fixed-wing drones, they require operator training and high costs [59].

By combining the two mentioned classifications, nine alternatives (variants) were defined, i.e., types of drones: D_1—fixed-wing microdrone, D_2—multi-rotor microdrone, D_3—single-rotor microdrone, D_4—fixed-wing mini drone, D_5—multirotor mini drone, D_6—single-rotor mini drone, D_7—small fixed-wing drone, D_8—multirotor small drone, D_9—single-rotor small drone.

The criteria, according to which the listed variants will be evaluated and the most favorable of them selected from the aspect of risk, are defined as the possibility of occurrence of certain unwanted events [57]: loss of control, leaving the intended flight zone, loss of communication, loss of navigation, unsuccessful landing, unintentional termination of flight, inability to avoid collision with terrain/moving obstacles.

The first criterion according to which the alternatives will be evaluated is the possibility of losing control of the drone (C_1). The most common reason for losing control of a drone is operator error, but loss of control can occur for other reasons: too high speed, flying indoors, engine problems, wind gusts, other weather conditions, flying obstacles, etc. Drones should also be evaluated from the aspect of the possibility of leaving the intended flight zone (C_2). This phenomenon is prevented by the use of geofencing, i.e., by setting virtual borders to limit the operation of drones in a certain zone, thereby preventing unauthorized entry into the air proctor [60]. Loss of communication with the drone (C_3) occurs more often in remote and rural areas, with low demand density, during manual control by the operator, and the consequences of this event can be collisions with other aircraft, objects, injuries to people, etc. [57]. In case of loss of navigation (C_4), the drone also poses a danger to the environment. Based on one or more global navigation satellite systems, autonomous navigation control is performed, which helps the drone to move without human control and to minimize the drone's flight time [61]. Unsuccessful landing (C_5) represents inadequate contact with the runway or a crash during landing, which can cause the vehicle to break, catch fire, injure people, etc. [57]. Unintended or unsuccessful flight disruption (C_6) may occur during delivery and its consequences such as fire may endanger people, the environment, etc. The final criterion is the inability to avoid collisions with terrain, or fixed or moving obstacles (C_7), such as buildings, infrastructure, means of transport, people, animals, etc. It is also an important criterion against which any alternative should be evaluated.

4. Methodology

To solve the problem, i.e., the selection of the least risky drone, a combined model was used that implies the application of two MCDM methods, one for determining the weight of the criteria (fuzzy FARE), and the other for evaluating and obtaining the final ranking of alternatives (ADAM) (Figure 1).

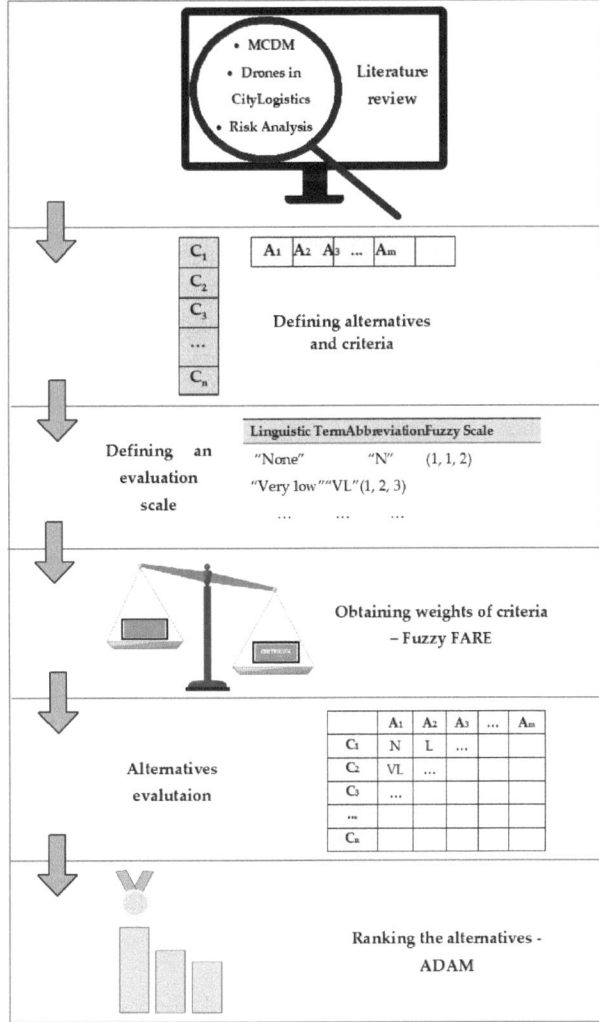

Figure 1. Methodology of the study.

The model comprises the following sequential phases:

Phase 1: Defining the structure of the problem. The sets of alternatives and criteria for their evaluation (shown in the previous section) need to be established.

Phase 2: Defining a scale for evaluating criteria and alternatives. Decisionmakers describe the importance of criteria and alternatives using linguistic ratings that can be transformed into numerical values or triangular fuzzy numbers (TFNs) as shown in Table 2. The evaluation of criteria depends to a greater extent on the subjective ratings of decisionmakers, in contrast to the evaluations of the alternative, which are based more on the concrete characteristics of the alternative about the criteria; fuzzy evaluations were used to evaluate the criteria, that is, to apply the fuzzy FARE method, whereas ordinary numerical values were used to rank the alternative by changing the ADAM method.

Table 2. Evaluation scale [13,17].

Linguistic Term	Abbreviation	Fuzzy Scale	Numerical Value
"None"	"N"	(1, 1, 2)	1
"Very low"	"VL"	(1, 2, 3)	2
"Low"	"L"	(2, 3, 4)	3
"Fairly low"	"FL"	(3, 4, 5)	4
"Medium"	"M"	(4, 5, 6)	5
"Fairly high"	"FH"	(5, 6, 7)	6
"High"	"H"	(6, 7, 8)	7
"Very high"	"VH"	(7, 8, 9)	8
"Extremely high"	"EH"	(8, 9, 10)	9

Phase 3: Obtaining weights of criteria.

Phase 3.1: Creating the criteria evaluation matrix $\widetilde{A}$. Decisionmakers' linguistic assessments are converted into TFNs by applying the relationships specified in Table 2.

$$\widetilde{A} = [\widetilde{a}_{ij}]_{nxn} \quad (1)$$

where $\widetilde{a}_{ij} = (l, m, u) = (l, m, n)$ is the evaluation of the importance of criterion i over criterion j. Items l, m, and u are the lower, middle, and upper values of the TFNs. Item n is the number of criteria taken into account. When forming the matrix $\widetilde{A}$, the following applies:

$$\widetilde{a}_{ji} = -\widetilde{a}_{ij} \quad (2)$$

and the evaluation is considered consistent if:

$$\sum_{j=1}^{n} u = -\sum_{j=1}^{n} l \quad (3)$$

Phase 3.2: Obtaining the potential criteria impact $\widetilde{P}$ as:

$$P = H(n-1) \quad (4)$$

where H is the highest value of the scale used for the evaluations.

Phase 3.3: Obtaining the total impact (importance) of criterion $\widetilde{P}_j$ as:

$$\widetilde{P}_j = \sum_{j=1}^{n} \widetilde{a}_{ij}, \forall j = 1, \ldots, n, \ j \neq i \quad (5)$$

Phase 3.4: Obtaining the final fuzzy criteria weights:

$$W = \widetilde{P}_j / \widetilde{P}_H, \ \forall j = 1, \ldots, n \quad (6)$$

where P_H is the total potential importance of criteria obtained as:

$$\widetilde{P}_H = (\min_j l^{\widetilde{P}_j r}, \operatorname{mean}_j m^{\widetilde{P}_j r}, \max_j u^{\widetilde{P}_j r}) \quad (7)$$

where P_j is the real total impact of the criterion j obtained as:

$$\widetilde{P}_j^r = \widetilde{P}_j + \widetilde{P}, \ \forall j = 1, \ldots, n \quad (8)$$

Phase 4: Evaluation of alternatives. The ADAM method is used to evaluate alternatives according to criteria.

Phase 4.1: Defining the decision matrix E, elements of which are evaluations e_{qj} of the alternatives q regarding criteria j, i.e., vector magnitudes that correspond to the evaluations of the alternatives regarding the criteria:

$$E = [e_{qj}]_{mxn} \qquad (9)$$

where m is the total number of alternatives and n is the total number of criteria.

Phase 4.2: Defining the sorted decision matrix S elements, which are s_{qj}, indicating the sorted evaluations e_{qj} in descending order according to the importance (weight) of the criterion:

$$S = [s_{qj}]_{mxn} \qquad (10)$$

Phase 4.3: Defining the normalized sorted matrix N elements, which are normalized evaluations n_{qj} obtained as:

$$n_{qj} = \begin{cases} \dfrac{s_{qj}}{\max\limits_q s_{qj}}, & za\ j \in B \\ \dfrac{\min\limits_q s_{qj}}{s_{qj}}, & za\ j \in C \end{cases} \qquad (11)$$

where B is the set of benefits and C is the set of cost criteria.

Phase 4.4: Finding the coordinates (x, y, z) of the reference (R_{qj}) and weighted reference (P_{qj}) points that define the complex polyhedron in the following way:

$$X_{qj} = n_{qj} \times \sin \alpha_j, \forall j = 1, \ldots, n; \forall q = 1, \ldots, m \qquad (12)$$

$$Y_{qj} = n_{qj} \times \cos \alpha_j, \forall j = 1, \ldots, n; \forall q = 1, \ldots, m \qquad (13)$$

$$Z_{qj} = \begin{cases} 0, & za\ R_{qj} \\ w_j, & za\ R_{qj} \end{cases}, \forall j = 1, \ldots, n; \forall q = 1, \ldots, m \qquad (14)$$

where α_j is the angle that determines the direction of the vector that defines the value of the alternative, which is obtained as:

$$\alpha_j = (j-1)\frac{90°}{n-1}, \forall j = 1, \ldots, n \qquad (15)$$

Phase 4.5: Finding the volumes of complex polyhedra V_q^C as the sum of the volumes of the pyramids of which it is composed using the following equation:

$$V_q^C = \sum_{k=1}^{n-1} V_k, \forall q = 1, \ldots, m \qquad (16)$$

where V_k is the volume of the pyramid obtained by applying the following equation:

$$V_k = \frac{1}{3} B_k \times h_k, \forall k = 1, \ldots, (n-1) \qquad (17)$$

where B_k is the surface of the base of the pyramid defined by the reference and weighted reference points of two consecutive criteria and is obtained by applying the following equation:

$$B_k = c_k \times a_k + \frac{a_k \times (b_k - c_k)}{2} \qquad (18)$$

where a_k is the Euclidean distance between the reference points of two consecutive criteria, which is obtained by applying the following equation:

$$a_k = \sqrt{(x_{j+1} - x_j)^2 + (y_{j+1} - y_j)^2} \qquad (19)$$

b_k and c_k are the magnitudes of the vectors corresponding to the weights of two consecutive criteria, that is:

$$b_k = z_j \tag{20}$$

$$c_k = z_{j+1} \tag{21}$$

h_k is the height of the pyramid from the defined base to the top of the pyramid located in the coordinate origin (O) and is obtained by applying the following equation:

$$h_k = \frac{2\sqrt{s_k(s_k - a_k)(s_k - d_k)(s_k - e_k)}}{a_k} \tag{22}$$

where s_k is the semicircumference of the triangle defined by the x and y coordinates of two consecutive criteria and the coordinate origin and is obtained as:

$$s_k = \frac{a_k + d_k + e_k}{2} \tag{23}$$

where d_k and e_k are the Euclidean distances of the reference points of two consecutive criteria from the coordinate origin, obtained as:

$$d_k = \sqrt{x_j^2 + y_j^2} \tag{24}$$

$$e_k = \sqrt{x_{j+1}^2 + y_{j+1}^2} \tag{25}$$

Phase 5: Ranking the alternatives according to the decreasing values of the volumes of complex polyhedra V_q^C ($q = 1, \ldots, m$). The best alternative is the one with the highest volume value.

Evaluation and ranking of alternatives are performed using the software ADAM 1.2-beta, http://adam-mcdm.com/ (accessed on 19 March 2024).

5. Risk Assessment and Ranking

The methods described were applied to obtain results, which are presented below. Additionally, to examine the stability of the solution, an analysis of the methods' sensitivity to changes in criteria weights through multiple iterations is also reported.

The fuzzy FARE method was used to obtain the comparison scores of the criteria (Table 3), and their weights were then normalized (Table 4).

Table 3. Criterion comparison ratings.

	C_1	C_2	C_3	C_4	C_5	C_6	C_7
C_1		"EH"	"VH"	"FH"	"M"	"H"	"FL"
C_2			"N"	"L"	"FL"	"VL"	"M"
C_3				"VL"	"L"	"N"	"FL"
C_4					"N"	"N"	"VL"
C_5						"L"	"N"
C_6							"FL"
C_7							

To define the evaluations of the alternatives according to the criteria, it was first necessary to form a focus group and interview the members. This consisted of 29 experts with different scientific/professional interests (city logistics, drones/air transport, risk analysis/management) (Table 5).

Table 4. Criterion weights.

	P_J			P_{jr}			w_j			Crisp (w_j)
C_1	33.00	39.00	45.00	81	93	105	0.77	1.40	2.12	1.4179
C_2	11.10	15.11	20.13	59.1	69.11	80.13	0.56	1.04	1.62	1.059
C_3	7.61	11.13	15.14	55.61	65.13	75.14	0.53	0.98	1.51	0.9965
C_4	3.73	5.00	8.70	51.73	59	68.7	0.49	0.89	1.39	0.9071
C_5	4.12	5.78	8.08	52.12	59.78	68.08	0.50	0.90	1.37	0.9135
C_6	4.71	6.98	8.67	52.71	60.98	68.67	0.50	0.92	1.38	0.9284
C_7	1.60	2.45	3.17	49.6	56.45	63.17	0.47	0.85	1.27	0.8594

Table 5. The focus group members' characteristics.

Sector	Number of Experts	Years of Experience
City logistics	4	up to 5
	3	from 5 to 15
	3	over 15
Drones/air transport	1	up to 5
	3	from 5 to 15
	5	over 15
Risk analysis	1	up to 5
	7	from 5 to 15
	2	over 15

Based on the risk assessment for smaller drones [57] and the subjective opinion of decisionmakers (focus group), the alternatives were evaluated according to the criteria (Table 6). The normalized weights of the criteria together with the normalized scores of the alternatives per criteria (Table 6) were given to the ADAM 1.2-beta software.

Table 6. Evaluations and normalized numerical evaluations of alternatives according to criteria (ADAM method).

	Evaluations							Normalized Numerical Evaluations						
	C_1	C_2	C_3	C_4	C_5	C_6	C_7		C_1	C_2	C_3	C_4	C_5	C_6	C_7
D_1	"H"	"M"	"FL"	"FL"	"EH"	"FL"	"FL"	D_1	0.8	0.6	0.5	0.6	1.0	0.8	0.6
D_2	"VH"	"VH"	"M"	"H"	"L"	"M"	"FH"	D_2	0.9	0.9	0.6	1.0	0.3	1.0	0.9
D_3	"EH"	"EH"	"H"	"VL"	"FH"	"FL"	"H"	D_3	1.0	1.0	0.9	0.3	0.7	0.8	1.0
D_4	"FL"	"M"	"L"	"L"	"VH"	"VL"	"VL"	D_4	0.4	0.6	0.4	0.4	0.9	0.4	0.3
D_5	"M"	"H"	"FH"	"FH"	"VL"	"L"	"FL"	D_5	0.6	0.8	0.8	0.9	0.2	0.6	0.6
D_6	"FH"	"VH"	"VH"	"VL"	"M"	"VL"	"L"	D_6	0.7	0.9	1.0	0.3	0.6	0.4	0.4
D_7	"N"	"M"	"VL"	"L"	"H"	"N"	"N"	D_7	0.1	0.6	0.3	0.4	0.8	0.2	0.1
D_8	"VL"	"FH"	"L"	"M"	"N"	"VL"	"L"	D_8	0.2	0.7	0.4	0.7	0.1	0.4	0.4
D_9	"L"	"H"	"L"	"N"	"FL"	"N"	"N"	D_9	0.3	0.8	0.4	0.1	0.4	0.2	0.1

As a result, the software provides numerical values and ranking of alternatives (Table 7), as well as a graphical display of obtained complex polyhedra corresponding to each of the alternatives.

The obtained complex polyhedra of drone alternatives used for their ranking are shown in Figure 2.

Table 7. Ranking of alternatives according to criteria (ADAM method).

Alternatives	Volume	Rank
D_1	0.175692	3
D_2	0.211696	2
D_3	0.233089	1
D_4	0.089025	6
D_5	0.150036	5
D_6	0.157237	4
D_7	0.048132	9
D_8	0.058588	7
D_9	0.050106	8

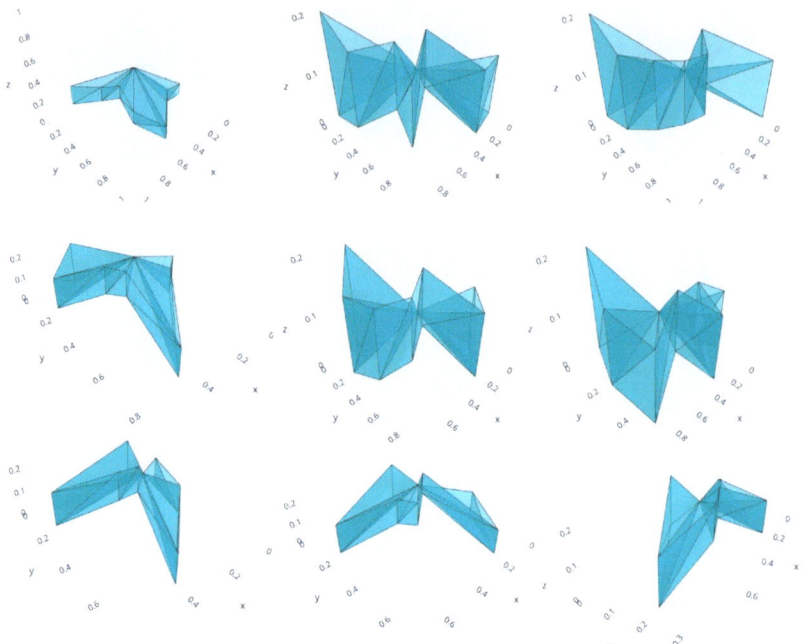

Figure 2. Complex polyhedra of drone alternatives.

Based on the ranking of alternatives, the final solution to the problem is obtained. The best-ranked alternative is the A_3 alternative, which means that the least risky drone for use in city logistics is a single-rotor microdrone, which is expected given the characteristics of this aircraft.

To ensure the reliability of the solution, 10 scenarios were implemented in which the weights of the criteria were reduced. First, the weight of all criteria was reduced by 15%, then by 30%, 45%, 60%, 75%, 90%, and finally by 100%. Following that, the weight of criteria C_1, C_7, and C_5 was reduced. The obtained rankings for all scenarios are presented in Table 8 and Figure 3. Additionally, Spearman's correlation coefficient (SCC) was calculated to determine the correlation between the initial and other scenarios.

Table 8. Alternatives ranking by the scenarios.

	D_1	D_2	D_3	D_4	D_5	D_6	D_7	D_8	D_9	SCC
Sc.0	3	2	1	6	5	4	9	7	8	/
Sc.1	3	2	1	6	5	4	9	7	8	1
Sc.2	3	2	1	6	4	5	9	7	8	0.983
Sc.3	3	2	1	6	5	4	9	7	8	1
Sc.4	3	2	1	6	5	4	9	7	8	1
Sc.5	3	2	1	5	6	4	9	8	7	0.967
Sc.6	4	2	1	6	5	3	9	7	8	0.983
Sc.7	3	2	1	6	5	4	9	7	8	1
Sc.8	3	2	1	6	5	4	9	7	8	1
Sc.9	3	2	1	6	5	4	9	7	8	1
Sc.10	3	2	1	7	5	4	9	6	8	0.983

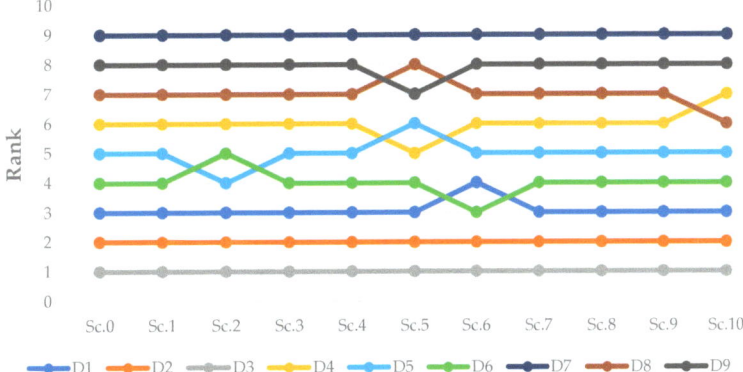

Figure 3. Sensitivity analysis.

Given that a large number of MCDM methods have been developed in recent decades, which can provide different solutions when making the same decisions, the results obtained by applying the ADAM method within the defined model for the basic scenario (Sc.0) were compared with the results of applying the TOPSIS, VIKOR, SAW, COPRAS, AHP, and COBRA methods for identical problem and input data. The obtained ranking and SCCs for cases of application of all listed methods compared to the results obtained with the ADAM method are shown in Table 9 and Figure 4. The average value of SCCs for all methods is 0.969, which confirms the high degree of correlation in the results between the ADAM method and other methods and the validity of the defined model.

Table 9. Comparing results of the model with other MCDM methods.

	ADAM	TOPSIS	VIKOR	SAW	COPRAS	AHP	COBRA
D_1	3	3	5	3	3	3	3
D_2	2	2	2	2	2	2	2
D_3	1	1	1	1	1	1	1
D_4	6	6	6	6	6	6	6
D_5	5	4	4	4	4	4	5
D_6	4	5	3	5	5	5	4
D_7	9	8	9	8	8	8	8
D_8	7	7	8	7	7	7	7
D_9	8	9	7	9	9	9	9
SCC	1	0.96667	0.93333	0.96667	0.96667	0.96667	0.98333

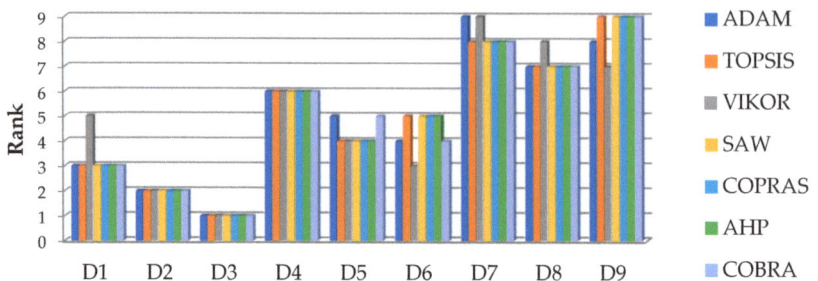

Figure 4. Rankingcomparison obtained by various MCDM methods.

6. Discussion

The model's limitations stem from the shortcomings of the methods used to create it. The recently developed ADAM method requires the direct input of criteria weights. Consequently, in scenarios involving complex interdependencies among criteria, it becomes impractical to independently derive weights. To address this, it is recommended to extend the ADAM method with other approaches [13]. Conversely, the fuzzy FARE method heavily depends on subjective assessments, introducing a potential for unreliability and bias. Additionally, the method proves unsuitable for a substantial number of criteria due to its protracted application process, making it challenging for decisionmakers to facilitate comparisons effectively [13]. Moreover, a notable limitation of the model is its failure to explicitly consider the unique requirements and objectives of various stakeholders during the decision-making process. The decision is made by an individual who can influence the solution of the problem he is dealing with to be in his favor.

The work presented in this study has significant theoretical implications for the fields of MCDM theory, air traffic, logistics, and risk management. The study introduces a new MCDM method, a hybrid model that can be applied to any research field. However, specific adjustments are necessary for criteria, interest groups, and evaluation scales to solve a particular problem. This study can be a starting point for new studies that define and analyze ecologically based models. For example, it can be used to determine which aircraft poses the most risk for traffic and transport in terms of environmental pollution from exhaust gases. Moreover, this method can be used to address numerous problems in traffic and logistics, economy, management, and other areas [13]. Regarding practical implications, the developed model can be used as a tool for decisionmakers, managers, planners, designers, and policymakers at different levels while dealing with problems involving many alternatives and criteria in any field. The ADAM method allows for an effective display of results, making it particularly suitable for managers. On the other hand, the fuzzy FARE method can benefit decisionmakers in companies, firms, and other institutions in employment, purchasing goods, investing in business, etc. [13].

7. Conclusions

The focus of this study was on analyzing the risks associated with using various types of drones in city logistics. The primary objective was to identify the least risky type of drone. To achieve this goal, a hybrid model combining two MCDM methods—fuzzy FARE and ADAM—was employed to evaluate the different types of drones. This model was designed to address the limitations of using these methods individually. Following the evaluation of nine alternatives based on seven criteria, the single-rotor microdrone, weighing up to 4.4 lb, also known as alternative D_3, was found to be the least risky option.

The application of this hybrid model, in addition to in the field of transport and logistics, can help in the fields of environmental protection, management, economy, new technologies in companies, agriculture, food and chemicals, etc. In future research, the model can be applied to solve other problems in the areas covered by this study. The model holds potential for application in addressing additional challenges within the domains explored in this study. Furthermore, it may find utility in resolving analogous issues within intermodal transport and other areas of logistics. A crucial direction of future research, i.e., upgrading the model, is the incorporation of interest groups in the decision-making process. Some areas of application of drones in logistics have not yet been sufficiently considered. Thus, although the topic of the application of drones for delivery in urban areas has been largely discussed in the literature, the characteristics, challenges, and problems of application in rural areas have not received adequate attention, and represent a potential area of application of models similar to the one defined in this paper.

Author Contributions: Conceptualization, S.T., M.K., M.V., O.Č. and M.M.; methodology, S.T., M.K., M.V., O.Č. and M.M.; software, M.K. and M.M.; validation, S.T., M.K., M.V., O.Č. and M.M.; formal analysis, S.T., M.K., M.V., O.Č. and M.M., writing—original draft preparation, S.T., M.K., M.V. and M.M.; writing—review and editing, S.T., M.K., M.V. and O.Č.; visualization, S.T., M.K. and M.V.; supervision, S.T., M.K. and O.Č. All authors have read and agreed to the published version of the manuscript.

Funding: This research received no external funding.

Data Availability Statement: The original contributions presented in the study are included in the article, further inquiries can be directed to the corresponding author.

Conflicts of Interest: The authors declare no conflicts of interest.

References

1. Tadić, S.R. City Logistics Initiatives for Central Urban Zones. *Tehnika* **2019**, *74*, 585–594. [CrossRef]
2. Benarbia, T.; Kyamakya, K. A Literature Review of Drone-Based Package Delivery Logistics Systems and Their Implementation Feasibility. *Sustainability* **2021**, *14*, 360. [CrossRef]
3. Moshref-Javadi, M.; Winkenbach, M. Applications and Research Avenues for Drone-Based Models in Logistics: A Classification and Review. *Expert Syst. Appl.* **2021**, *177*, 114854. [CrossRef]
4. Vlahović, N.; Knežević, B.; Batalić, P. Implementing Delivery Drones in Logistics Business Process: Case of Pharmaceutical Industry. *Int. J. Mech. Ind. Eng.* **2017**, *10*, 4026–4031.
5. Roca-Riu, M.; Menendez, M. Logistic Deliveries with Drones: State of the Art of Practice and Research. In Proceedings of the 19th Swiss Transport Research Conference (STRC 2019), Monte Verità, Ascona, Switzerland, 15–17 May 2019.
6. Lu, F.; Jiang, R.; Bi, H.; Gao, Z. Order Distribution and Routing Optimization for Takeout Delivery under Drone–Rider Joint Delivery Mode. *J. Theor. Appl. Electron. Commer. Res.* **2024**, *19*, 774–796. [CrossRef]
7. Aurambout, J.P.; Gkoumas, K.; Ciuffo, B. Last mile delivery by drones: An estimation of viable market potential and access to citizens across European cities. *Eur. Transp. Res. Rev.* **2019**, *11*, 1–21. [CrossRef]
8. Shao, Q.; Li, J.; Li, R.; Zhang, J.; Gao, X. Study of Urban Logistics Drone Path Planning Model Incorporating Service Benefit and Risk Cost. *Drones* **2022**, *6*, 418. [CrossRef]
9. Han, P.; Yang, X.; Zhao, Y.; Guan, X.; Wang, S. Quantitative Ground Risk Assessment for Urban Logistical Unmanned Aerial Vehicle (UAV) Based on Bayesian Network. *Sustainability* **2022**, *14*, 5733. [CrossRef]
10. Büyüközkan, G.; Mukul, E. Evaluation of smart city logistics solutions with fuzzy MCDM methods. *Pamukkale Üniversitesi Mühendislik Bilim. Derg.* **2019**, *25*, 1033–1040. [CrossRef]
11. Tadić, S.; Radovanović, L.J.; Krstić, M.; Veljović, M. Study of barriers for the use of drones in the last mile logistics. In Proceedings of the 2nd International Conference on Advances in Traffic and Communication Technologies, ATCT 2023, Sarajevo, Bosnia and Herzegovina, 11–12 May 2023.
12. Tadić, S.; Krstić, M.; Radovanović, L. Assessing Strategies to Overcome Barriers for Drone Usage in Last-Mile Logistics: A Novel Hybrid Fuzzy MCDM Model. *Mathematics* **2024**, *12*, 367. [CrossRef]
13. Krstić, M.; Agnusdei, G.P.; Tadić, S.; Kovač, M.; Miglietta, P.P. A Novel Axial-Distance-Based Aggregated Measurement (ADAM) Method for the Evaluation of Agri-Food Circular-Economy-Based Business Models. *Mathematics* **2023**, *11*, 1334. [CrossRef]
14. Girdzijauskaitė, E.; Radzevičienė, A.; Jakubavičius, A. Impact of international branch campus KPIs on the university competitiveness: FARE method. *Insights Reg. Dev.* **2019**, *1*, 171–180. [CrossRef] [PubMed]
15. Sahoo, S.K.; Goswami, S.S. A comprehensive review of multiple criteria decision-making (MCDM) Methods: Advancements, applications, and future directions. *Decis. Mak. Adv.* **2023**, *1*, 25–48. [CrossRef]
16. Ginevičius, R. A New Determining Method for the Criteria Weights in Multicriteria Evaluation. *Int. J. Inf. Technol. Decis. Mak.* **2011**, *10*, 1067–1095. [CrossRef]
17. Kazan, H.; Özçelik, S.; Hobikoğlu, E.H. Election of deputy candidates for nomination with AHP-Promethee methods. *Procedia-Soc. Behav. Sci.* **2015**, *195*, 603–613. [CrossRef]
18. Ginevicius, R.; Szczepanskawoszczyna, K.; Szarucki, M.; Stasiukynas, A. Assessing Alternatives to the Development of Administrative-Economic Units Applying the FARE. *Adm. Manag. Public* **2021**, *36*, 6–24.

19. Roy, J.; Pamučar, D.; Kar, S. Evaluation and Selection of Third Party Logistics Provider under Sustainability Perspectives: An Interval Valued Fuzzy-Rough Approach. *Ann. Oper. Res.* **2020**, *293*, 669–714. [CrossRef]
20. Krstić, M.; Tadić, S. Hybrid Multi-Criteria Decision-Making Model for Optimal Selection of Cold Chain Logistics Service Providers. *J. Organ. Technol. Entrep.* **2023**, *1*, 77–87. [CrossRef]
21. Alguliyev, R.; Aliguliyev, R.; Yusifov, F. MCDM for candidate selection in e-voting. *Int. J. Public Adm. Digit. Age (IJPADA)* **2019**, *6*, 35–48. [CrossRef]
22. Yazdani, M. New Approach to Select Materials Using MADM Tools. *Int. J. Bus. Syst. Res.* **2018**, *12*, 25. [CrossRef]
23. Chatterjee, P.; Mondal, S.; Boral, S.; Banerjee, A.; Chakraborty, S. A Novel Hybrid Method for Non-Traditional Machining Process Selection Using Factor Relationship and Multi-Attributive Border Approximation Method. *Facta Univ. Ser. Mech. Eng.* **2017**, *15*, 439–456. [CrossRef]
24. Stankevičienė, J.; Kraujalienė, L.; Vaiciukevičiūtė, A. Assessment of Technology Transfer Office Performance for Value Creation in Higher Education Institutions. *J. Bus. Econ. Manag.* **2017**, *18*, 1063–1081. [CrossRef]
25. Pitchipoo, P.; Vincent, D.S.; Rajini, N.; Rajakarunakaran, S. COPRAS Decision Model to Optimize Blind Spot in Heavy Vehicles: A Comparative Perspective. *Procedia Eng.* **2014**, *97*, 1049–1059. [CrossRef]
26. Agnusdei, L.; Krstić, M.; Palmi, P.; Miglietta, P.P. Digitalization as Driver to Achieve Circularity in the Agroindustry: A SWOT-ANP-ADAM Approach. *Sci. Total Environ.* **2023**, *882*, 163441. [CrossRef] [PubMed]
27. Krstić, M.; Agnusdei, G.P.; Tadić, S.; Miglietta, P.P. Prioritization of E-Traceability Drivers in the Agri-Food Supply Chains. *Agric. Food Econ.* **2023**, *11*, 42. [CrossRef]
28. Tadić, S.; Krstić, M.; Veljović, M.; Kovač, M. Selection of the starting point of e-order delivery using ADAM method. In Proceedings of the 50th International Symposium on Operational Research, SYM-OP-IS 2023, Tara, Serbia, 18–21 September 2023.
29. Popovic, G.; Fedajev, A.; Mitic, P.; Meidute-Kavaliauskiene, I. An ADAM-based approach to unveiling entrepreneurial ecosystems in selected European countries. *Manag. Decis.* **2024**. ahead-of-print. [CrossRef]
30. Krstić, M.; Tadić, S.; Brnjac, N. Strategic Application of Industry 4.0 Technologies in Enhancing Intermodal Transport Terminal Efficiency. *J. Organ. Technol. Entrep.* **2023**, *1*, 98–109. [CrossRef]
31. Krstić, M.; Tadić, S.; Jolović, M. Evaluation of Transshipment Technologies in Intermodal Terminals: A Hybrid FSWARA-ADAM Approach. *J. Organ. Technol. Entrep.* **2024**, *2*, 27–38. [CrossRef]
32. Chan, K.W.; Nirmal, U.; Cheaw, W.G. Progress on Drone Technology and Their Applications: A Comprehensive Review. In Proceedings of the 4th International Conference on Green Design and Manufacture, Ho Chi Minh, Vietnam, 29–30 April 2018. [CrossRef]
33. Garg, P.K. Characterisation of Fixed-Wing Versus Multirotors UAVs/Drones. *J. Geomat.* **2022**, *16*, 152–159. [CrossRef]
34. Melo, S.; Silva, F.; Abbasi, M.; Ahani, P.; Macedo, J. Public Acceptance of the Use of Drones in City Logistics: A Citizen-Centric Perspective. *Sustainability* **2023**, *15*, 2621. [CrossRef]
35. Li, Y.; Liu, M.; Jiang, D. Application of Unmanned Aerial Vehicles in Logistics: A Literature Review. *Sustainability* **2022**, *14*, 14473. [CrossRef]
36. Li, X.; Tupayachi, J.; Sharmin, A.; Martinez Ferguson, M. Drone-aided delivery methods, challenge, and the future: A methodological review. *Drones* **2023**, *7*, 191. [CrossRef]
37. Wang, Z.; Sheu, J.-B. Vehicle Routing Problem with Drones. *Trans. Res. Part B Methodol.* **2019**, *122*, 350–364. [CrossRef]
38. Bachofner, M.; Lemardelé, C.; Estrada, M.; Pagès, L. City logistics: Challenges and opportunities for technology providers. *J. Urban Mobil.* **2022**, *2*, 100020. [CrossRef]
39. Gabani, P.R.; Gala, U.B.; Narwane, V.S.; Raut, R.D.; Govindarajan, U.H.; Narkhede, B.E. A viability study using conceptual models for last mile drone logistics operations in populated urban cities of India. *IET Collab. Intell. Manuf.* **2021**, *3*, 262–272. [CrossRef]
40. Xydianou, T.; Nathanail, E. The Use of Drones in City Logistics—A Case Study Application. In Proceedings of the Conference on Sustainable Urban Mobility (CSUM 2022): Smart Energy for Smart Transport, Skiathos Island, Greece, 31 August–2 September 2022.
41. Rejeb, A.; Rejeb, K.; Simske, S.J.; Treiblmaier, H. Drones for Supply Chain Management and Logistics: A Review and Research Agenda. *Int. J. Logist.* **2023**, *26*, 708–731. [CrossRef]
42. Sah, B.; Gupta, R.; Bani-Hani, D. Analysis of Barriers to Implement Drone Logistics. *Int. J. Logist.* **2021**, *24*, 531–550. [CrossRef]
43. Čokorilo, O. *Aircraft Safety*, 2nd ed.; University of Belgrade, Faculty of Transport & Traffic Engineering: Belgrade, Serbia, 2020. (In Serbian)
44. Boudville, N.; Ramesh Prasad, G.V.; Knoll, G.; Muirhead, N.; Thiessen-Philbrook, H.; Yang, R.C.; Rosas-Arellano, M.P.; Housawi, A.; Garg, A.X. Meta-Analysis: Risk for Hypertension in Living Kidney Donors. *Ann. Intern. Med.* **2006**, *145*, 185. [CrossRef] [PubMed]
45. Milovanović, M.; Čokorilo, O.; Čokorilo, S. Analysis of the impact of lightning strikes on flight safety. *Int. J. Traffic Transp. Eng.* **2022**, *12*, 352–360.
46. Ayyub, B.M. *Risk Analysis in Engineering and Economics*, 1st ed.; Chapman and Hall/CRC: London, UK; Boca Raton, FL, USA; New York, NY, USA; Washington, DC, USA, 2003. [CrossRef]
47. Choi, T.M. Risk Analysis in Logistics Systems: A Research Agenda during and after the COVID-19 Pandemic. *Transp. Res. Part E Logist. Trans. Rev.* **2021**, *145*, 102190. [CrossRef]

48. Choi, T.M.; Chiu, C.-H.; Chan, H.-K. Risk Management of Logistics Systems. *Transp. Res. Part E Logist. Trans. Rev.* **2016**, *90*, 1–6. [CrossRef]
49. Chung, S.H.; Tse, Y.K.; Choi, T.M. Managing Disruption Risk in Express Logistics via Proactive Planning. *Ind. Manag. Data Syst.* **2015**, *115*, 1481–1509. [CrossRef]
50. Kulińska, E. Selected Tools for Risk Analysis in Logistics Processes. *Arch. Transp.* **2012**, *24*, 27–42. [CrossRef]
51. Kulińska, E. *Aksjologicznywymiarzarządzaniaryzykiemprocesówlogistycznych: Modeleieksperymentyekonomiczne*; OficynaWydawnicza-PolitechnikiOpolskiej: Opole, Poland, 2011.
52. Sodhi, M.S.; Son, B.-G.; Tang, C.S. Researchers' Perspectives on Supply Chain Risk Management. *Prod. Oper. Manag.* **2012**, *21*, 1–13. [CrossRef]
53. Fuchs, H.; Wohinz, J.W. Risk management in logistics systems. *Adv. Prod. Eng. Manag.* **2009**, *4*, 233–242.
54. Hesse, M. City logistics. network modelling and intelligent transport systems. *J. Transp. Geogr.* **2002**, *10*, 158–159. [CrossRef]
55. Taniguchi, E.; Thompson, R.G.; Yamada, T. Incorporating Risks in City Logistics. *Procedia Soc. Behav. Sci.* **2010**, *2*, 5899–5910. [CrossRef]
56. Ren, X.; Cheng, C. Model of Third-Party Risk Index for Unmanned Aerial Vehicle Delivery in Urban Environment. *Sustainability* **2020**, *12*, 8318. [CrossRef]
57. Barr, L.C.; Newman, R.; Ancel, E.; Belcastro, C.M.; Foster, J.V.; Evans, J.; Klyde, D.H. Preliminary Risk Assessment for Small Unmanned Aircraft Systems. In Proceedings of the 17th AIAA Aviation Technology, Integration, and Operations Conference, Denver, CO, USA, 5–9 June 2017.
58. Vergouw, B.; Nagel, H.; Bondt, G.; Custers, B. Drone Technology: Types, Payloads, Applications, Frequency Spectrum Issues and Future Developments. In *The Future of Drone Use: Opportunities and Threats from Ethical and Legal Perspectives; Information Technology and Law Series (ITLS)*; Custers, B., Ed.; T.M.C. Asser Press: The Hague, The Netherlands, 2016; Volume 27, pp. 21–45.
59. Dileep, M.R.; Navaneeth, A.V.; Ullagaddi, S.; Danti, A. A study and analysis on various types of agricultural drones and its applications. In Proceedings of the Fifth International Conference on Research in Computational Intelligence and Communication Networks (ICRCICN), Bangalore, India, 26–27 November 2020.
60. Hermand, E.; Nguyen, T.W.; Hosseinzadeh, M.; Garone, E. Constrained control of UAVs in geofencing applications. In Proceedings of the 26th Mediterranean Conference on Control and Automation (MED), Zadar, Croatia, 19–22 June 2018.
61. Kim, T.H.; Toazza, D. Navigation Control of an Unmanned Aerial Vehicle (UAV). Bachelor's Thesis, School of Information Science, Computer and Electrical Engineering Halmstad University, Halmstad, Sweden, 2009.

Disclaimer/Publisher's Note: The statements, opinions and data contained in all publications are solely those of the individual author(s) and contributor(s) and not of MDPI and/or the editor(s). MDPI and/or the editor(s) disclaim responsibility for any injury to people or property resulting from any ideas, methods, instructions or products referred to in the content.

Article

An Efficient Tour Construction Heuristic for Generating the Candidate Set of the Traveling Salesman Problem with Large Sizes

Boldizsár Tüű-Szabó [1,*], Péter Földesi [2] and László T. Kóczy [1]

[1] Department of Information Technology, Szechenyi Istvan University, 9026 Gyor, Hungary; koczy@sze.hu
[2] Department of Logistics, Szechenyi Istvan University, 9026 Gyor, Hungary; foldesi@sze.hu
* Correspondence: tuu.szabo.boldizsar@sze.hu

Abstract: In this paper, we address the challenge of creating candidate sets for large-scale Traveling Salesman Problem (TSP) instances, where choosing a subset of edges is crucial for efficiency. Traditional methods for improving tours, such as local searches and heuristics, depend greatly on the quality of these candidate sets but often struggle in large-scale situations due to insufficient edge coverage or high time complexity. We present a new heuristic based on fuzzy clustering, designed to produce high-quality candidate sets with nearly linear time complexity. Thoroughly tested on benchmark instances, including VLSI and Euclidean types with up to 316,000 nodes, our method consistently outperforms traditional and current leading techniques for large TSPs. Our heuristic's tours encompass nearly all edges of optimal or best-known solutions, and its candidate sets are significantly smaller than those produced with the POPMUSIC heuristic. This results in faster execution of subsequent improvement methods, such as Helsgaun's Lin–Kernighan heuristic and evolutionary algorithms. This substantial enhancement in computation time and solution quality establishes our method as a promising approach for effectively solving large-scale TSP instances.

Keywords: fuzzy clustering; candidate set; TSP; heuristic

MSC: 90C27

Citation: Tüű-Szabó, B.; Földesi, P.; Kóczy, L.T. An Efficient Tour Construction Heuristic for Generating the Candidate Set of the Traveling Salesman Problem with Large Sizes. *Mathematics* **2024**, *12*, 2960. https://doi.org/10.3390/math12192960

Academic Editors: Momčilo Dobrodolac, Stefan Jovčić and Marjana Čubranić-Dobrodolac

Received: 16 August 2024
Revised: 18 September 2024
Accepted: 22 September 2024
Published: 24 September 2024

Copyright: © 2024 by the authors. Licensee MDPI, Basel, Switzerland. This article is an open access article distributed under the terms and conditions of the Creative Commons Attribution (CC BY) license (https://creativecommons.org/licenses/by/4.0/).

1. Introduction

The Traveling Salesman Problem (TSP) is one of the most extensively studied problems in combinatorial optimization, with applications ranging from logistics and manufacturing to telecommunications and DNA sequencing. The TSP involves finding the shortest possible route that visits a set of nodes exactly once and returns to the original city. Despite its apparent simplicity, the TSP is NP-hard, making it computationally challenging to solve, especially as the number of nodes increases.

In this study, we focus specifically on the symmetric TSP (sTSP), a variant where the distance between any two nodes is identical regardless of the direction of travel. The sTSP is a common representation of real-world problems where the travel cost between locations is the same in both directions, such as in road networks or communication systems. This symmetry allows for certain algorithmic simplifications, but it also presents unique challenges in terms of efficiently finding optimal or near-optimal solutions for large problem instances.

In the last few decades, many efficient methods were presented in the literature for solving the TSP. The most efficient exact method is the Concorde solver, which has been used to obtain the optimal solutions to TSPLIB instances up to 85,900 nodes [1]. One possible solution for tackling larger problems with hundreds of thousands of vertices is to use heuristics and metaheuristics which can provide near-optimal solutions within a reasonable amount of time.

Among these methods, Helsgaun's implementation of the Lin–Kernighan (LKH) heuristic is one of the most effective and widely recognized techniques for solving the TSP [2]. The LKH algorithm, an advanced variant of the original Lin–Kernighan heuristic developed by Helsgaun, incorporates several improvements and new strategies that significantly enhance its performance. The LKH heuristic extends the Lin–Kernighan approach by adapting the number of edges involved in the optimization process, allowing it to explore more complex edge rearrangements and achieve high-quality solutions. Notably, LKH is renowned for achieving the best-known solutions for many large TSP instances, demonstrating its exceptional capability in solving complex and large-scale problems.

A class of metaheuristics called "memetic algorithms" [3] that combine evolutionary-based algorithms with local search are effective in solving the TSP and closely related optimization problems [4]. Dinh Nguyen et al. introduced an effective memetic algorithm for large-scale TSP problems in 2007 [5]. This approach integrates a parallel multipopulation steady-state genetic algorithm with Lin–Kernighan local search, including variants like maximal preservative crossover and double-bridge move mutation. By balancing exploration through the genetic algorithm and exploitation via local search, the method proves highly efficient and has achieved new best solutions for numerous large-scale problems, outperforming the LKH heuristic in several cases. Another effective metaheuristic is the Fast Ant Colony Optimization (FACO) algorithm, which leverages a hybrid approach combining constructive and perturbation-based strategies [6]. FACO efficiently finds solutions within 1% of the best-known results for TSP Art instances with up to 200,000 nodes on an 8-core CPU, demonstrating notable speed and performance improvements over recent ACO-based methods. However, while FACO offers competitive performance, it generally does not surpass the state-of-the-art LKH heuristic, which remains superior for most TSP instances. Nonetheless, FACO has occasionally outperformed LKH on particularly challenging instances, showcasing its potential for specific problem scenarios. In addition to solving TSP and other optimization problems, metaheuristic algorithms have found significant application in enhancing the security of AI-based systems. For example, combining AI, machine learning (ML), and metaheuristic techniques has proven effective in detecting and mitigating dynamic security threats like intrusion detection and real-time malware detection [7]. Another notable application of metaheuristics is in optimizing supply chain management, where techniques like genetic algorithms [8] and simulated annealing [9] are used to improve logistics efficiency and reduce operational costs.

To implement a fast and efficient heuristic or metaheuristic approach for the TSP, the key point is to use a limited size neighborhood (candidate sets) during the search especially for large-size TSP instances. Candidate sets help to limit the search space by reducing the number of moves evaluated during the search, which speeds up the computation.

When solving geometric problems, there are several methods for creating the candidate set. For 2D Euclidean instances, a Delaunay triangulation can be created with $O(nlog(n))$ time complexity, where n is the number of nodes involved in the problem. If the nodes are defined by their K-dimensional coordinates, an alternative is to construct a KD-tree [10] with an $O(Knlog(n))$ time complexity. This method involves selecting only a few of the closest nodes in each quadrant. The Nearest Neighbor heuristic is a well-known and frequently used approach, although not so efficient, for generating candidate sets. Limiting the candidate set to only the closest vertices may prevent finding the optimal solution in the tour improvement phase [11]. To illustrate this, in a problem that involves 532 nodes (att532), one of the connections in the optimal solution is with the node that is the 22nd closest to a particular endpoint. However, including more nodes in the pool of potential connections significantly increases the runtime.

To limit the moves, one can use a fast randomized heuristic to generate a few dozen TSP solutions of moderate quality. The edges of a specified number of these tours can be merged to create a candidate set. Only the edges contained in these tours are utilized for building moves. This technique, known as tour merging, was introduced in 2007 [12]. Blazinskas and Misevicius utilized a multi-random-start technique incorporating fast 3-opt and the simplified LKH heuristic to create high-quality candidate sets in 2012 [13]. However, its more than quadratic time complexity limits its usability for large-scale instances. Ali et al. presented an efficient tour construction heuristic called Circle Group Heuristic in 2022 which creates better tours compared with the well-known tour construction methods [14].

One way to create high-quality solutions with low time complexity is to use the POPMUSIC template, formalized by Taillard and Voss in 2002 [15]. It has been shown to be very efficient for solving hard combinatorial problems such as p-median [16], sum of squares clustering [16], vehicle routing [17], and map labeling [18]. The concept of POPMUSIC is to optimize sub-parts of a solution locally, after obtaining a solution for the problem. These local optimizations are repeated until no further improvements are found. Helsgaun and Taillard first used this idea for the TSP and proposed a new efficient tour construction method [19]. This method consists of two main steps: creating a feasible tour based on clustering and 2-opt local search and optimizing every subpath of the initial solution with a Lin–Kernighan local search. It has been proven that this method has low empirical complexity, typically $O(n^{1.6})$. Taillard proposed an improved version of the POPMUSIC heuristic. Instead of the initial tour construction phase, a recursive randomized procedure is used to build the tour, which takes $O(nlog(n))$ time [20]. Additionally, the subpath optimization (fast POPMUSIC) has been made faster by reducing the number of examined subpaths. Although the time required to improve the initial tour still depends on the problem size, it has been reduced by a factor of 10 to 20 compared to the previous implementation. Since the overall time complexity of the method is near-linear, it can be used to solve extremely large instances on a standard personal computer.

This improved POPMUSIC heuristic was compared with two other candidate set generating techniques, the alpha and Delaunay methods. While the POPMUSIC and alpha candidate set generating methods are generally applicable, Delaunay triangulation works only on Euclidean instances. However, the Delaunay triangulation method is the fastest, but POPMUSIC always produced candidate sets with better quality (the number of missing edges from the best-known tours are lower). Helsgaun proposed the alpha candidate set generating method as an alternative to the Nearest Neighbor candidate set generating approach in his effective implementation of the Lin–Kernighan heuristic [2]. This method, which is both widely used and efficient, relies on the minimum 1-tree. It generates high-quality candidate sets that include nearly all the edges of optimal solutions. Candidate sets with fewer edges typically have average vertex degrees of about 5–6. However, the preprocessing step involving 1-trees, when integrated into the LKH algorithm, exhibits empirical complexity that seems to be quadratic. This makes it impractical for instances with more than 100,000 nodes.

As highlighted by Queiroga et al. in 2021, in their study on the capacitated vehicle routing problem, POPMUSIC remains a robust and adaptable heuristic for a range of optimization problems, showcasing its effectiveness even for very large instances [17].

The methods developed for solving the Traveling Salesman Problem (TSP) have achieved notable progress, yet significant challenges remain, particularly with large-scale instances. While exact methods like the Concorde solver provide optimal solutions, and heuristics such as Nearest Neighbor and Delaunay triangulation offer practical approaches, they often fall short in terms of efficiency or scalability for larger problems. The quadratic time complexity of some candidate set generation methods and the limitations of existing heuristics underscore the need for more effective solutions. This research addresses these challenges by proposing a novel heuristic aimed at generating high-quality candidate sets specifically for large-scale TSP problems.

The primary goal of this research is to develop an efficient heuristic with low time complexity that can generate high-quality candidate sets for large-scale TSP instances. By leveraging fuzzy clustering techniques, the proposed approach seeks to partition the problem into manageable subproblems and optimize connections between subpaths. This method is designed to address the limitations of current techniques, offering a more effective alternative for large-scale TSP instances and contributing significantly to the field.

This paper is organized as follows: Section 2 introduces the novel tour construction heuristic, detailing its methodology and the integration of fuzzy clustering techniques. Section 3 presents the results of extensive experimentation, including parameter tuning and comparative analysis with existing methods like POPMUSIC. This paper concludes with a discussion of the strengths and limitations of the proposed heuristic, as well as suggestions for future research directions.

2. From Clustering to Tour Construction: An Innovative Approach to TSP

The first part of this section offers a comprehensive overview of clustering techniques, with a detailed focus on the Fuzzy C-means (FCM) algorithm, which is crucial for partitioning large-scale TSP instances in our heuristic. We explore the mechanics of FCM, emphasizing its advantages over traditional clustering methods, particularly in handling overlapping clusters and providing nuanced membership information.

In the second part, we present the step-by-step process of our novel tour construction heuristic, designed to effectively handle large TSP instances. This heuristic uses clustering to break down complex problems into manageable subproblems and employs optimization techniques to generate high-quality candidate sets.

2.1. Clustering Techniques: Theory and Principles

The Traveling Salesman Problem (TSP) is a well-known NP-hard problem, which means it is computationally challenging to solve, particularly for large instances. The complexity of TSP grows exponentially with the size of the problem, making it increasingly difficult to find optimal solutions as the number of cities increases. One effective strategy for managing such large-scale problems is to break them down into smaller, more manageable subproblems. This approach, known as "divide and conquer", simplifies the overall problem by partitioning it into smaller parts that can be solved independently before combining their solutions.

In this context, clustering techniques offer a practical method for partitioning large TSP instances into smaller subproblems. Clustering involves grouping data points into clusters such that points within the same cluster are more similar to each other than to those in other clusters. Clustering can be classified as either hard or fuzzy. In hard clustering, patterns are separated by well-defined cluster boundaries. However, due to the overlapping nature of these boundaries, some patterns may fall into a single cluster or a dissimilar group. This limitation makes hard clustering less suitable for real-life applications. To address this issue, fuzzy clustering was introduced [21]. Fuzzy clustering provides more information about the pattern memberships, reducing the limitations of hard clustering. We investigated two clustering methods for partitioning the problem: k-means clustering and Fuzzy C-means clustering (FCM) [22]. The k-means clustering method involves an iterative data-partitioning algorithm that assigns data points to clusters defined by centroids. Fuzzy clustering, on the other hand, allows data points to belong to more than one cluster with different degrees of membership. Fuzzy C-means clustering is a popular fuzzy method for clustering, introduced in 1973 [21] and improved in 1981 [22], but the method has some disadvantages, such as sensitivity to the initialization of cluster centers, the given number of expected clusters, and convergence to the optimal local response [23]. It has been widely applied in various fields such as clustering [24], classification [25], image analysis [26], etc.

The pseudo-code of the FCM method is shown in Figure 1, starting with the determination of the initial cluster centers. Figure 2 shows the flowchart of the algorithm.

Afterwards, in an iterative process, the membership matrix and the cluster centers are updated, and the value of objective function is calculated. The membership grades are calculated with Equation (1). In our implementation, the Euclidean distance metric was used. In this equation, each data point x_i is assigned a membership grade w_{ij} to cluster c_j based on its distances to all cluster centers. The fuzzy membership value w_{ij} is inversely related to the distances: points closer to the cluster center will have higher membership grades for that cluster. The term in the denominator normalizes the membership values across all clusters for the given data point:

$$w_{ij} = \frac{1}{\sum_{k=1}^{c} \left(\frac{\|x_i - c_j\|}{\|x_i - c_k\|} \right)^{\frac{2}{m-1}}}, \tag{1}$$

where $w_{ij} \in [0,1]$ represents a fuzzy membership value that quantifies the grade of membership of data point x_i belongs to the fuzzy cluster c_j; m is the weighing exponent parameter that determines the degree of fuzziness of the clustering; c is the number of the clusters.

```
begin
fix parameters: c number of clusters, m, ε and maxIterations
initialize C₀ = c₁,c₂,...,c_c cluster centers
for t=1 to maxIterations do
    update the membership matrix W using the Equation 1
    calculate the new cluster centers C_t using the Equation 2
    calculate the new objective function J_m^t using Equation 3
    if abs(J_m^t − J_m^{t−1}) < ε) then
        break;
    end if
end for
end
```

Figure 1. The pseudo-code of the FCM method.

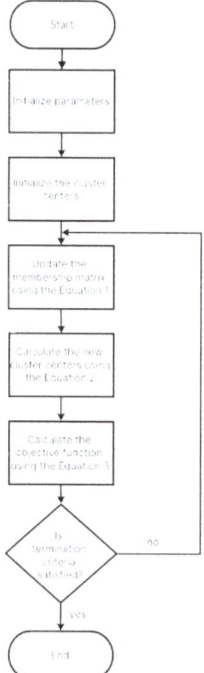

Figure 2. The flowchart of the FCM method.

The cluster centers are updated with the following equation:

$$c_j = \frac{\sum_{i=1}^{n} w_{ij} x_i}{\sum_{i=1}^{n} w_{ij}}. \tag{2}$$

This formula calculates the new cluster center c_j as the weighted average of all data points, where the weights are given by the membership grades. The more a data point belongs to a cluster (i.e., the higher its membership grade w_{ij}) the more influence it has on the position of the cluster center.

Finally, the value of the objective function is calculated in each iteration:

$$J_m = \sum_{j=1}^{c} \sum_{i=1}^{n} w_{ij} \|x_i - c_j\|^2. \tag{3}$$

The objective function J_m measures the overall quality of the clustering by calculating the weighted sum of squared distances between data points and their cluster centers. This value is minimized during the iterative process to achieve better clustering. The weights w_{ij} affect how much each point contributes to the total distance, reflecting the degree of its membership to each cluster.

2.2. Our Novel Tour Construction Heuristic

In this section, our new heuristic will be presented in detail. This method consists of five main steps:

1. Splitting the problem into subproblems with fuzzy clustering (k subproblems);
2. Solving each subproblem with Helsgaun's Lin–Kernighan heuristic;
3. Splitting the tours found at step 2 into two paths ($2k$ paths in total);
4. Connecting the paths into a solution for the entire problem with Helsgaun's Lin–Kernighan heuristic;
5. Post-optimization of randomly selected segments of the solution found at step 4 with Helsgaun's Lin–Kernighan heuristic.

In our research, we explored both k-means and Fuzzy C-means (FCM) clustering techniques to partition large TSP instances into smaller, more manageable subproblems. K-means clustering, a widely used approach, resulted in a slightly smaller candidate set but was limited by its rigid cluster boundaries and inability to handle overlapping clusters effectively.

In contrast, Fuzzy C-means clustering proved to be more advantageous. FCM allows data points to belong to multiple clusters with varying degrees of membership, addressing the limitations of traditional k-means and better accommodating the overlapping nature of real-world problems. Our experiments demonstrated that while k-means produced a smaller candidate set, Fuzzy C-means yielded faster convergence in reducing the number of missing edges in the candidate set. Consequently, we chose Fuzzy C-means for partitioning the problem, as it offered superior performance and efficiency. In the FCM algorithm, each node is assigned a fuzzy membership grade between 0 and 1 for each cluster, which indicates the degree of belonging to each cluster. The subsequent step of our method involves assigning each node to a single cluster proportionally based on these membership grades, meaning that the assignment reflects the relative probabilities of the node belonging to each cluster. This means that a node is more likely to be assigned to a cluster where its membership grade is higher. When applying a small degree of fuzziness and assigning nodes proportionally to a single cluster based on their membership grades, nodes are typically allocated to the nearest or a nearby cluster. This happens because, with reduced fuzziness, membership grades become more extreme. As a result, nodes are usually assigned to the cluster closest to them or to one of the nearby clusters, where the membership grades are higher. Figure 3 exemplifies this process using a small fuzziness parameter (m = 1.05) in the FCM algorithm, showing the clusters for the dkc3938 instance with 10 clusters after this allocation method. The dkc3938 instance is a Very-Large-Scale

Integration (VLSI) instance consisting of 3938 points, where the distances between points are Euclidean. The x-axis and y-axis represent the spatial coordinates of the points in the 2D Euclidean plane.

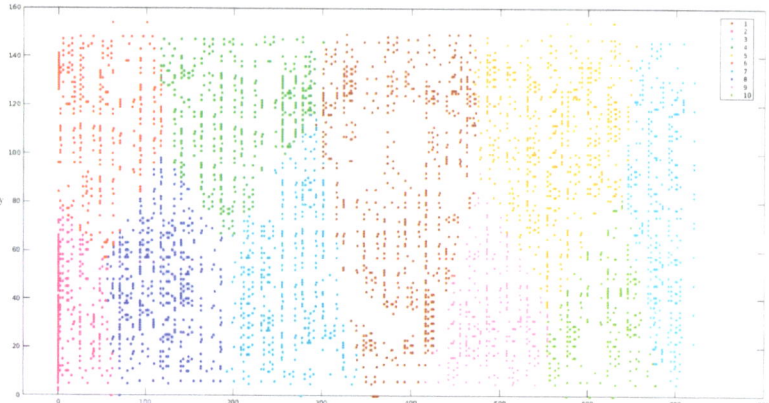

Figure 3. The 10 clusters on the dkc3938 instance.

In order to increase the convergence speed in our implementation, the initial cluster centers were selected with the following process:

- The first cluster center is chosen uniformly at random from the vertices;
- All other cluster centers are chosen as follows: select 100 vertices uniformly at random and choose the one that is the furthest away from the cluster centers that have already been determined. This method aims to ensure that the new cluster centers are as far apart as possible from the existing ones, which can help in achieving a more diverse and well-distributed set of cluster centers.

As part of the new tour construction heuristics, the second main step is to solve the subproblems created by fuzzy clustering separately. The aim of this step is not to search for the optimal solution to the subproblems, as this would take a significant amount of time and could result in missing numerous edges in the candidate set that are part of the optimal solution of the entire problem. Instead, the goal is to generate high-quality solutions in the shortest time possible. To achieve this, the Lin–Kernighan heuristic implemented by Helsgaun was chosen (LKH-2.0.10 version), which is currently the most efficient heuristic in the literature for solving the TSP and holds the best-known solutions for many instances with thousands of nodes. When setting the parameters of the LKH, the aforementioned goal was kept in mind. The initial tours of the subproblems were generated with the Nearest Neighbor heuristic, which is a simple algorithm that always visits the closest unvisited point. For generating the candidate sets of the subproblems (five candidates for each vertex), the Nearest Neighbor heuristic was also used. During the search, based on our experiments, 3-opt sequential moves were applied as sub-moves instead of the 5-opt suggested by Helsgaun. The number of trials was set to 1, so the search consists of generating the initial subtour and improving it with LKH.

After creating the subtours, each of them was divided into two subpaths. The splitting points were determined with the following three-steps process:

1. Determining the closest and second-closest clusters to each cluster based on the distances of the clusters' centers;
2. Determining the two splitting points by finding the closest vertices to the closest and second-closest clusters;
3. Deleting for each splitting point one of the two edges in which the splitting point appears.

Figure 4 shows the 20 subpaths obtained on the dkc3938 instance after solving the 10 subproblems from Figure 3 with LKH and then splitting each into two subpaths.

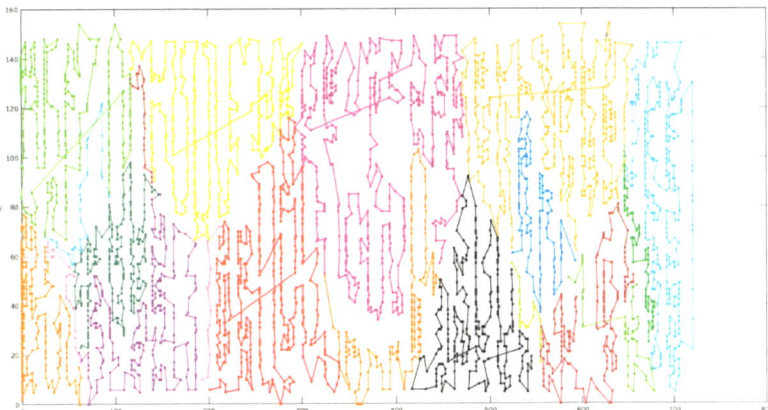

Figure 4. The subpaths of the dkc3938 instance.

The next step connects the subpaths into a complete tour which is a solution for the entire problem. The LKH (2.0.10 version) was also applied to find the optimal connection of the subpaths with the default parameters. The LKH adds $2k$ edges (where k is the number of the clusters) to form a valid tour for the entire problem. All edges in the subpaths were fixed during the search. Here, 5-opt sequential moves were applied in order to find the optimal connection of the subpaths. For such small-sized problems, specifically finding the optimal order of the $2k$ subpath connections, LKH consistently finds the optimal solution.

Figure 5 shows the complete tour on the dkc3938 instance after connecting the subpaths. There are some long edges in this tour, but their number can be reduced by using post-optimization with LKH (2.0.10 version). It improves subpaths starting with a randomly selected vertex. The first and last vertex of the subpath is fixed ensuring that improving the subpath leads to an improvement in the entire tour. As basic steps, 3-opt sequential moves were applied in LKH.

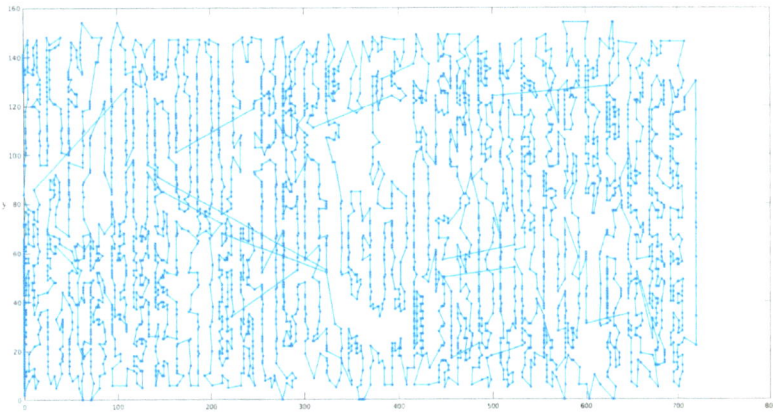

Figure 5. A complete tour of the dkc3938 instance after connecting the subpaths.

Figure 6 shows the tour after post-optimization on the dkc3938 instance. A comparison of Figures 5 and 6 demonstrates that post-optimization has successfully eliminated several long edges from the final solution. This indicates that the post-optimization process has effectively reduced the number of long edges present in the solution. This is beneficial because long edges are typically unlikely to be included in the optimal solution, and their presence can unnecessarily inflate the size of the candidate set. By eliminating these long edges, the candidate set becomes more refined, thereby improving the overall performance of the tour construction heuristic.

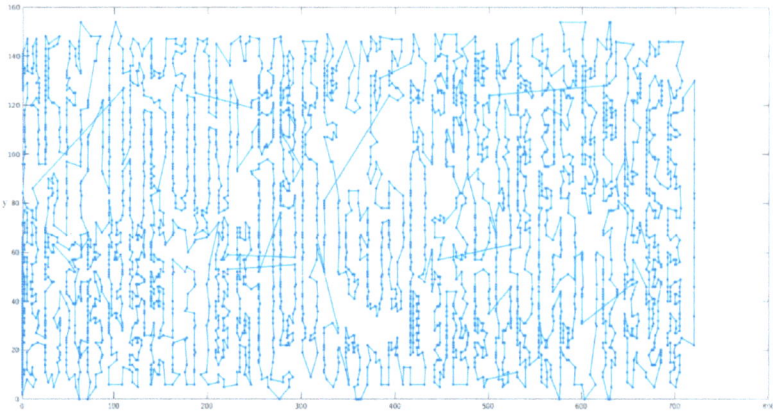

Figure 6. A final tour of the dkc3938 instance after post-optimization.

3. Results

In this section, we present the results of our extensive experimentation aimed at optimizing the parameters of our tour construction heuristic. We explore the effects of various parameter settings on the performance of the heuristic. Our analysis is based on multiple benchmark instances, both Euclidean and VLSI, to illustrate the impact of these parameters on solution quality and runtime. We also compare our heuristic's performance with the POPMUSIC method in Section 3.2.

3.1. Parameter Tuning and Its Impact on Heuristic Performance

We have conducted extensive investigations in order to set the parameters of the heuristic (fuzzy or traditional clustering, parameter m of the Fuzzy C-means clustering, the number of clusters $n_{cluster}$, a binary variable determining whether post-optimization is applied or not, the segment size of post-optimization $postopt$, and the number of times the post-optimization is performed $n_{postopt}$) appropriately. The experiments were carried out on the following computer configuration (Core i7-7500U 2.7 GHz, 8GB of RAM memory running under Linux Mint 18.2). Seven instances were selected for tuning the parameters of our tour construction heuristic, including ei8246, vm22775, sw24978, bm33708, ics39603, E10k0, and dan59296. These instances encompass a range of problem types: Euclidean, VLSI, and national instances. This diverse selection ensures that the parameter tuning process considers various types of problems, allowing for a more comprehensive evaluation of the heuristic's performance across different scenarios. The number in each instance name refers to the number of nodes. Similar trends were observed in the parameter tuning across these seven benchmarks. Consequently, the results for one Euclidean benchmark (E10k0) and one Very-Large-Scale Integration (VLSI) benchmark (dan59296) are presented in detail to illustrate these trends comprehensively. While the optimal solution is known for the E10k0, dan59296 has not yet been solved optimally, so in this case, the candidate set was compared with the best-known solution.

Some of our results with different parameter settings can be seen in Tables 1 and 2. Two indicators were used to evaluate the quality of the candidate set, the number of missing edges, and the average vertex degree of the candidate set. "Missing edges" refers to the set of edges that are present in the best-known solution (or the optimal solution, if available) but are not included in the candidate set. Finding the optimal or a near-optimal solution during the tour improvement phase can be hindered by a significant number of missing edges. On the other side, generating a larger candidate set can lead to longer run times reducing the efficiency of the tour improvement algorithm. Therefore, it is necessary to develop a candidate set generating method that can produce a relatively small set with a low number of missing edges. In Tables 1 and 2, ME stands for missing edges, and AVD stands for average vertex degree of the candidate set. The tables highlight results for a subset of parameter settings, while constant parameters across the experiments include the use of post-optimization (*postopt* = yes) with $n_{postopt}$ = 10 and *postopt* = nodes/10. For the hard clusters, the number of clusters is fixed at 10, while for the fuzzy clusters, the number of clusters varies between 5, 10, 15, and 20, with a constant m = 1.05. In the case of fuzzy clusters with $n_{cluster}$ = 20, two scenarios are considered: with and without post-optimization, highlighting how this specific setting impacts the results.

Table 1. Results with different parameter settings on the E10k0 instance.

Parameters (Constant Values: m = 1.05, $n_{postopt}$ = 10, postopt = Nodes/10)	After 50 Tours		After 100 Tours		After 150 Tours				
	ME	AVD	ME	AVD	ME	AVD	Best Tour	Avg. Tour	Time [s]
hard clusters, $n_{cluster}$ = 10, post_opt = yes	10	5	1	5.8	0	6.5	74,497,318	76,030,799.3	49.573
fuzzy clusters, $n_{cluster}$ = 5, post_opt = yes	2	5.1	1	6.1	0	7	74,311,481	75,780,634.5	53.286
fuzzy clusters, $n_{cluster}$ = 10, post_opt = yes	1	5.3	0	6.4	0	7.3	74,886,400	76,277,249.4	53.162
fuzzy clusters, $n_{cluster}$ = 15, post_opt = yes	3	5.5	0	6.7	0	7.5	75,375,746	76,883,980	52.013
fuzzy clusters, $n_{cluster}$ = 20, post_opt = no	4	5.6	1	6.8	0	7.7	75,496,760	77,081,900.7	33.835
fuzzy clusters, $n_{cluster}$ = 20, post_opt = yes	3	5.5	0	6.5	0	7.5	74,936,874	76,749,658.4	54.801

Table 2. Results with different parameter settings on the dan59296 instance.

Parameters (Constant Values: m = 1.05, $n_{postopt}$ = 10, postopt = Nodes/10)	After 50 Tours		After 100 Tours		After 150 Tours				
	ME	AVD	ME	AVD	ME	AVD	Best Tour	Avg. Tour	Time [s]
hard clusters, $n_{cluster}$ = 10, post_opt = yes	236	4.78	102	5.88	68	6.75	183,385	186,523	224.42
fuzzy clusters, $n_{cluster}$ = 5, post_opt = yes	227	5.22	128	6.70	59	7.60	184,360	187,635	331.22
fuzzy clusters, $n_{cluster}$ = 10, post_opt = yes	182	5.61	72	7.32	44	8.63	185,815	188,579	231.07
fuzzy clusters, $n_{cluster}$ = 15, post_opt = yes	173	5.64	70	7.37	36	8.78	185,531	189,331	229.51
fuzzy clusters, $n_{cluster}$ = 20, post_opt = no	198	6.02	81	7.90	59	9.38	186,064	189,873	174.03
fuzzy clusters, $n_{cluster}$ = 20, post_opt = yes	159	5.79	70	7.66	30	9.04	185,997	189,153	238.56

For the E10k0 instance, our heuristic was able to find all the edges present in the optimal solution across all parameter settings (see Table 1). However, the dan59296 VLSI instance proved to be a much more challenging task (see Table 2). In this case, the impact of different parameter settings on the number of missing edges becomes evident.

The following subsections detail the effects of various parameters on the performance of the heuristic. Each subsection focuses on a specific aspect of the parameter adjustments and their impact on solution quality and runtime.

3.1.1. Effect of Cluster Numbers on Solution Quality and Runtime

Smaller numbers of clusters (5) lead to longer computation times without significant improvements in solution quality. This is because fewer clusters result in routes that are "too good", leading to a higher number of missing edges compared to using a larger number of clusters. Although solving smaller subproblems takes less time, creating clusters and connecting subpaths into a complete solution requires additional time resources. These opposing effects seem to balance each other out when using cluster numbers between 10 and 20, resulting in nearly identical runtimes. Increasing the number of clusters also raises the average vertex degree. Considering this, choosing 10 clusters appears to be a good compromise in terms of the number of missing edges and the average vertex degree.

3.1.2. Impact of Basic Moves in the Lin–Kernighan Heuristic

Helsgaun's Lin–Kernighan heuristic was employed in three phases of our novel method: for solving the subproblems, connecting the tours, and for post-optimization. The impact of the basic move on the method's effectiveness was thoroughly analyzed. The choice of basic move significantly influences both the run time and the quality of the solution. Table 3 shows the average gap percentages relative to the optimal solution and the average computation time per tour for various basic moves used in the LKH heuristic. As indicated, increasing the complexity of the move affects both tour quality and computational efficiency. Specifically, the 2-opt move results in a higher average gap of 10.79% but has the shortest average computation time of 0.229 s per tour. Conversely, the 3-opt move improves tour quality to an average gap of 6.14%, with a slightly increased computation time of 0.354 s. The 4-opt and 5-opt moves further enhance tour quality, reducing the average gap to 4.83% and 4.38%, respectively, but they also lead to longer computation times of 0.853 s and 2.562 s per tour. Thus, while more complex moves generally yield better solutions, they require more computational resources. It can be concluded that the 3-opt move is the optimal choice. Although increasing the complexity of the basic move slightly reduces the size of the candidate set (as shown in Figure 7), it does not improve significantly the rate of decrease in the missing edges (Figure 8). Furthermore, using 4-opt and 5-opt requires longer runtimes and more iterations compared to the 3-opt move to ensure that the candidate set includes all edges of the optimal solution. This is because while more complex moves generate better routes, they may also exclude some edges of the optimal solution from the candidate set. For the E10k0 instance, identifying all the edges included in the optimal solution requires 73 iterations with the 4-opt move, while only 64 iterations are needed with the 3-opt move (Figure 7). When accounting for the average time required to generate a single tour with both the 3-opt and 4-opt moves (Table 3), it is observed that finding all the optimal edges with the 4-opt move takes approximately 2.75-times longer than with the 3-opt move.

Table 3. Results with using different basic moves on the E10k0 instance (fuzzy clusters, $m = 1.05$, $n_{cluster} = 10$, post_opt = yes, $n_{postopt} = 10$, and $postopt$ = nodes/10).

Basic Move	Avg. Gap [%]	Avg. Time [s]/Tour
2-opt	10.79	0.229
3-opt	6.14	0.354
4-opt	4.83	0.853
5-opt	4.38	2.562

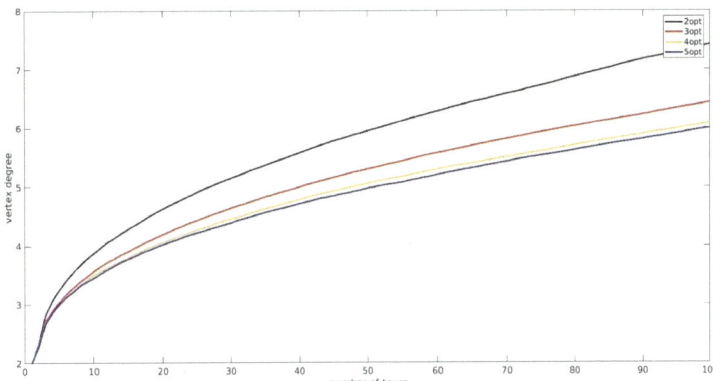

Figure 7. The candidate set size with different basic steps on the E10k0 instance (fuzzy clusters, $m = 1.05$) vs. hard clusters ($n_{cluster} = 10$, post_opt = yes, $n_{postopt} = 10$, and $postopt$ = nodes/10).

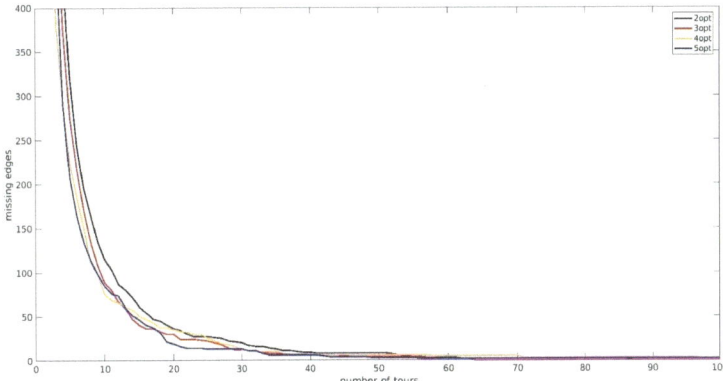

Figure 8. The reduction in the number of missing edges with different basic steps on the E10k0 instance (fuzzy clusters, $m = 1.05$, $n_{cluster} = 10$, post_opt = yes, $n_{postopt} = 10$, and $postopt$ = nodes/10).

3.1.3. Fuzzy Clustering vs. Traditional Clustering

Based on the simulations, it can be concluded that fuzzy clustering offers significant advantages over traditional clustering methods (see Figures 9 and 10). While standard clustering can also produce a high-quality candidate set, it typically requires merging more tours and thus demands more computational time. For example, with the E10k0 instance, the fuzzy clustering approach identified all the edges of the optimal solution after merging 64 tours, whereas the traditional clustering method needed 97 iterations to achieve similar results. Allowing a small degree of fuzziness in the clustering process not only facilitates the rapid reduction in missing edges relative to the number of iterations but also provides an efficient balance between solution quality and computational effort. This is evident from the faster decrease in the number of missing edges observed with fuzzy clustering (see Figure 9).

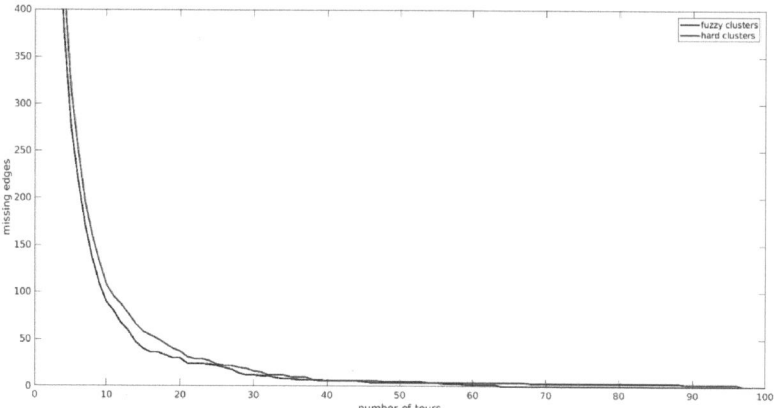

Figure 9. The reduction in the number of missing edges on the E10k0 instance fuzzy ($m = 1.05$) vs. hard clusters ($n_{cluster} = 10$, post_opt = yes, $n_{postopt} = 10$, and $postopt$ = nodes/10).

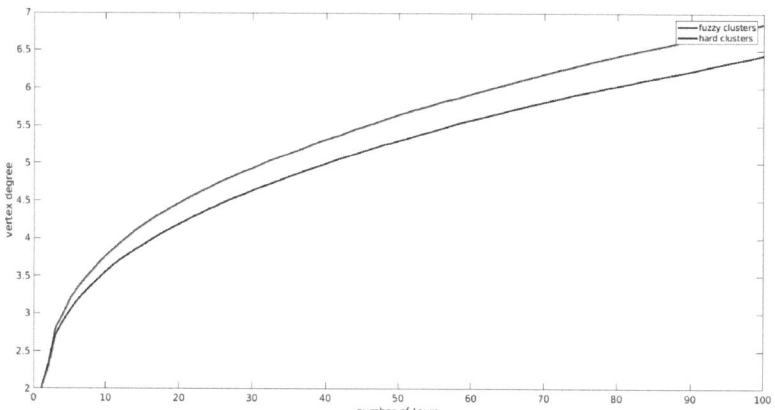

Figure 10. The candidate set size on the E10k0 instance fuzzy ($m = 1.05$ vs. normal clusters ($n_{cluster} = 10$, post_opt = yes, $n_{postopt} = 10$, and $postopt$ = nodes/10).

3.1.4. Effects of the Fuzziness Parameter

Increasing the fuzziness parameter m resulted in a somewhat faster reduction in missing edges as the number of iterations increased (Figure 11). However, it is crucial to consider that a higher m value significantly enlarges the candidate set, as depicted in Figure 12. This increase in candidate set size occurs because, with higher fuzziness, points that are far from each other can be assigned to the same cluster. Consequently, this broader clustering leads to a larger candidate set. Therefore, it is advisable to choose a small degree of fuzziness, close to 1 (e.g., m = 1.05, which is used as the default value), to strike a balance between the efficiency of edge inclusion and the size of the candidate set.

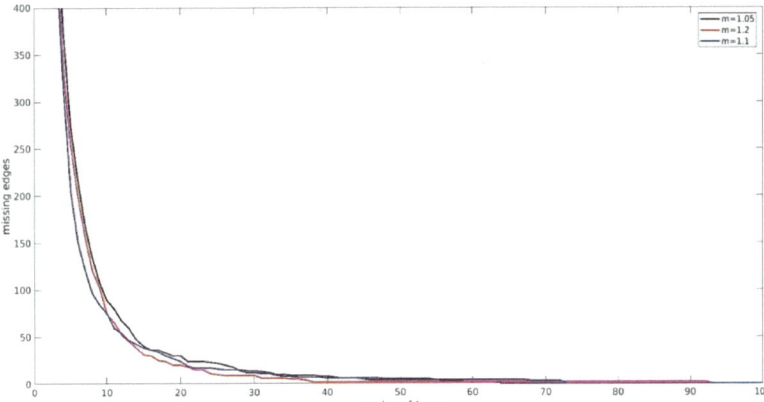

Figure 11. The reduction in the number of missing edges with different parameter m values on the E10k0 instance (fuzzy clusters, $n_{cluster}$ = 10, post_opt = yes, $n_{postopt}$ = 10, and $postopt$ = nodes/10).

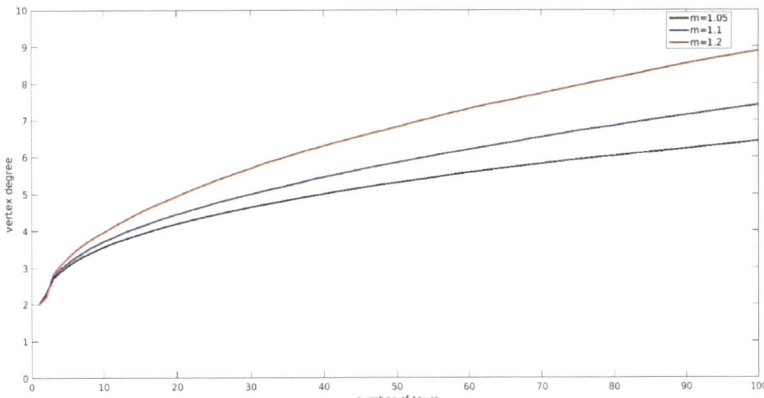

Figure 12. The candidate set size with m parameter values on the E10k0 instance (fuzzy clusters, $n_{cluster}$ = 10, post_opt = yes, $n_{postopt}$ = 10, and $postopt$ = nodes/10).

3.1.5. Post-Optimization Impact

With post-optimization, the number of missing edges and the size of the candidate set can be reduced. Although the post-optimization of longer segments usually results in a greater improvement in the length of the route, this does not necessarily mean an improvement in the quality of the candidate set (in fact, in some cases, it can even make it worse missing more edges of the optimal or best-known solution); moreover, it takes longer time to perform. Although the longest segment length initially shows the fastest reduction in missing edges for the E10k0 instance, it still requires more iterations than the other two parameter settings to find all edges in the optimal solution (see Figure 13). On the other hand, increasing the length of the segment slightly increases the size of the candidate set (see Figure 14). For these reasons, the default parameter values are set to segment length $postopt$ = nodes/10 and number of post-optimization iterations $n_{postopt}$ = 10, balancing the convergence speed and the candidate set size.

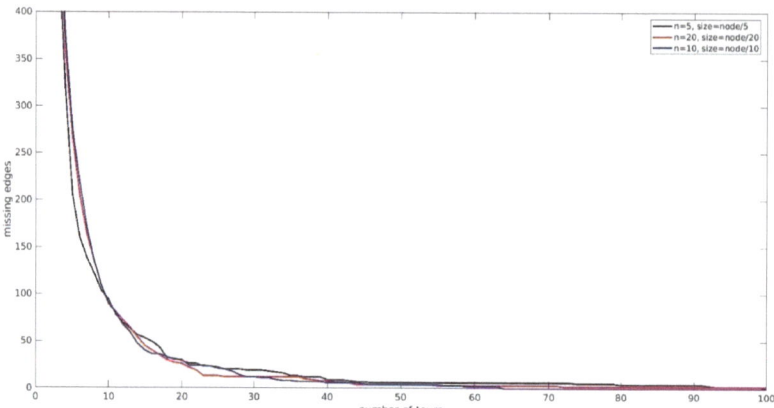

Figure 13. The reduction in the number of missing edges with different parameter values of the post-optimization on the E10k0 instance (fuzzy clusters, $m = 1.05$, $n_{cluster} = 10$, and post_opt = yes).

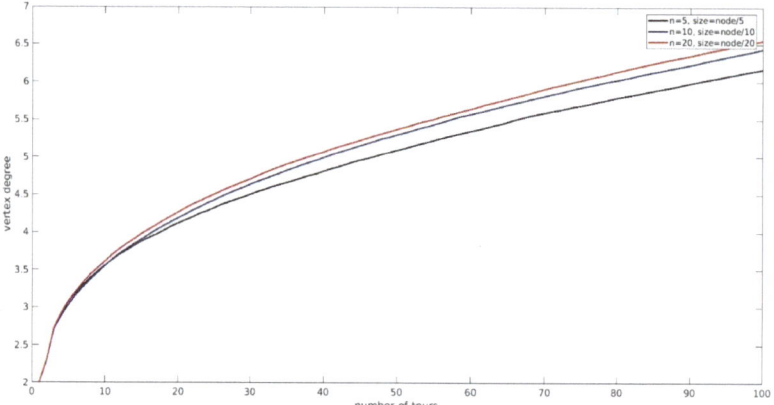

Figure 14. The candidate set size with different parameter values of the post-optimization on the E10k0 instance (fuzzy clusters, $m = 1.05$, $n_{cluster} = 10$, and post_opt = yes).

3.2. Comparison with the POPMUSIC Heuristic

Based on the parameter tuning experience, our comparative analysis uses and recommends the following parameter values for our new heuristic:

- Fuzzy clusters with $m = 1.05$ and $n_{cluster} = 10$;
- LKH with 3-opt basic moves;
- post_opt = yes;
- $n_{postopt} = 10$;
- $postopt = $ nodes/10.

Using these parameters, our tour construction heuristic produced high-quality candidate sets, achieving a good compromise between the number of missing edges and the size of the candidate set (see Tables 1 and 2).

3.2.1. Evaluation on Benchmark Instances

We compared our heuristic's performance with the improved POPMUSIC method using VLSI and national TSP instances (see Tables 4 and 5). The simulations were conducted on the same computer. The VLSI instances represent real-world challenges in integrated circuit design. VLSI design requires the efficient placement and routing of a vast number of components on a chip, often involving tens or even hundreds of thousands of connections. The complexity of these instances is comparable to large-scale TSP problems, where finding near-optimal routing solutions is critical for minimizing wire length, reducing signal delay, and improving overall chip performance. Given the scale of modern VLSI problems, where the number of components can easily exceed 100,000, a highly efficient heuristic is essential. Our method demonstrated strong performance on these VLSI instances, making it a promising tool for optimizing large-scale integrated circuit layouts in a feasible time frame, which is crucial for advancing the efficiency and cost-effectiveness of semiconductor manufacturing. The national TSP instances simulate real-world geographic routing problems. These instances are designed to reflect the challenges faced in logistics, transportation, and supply chain management, where the goal is to optimize routes across vast geographical regions. In these scenarios, minimizing travel distance is critical for reducing operational costs and improving delivery efficiency. National TSP instances often involve thousands or even tens of thousands of locations, making the ability to efficiently handle large-scale problems essential. Our method showed strong performance for these instances, demonstrating its practical applicability in optimizing complex logistics and transportation networks, where the scale and complexity of the problem can have a significant impact on real-world operations. The candidate set for our method was generated by merging the edges from 100 tours created with our fuzzy clustering-based approach. We evaluated the fast POPMUSIC method using the recommended default parameters from the literature. Our comparison revealed that although POPMUSIC is faster, our method produces smaller candidate sets with a comparable number of missing edges. Additionally, the results show that VLSI problems are significantly more challenging than national TSP instances. Specifically, the constructed tours for VLSI problems are further from the optimal solution, and the number of missing edges is higher compared to those for world TSP problems (e.g., bm33708 versus dan59296). The average gap [%] represents the deviation from the optimal or best-known solution. The results indicate that our heuristic consistently produces better-quality tours, as evidenced by the lower average gap percentages compared to those obtained using the fast POPMUSIC method.

Table 4. Comparison of candidate sets on VLSI instances.

	Fuzzy Cluster Based				Fast POPMUSIC			
	Candidate Set		Time [s]	Avg. Gap [%]	Candidate Set		Time [s]	Avg. Gap [%]
	Size	Missing Edges			Size	Missing Edges		
dkc3938	7.1	3	12.99	13.44	7.8	5	7.38	17.04
xmc10150	7.7	14	34.82	16.06	8.7	18	16.10	20.06
pba38478	7.9	81	115.37	13.79	8.4	63	60.99	19.41
ics39603	6.9	48	125.78	14.09	8.4	34	63.69	20.44
dan59296	7.3	72	150.01	14.03	8.6	62	88.64	19.45
sra104815	7.6	140	511.78	15.98	8.6	98	170.86	19.29
ara238025	7.7	320	1298.22	13.29	8.6	221	376.76	19.94

Table 5. Comparison of candidate sets on national instances.

	Fuzzy Cluster Based				Fast POPMUSIC			
	Candidate Set		Time [s]	Avg. Gap [%]	Candidate Set		Time [s]	Avg. Gap [%]
	Size	Missing Edges			Size	Missing Edges		
ei8246	4.9	0	25.76	6.76	6.3	0	13.59	12.26
fi10639	6.3	3	36.58	7.69	7.1	2	18.56	13.15

Table 5. *Cont.*

	Fuzzy Cluster Based				Fast POPMUSIC			
	Candidate Set		Time [s]	Avg. Gap [%]	Candidate Set		Time [s]	Avg. Gap [%]
	Size	Missing Edges			Size	Missing Edges		
mo14185	6.3	0	42.61	8.19	7.1	3	28.69	13.57
it16862	5.8	3	60.31	6.86	7.0	0	27.14	12.86
vm22775	5.7	6	72.30	4.83	7.0	3	24.55	12.93
sw24978	6.0	3	73.91	6.87	7.1	5	24.91	13.31
bm33708	5.9	13	97.72	5.80	7.1	6	50.28	13.28
ch71009	6.2	18	281.18	5.55	7.1	9	114.14	11.72

3.2.2. Time Complexity Analysis

To determine the empirical time complexity of our novel tour construction heuristic, a polynomial curve was fit on the run times. The parameters of the polynomial model were determined by minimizing the RMSE with 95% confidence bounds (in Table 6). The time complexity is near linear, similar to the improved version of the POPMUSIC heuristic, so it can be used for creating the candidate sets of even large-sized instances with several hundred thousand nodes. Figure 15 shows the fitted curve.

Table 6. The parameters of the polynomial curve fitting.

a	b	R^2
0.0001741 (2.26×10^{-6}, 0.0003459)	1.279 (1.198, 1.36)	0.994

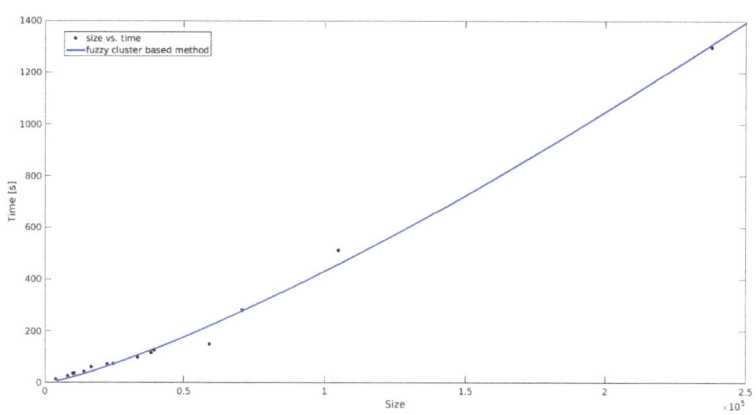

Figure 15. The polynomial curve fitted to our tour construction heuristic.

3.2.3. Tour Improvement Performance

Our proposed method is designed to generate high-quality candidate edges to enhance the performance of heuristic or metaheuristic approaches during the tour improvement phase. To evaluate its efficiency, we used the state-of-the-art TSP heuristic, the LKH algorithm (version LKH-2.0.10), with candidate sets generated by our heuristic. The LKH algorithm was configured with 5-opt steps as basic moves and was run with a termination condition set to 1000 trials, with each instance tested 10 times. Additionally, simulations were conducted using candidate sets from the improved version of the POPMUSIC heuristic, with a time limit set for fair comparison.

The results, summarized in Table 7, reveal that LKH using candidate sets from our fuzzy clustering-based method consistently produced high-quality solutions, with tour gaps of less than 0.1% from the best-known solutions. In contrast, while the fast POPMUSIC method generates candidate sets more quickly, our method provides higher quality candidate sets, leading to superior tour improvement. This suggests that our method offers a more effective solution for enhancing tour optimization.

Table 7. Comparison of results on Euclidean instances. (The better results are highlighted in bold).

Instance	Fuzzy Cluster Based (100 Tours)					POPMUSIC				Time Limit[s]
	Candidate Set		LKH (1000 Trials)			Candidate Set		LKH		
	Size	Time [s]	Avg. Time [s]	Best Gap	Avg. Gap	Size	Time [s]	Best Gap	Avg. Gap	
E10k0	6.4	36.483	255.49	0.01%	0.02%	7.1	17.82	**0.00%**	**0.01%**	300
E31k0	6.2	124.652	1880.12	**0.01%**	**0.02%**	7.2	55.67	0.01%	0.03%	2000
E100k0	6.1	419.819	14,462.18	**0.03%**	**0.04%**	7.2	136.53	0.05%	0.06%	15,000
E316k0	6	1642.85	102,750.02	**0.09%**	**0.09%**	7.3	569.87	0.10%	0.10%	110,000

Figure 16 illustrates the convergence speed to the best-known solution using candidate sets from both our approach and the POPMUSIC method for the E100k0 instance. The graph displays the gap between the average tour length of 10 runs and the best-known solution over time. Initially, the LKH algorithm with candidate sets from the POPMUSIC heuristic shows superior performance, achieving better results up to approximately 1000 s. However, beyond this point, the LKH algorithm utilizing candidate sets from our approach begins to outperform the POPMUSIC-based sets. This shift occurs because the LKH algorithm with the larger candidate set initially finds better tours more quickly. Over time, though, the candidate sets generated by our approach enable the LKH algorithm to overcome this initial advantage and achieve better results overall.

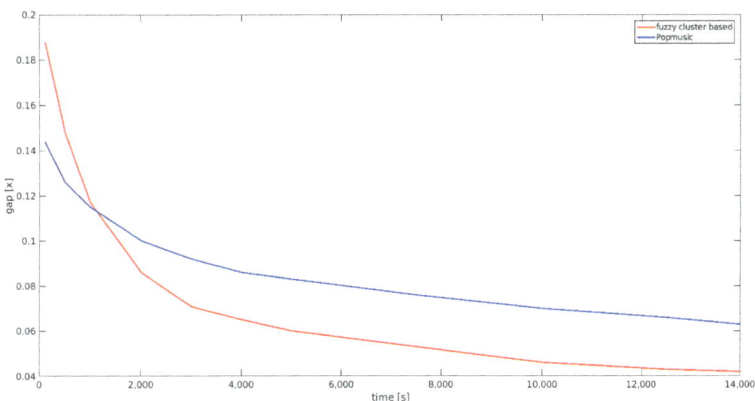

Figure 16. The comparison of reduction in gap over time using our fuzzy cluster-based and POPMUSIC candidate set generating methods.

3.3. Discussion

In this section, we evaluate the strengths and weaknesses of our proposed heuristic in comparison with the POPMUSIC method, highlighting how each method's characteristics impact their performance in practical scenarios.

One of the main advantages of our heuristic over POPMUSIC is the quality of the candidate sets it generates. While POPMUSIC is efficient in producing candidate sets quickly, this speed comes at the cost of generating larger candidate sets. The downside of these larger sets becomes apparent during the optimization phase, as more unnecessary options need to be considered and processed. This increases the computational load and time required to handle the excess candidate edges, ultimately affecting the efficiency of finding high-quality solutions.

In contrast, our heuristic is designed to create smaller, more refined candidate sets that are more manageable during the optimization process. By focusing on quality rather than quantity, our method tends to produce candidate sets that lead to better performance in the subsequent optimization phases. This is particularly evident when using the LKH algorithm with candidate sets generated by our approach. The LKH algorithm demonstrated superior results in terms of tour quality and convergence speed when given the candidate sets from our heuristic, compared to those generated via POPMUSIC. Reinelt, in his studies on 2-opt and 3-opt local searches, similarly observed the impact of candidate set size and quality on optimization results. It was found that larger candidate sets for 2-opt and 3-opt are not worthwhile, as they significantly increase computational time. This is consistent with our approach, where smaller candidate sets lead to faster convergence and better optimization performance when using the Lin–Kernighan heuristic [27].

For example, the LKH algorithm demonstrates the impact of high-quality candidate sets on optimization performance [2]. In the earlier versions of the Lin–Kernighan heuristic, the Nearest Neighbor (NN) algorithm was used to generate candidate sets, which often resulted in larger and less-refined sets [28]. However, Helsgaun introduced a shift to using alpha candidate sets in his implementation. The alpha candidate sets are defined by an alpha parameter that limits the candidate edges to those within a specified distance, leading to smaller and more targeted sets compared to the NN approach. This transition to alpha candidate sets significantly improved the LKH algorithm's performance, as evidenced by superior tour quality and faster convergence rates [2]. Similarly, our heuristic's focus on generating smaller, high-quality candidate sets mirrors this approach and achieves comparable improvements in performance during the optimization phase. Our results align with Helsgaun's findings, illustrating that refining candidate sets can lead to more effective optimization, particularly in terms of tour quality and convergence speed.

However, it is important to note that the trade-off for this improved performance is an increase in computational time for generating the candidate sets. Our heuristic requires more time to produce candidate sets compared to POPMUSIC, which can be a significant consideration in time-sensitive applications or scenarios where rapid results are needed. Despite this, the benefit of higher-quality candidate sets often outweighs the additional time investment, especially in cases where achieving near-optimal solutions is crucial.

In summary, while POPMUSIC is faster and may be preferable in situations where time is of essential importance, our proposed heuristic offers notable advantages in terms of the quality of the candidate sets and the effectiveness of the tour improvement phase. The trade-off between the speed of candidate set generation and the quality of the resulting tours highlights the importance of selecting the appropriate heuristic based on the specific requirements and constraints of the problem at hand.

4. Conclusions

The research presented in this paper highlights the critical role of candidate set quality in the success of tour improvement methods for solving the Traveling Salesman Problem (TSP), particularly as problem instances scale up. We introduced a novel tour construction heuristic grounded in fuzzy clustering, which proves to be highly effective for generating candidate sets in a nearly linear time complexity framework. Our extensive experimentation on large-scale TSP instances, including Euclidean and VLSI datasets, confirms that the proposed method covers almost all edges of the best-known solutions. Moreover, when integrated with Helsgaun's Lin–Kernighan heuristic, the method not only accelerates convergence but also achieves superior results compared to the improved POPMUSIC algorithm. These findings suggest that our approach offers a robust and scalable solution for addressing large-scale TSP challenges, paving the way for more efficient optimization in combinatorial problems. Future work may explore further refinements of the heuristic and its application to other complex optimization problems.

Author Contributions: Conceptualization, B.T.-S., P.F. and L.T.K.; methodology, B.T.-S.; software, B.T.-S.; validation, B.T.-S.; writing—original draft preparation, B.T.-S.; writing—review and editing, L.T.K.; visualization, B.T.-S.; supervision, L.T.K. and P.F.; funding acquisition, B.T.-S. All authors have read and agreed to the published version of the manuscript.

Funding: This work was supported by the ÚNKP-22-4 New National Excellence Program of the Ministry of Human Capacities.

Data Availability Statement: The source code of our algorithm and the instances used in the experiments will be made available upon request. A subset of the tested instances is publicly accessible at https://www.math.uwaterloo.ca/tsp/data/index.html (accessed on 18 September 2024).

Conflicts of Interest: The authors declare no conflicts of interest.

References

1. Applegate, D.L.; Bixby, R.E.; Chvátal, V.; Cook, W.J.; Espinoza, D.; Goycoolea, M.; Helsgaun, K. Certification of an optimal tour through 85,900 cities. *Oper. Res. Lett.* **2009**, *37*, 11–15. [CrossRef]
2. Helsgaun, K. An effective implementation of the Lin-Kernighan traveling salesman heuristic. *Eur. J. Oper. Res.* **2000**, *126*, 106–130. [CrossRef]
3. Moscato, P. On Evolution, Search, Optimization, Genetic Algorithms and Martial Arts—Towards Memetic Algorithms. In *Technical Report Caltech Concurrent Computation Program, Report 826*; California Institute of Technology: Pasadena, CA, USA, 1989.
4. Kóczy, L.T.; Földesi, P.; Tüű-Szabó, B. Enhanced discrete bacterial memetic evolutionary algorithm—An efficacious metaheuristic for the traveling salesman optimization. *Inf. Sci.* **2018**, *460–461*, 389–400. [CrossRef]
5. Nguyen, H.D.; Yoshihara, I.; Yamamori, K.; Yasunaga, M. Implementation of an effective hybrid GA for large-scale traveling salesman problems. *IEEE Trans. Syst. Man Cybern. Part B (Cybern.)* **2007**, *37*, 92–99. [CrossRef] [PubMed]
6. Skinderowicz, R. Improving Ant Colony Optimization efficiency for solving large TSP instances. *Appl. Soft Comput.* **2022**, *120*, 108653. [CrossRef]
7. Singh, S.P.; Kumar, N.; Dhiman, G.; Vimal, S.; Viriyasitavat, W. AI-Powered Metaheuristic Algorithms: Enhancing Detection and Defense for Consumer Technology. *IEEE Consum. Electron. Mag.* **2024**, 1–8. [CrossRef]
8. Jauhar, S.K.; Pant, M. Genetic algorithms in supply chain management: A critical analysis of the literature. *Sādhanā* **2016**, *41*, 993–1017. [CrossRef]
9. Balaji, A.N.; Jawahar, N. A simulated annealing algorithm for a two-stage fixed charge distribution problem of a supply chain. *Int. J. Oper. Res.* **2010**, *7*, 192–215. [CrossRef]
10. Bentley, J.L. Multidimensional binary search trees used for associative searching. *Commun. ACM* **1975**, *18*, 509–517. [CrossRef]
11. Padberg, M.W.; Rinaldi, G. Optimization of a 532-city symmetric traveling salesman problem by branch and cut. *Oper. Res. Lett.* **1987**, *6*, 1–7. [CrossRef]
12. Applegate, D.L.; Bixby, R.E.; Chvátal, V.; Cook, W.J. *The Traveling Salesman Problem: A Computational Study*, 1st ed.; Princeton University Press: Princeton, NJ, USA, 2007; pp. 469–489.
13. Blazinskas, A.; Misevicius, A. Generating High Quality Candidate Sets by Tour Merging for the Traveling Salesman Problem. In *Information and Software Technologies. ICIST 2012 Communications in Computer and Information Science*; Skersys, T., Butleris, R., Butkiene, R., Eds.; Springer: Berlin/Heidelberg, Germany, 2012; Volume 319.
14. Ali, I.J.; Tüű-Szabó, B.; Kóczy, L.T. Effect of the initial population construction on the DBMEA algorithm searching for the optimal solution of the traveling salesman problem. *Infocommun. J.* **2022**, *14*, 72–78.
15. Taillard, E.D.; Voss, S. Popmusic—Partial Optimization Metaheuristic under Special Intensification Conditions. In *Essays and Surveys in Metaheuristics*; Operations Research/Computer Science Interfaces Series; Springer: Boston, MA, USA, 2002; Volume 15.
16. Taillard, E.D. Heuristic methods for large centroid clustering problems. *J. Heuristics* **2003**, *9*, 51–73. [CrossRef]
17. Queiroga, E.; Sadykov, R.; Uchoa, E. A POPMUSIC matheuristic for the capacitated vehicle routing problem. *Comput. Oper. Res.* **2021**, *136*, 105475. [CrossRef]
18. Alvim, A.C.F.; Taillard, E.D. POPMUSIC for the point feature label placement problem. *Eur. J. Oper. Res.* **2009**, *192*, 396–413. [CrossRef]
19. Taillard, E.D.; Helsgaun, K. POPMUSIC for the travelling salesman problem. *Eur. J. Oper. Res.* **2019**, *272*, 420–429. [CrossRef]
20. Taillard, E.D. A linearithmic heuristic for the travelling salesman problem. *Eur. J. Oper. Res.* **2022**, *297*, 442–450. [CrossRef]
21. Dunn, J.C. A fuzzy relative ISODATA process and its use in detecting compact well-separated clusters. *J. Cybern.* **1974**, *3*, 32–57. [CrossRef]
22. Bezdek, J.C. *Pattern Recognition with Fuzzy Objective Function Algorithms*; Springer: New York, NY, USA, 1981.
23. Suganya, R.; Shanthi, R. Fuzzy c-means algorithm—A review. *Int. J. Sci. Res. Publ.* **2012**, *2*, 1.

24. Kim, W.D.; Lee, K.H.; Lee, D. A novel initialization scheme for the fuzzy c-means algorithm for color clustering. *Pattern Recognit. Lett.* **2004**, *25*, 227–237. [CrossRef]
25. Yu, X.C.; He, H.; Hu, D.; Zhou, W. Land cover classification of remote sensing imagery based on interval-valued data fuzzy c-means algorithm. *Sci. China Earth Sci.* **2014**, *57*, 1306–1313. [CrossRef]
26. Chuang, K.-S.; Tzeng, H.-L.; Chen, S.; Wu, J.; Chen, T.J. Fuzzy c-means clustering with spatial information for image segmentation. *Comput. Med. Imaging Graph.* **2006**, *30*, 9–15. [CrossRef] [PubMed]
27. Reinelt, G. *Improving Solutions. The Traveling Salesman: Computational Solutions for TSP Applications*; Springer: Berlin/Heidelberg, Germany, 1994; pp. 100–132.
28. Lin, S.; Kernighan, B.W. An effective heuristic algorithm for the traveling-salesman problem. *Oper. Res.* **1973**, *21*, 498–516. [CrossRef]

Disclaimer/Publisher's Note: The statements, opinions and data contained in all publications are solely those of the individual author(s) and contributor(s) and not of MDPI and/or the editor(s). MDPI and/or the editor(s) disclaim responsibility for any injury to people or property resulting from any ideas, methods, instructions or products referred to in the content.

Article

Location and Size Planning of Charging Parking Lots Based on EV Charging Demand Prediction and Fuzzy Bi-Objective Optimization

Qiong Bao *, Minghao Gao, Jianming Chen and Xu Tan

School of Transportation, Southeast University, Nanjing 211189, China; 220233378@seu.edu.cn (M.G.); chenjm129@163.com (J.C.); tanxu6@hikvision.com (X.T.)
* Correspondence: baoqiong@seu.edu.cn

Abstract: The market share of electric vehicles (EVs) is growing rapidly. However, given the huge demand for parking and charging of electric vehicles, supporting facilities generally have problems such as insufficient quantity, low utilization efficiency, and mismatch between supply and demand. In this study, based on the actual EV operation data, we propose a driver travel-charging demand prediction method and a fuzzy bi-objective optimization method for location and size planning of charging parking lots (CPLs) based on existing parking facilities, aiming to reduce the charging waiting time of EV users while ensuring the maximal profit of CPL operators. First, the Monte Carlo method is used to construct a driver travel-charging behavior chain and a user spatiotemporal activity transfer model. Then, a user charging decision-making method based on fuzzy logic inference is proposed, which uses the fuzzy membership degree of influencing factors to calculate the charging probability of users at each road node. The travel and charging behavior of large-scale users are then simulated to predict the spatiotemporal distribution of charging demand. Finally, taking the predicted charging demand distribution as an input and the number of CPLs and charging parking spaces as constraints, a bi-objective optimization model for simultaneous location and size planning of CPLs is constructed, and solved using the fuzzy genetic algorithm. The results from a case study indicate that the planning scheme generated from the proposed methods not only reduces the travelling and waiting time of EV users for charging in most of the time, but also controls the upper limit of the number of charging piles to save construction costs and increase the total profit. The research results can provide theoretical support and decision-making reference for the planning of electric vehicle charging facilities and the intelligent management of charging parking lots.

Keywords: electric vehicles; charging demand; charging parking lots; position and size planning; fuzzy bi-objective optimization

MSC: 90-10; 90B20

Citation: Bao, Q.; Gao, M.; Chen, J.; Tan, X. Location and Size Planning of Charging Parking Lots Based on EV Charging Demand Prediction and Fuzzy Bi-Objective Optimization. *Mathematics* **2024**, *12*, 3143. https://doi.org/10.3390/math12193143

Academic Editors: Momcilo Dobrodolac, Stefan Jovcic and Marjana Čubranić-Dobrodolac

Received: 6 September 2024
Revised: 28 September 2024
Accepted: 7 October 2024
Published: 8 October 2024

Copyright: © 2024 by the authors. Licensee MDPI, Basel, Switzerland. This article is an open access article distributed under the terms and conditions of the Creative Commons Attribution (CC BY) license (https://creativecommons.org/licenses/by/4.0/).

1. Introduction

Nowadays, road transportation with fuel vehicles as the main body has aggravated the problems of fossil fuel resource shortage, carbon emissions and air pollution. Electric vehicles (EVs) have been considered as one of the most promising solutions to these problems [1,2]. Subsidies and related policies for EVs in China, Europe, and other countries over the past decade have led to a continuous increase in the penetration rate of EVs [3–5]. According to the global outlook and prediction in 2018, the number of new energy vehicles in the whole world will exceed 130 million by 2030 [6]. Compared with the fuel vehicles, the driving mileage of EVs is vulnerable to the impact of temperature and battery energy storage characteristics, which leads to electricity anxiety and increases the dependence of EVs on charging facilities [7]. Therefore, the layout of charging facilities is particularly important. Meanwhile, the construction cost, construction cycle and other issues should be considered as well.

The underdevelopment of charging infrastructure is one of the main obstacles to the popularization of EVs worldwide. Given the large parking and charging demand, there are currently insufficient charging facilities in many countries and unbalanced supply and demand in time and space; moreover, the construction period of new charging stations is long and the construction costs are high [8]. Therefore, transforming the existing traditional public parking lots into the charging parking lots (CPLs) an efficient and effective way to solve this issue. The question now is how to decide the location of these CPLs and their size. The traditional way to do so is from a macro perspective, that is, to determine the location and size of charging facilities based on some socio-economic indicators such as vehicle ownership, population, and land use. However, the results based on such an approach are often inaccurate or even wrong [9,10]. Therefore, in this study, we propose a new framework to predict the spatial–temporal distribution of EV charging demand, from the perspective of individual travel-charging behavior. More specifically, we analyze the travel and charging behavior of EV users according to their real vehicle usage data, based on which an EV charging demand prediction model is built, and it can then be used to simulate the daily travel and charging process of each vehicle. By aggregating the results of all vehicles under consideration, the spatial–temporal distribution of charging demand of all the EVs in the study area can be estimated.

Moreover, as an important urban infrastructure, the planning and reconstruction of a charging parking lot should consider both the benefit of EV drivers and the profit of CPL operators [11,12]. Therefore, in this study, we propose a fuzzy bi-objective optimization method for the location and size planning of CPLs, which takes the extra time spent by EV drivers for charging, the income of the operators due to this charging service, and the construction cost of CPLs into account. Such a method not only considers the balance between multiple objectives but also improves the model solving speed by introducing a fuzzy membership as the individual fitness function.

The rest of the paper is organized as follows: Section 2 provides a literature review on EV charging demand prediction and charging facility planning. Section 3 presents the modeling process of EV charging demand prediction. Section 4 describes the fuzzy bi-objective optimization model for the location and size planning of CPLs. A case study and the results are given in Section 5, and Section 6 summarizes the key findings from this study.

2. Literature Review
2.1. EV Charging Demand Prediction

The charging demand of electric vehicles generally refers to the sum of the charging power demand generated at a specific time and place after large-scale EVs operate and consume electricity. Previous studies have revealed that the spatial–temporal distribution of EV charging demand is mainly affected by objective factors such as vehicle types, power batteries, charging facilities, charging price, etc., and subjective factors such as user travel and charging psychology [7,13]. Based on the on-board GPS data, Ashtari [9] screened out key influencing factors that influence the charging demand of EV, involving vehicle power type, parking duration, parking type and state of charge (SOC). By exploring the correlation between charging demand and external characteristics, Gopalakrishnan [14] found that point of interest (POI) and traffic density are highly correlated with charging demand.

At present, there are three kinds of charging demand prediction methods. The first type of research method is direct estimation through external data. Dong [15] predicted the spatial–temporal distribution of EV charging demand density in London through geographic information such as POI density, population, and traffic volume. Assuming that there is an equal proportion between the charging demand and traffic flow, Shuai [16] proposed a Voronoi polygon spatial partitioning method based on charging demand clustering and two spatial econometric models, spatial lag model and spatial error model, to quantitatively analyze the influences of various elements on charging demands.

The second type of research method is driver choice prediction, which focuses on predicting which charging station will be selected by drivers for charging. Tian [17] sorted the charging stations in descending order through the two dimensions of distance and historical visit frequency and selected the top-ranked station as the charging station. Jiang [18] proposed a public charging demand prediction based on travel trajectory prediction, taking into account the supply and demand randomness of the transportation system and the heterogeneity of charging behavior of EV users.

The third type of research method is data-driven regression prediction. Data-driven models are free of many parameters and are essential to fully exploit the information contained in the data. Kuang [19] proposed a learning approach for accurate EV charging demand prediction and reasonable pricing, which enabled the integration of convolutional feature engineering, spatial–temporal dual attention mechanism and physics-informed neural network training. Ge [20] proposed a method based on improved random forest to predict the spatial–temporal distribution of EV cluster charging load.

According to the above introduction and analysis, most previous studies assume that fuel vehicles and EVs have the same travel characteristics. The electricity consumption behavior model based on resident travel survey data lacks the support of actual data. In addition, the existing prediction models do not dig deeply into the user travel behavior, resulting in high granularity in spatial distribution prediction.

2.2. Charging Facility Planning

The macro layout and service scope division of EV charging facilities are mainly realized based on spatial analysis, Voronoi diagrams and other methods. Luo [21] offered a strategic approach to EV charging network planning, emphasizing the integration of demand and supply dynamics. This method is accomplished through the utilization of continuous-time fluid queue models alongside discrete flow refueling location modeling, all in the context of innovation diffusion principles. Ip [22] proposed a two-stage model for the planning of EV charging stations. In the first stage, the cluster analysis method was employed to transform road information into charging demand clusters, and in the second stage, the optimization algorithm was utilized to determine the optimal locations for charging stations. Xi [23] built a stochastic charging model to estimate the expected number of EVs, and then used linear integer programming to conduct location and capacity determination to maximize the use of privately owned EVs.

The site selection and capacity determination of EV charging facilities need to consider multiple interests and coordinate multiple objectives. Wang [24] modeled the behavior of EV drivers from two aspects, path selection and charging behavior, to design the location and capacity of charging stations to support long-distance travel of EVs. Zeng [25] developed a metanetwork-based two-stage model for uncongested networks and a network-based bi-level model for congested networks to address the issue of charging station location. At the level of the solution algorithm, Yin [26] proposed particle swarm optimization based on deep neural network modified boundaries (DNNMBPSO) to calculate the optimal solution for charging station siting. In addition to the benefits of EV drivers, the construction cost and revenue of charging stations should also be focused on. Chen [12] established a multi-level programming model for determining the location and capacity of charging facilities. The model aims to minimize the construction costs of these facilities, as well as the travel and waiting times for EV drivers within the transportation network.

The limitation of the recent research is that it mainly focused on solving the problems of service scope division, location and size planning of new charging stations, but urban space demand is strictly limited by cost, land type and other conditions, lacking consideration of establishing planning model combining existing parking facilities and designing effective solution algorithm for this problem.

3. EV Charging Demand Prediction

In this study, the modeling framework for EV charging demand prediction consists of four parts: (i) data feature extraction, (ii) travel behavior modeling, (iii) charging behavior modeling, and (iv) charging demand distribution estimation, which is shown in Figure 1. First, data feature extraction is carried out to obtain the information of users' travel and charging process based on their daily vehicle usage data. Next, travel behavior models and charging behavior models are established to analyze the characteristics of users' travel and charging patterns, respectively, and construct a travel-charging behavior chain, based on which the spatial–temporal distribution of charging demand in the study area can be estimated by simulating the travel and charging behavior of all the EV drivers in this study area.

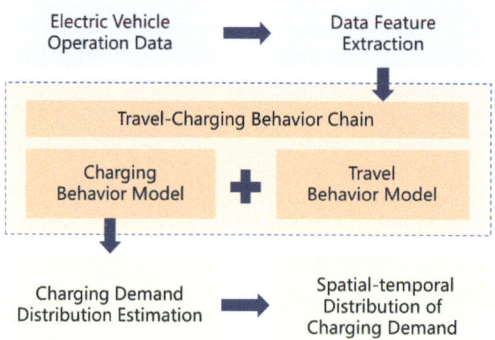

Figure 1. EV charging demand prediction modeling framework.

3.1. Data Feature Extraction

In this study, the usage data of 50 Roewe E50 (with a battery capacity of 22.4 kwh and a rough driving distance of 100 km in normal operating conditions) were provided by the Shanghai New Energy Vehicle Public Data Collection and Monitoring Research Center [27]. The data span from June 2015 to June 2016, with an average record duration of 214 days per vehicle.

Table 1 shows an example of the original data. For each vehicle, the accumulated mileage, SOC, location, and time are recorded, with a data acquisition interval of 30~60 s. The vehicle has several statuses, and a value of 1 and 3 corresponds to normal operation and charging, respectively. Due to personal privacy protection, no information about the driver is provided.

The start and ending time of a vehicle's travel and charging can be identified according to the change in the vehicle status shown in Table 1. Hence, the specific information of the vehicle's travel and charging process can be extracted. One trip may be identified as multiple different trips due to driver operation errors, queuing at intersections and other reasons. In this study, the trips with an interval of less than 10 min were considered as one trip, and a charging time interval of less than 15 min was considered as one single charging behavior. In addition, the data with vacancy and abnormal recording time were discarded. In total, 15,137 trips and 8498 charging sessions were extracted. Tables 2 and 3 show the data extracted during travel and charging, respectively.

Table 1. Recording form of original data (partial).

Vehicle ID	Acquisition Time	Accumulated Mileage	SOC	Longitude	Latitude	Status Start Time	Vehicle Status
1	5 December 2015 22:11:59	748	4	121.2073	31.2901	5 December 2015 22:11:46	3
1	5 December 2015 22:13:42	748	5	121.2073	31.2902	5 December 2015 22:11:46	3
...	...	...	...	...	...	...	...
1	6 December 2015 7:27:32	748	100	121.2073	31.2902	5 December 2015 22:11:46	3
1	6 December 2015 7:28:35	748	100	121.2073	31.2902	5 December 2015 22:11:46	3
1	6 December 2015 7:29:20	748	100	121.2118	31.2883	6 December 2015 7:28:47	1
1	6 December 2015 7:29:53	748	100	121.2154	31.2862	6 December 2015 7:28:47	1

Table 2. Travel behavior data of EV drivers (partial).

Travel ID	Vehicle ID	Departure Time	Travel Duration (min)	Driving Mileage (km)	Power Consumption (%)
630	2	25 July 2015 06:38:23	15.87	4	3
631	2	25 July 2015 12:46:45	89.40	55	58
632	2	25 July 2015 17:18:39	56.30	38	39

Table 3. Charging behavior data of EV drivers (partial).

Charging ID	Vehicle ID	Charging Start Time	Charging Duration (h)	SOC before Charging (%)	SOC after Charging (%)
300	3	31 August 2015 08:22:13	1.06	57	67
301	3	11 September 2015 08:58:06	6.64	18	97
302	3	14 September 2015 09:09:03	6.07	34	64

3.2. Travel Behavior Modeling

Based on the data, the activity–travel chain for daily commuters can be divided mainly into two types: one is from home to work and then back to home, which is recorded as an 'H–W–H' chain, and the other is from home to work, then to commercial leisure places, and finally back to home, which is recorded as an 'H–W–C–H' chain. In both types of activity–travel chain, although daily commuters always leave from their places of residence, the departure time of individual's first trip is uncertain; moreover, although the user's travel distance can be determined after the route selection is completed, the travel speed may vary according to different people and traffic environments, resulting in different travel times for each individual. In addition, when users arrive at the destination, their parking time is also heterogeneous and random due to travel purpose, charging demand and other factors. Therefore, we analyzed these travel behavior characteristics and estimated their probability distribution, respectively.

3.2.1. The Departure Time of the First Trip

Given the collected data, the mixed Gaussian distribution is used to fit drivers' departure time of the first trip, and its probability density function is shown in Formula (1):

$$pdf_T(x) = \sum_{i=1}^{m} \varepsilon_i \frac{1}{\sqrt{2\pi\sigma_i^2}} \exp\left[-\frac{(x-u_i)^2}{2\sigma_i^2}\right] \quad (1)$$

where m is the number of the Gaussian distribution used and u_i, σ_i^2, and ε_i are the mean, variance, and proportion of the Gaussian distribution i, respectively. $\varepsilon_i \in (0,1)$ and $\sum_i \varepsilon_i = 1$.

The fitting result is shown in Figure 2a, and the values of the corresponding parameters are as follows: $m = 2$, $\mu_1 = 12.033$, $\mu_2 = 7.866$, $\sigma_1 = 27.206$, $\sigma_2 = 0.403$, $\varepsilon_1 = 0.747$, and $\varepsilon_2 = 0.253$.

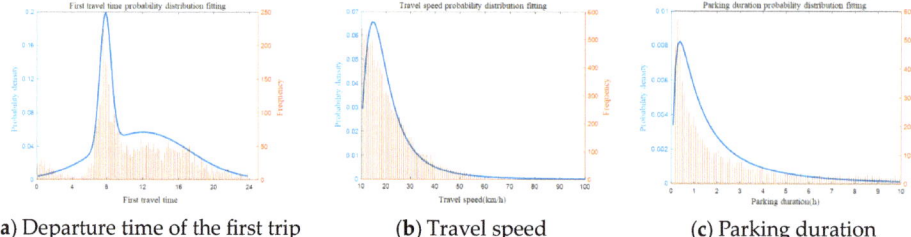

(a) Departure time of the first trip (b) Travel speed (c) Parking duration

Figure 2. Probability distribution fitting of different travel characteristics.

3.2.2. Travel Speed

Given the fact that the travel speed is relatively concentrated at the low-speed range, the generalized extreme value distribution is used to fit the data, and its probability density function is shown in Formula (2).

$$pdf_V(x) = \frac{1}{\sigma}\exp\left\{-\left[1+k\frac{(x-\mu)}{\sigma}\right]^{-\frac{1}{k}}\right\}\left[1+k\frac{(x-\mu)}{\sigma}\right]^{-1-\frac{1}{k}} \quad (2)$$

where μ, σ, and k are three parameters and $k \neq 0$.

The fitting result is shown in Figure 2b, and the values of the corresponding parameters are as follows: $\mu = 16.290$, $\sigma = 5.882$, and $k = 0.337$.

3.2.3. Parking Duration

Based on the characteristics of data distribution, the log normal distribution is applied to fit the data of parking time. The probability density function is shown in Formula (3). By setting $\mu = 5.097$ and $\sigma = 1.568$, the fitting result is shown in Figure 2c.

$$pdf_P(x) = \begin{cases} \frac{1}{x\sqrt{2\pi}\sigma}\exp\left[-\frac{1}{2\sigma^2}(\ln x - \mu)^2\right], & x > 0 \\ 0, & x \leq 0 \end{cases} \quad (3)$$

3.3. Charging Behavior Modeling

3.3.1. Energy Consumption

The travel energy consumption of EVs is mainly determined by the driving distance. The relationship between battery state of charge consumption and driving distance is shown in Formula (4).

$$\Delta SOC = E_{100} * (l/100)/C * 100\% \quad (4)$$

where ΔSOC is the percentage power consumption in one trip (%), l is the travel mileage (km), E_{100} is the vehicle power consumption per hundred kilometers (kwh/100 km), and C is the battery capacity (kwh). For the Roewe E50s, its battery capacity is 22.4 kwh, and its power consumption is 20.4 kwh/100 km according to linear fitting. Regarding its charging power, the average value of 3.8 kw is utilized.

3.3.2. Charging Decision-Making

Charging decision is made by EV drivers based on the comprehensive evaluation of subsequent travel demand, current parking and charging conditions, and so on. Generally, the charging demand is divided into rigid charging demand and elastic charging demand.

Rigid charging is the charging behavior that EV drivers must carry out in order to meet the needs of travel power consumption. If the current remaining power is less than the power consumption of completing the remaining mileage to the destination, drivers must choose to charge until the battery power can meet the remaining mileage or be fully charged. On the contrary, if the remaining power can meet the demand for the next trip, the driver can choose whether to charge or not, so it is called the elastic charging demand.

For elastic charging, a fuzzy logic inference system is established to simulate driver charging decisions based on the factors such as maximum rechargeable capacity during parking (ΔSOC_{max}) and charging price ($c(t)$). The former is related to the parking duration and the current SOC of the battery, which can be calculated using Formula (5), where P is the charging power (kw) and T is the parking duration (h). If the parking duration is brief, users with charging needs may still opt not to charge their vehicles. The current SOC of the battery significantly influences the amount of power that can be accepted. When the battery is nearly fully charged, users are less likely to choose to charge. Additionally, charging cost is directly influenced by the charging price. During peak hours, when electricity prices are elevated, users may opt to delay charging to reduce expenses.

$$\Delta SOC_{max} = \min(P * T/C * 100, 100 - SOC) \tag{5}$$

In the fuzzy logic inference system of elastic charging decision-making, ΔSOC_{max} and $c(t)$ are input variables, and the charging probability is the output variable. For ΔSOC_{max}, three fuzzy sets are defined to express drivers' general judgment on maximum rechargeability, which are low, medium and high. For $c(t)$, the peak–valley charge prices are considered. For the charging probability, five fuzzy sets, i.e., very low, low, medium, high, and very high, are defined to reflect drivers' willingness to charge. Figure 3 shows the corresponding fuzzy membership functions of these input and output variables.

In combination with the actual charging behavior characteristics, six fuzzy inference rules are defined, as shown in Table 4.

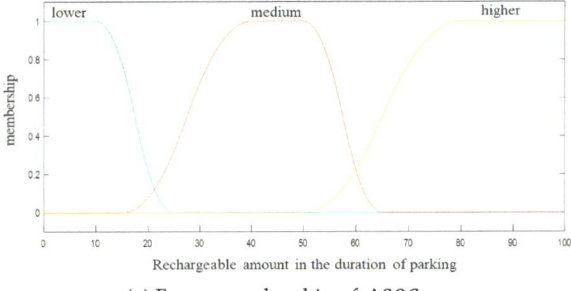

(**a**) Fuzzy membership of ΔSOC_{max}

Figure 3. *Cont.*

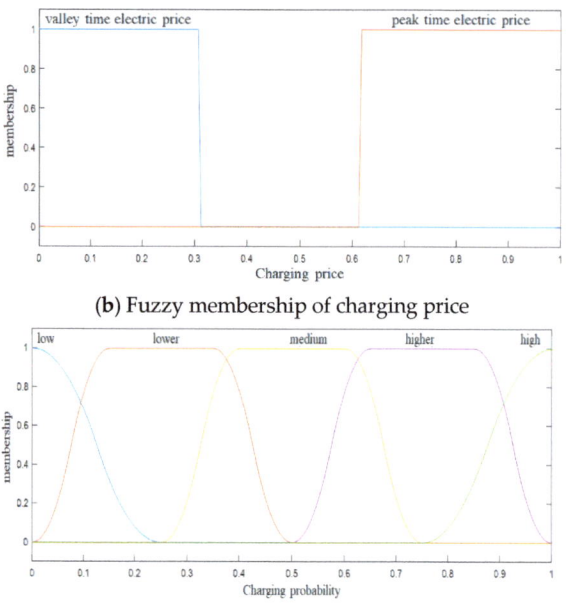

(b) Fuzzy membership of charging price

(c) Fuzzy membership of charging probability

Figure 3. Fuzzy membership functions of the input and output variables.

Table 4. Fuzzy inference rules for charging decision-making.

ID	Rule
Rule 1	IF ΔSOC_{max} == high AND $c(t)$ == c_{valley} THEN charging probability == very
Rule 2	IF ΔSOC_{max} == high AND $c(t)$ == c_{peak} THEN charging probability == high
Rule 3	IF ΔSOC_{max} == medium AND $c(t)$ == c_{valley} THEN charging probability == high
Rule 4	IF ΔSOC_{max} == medium AND $c(t)$ == c_{peak} THEN charging probability == medium
Rule 5	IF ΔSOC_{max} == low AND $c(t)$ == c_{valley} THEN charging probability == low
Rule 6	IF ΔSOC_{max} == low AND $c(t)$ == c_{peak} THEN charging probability == very low

To sum up, after each trip, EV drivers will judge whether the current remaining power can meet the next trip. If not, they have to charge until the battery can meet the remaining mileage or full charge. Otherwise, the charging probability will be estimated according to the elastic charging decision-making system. The travel chain and the charging decision-making system constitute the final travel-charging behavior chain of EV drivers.

3.4. Spatial–Temporal Distribution of Charging Demand

Based on the travel-charging behavior chain generated from the above section, as well as the topological structure of the road network and the classification of land use types in the study area, the Monte Carlo method can be used to simulate the travel and charging behavior of individual EV drivers, based on which the spatial–temporal distribution of the charging demand in this study area can be predicted. This method is widely used in charging demand prediction and large-scale user travel simulation [28]. More specifically, for each individual EV driver, their spatial location of residence, workplace and leisure place (if any) are generated randomly according to the classification of land use types and their travel chain category, and the route of each trip is determined by applying the Logit model, based on which the travel distance can be estimated. Furthermore, the departure time of their first trip, the travel speed (or travel time) of each trip, and the park time after each trip are drawn randomly from the probability distribution functions shown in Figure 2. Thus, the overall time schedule of a driver's one-day trips can be generated.

Meanwhile, assume that the initial SOC of all EV drivers when leaving from home every day is subject to a uniform distribution of 80~100%. When the driver arrives at a destination after one trip, it is determined whether to charge according to the current SOC, as well as the parking time and the distance to the next destination. With respect to the elastic charging, the fuzzy logic inference system introduced in the previous section is applied to make charging decisions. After the whole day trips, the driver arrives at home and charge for the trips of the next day.

In the simulation process, if the driver has charging behavior, their charging location, charging amount, charging power, charging start time, and charging duration are recorded. Finally, the charging power of all drivers is superimposed in space and time to obtain the spatial–temporal distribution characteristics of the charging demand. The overall simulation process of EV charging demand prediction based on the Markov chain Monte Carlo method is shown in Figure 4.

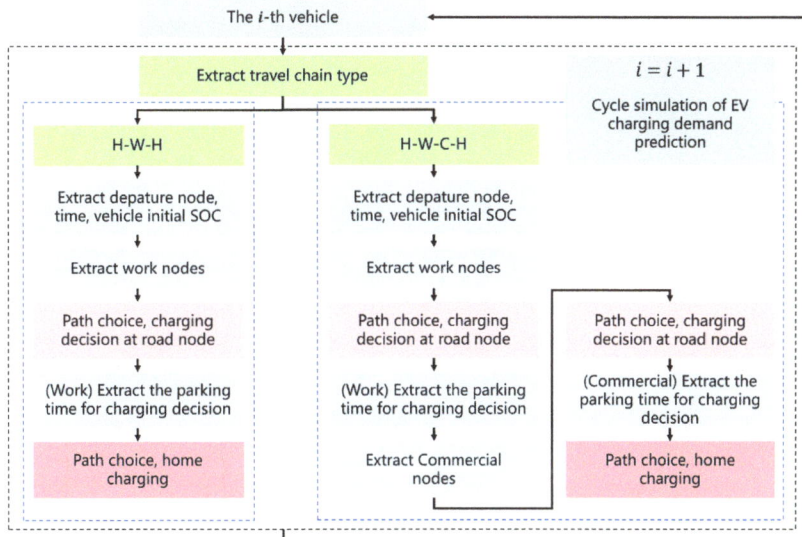

Figure 4. Simulation of EV charging demand.

4. Location and Size Planning of Charging Parking Lots

4.1. Problem Description and Model Assumption

Suppose that there are M public parking lots in the study area, N of which will be transformed into CPLs. In consideration of controlling the construction cost and meeting the parking demand of fuel vehicles, the number of charging piles C_k in each alternative parking lot k ($k = 1, 2, \ldots, N$) should not exceed C_k^{max}. Taking both the benefit of EV drivers and the profit of CPL operators into account, an optimization model is established to determine the optimal location of CPLs and the optimal number of charging piles. In doing so, the following assumptions are proposed:

1. All charging demand points and alternative public parking lots are located at the nodes of the road network;
2. Each charging demand point will be charged at its nearest CPL;
3. Drivers shall follow the shortest path in the road network from the point where the charging demand is generated to the nearest CPL;
4. Drivers are driving at a constant speed v regardless of the road traffic conditions;

5. Considering the capacity of CPLs, when the number of charging vehicles is greater than the number of charging piles in a CPL, the vehicles will have to wait until a charging pile is free to use.

4.2. The Objective Functions

The objectives of the aforementioned problem are twofold. First, the sum of the extra travel time and waiting time of the EVs that have charging demand should be minimized, which is denoted as Objective 1; second, the profit of the CPLs, i.e., the difference between the charging income and the cost of charging facility construction, should be maximized, which is denoted as Objective 2.

The objective function f_1 of Objective 1 can be expressed by Formula (6).

$$f_1 = \min \sum_i (\frac{d_i}{v_i} + Wt_i) \tag{6}$$

where d_i is the distance from the road node where vehicle i generates the charging demand to the nearest CPL, v_i is its travel speed, and Wt_i is the waiting time of vehicle i for charging service.

As for the calculation of waiting time, real-time monitoring of each charging piles is required. To simplify the solution process, we take the calculation of vehicle queuing delay at bottleneck sections as a reference and set the time distribution curve of the number of vehicles required for charging in CPL k as $\varphi_k(t)$. When the amount of charging demand exceeds C_k in the time period t_a to t_b, the area of the charging demand time distribution curve beyond the horizontal line C_k can approximately represent the charging delay in this period, which is recorded as D_k^{ab}, as shown in Formula (7):

$$D_k^{ab} = \int_{t_a}^{t_b} [\varphi_k(t) - C_k] dt \tag{7}$$

The total vehicle waiting time can then be obtained approximately by summing the area of all CPL demand curves exceeding the facility capacity, as shown in Formula (8).

$$\sum_i Wt_i \approx \sum_k \int [\varphi_k(t) - C_k] dt \tag{8}$$

The objective function f_2 of Objective 2 can be expressed by Formula (9).

$$f_2 = \max(\sum_i c_i - \frac{P_c}{T_c} \sum_k C_k) \tag{9}$$

where c_i is the charging cost to be paid by the i-th driver, P_c is the price of a charging pile, and T_c is the service life of a charging pile. Since the charging cost is calculated based on the spatial–temporal distribution of 24 h charging demand, the cost of the charging piles including the total construction price and service life of a charging pile needs to be converted into the daily consumption cost. The Objective 2 is actually to maximize the daily average profit of the charging facilities.

To calculate the value of c_i, it can be estimated from the number of charging vehicles at different times, and subject to the supply quantity of charging piles in the CPL, which is shown in Formula (10).

$$\sum_i c_i = \sum_k \min(\int_{0:00}^{24:00} \varphi_k(t) * P * c_k(t) dt, \int_{0:00}^{24:00} C_k * P * c_k(t) dt) \tag{10}$$

where $c_k(t)$ is the price of timed electricity in the kth CPL and P is the maximum charging power provided by each charging pile.

In summary, Objective 1 and Objective 2 have both synergistic and restrictive relationships with each other. Minimizing the charging distance for users in Objective 1 is to make

CPLs located at the place where the charging demand is most concentrated within its service scale, so as to optimize the spatial layout of the charging facilities. Moreover, the goals of minimizing the waiting time of users in Objective 1 and maximizing the charging income of CPL operators in Objective 2 can be met by increasing the number of charging piles in each CPL. However, the construction cost will increase as well, which will reduce the total profit of CPL operators to a certain extent. Therefore, by satisfying both the objectives, the optimal location and size of CPLs can be determined. The established optimization model considering location and size planning is summarized in Formula (11):

$$\begin{cases} \min\left(\sum_i \frac{d_i}{v_i} + \sum_k^N \int [\varphi_k(t) - C_k] dt\right) \\ \max\left(\sum_k^N \min\left(\int_{0:00}^{24:00} \varphi_k(t) * P * c_k(t) dt, \int_{0:00}^{24:00} C_k * P * c_k(t) dt\right) - \frac{P_c}{T_c} C_k\right) \\ \text{s.t.} \begin{cases} N \leq M \\ C_k \leq C_k^{max}, \; k = 1, 2, \ldots, N \end{cases} \end{cases} \quad (11)$$

4.3. The Fuzzy Genetic Algorithm

For the above bi-objective programming problem, due to the existence of integral and comparative values in the objective functions, it is difficult to obtain to obtain the optimal solution using the conventional numerical optimization method, and the problem-solving efficiency is low. Therefore, in this study, we propose a fuzzy genetic algorithm (FGA) to solve the problem. More specifically, a fuzzy fitness function is established so as to provide a single standard fitness value for assessing the genetic algorithm solution of the bi-objective optimization problem. The core idea of this method is to calculate the membership degree of the optimal solution of each objective and take the minimum value of the membership degree of the optimal solution of each objective as its fitness value in Formula (12).

$$F = \min\{\mu_1(F_1), \mu_2(F_2)\}$$

$$\mu_1(F_1) = \begin{cases} 1, & F_1 \leq F_{1m} \\ \frac{F_{1M} - F_1}{F_{1M} - F_{1m}}, & F_{1m} < F_1 < F_{1M} \\ 0, & F_1 \geq F_{1M} \end{cases}$$

$$\mu_2(F_2) = \begin{cases} 1, & F_2 \geq F_{2M} \\ \frac{F_{2m} - F_2}{F_{2m} - F_{2M}}, & F_{1m} < F_1 < F_{1M} \\ 0, & F_2 \leq F_{2m} \end{cases} \quad (12)$$

where F is the fitness of a solution, F_1 is the solution value of the corresponding objective function f_1, and $\mu_1(F_1)$ is the membership degree of the optimal solution of Objective 1. Similarly, F_2 is the solution value of the corresponding objective function f_2, and $\mu_2(F_2)$ is the membership degree of the optimal solution of Objective 2. When only Objective 1 is considered, the value of the optimal solution corresponding to the objective function f_1 is F_{1m}. That is, the total travel and waiting time for charging is minimized, but the value of objective function f_2 corresponding to this solution, i.e., the profit of the parking lots, is not necessarily maximized, which is recorded as F_{2m}. Similarly, when only Objective 2 is considered, the value of the optimal solution corresponding to the objective function f_2 is F_{2M}. At this time, the profit of the parking lots is maximized, but the value of the objective function f_1 is not necessarily minimized, which is recorded as F_{1M}.

The value of the above fuzzy fitness function is between 0 and 1, with a higher value indicating a better performance in both objectives. Therefore, the main purpose of the genetic algorithm is to search for a solution achieving the highest fitness value F. The algorithm flow chart is shown in Figure 5, and the specific process is given as follows:

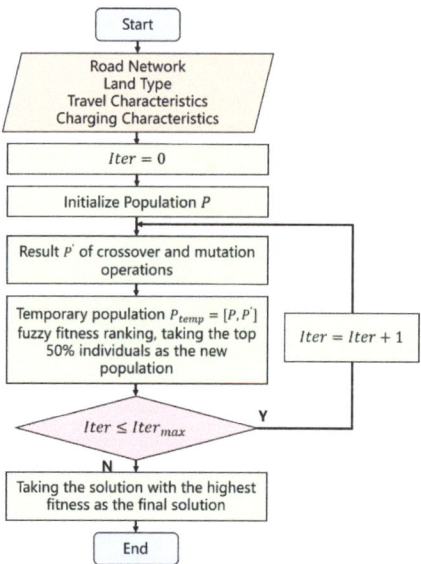

Figure 5. FGA process.

Step 1: Population initialization. Define the basic parameters of the genetic algorithm, including encoding mode, population size Q, individual size M, and maximum iteration number $Iter_{max}$. Here, real number coding is adopted, and the model individual solution is a vector X with a size of $2 \times M$, as shown in Formula (13). The first row represents the locating solution of CPLs, and a value of 0 or 1 is used to indicate whether the corresponding public parking lot is transformed into a CPL. The second row represents the sizing solution of CPLs.

$$X = \begin{bmatrix} \delta_1 & \delta_2 & \cdots & \delta_k & \cdots & \delta_M \\ C_1 & C_2 & \cdots & C_k & \cdots & C_M \end{bmatrix} \quad (13)$$

where $\sum_{k=1}^{M} \delta_k = N$. When $\delta_k = 0$, $C_k = 0$, and when $\delta_k = 1$, $0 < 0 \leq C_k$.

Step 2: Crossover and mutation operation. When the number of iterations does not reach the preset maximum value, crossover operation and mutation operation are performed on individual vector X. The crossover operation is divided into locating solution crossover operation and sizing solution crossover operation, as shown in Figure 6a. For the locating solution crossover operation, two columns of the decision variables are selected and exchanged their position with a probability of P_{c1}. For the sizing solution crossover operation, a column with the locating solution value of 1 is selected, and a linear crossover of real values is conducted with a probability of P_{c2}. For the mutation operation, as shown in Figure 6b, a locating variable is selected with probability P_{m1} to invert it, together with its associated sizing variable. And for the sizing variable with the locating variable equaling to 1, it floats up and down to a certain extent with a probability of P_{m2}.

Step 3: Individual selection. Randomly generate Q feasible solutions that meet the locating and sizing constraints as the first generation of parent population P. Then, all individuals in the population are randomly matched. Each pair of individuals first carries out the locating solution crossover operation with a probability of P_{c1}, and then carries out the sizing solution crossover operation with a probability of P_{c2}. After that, all individuals in the population are selected with a probability of P_{m1} and P_{m2} for the locating and sizing solution mutation operation, respectively. Thus, the new population P' with M individuals can be obtained, and the temporary population $P_{temp} = [P, P']$ together with the parent population P can be constituted. Thereafter, the fitness value of all individuals in P_{temp} is calculated and ranked, and the top Q individuals are selected as the new population of the next generation.

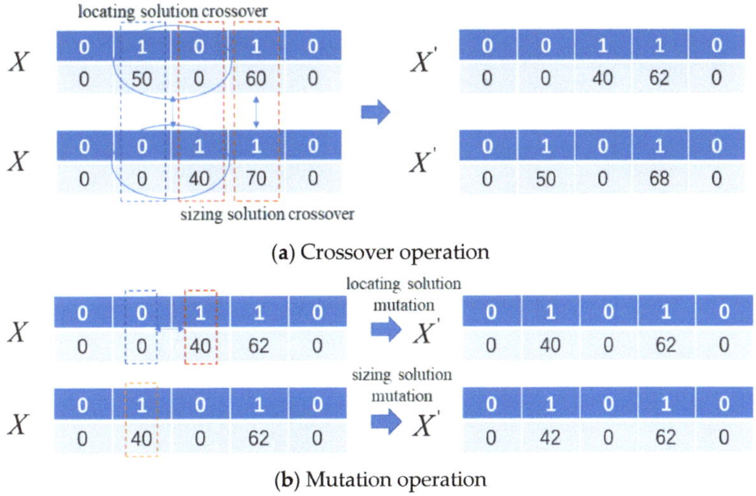

(a) Crossover operation

(b) Mutation operation

Figure 6. Schematic diagram of crossover and mutation operation.

Step 4: Result obtainment. Such an iteration is repeated until the number of iterations reaches $Iter_{max}$. Finally, in the final generation population, the individuals with the highest fitness value are found to reach the optimal solution of the problem.

5. A Case Study
5.1. The Simulation Scenario

Taking the Nguyen–Dupuis road network as the simulation scenario, which has 13 nodes and 19 two-way road sections, assume that nodes 1, 4, 5 and 12 are residential sites, nodes 2, 3, 8 and 13 are working sites, and nodes 6, 7, 9, 10 and 11 are commercial leisure sites (see Figure 7). The distances between two adjacent nodes are given in Table 5.

Suppose that there are 2000 EVs in this study area, and the H–W–H and H–W–C–H travel chains each account for 50%. The proportion of drivers living in nodes 1, 4, 5 and 12 is 0.4, 0.3, 0.2 and 0.1, respectively. The probability matrix of drivers transferring from residential node to working node and from working node to commercial leisure node is shown in Formulas (14) and (15).

Now, suppose that there are five public parking lots located at the five commercial leisure sites, and it is decided to transform two of them into CPLs so as to meet the increasing charging demand of these EVs. The question now is how to choose the appropriate location of these two CPLs and the optimal number of charging piles in each CPL.

$$\begin{array}{c} \\ 1 \\ 4 \\ 5 \\ 12 \end{array} \begin{array}{cccc} 2 & 3 & 8 & 13 \\ \begin{bmatrix} 0.4 & 0.3 & 0.2 & 0.1 \\ 0.1 & 0.3 & 0.2 & 0.4 \\ 0.2 & 0.4 & 0.1 & 0.3 \\ 0.3 & 0.2 & 0.4 & 0.1 \end{bmatrix} \end{array} \quad (14)$$

$$\begin{array}{c} \\ 2 \\ 3 \\ 8 \\ 13 \end{array} \begin{array}{ccccc} 6 & 7 & 9 & 10 & 11 \\ \begin{bmatrix} 0.3 & 0.2 & 0.2 & 0.1 & 0.2 \\ 0.4 & 0.2 & 0.1 & 0.2 & 0.1 \\ 0.3 & 0.2 & 0.1 & 0.3 & 0.1 \\ 0.2 & 0.2 & 0.3 & 0.1 & 0.2 \end{bmatrix} \end{array} \quad (15)$$

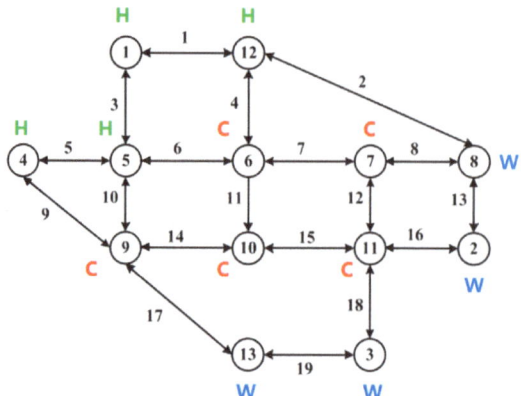

Figure 7. Topological structure of the Nguyen–Dupuis road network.

Table 5. Distance of the road section in the Nguyen–Dupuis road network.

Road Section	Node	Distance (km)	Road Section	Node	Distance (km)
1	1–5	11.2	11	6–7	8
2	1–12	13.6	12	6–10	20.8
3	2–8	14.4	13	6–12	11.2
4	2–11	14.4	14	7–8	8
5	3–11	12.8	15	7–11	14.4
6	3–13	17.6	16	8–12	22.4
7	4–5	14.4	17	9–10	10
8	4–9	19.2	18	9–13	14.4
9	5–6	4.8	19	10–11	10
10	5–9	14.4			

5.2. Results

5.2.1. Spatial–Temporal Distribution of EV Charging Demand

Based on the charging demand prediction model introduced in Section 3, 3673 charging demands with a total of 42,511 kwh are generated from the simulated travel-charging behavior of these 2000 EVs during a working day. Figure 8a shows that there are two peak values in the total charging power. The highest peak happens at 21:00 pm with a value of 5232.6 kw, and the second peak occurs at 10:27 am with a value of 4316.8 kw. A maximum of 1377 vehicles (68.9%) are charging at the same time.

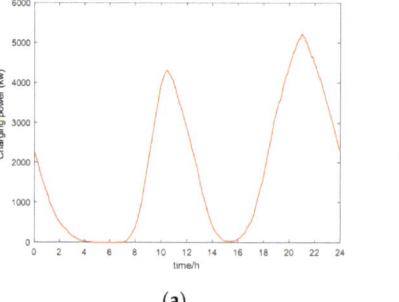

(a)

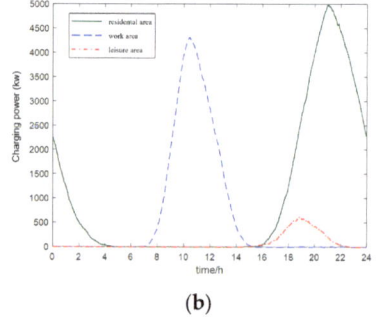

(b)

Figure 8. Load curve of charging demand. (a) Total load curve of regional charging demand during a working day; (b) charging demand load curve of each land use type.

In terms of the spatial distribution, the charging demand load curves of different land use types are shown in Figure 8b. In the residential area, the charging load gradually accumulates from about 16:00 pm to the peak of 21:00 pm, and continues until 4:43 am, accounting for 59.8% of the total charging demand. The work area acts as the first charging place of the travel-charging behavior chain of the EV drivers, and the charging time in this area lasts from 6:36 am to 15:32 pm, completing 35.7% of the total charging demand. Such a result is in line with the basic spatial–temporal rule of EV drivers' travel and charging behavior.

Considering the commercial leisure area, in which the five public parking lots are located, it is the parking place for the EV users with the "H–W–C–H" travel chain. As can be seen from Figure 8b, the charging demand in this area lasts from about 16 pm to 22 pm, with the peak value at 18:50 pm, and 164 vehicles are charging at this moment. Furthermore, the temporal distribution of the charging demand at each node is shown in Figure 9. The numbers of charging requirements at these five nodes (i.e., nodes 6, 7, 9, 10, and 11) are 99, 73, 70, 74 and 73, respectively. It can be seen from (15) that compared with the other four commercial leisure nodes, node 6 undertakes more EV drivers, so its charging demand is also significantly higher than the other four nodes, while those four nodes have similar charging demands.

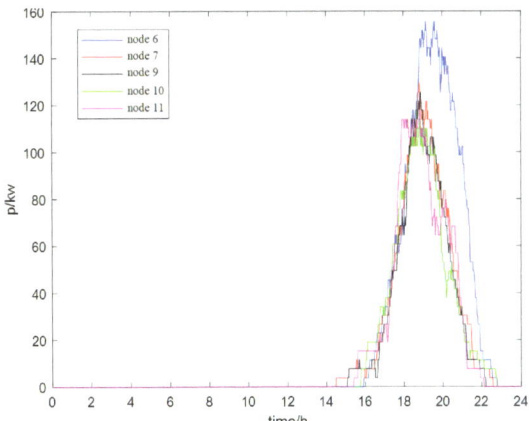

Figure 9. The temporal distribution of charging demand at five commercial leisure nodes.

5.2.2. Sensitivity Analysis of EV Charging Demand

Based on the above simulation conditions, the traffic factors and power consumption factors that affect the charging demand are integrated, and charging demand prediction model variables such as user scale, departure time of the first trip, parking duration, battery capacity and charging power, respectively, fluctuate by 10%. The changes in key indicators such as total charging demand, peak time and peak power of users in non-residential nodes were studied to conduct sensitivity analysis of influencing factors. The results are shown in Table 6.

When the user scale increases by 10%, the total charging demand and peak power of the user in the non-residential area will increase by close to the corresponding proportion, and vice versa. However, the change in user size has no effect on the peak time of charging demand load. In terms of user travel behavior, changes in the departure time of the first trip and travel speed may have little impact on the total charging demand or peak power in non-residential areas. It can be found that the user behavior variable mainly affects the time when the charging load peak occurs. For the departure time of the first trip, the peak time of the charging power of the user is correspondingly advanced or delayed with its advance and delay. The increase in travel speed will advance the charging peak in non-residential areas; the slower travel speed will significantly delay the peak charging time. The extension of parking duration will lead to slightly earlier charging peak times in non-residential areas, caused by users' increased willingness to charge and more concentrated choice of charging. The total charging demand also increases, but the peak charging power decreases due to the extension of the overall parking and charging duration. The change caused by shorter parking duration is the opposite to the change caused by longer parking duration.

Table 6. Sensitivity analysis results of influencing factors of charging demand.

Non-Residential Area		Total Demand (MWh)	Amplitude of Change %	Peak Time	Variation (min)	Peak Power (kw)	Amplitude of Change %
Original parameter		17.081		10:27		4316.8	
User scale	+10%	18.713	9.554 **	10:27	0	4743.8	9.892 **
	−10%	15.455	−9.519 **	10:27	0	3906.4	−9.507 **
Departure time of the first trip	+10%	17.122	0.240	10:46	+19 *	4031.8	−6.602 **
	−10%	16.772	−1.809 *	9:59	−28 **	4297.8	−0.440
Travel speed	+10%	17.067	−0.082	10:21	−6	4301.6	−0.352
	−10%	17.060	−0.123	10:50	+23 **	4199.0	−2.729 *
Parking duration	+10%	17.306	1.317 *	10:22	−5	4290.2	−0.616
	−10%	16.972	−0.638	10:28	+1	4373.8	1.320 *
Battery capacity	+10%	15.508	−9.209 **	10:26	−1	3959.6	−8.275 **
	−10%	18.422	7.851 **	10:26	−1	4727.2	9.507 **
Charging power	+10%	15.745	−7.822 **	10:26	−1	4145.8	−3.961 *
	−10%	18.654	9.209 **	10:32	+5	4434.6	2.729 *
Power consumption per 100 km	+10%	19.876	16.363 ***	10:36	+9	4791.8	11.004 ***
	−10%	13.998	−18.049 ***	10:26	−1	3750.6	−13.116 ***

*—The change amplitude is more than 1% or the change amount is more than 10min; **—The change amplitude is more than 5% or the change amount is more than 20min; ***—The change amplitude is more than 10%.

The increase in power consumption per 100 km will lead to faster power consumption of users, so the total charging demand of users and charging peak power are correspondingly increased, and vice versa. In addition, the increase in power consumption per 100 km will also affect the peak time of the charging load, which is due to the increase in power consumption leading to an increase in charging demand, which leads to an increase in the number of users charging and, thus, charging time, thus delaying the charging peak time. However, the reduction in power consumption per 100 km has little effect on peak charging power times. When the battery capacity is increased by 10%, the total charging demand and peak power of users will decrease, and the peak time of demand load will remain almost unchanged. This is because when the battery capacity rises, the proportion of electricity consumed per trip will decrease accordingly, so that the battery SOC is maintained at a relatively higher state, and the user has less charging demand, so the charging demand in the middle destination of the travel chain is reduced, and more is transferred to charging after going home. When the battery capacity is reduced, the situation is completely the opposite, because the proportion of power consumption of the user will increase. Finally, the increase in charging power can shorten the charging duration, and the ratio of users to concentrate on charging at a certain time is reduced, so that the peak power of charging load in each region is reduced to a certain extent, and the total charging demand of users is also reduced correspondingly, but it has almost no impact on the peak time. On the contrary, the reduction in charging power will lead to an increase in the total charging demand and the peak power of the user, and the charging peak time will be slightly delayed.

5.2.3. Fuzzy Bi-Objective Optimization

Set the genetic algorithm population size to 100, the maximum number of iterations to 100, and each feasible solution to a vector of 2×5. Given the charging demand distribution of five public parking lots, we apply the optimization models presented in Section 4. First, the single Objective 1 is considered, and the optimal solution is $X_1 = \begin{bmatrix} 1 & 0 & 0 & 1 & 0 \\ 89 & 0 & 0 & 92 & 0 \end{bmatrix}$, i.e., nodes 6 and 10 are selected as the locations of 2 CPLs, and 89 and 92 charging piles should be installed at these two nodes, respectively. The value of the objective functions f_1 and f_2, i.e., F_{1m} and F_{2m}, is 3356.7 min and CNY 1021.9, respectively, and the spatial–temporal distribution results of the number of charging vehicles in the CPL are shown in Figure 10.

Next, Objective 2 is individually considered, the optimal solution is $X_2 = \begin{bmatrix} 0 & 1 & 0 & 1 & 0 \\ 0 & 5 & 0 & 20 & 0 \end{bmatrix}$, i.e., nodes 7 and 10 are selected as the locations of 2 CPLs, and 5 and 20 charging piles should be installed at these 2 nodes, respectively. In this case, the value of F_{1m} and F_{2m} is 25,089 min and CNY 1150.1, respectively, the results are shown in the Figure 11. Since Objective 2 only takes the profit of CPL operators into account and ignores the time cost of EV users, the number of charging piles in this scheme is low. Now, if both Objective 1 and Objective 2 are considered, the optimal solution is $X = \begin{bmatrix} 1 & 0 & 0 & 1 & 0 \\ 37 & 0 & 0 & 45 & 0 \end{bmatrix}$. That is, nodes 6 and 10 are selected as the locations of 2 CPLs, and 37 and 45 charging piles should be installed at these 2 nodes, respectively. The value of F_{1m} and F_{2m} is 11,277 min and CNY 1103.3, respectively, and the final fitness is 0.6346, which can better meet the two optimization objectives at the same time. As can be seen, the result of X increases the profit of the CPL operators by 7.97% compared with the result of X_1. Compared with the result of X_2, the profit of the CPL operators only decreases by 4.07%, but the EV driver's extra time for charging decreases by 55.05%; the results are shown in the Figure 12. Thus, such a scheme not only reduces the travelling and waiting time of EV users for charging in most of the time but also controls the upper limit of the number of charging piles to save construction costs and expand total profit. It is a reasonable result and can be used as the optimal scheme for CPL location and size planning of this case study.

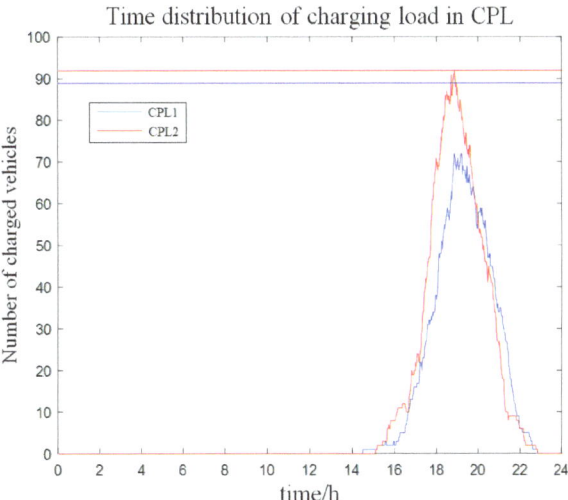

Figure 10. Charging load curve of CPLs based on Objective 1.

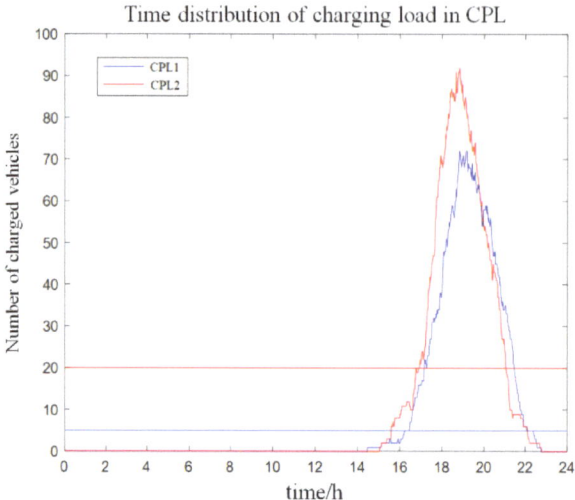

Figure 11. Charging load curve of CPLs based on Objective 2.

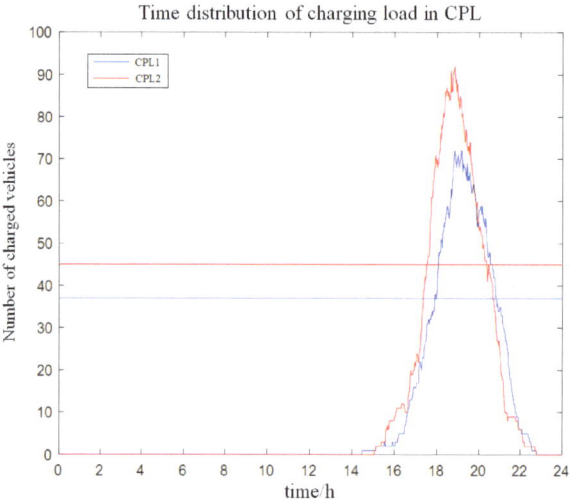

Figure 12. Charging load curve of CPLs based on fuzzy bi-objective optimization.

6. Discussion and Conclusions

This paper analyzes travel and charging behaviors of EV drivers according to the operation data of EVs, establishes a charging demand prediction model for EVs, and then obtains the spatial–temporal distribution of charging demand in the study area. Based on the predicted charging demand spatial–temporal distribution, a fuzzy bi-objective optimization model is built from the perspective of time cost and CPL profit so as to determine the optimal location of CPLs and the number of charging piles.

Compared with the previous studies, the method proposed in this paper is more accurate in predicting the charging demand spatial–temporal distribution of EVs. The travel characteristics extracted based on EVs operation data make the constructed travel-charging behavior chain more able to reflect the travel and charging behavior of actual EV drivers. In addition, the fuzzy elastic charging decision-making method further improves the accuracy of predicting the charging demand spatial–temporal distribution.

The transformation scheme of adding charging piles to some existing public parking lots reduces the construction cost and lowers the waiting time for charging. In terms of CPL location and size planning, the multi-objective optimization method can provide more appropriate results than the single-objective optimization method, and the fuzzy bi-objective optimization algorithm avoids the problems of the traditional algorithm, such as long solving time and high subjectivity of weight.

To sum up, aiming at the problem of insufficient charging facilities, this paper proposes a new planning method to renovate the public parking lot combined with predicting the spatial–temporal distribution of charging demand based on real travel data. The specific contributions are as follows:

1. This paper proposes a transformation scheme of adding charging piles to some existing public parking lots, so as to curtail the construction period, reduce the construction cost and lower the waiting time for charging;
2. A charging demand prediction model considering user travel behavior is constructed by using EV travel data of large sample size to predict charging demand spatial–temporal distribution that accurately considers the road network nodes;
3. According to the influencing factors of EV charging and historical charging data, a fuzzy inference system for elastic charging decision is proposed, which can truly reflect the charging decision-making process under the influence of different residual power and external factors;
4. The optimization model considers both drivers time cost and charging station profit. According to the calculation method of vehicle queuing delay, a method is proposed to calculate the waiting time of charging queuing vehicles;
5. The model proposed in this study considers the location and size planning of charging facilities at the same time, and the fuzzy bi-objective membership is used as the individual fitness function to speed up the solution.

Although the research method proposed in this paper achieves promising results in the planning of charging pile locations (CPLs) and their scale, further research is necessary to enhance the robustness and applicability of the method. Future research should consider the following directions: complex and realistic EV user travel scenarios: (1) incorporate more complex and realistic travel scenarios of EV users, including variations in travel patterns due to seasonal changes, special events, and different geographical regions. (2) Latest and diverse datasets: utilize the latest and diverse datasets to improve the accuracy and relevance of charging demand forecasting models. (3) Impact on the grid: investigate the impact of charging loads on the power grid, including grid dispatch, vehicle-to-grid (V2G) capabilities, and the integration of renewable energy sources. This will aid in developing strategies for grid stability and efficient energy management. (4) Traffic conditions: analyze the impact of road network traffic conditions on the time required for electric vehicles to reach charging stations, enabling more precise planning of CPL locations. (5) Multi-objective optimization improvements: further enhance the multi-objective optimization algorithm to reduce solution time and explore advanced optimization technologies and machine learning methods. By addressing these issues, future research can build on the foundation laid by this study and contribute to more efficient and user-centered EV charging infrastructure planning.

Author Contributions: Conceptualization, Q.B.; methodology, Q.B. and X.T.; formal analysis, X.T. and Q.B.; resources, Q.B.; writing—original draft preparation, M.G., J.C. and X.T.; writing—review and editing, Q.B.; supervision, Q.B.; funding acquisition, Q.B. All authors have read and agreed to the published version of the manuscript.

Funding: This research was funded by the National Natural Science Foundation of China (Grant No. 52002063).

Data Availability Statement: The data presented in this study are available on request from the corresponding author because the data are not publicly available due to privacy.

Conflicts of Interest: The authors declare no conflicts of interest.

References

1. Zhang, X.; Zhang, Z.; Liu, Y.; Xu, Z.; Qu, X. A review of machine learning approaches for electric vehicle energy consumption modelling in urban transportation. *Renew. Energy* **2024**, *234*, 121243. [CrossRef]
2. Ji, W.; Tal, G. Scenarios for transitioning cars from ICEV to BEVs and PHEVs using household level GPS travel data. *Transp. Res. Part D Transp. Environ.* **2020**, *88*, 102555. [CrossRef]
3. Peiseler, L.; Cabrera Serrenho, A. How can current German and EU policies be improved to enhance the reduction of CO_2 emissions of road transport? Revising policies on EVs informed by stakeholder and technical assessments. *Energy Policy* **2022**, *168*, 113124. [CrossRef]
4. Shang, W.; Zhang, J.; Wang, K.; Yang, H.; Ochieng, W. Can financial subsidy increase electric vehicle (EV) penetration—Evidence from a quasi-natural experiment. *Renew. Sustain. Energy Rev.* **2024**, *190*, 114021. [CrossRef]
5. Xiao, L.; Zhang, J.; Wang, C.; Han, R. Optimal fleet replacement management under cap-and-trade system with government subsidy uncertainty. *Multimodal Transp.* **2023**, *2*, 100077. [CrossRef]
6. Javad Mirzaei, M.; Siano, P. Dynamic long-term expansion planning of EV parking lots considering lost opportunity cost and energy saving. *Int. J. Electr. Power Energy Syst.* **2022**, *140*, 108066. [CrossRef]
7. Chu, W.; Im, M.; Song, M.; Park, J. Psychological and behavioral factors affecting EV adoption and satisfaction: A comparative study of early adopters in China and Korea. *Transp. Res. Part D Transp. Environ.* **2019**, *76*, 1–18. [CrossRef]
8. Wang, Z.; Zhang, J.; Liu, P.; Zhang, Z. Overview of Planning of Electric Vehicle Charging Stations. *China J. Highw. Transp.* **2022**, *35*, 230–252.
9. Ashtari, A.; Bibeau, E.; Shahidinejad, S.; Molinski, T. PEV charging profile prediction and analysis based on vehicle usage data. *IEEE Trans. Smart Grid.* **2012**, *3*, 341–350. [CrossRef]
10. Amini, M.H.; Moghaddam, M.P. Probabilistic modelling of EVs' parking lots charging demand. In Proceedings of the 2013 21st Iranian Conference on Electrical Engineering (ICEE), Mashhad, Iran, 14–16 May 2013; pp. 1–4.
11. Haji-Aghajani, E.; Hasanzadeh, S.; Heydarian-Forushani, E. A novel framework for planning of EV parking lots in distribution networks with high PV penetration. *Electr. Pow. Syst. Res.* **2023**, *217*, 109156. [CrossRef]
12. Chen, R.; Qian, X.; Miao, L.; Ukkusuri, S.V. Optimal charging facility location and capacity for electric vehicles considering route choice and charging time equilibrium. *Comput. Oper. Res.* **2020**, *113*, 104776. [CrossRef]
13. Zhao, D.; Liu, Y.; Chen, H. Are Mini and full-size electric vehicle adopters satisfied? An application of the regression with dummy variables. *Travel. Behav. Soc.* **2024**, *35*, 100744. [CrossRef]
14. Gopalakrishnan, R.; Biswas, A.; Lightwala, A.; Vasudevan, S.; Dutta, P.; Tripathi, A. Demand prediction and placement optimization for EV charging stations. *arXiv* **2016**, arXiv:1604.05472.
15. Dong, G.; Ma, J.; Wei, R.; Haycox, J.R. EV charging point placement optimization by exploiting spatial statistics and maximal coverage location models. *Transp. Res. Part D Transp. Environ.* **2019**, *67*, 77–88. [CrossRef]
16. Shuai, C.; Zhang, X.; Xin, O.; Liu, K.; Yang, Y. Research on charging demands of commercial electric vehicles based on Voronoi diagram and spatial econometrics model: An empirical study in Chongqing China. *Sustain. Cities Soc.* **2024**, *105*, 105335. [CrossRef]
17. Tian, Z.; Jung, T.; Wang, Y.; Zhang, F.; Tu, L.; Xu, C.; Tian, C.; Li, X. Real-time charging station recommendation system for EV taxis. *IEEE Trans. Intell. Transp. Syst.* **2016**, *17*, 3098–3109. [CrossRef]
18. Jiang, Q.; Zhang, N.; Yueshuai He, B.; Lee, C.; Ma, J. Large-scale public charging demand prediction with a scenario- and activity-based approach. *Transp. Res. Part A Policy Pract.* **2024**, *179*, 103935. [CrossRef]
19. Kuang, H.; Qu, H.; Deng, K.; Li, J. A physics-informed graph learning approach for citywide electric vehicle charging demand prediction and pricing. *Appl. Energy* **2024**, *363*, 123059. [CrossRef]
20. Ge, X.; Shi, L.; Fu, Y.; Muyeen, S.M.; Zhang, Z.; He, H. Data-driven spatial-temporal prediction of electric vehicle load profile considering charging behavior. *Electr. Power Syst. Res.* **2020**, *187*, 106469. [CrossRef]
21. Luo, X.; Kuby, M.J.; Honma, Y.; Kchaou-Boujelben, M.; Zhou, X. Innovation diffusion in EV charging location decisions: Integrating demand & supply through market dynamics. *Transp. Res. Part C Emerg. Technol.* **2024**, *165*, 104733. [CrossRef]
22. Ip, A.; Fong, S.; Liu, E. Optimization for allocating BEV recharging stations in urban areas by using hierarchical clustering. In Proceedings of the 2010 6th International Conference on Advanced Information Management and Service (IMS 2010), Seoul, Republic of Korea, 30 November–2 December 2010; pp. 460–465.
23. Xi, X.; Sioshansi, R.; Marano, V. Simulation–optimization model for location of a public EV charging infrastructure. *Transp. Res. Part D Transp. Environ.* **2013**, *22*, 60–69. [CrossRef]
24. Wang, C.; He, F.; Lin, X.; Shen, Z.M.; Li, M. Designing locations and capacities for charging stations to support intercity travel of EVs: An expanded network approach. *Transp. Res. Part C Emerg. Technol.* **2019**, *102*, 210–232. [CrossRef]
25. Zeng, X.; Xie, C. A comparative analysis of modeling and solution methods for the en-route charging station location problems within uncongested and congested highway networks. *Multimodal Transp.* **2024**, *3*, 100150. [CrossRef]
26. Yin, L.; Zhang, Y. Particle swarm optimization based on data driven for EV charging station siting. *Energy* **2024**, *310*, 133197. [CrossRef]

27. Yang, J.; Dong, J.; Zhang, Q.; Liu, Z.; Wang, W. An investigation of battery EV driving and charging behaviors using vehicle usage data collected in Shanghai, China. *Transp. Res. Rec. J. Transp. Res. Board* **2018**, *2672*, 20–30. [CrossRef]
28. Guo, D.; Liu, R.; Li, M.; Tan, X.; Ma, P.; Zhang, H. An approach to optimizing the layout of charging stations considering differences in user range anxiety. *Sustain. Energy Grids* **2024**, *38*, 101292. [CrossRef]

Disclaimer/Publisher's Note: The statements, opinions and data contained in all publications are solely those of the individual author(s) and contributor(s) and not of MDPI and/or the editor(s). MDPI and/or the editor(s) disclaim responsibility for any injury to people or property resulting from any ideas, methods, instructions or products referred to in the content.

Article

Solving a Fully Intuitionistic Fuzzy Transportation Problem Using a Hybrid Multi-Objective Optimization Approach

Sadegh Niroomand [1], Tofigh Allahviranloo [2,3], Ali Mahmoodirad [4], Alireza Amirteimoori [2], Leo Mršić [5,6] and Sovan Samanta [2,5,7,*]

[1] Department of Industrial Engineering, Firouzabad Higher Education Center, Shiraz University of Technology, Shiraz 7155713876, Iran; sadegh.niroomand@yahoo.com
[2] Research Center of Performance and Productivity Analysis, Istinye University, Istanbul 34010, Turkey; tofigh.allahviranloo@istinye.edu.tr (T.A.); alireza.amirteimoori@istinye.edu.tr (A.A.)
[3] Quantum Technologies Research Center (QTRC), Science and Research Branch, Islamic Azad University, Tehran 1477893780, Iran
[4] Department of Mathematics, Babol Branch, Islamic Azad University, Babol 3738147471, Iran; alimahmoodirad@yahoo.com
[5] Department of Technical Sciences, Algebra University, Gradiscanska 24, 10000 Zagreb, Croatia; leo.mrsic@algebra.hr
[6] Rudolfovo Science and Technology Centre, Podbreznik 15, 8000 Novo Mesto, Slovenia
[7] Department of Mathematics, Tamralipta Mahavidyalaya, Tamluk 721636, India
* Correspondence: ssamantavu@gmail.com

Abstract: In this study, a typical transportation problem involving intuitionistic fuzzy-type variables and parameters is focused on. The approaches proposed in the literature for such transportation problems have many shortcomings, such as the use of ranking functions and obtaining an infeasible solution with negative values for variables and objective functions in the presence of non-negative unit transportation charges. To overcome such weaknesses, a new approach without a ranking function is introduced in this paper. The proposed approach first constructs an equivalent crisp multi-objective form of the intuitionistic fuzzy transportation problem and then proposes a new hybrid multi-objective solution procedure to tackle the obtained crisp multi-objective problem. The conducted computer experiments with benchmark problems from the existing studies of the literature reflect the effectiveness of the proposed solution approach of this study in terms of the quality of the results when compared to the available approaches of the literature.

Keywords: transportation problem; fuzzy theory; intuitionistic fuzzy sets and numbers; intuitionistic fuzzy transportation problem; multi-objective optimization

MSC: 03B52; 90C29

1. Introduction

Transportation problems could be mentioned as a well-known application area of linear programming techniques. This problem considers a network of sources and destinations. In this problem, decisions are generally made about the amount of product sent between any pair of sources and destinations to reduce the overall transportation cost of the network [1–5]. These decisions are made as a function of the supplying capacity of each source (availability) and the product amount needed at each destination (demand). A basic condition is that the total availability of a network cannot be less than the total demands of the network. If these total values are equal, the problem is called a balanced transportation problem. In such cases, the problem is converted into a balanced form using dummy sources or destinations (see [6–10]).

Fuzzy theory [11] is an approach that represents problems in engineering, society, medicine, etc. Fields are mathematical models. This theory was first used in [12] for optimization problems. In traditional fuzzy numbers, the summation of membership and non-membership function degrees always becomes 1. Such a case may not be true in some real-world cases, where this sum value may take a value between zero and one due to vague and insufficient information. This deficiency motivated [13] to introduce a new version of fuzzy numbers, intuitionistic fuzzy numbers (IFNs), that can be applied to real-world cases with insufficient data and information. One advantage is that the summation of membership and non-membership function degrees of an intuitionistic fuzzy number is at least zero and at most one. One of the most important applications of an IFS is to estimate parameters in cases where there is a high degree of vagueness. In a transportation problem encountered in the real world, some information about demand, supply, and transportation costs may have a high degree of vagueness and inadequacy. Due to these inadequacies, the membership function and non-membership function degrees of these parameters cannot be accurately estimated. Therefore, IFN can be very useful in solving transportation problems. Some important applications of the intuitionistic fuzzy sets (IFSs) and IFNs can be seen in studies such as [14–19].

Many optimization problems, like transportation planning and scheduling theory with an uncertain nature, have been formulated by the intuitionistic fuzzy sets and numbers (for this purpose, the studies of [20–22]. The values of input data in a transportation problem may not be deterministic in real-world cases [23]. Authors [24] solved the transportation problem with trapezoidal fuzzy-type parameters. Authors [25] studied a transportation problem with two stages with fuzzy input data, such as supply and demand amounts. Authors [26] considered a fuzzy form-of-transportation problem and presented a solution procedure to achieve its optimal solution. A comparative study was conducted in [27] on transportation problems with fuzzy parameters, such as cost, availabilities, and demands. Authors [28] solved the fuzzy transport problem by introducing a new approach. Authors [29] dealt with a fuzzy transport problem involving trapezoidal fuzzy-type input data.

Authors [30] considered a fully intuitionistic fuzzy transportation problem in which the parameters are triangular intuitionistic fuzzy numbers. To solve this, first, the intuitionistic fuzzy branch and bound technique are applied to obtain the initial basic feasible solution and then the intuitionistic fuzzy modified distribution method is applied to acquire the optimal solution to the fully intuitionistic fuzzy transportation problem. Authors [31] studied the transportation problem with a generalized triangular intuitionistic fuzzy transportation problem. To handle this transportation problem, they proposed some criteria for ordering the generalized triangular intuitionistic fuzzy numbers. Authors [32] proposed a new approach to solve the transportation problem where transportation cost, supply values, and demand values are of the fuzzy type. Authors [33] formulated and solved a transportation problem when all parameters are interval-valued trapezoidal fuzzy numbers. Authors [34] proposed an algorithm for solving fully fuzzy transportation problems. The proposed algorithm deals with finding a starting basic feasible solution to the transportation problem with fuzzy parameters. The proposed algorithm is an amalgamation of two existing approaches that can be applied to a balanced fuzzy transportation problem where uncertainties are represented by the trapezoidal fuzzy numbers. Instead of transforming these uncertainties into crisp values, the proposed algorithm directly handles the fuzzy nature of the problem.

As mentioned in the above sections, the transportation problem involves a high degree of inconclusiveness and vagueness in estimating its parameters, e.g., transportation costs, supply values, and demand quantities. Because of this difficulty, these parameters can be estimated as intuitionistic fuzzy values. In such a problem, if, in addition to the intuitionistic fuzzy parameters, the variables are also defined by intuitionistic fuzzy values, the fully intuitionistic fuzzy transportation problem (FIFTP) is introduced, which has also been studied by [35]. In our study, we focus on a FIFTP where all decision variables and all input data (parameters) take triangular intuitionistic fuzzy-type numbers (TIFNs). In the study performed by [35], ranking functions are used to solve the FIFTP. This approach has the disadvantage that applying various ranking functions leads to different results. In the current study, a new solution approach based on multiple objectives is developed to overcome the shortcomings of the available approaches. The effectiveness of the developed solution method compared to the available solution methods is demonstrated by solving some numerical examples.

The rest of this paper is developed in five other sections. Section 2 contains some useful concepts of intuitionistic fuzzy numbers from the literature. Section 3 presents the transportation problem in its intuitionistic fuzzy form and shows its mathematical formulation. The proposed solution approach and some weaknesses of existing solution methodologies are mentioned in Section 4. In Section 5, computer experiments are performed on some examples from the literature. The paper ends in Section 6.

2. Basic Concepts

Some basic definitions and theorems of the intuitionistic fuzzy sets and numbers are presented in this section. These concepts later will be used in the paper.

Definition 1 ([13]). *Intuitionistic fuzzy set $\tilde{A}$ (IFS) is mentioned as $\tilde{A} = \{\langle x, \mu_{\tilde{A}}(x), v_{\tilde{A}}(x)\rangle : x \in X\}$, where:*

- $\mu_{\tilde{A}}(x)$ *is a membership function of x and* $v_{\tilde{A}}(x)$ *is a non-membership function of x;*
- $\mu_{\tilde{A}}, v_{\tilde{A}} : X \to [0,1]$;
- $0 \leq \mu_{\tilde{A}}(x) + v_{\tilde{A}}(x) \leq 1$;
- *for $x \in X$, the hesitation degree of $h(x) = 1 - \mu_{\tilde{A}}(x) - v_{\tilde{A}}(x)$ is calculated.*

Definition 2 ([13]). *Intuitionistic fuzzy set $\tilde{A}$ (IFS) should have the below pair of conditions:*

- *there must exist a real number (say r) in which $\mu_{\tilde{A}}(r) = 1$ and $v_{\tilde{A}}(r) = 0$;*
- *considering $\mu_{\tilde{A}}, v_{\tilde{A}} : X \to [0,1]$, for any $x \in X$, there should be $0 \leq \mu_{\tilde{A}}(x) + v_{\tilde{A}}(x) \leq 1$.*

Definition 3 ([13,36]). *Triangular intuitionistic fuzzy number $\tilde{A}$(TIFN) is shown by $\tilde{A} = (a_1, a_2, a_3; a'_1, a_2, a'_3)$ and its membership and non-membership functions are determined as below:*

$$\mu_{\tilde{A}}(x) = \begin{cases} \frac{x-a_1}{a_2-a_1} & a_1 \leq x \leq a_2 \\ \frac{a_3-x}{a_3-a_2} & a_2 \leq x \leq a_3 \\ 0 & \text{otherwise} \end{cases} \quad (1)$$

$$v_{\tilde{A}}(x) = \begin{cases} \frac{a_2-x}{a_2-a'_1} & a_1 \leq x \leq a_2 \\ \frac{x-a_2}{a'_3-a_2} & a_2 \leq x \leq a_3 \\ 1 & \text{otherwise} \end{cases} \quad (2)$$

The above-mentioned functions are depicted in Figure 1.

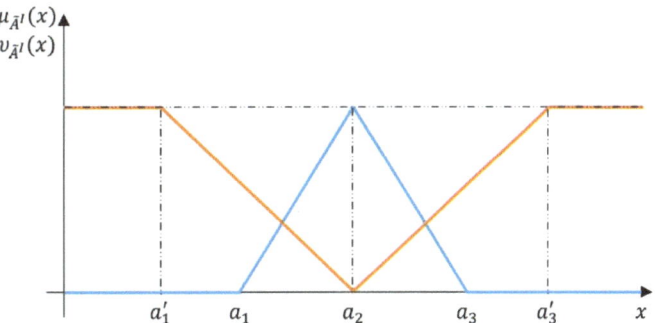

Figure 1. A triangular intuitionistic fuzzy number and its functions.

Definition 4 ([13,36]). *For the TIFNs* $\tilde{A} = (a_1, a_2, a_3; a'_1, a_2, a'_3)$ *and* $\tilde{B} = (b_1, b_2, b_3; b'_1, b_2, b'_3)$, *the below operators are defined:*

$$\tilde{A} \oplus \tilde{B} = (a_1 + b_1, a_2 + b_2, a_3 + b_3; a'_1 + b'_1, a_2 + b_2, a'_3 + b'_3) \qquad (3)$$

$$\tilde{A} \ominus \tilde{B} = (a_1 - b_3, a_2 - b_2, a_3 - b_1; a'_1 - b'_3, a_2 - b_2, a'_3 - b'_1) \qquad (4)$$

$$\tilde{A} \otimes \tilde{B} = (l_1, l_2, l_3; l'_1, l_2, l'_3) \qquad (5)$$

$$k\tilde{A} = (ka_1, ka_2, ka_3; ka'_1, ka_2, ka'_3) \qquad k \geq 0 \qquad (6)$$

$$k\tilde{A} = (ka_3, ka_2, ka_1; ka'_3, ka_2, ka'_1) \qquad k < 0 \qquad (7)$$

In Equation (5), the below declarations are given:

- $l_1 = min\{a_1 b_1, a_1 b_3, a_3 b_1, a_3 b_3\}$;
- $l_2 = a_2 b_2$;
- $l_3 = max\{a_1 b_1, a_1 b_3, a_3 b_1, a_3 b_3\}$;
- $l'_1 = min\{a'_1 b'_1, a'_1 b'_3, a'_3 b'_1, a'_3 b'_3\}$;
- $l'_3 = max\{a'_1 b'_1, a'_1 b'_3, a'_3 b'_1, a'_3 b'_3\}$.

Theorem 1. *For the TIFNs* $\tilde{A} = (a_1, a_2, a_3; a'_1, a_2, a'_3)$ *and* $\tilde{B} = (b_1, b_2, b_3; b'_1, b_2, b'_3)$, *the relation* $\tilde{A} \leq \tilde{B}$ *is true if the conditions* $a_1 \leq b_1, a_2 \leq b_2, a_3 \leq b_3, a'_1 \leq b'_1$, *and* $a'_3 \leq b'_3$ *are held.*

Proof. The proof is straightforward. □

It can be mentioned that Theorem 1 is based on all operations of Definition 4. Also, it has reflexive, symmetry, and transitivity relations.

3. Fully Intuitionistic Fuzzy Transportation Problem (FIFTP)

The classical transportation problem (TP) is characterized by some sources and some destinations with given supply values in each source and given demand values of each destination. A route is defined between each source and each destination with a specified unit transportation cost. The supply values should be sent to the destinations via the given routes to fulfill the demand values. In this problem, the value sent by each route is determined to minimize the total transportation cost of all routes. Here, we represent the cost values, demand quantities, supply values, and decision variables by TIFNs. The notations used to formulate the FIFTP are defined as below:

- m: the number of sources where the index is i;
- n: the number of destinations where the index is j;
- $\tilde{a}_i^I = \left(a_{i,1}, a_{i,2}, a_{i,3}; a'_{i,1}, a'_{i,2}, a'_{i,3}\right)$: the TIFN for the amount of product supplied by source i;
- $\tilde{b}_j^I = \left(b_{j,1}, b_{j,2}, b_{j,3}; b'_{j,1}, b'_{j,2}, b'_{j,3}\right)$: the TIFN that is used to show the demand value of destination j;
- $\tilde{c}_{ij}^I = \left(c_{ij,1}, c_{ij,2}, c_{ij,3}; c'_{ij,1}, c'_{ij,2}, c'_{ij,3}\right)$: the TIFN for the unit transportation cost between source i and destination j;
- $\tilde{X}_{ij}^I = \left(X_{ij,1}, X_{ij,2}, X_{ij,3}; X'_{ij,1}, X'_{ij,2}, X'_{ij,3}\right)$: the TIFN variable for the product amount sent from source i to destination j.

It is notable to mention that the way to represent the TIFNs in this section is an easy form. This form can be reflected in the objective function and constraints of the transportation problem. Furthermore, the fuzzy operators of the IFNs defined in the previous section are more understandable.

Now the FIFTP is formulated as follows (see also [37]):

$$\min \tilde{Z}^I = \sum_{i=1}^{m} \sum_{j=1}^{n} \tilde{c}_{ij}^I \otimes \tilde{X}_{ij}^I \tag{8}$$

subject to

$$\sum_{j=1}^{n} \tilde{X}_{ij}^I = \tilde{a}_i^I \qquad \forall i \tag{9}$$

$$\sum_{i=1}^{m} \tilde{X}_{ij}^I = \tilde{b}_j^I \qquad \forall j \tag{10}$$

$$\tilde{X}_{ij}^I \geq 0 \qquad \forall i, j \tag{11}$$

The assumptions of the FIFTP are the same as those of the TP. It means that the parameters cannot be negative TIFNs. Formulations (10)–(13) (the FIFTP) are a balanced problem if $\sum_{i=1}^{m} \tilde{a}_i^I = \sum_{j=1}^{n} \tilde{b}_j^I$ and are an unbalanced problem if $\sum_{i=1}^{m} \tilde{a}_i^I \neq \sum_{j=1}^{n} \tilde{b}_j^I$.

Definition 5. *Problems (8)–(11) have an optimal solution, including the set of values $\left\{\tilde{X}_{ij}^{I\,*}\right\}$ that makes it feasible. For any other feasible set of values $\left\{\tilde{X}_{ij}^{I}\right\}$, the relation $\sum_{i=1}^{m}\sum_{j=1}^{n} \tilde{c}_{ij}^I \otimes \tilde{X}_{ij}^{I\,*} \leq \sum_{i=1}^{m}\sum_{j=1}^{n} \tilde{c}_{ij}^I \otimes \tilde{X}_{ij}^I$ is true.*

4. Solution Methodology

The fuzzy transportation problem proposed by formulations (8)–(11), which is denoted by the FIFTP, is tackled here. Therefore, a solution methodology is proposed to consider the fuzzy parameters and variables and fix the shortcomings of the existing solution methods.

A key difficulty is that a mathematical formulation with fuzzy parameters cannot be solved using the available commercial optimization solvers. Therefore, it must be transformed into an unambiguous form and then the optimal solution for the unambiguous form should be found. It is worth noting that the optimal solution that is obtained for the crisp form of any fuzzy problem is only a solution for the fuzzy problem and its optimality for the fuzzy problem cannot be proved. This assertion also holds for the case of the FIFTP (Formulations (8)–(11)), where some methods in the literature, such as [36–38], apply ranking functions to crisp the FIFTP. Therefore, the optimal solutions obtained for the crisp forms of the FIFTP in these studies are feasible solutions for the FIFTP and nothing can be said about their optimality in the FIFTP.

4.1. On the Existing Solution Approaches

Models (8)–(11) were also solved by [36,37]. They proposed ranking function-based approaches to this problem. They investigated their approaches using some examples and case studies with all positive parameters, e.g., availabilities, demands, and transportation costs of TIFNs. However, the solutions obtained have one or more of the following weaknesses:

- In the obtained solutions, the intuitionistic fuzzy variables may obtain a negative value;
- The obtained objective function value is negative;
- When summing up the values determined for intuitionistic fuzzy variables, the availability and requirements are not considered.

The above points violate the main assumptions that are known for the transportation problem. It is worth noting that in the study performed by [38], the above-mentioned shortcomings can be seen.

4.2. The Proposed Solution Approach

The solution methodology used in this paper is presented in this sub-section. In this approach, the shortcomings of the existing solution methods (mentioned in Section 4.1) are fixed. To explain this solution methodology, the below steps should be followed. It is notable to mention that the proposed approach here is detailed for the triangular intuitionistic fuzzy numbers but its formulations and steps can be easily extended to the trapezoidal and general intuitionistic fuzzy numbers as well.

Step 1. The balanced FIFTP with parameters of TIFNs is expanded as below:

$$\min \widetilde{Z}^I = \sum_{i=1}^{m}\sum_{j=1}^{n} \left(c_{ij}^1, c_{ij}^2, c_{ij}^3; c_{ij}^4, c_{ij}^2, c_{ij}^5\right) \otimes \left(X_{ij}^1, X_{ij}^2, X_{ij}^3; X_{ij}^4, X_{ij}^2, X_{ij}^5\right) \quad (12)$$

subject to

$$\sum_{j=1}^{n}\left(X_{ij}^1, X_{ij}^2, X_{ij}^3; X_{ij}^4, X_{ij}^2, X_{ij}^5\right) = \left(a_i^1, a_i^2, a_i^3; a_i^4, a_i^2, a_i^5\right) \quad \forall i \quad (13)$$

$$\sum_{i=1}^{m}\left(X_{ij}^1, X_{ij}^2, X_{ij}^3; X_{ij}^4, X_{ij}^2, X_{ij}^5\right) = \left(b_j^1, b_j^2, b_j^3; b_j^4, b_j^2, b_j^5\right) \quad \forall j \quad (14)$$

$$\left(X_{ij}^1, X_{ij}^2, X_{ij}^3; X_{ij}^4, X_{ij}^2, X_{ij}^5\right) \geq 0 \quad \forall i,j \quad (15)$$

Step 2. The model obtained in Step 1 is converted to the following model. In this transformation, the definitions and theorem of Section 2 of the paper are considered:

$$\min \widetilde{Z}^I = \sum_{i=1}^{m}\sum_{j=1}^{n}\left(c_{ij}^1 X_{ij}^1, c_{ij}^2 X_{ij}^2, c_{ij}^3 X_{ij}^3; c_{ij}^4 X_{ij}^4, c_{ij}^2 X_{ij}^2, c_{ij}^5 X_{ij}^5\right) \quad (16)$$

subject to

$$\sum_{j=1}^{n} X_{ij}^k = a_i^k \quad \forall i, k | k \in \{1,\ldots,5\} \quad (17)$$

$$\sum_{i=1}^{m} X_{ij}^k = b_j^k \qquad \forall j,k | k \in \{1,\ldots,5\} \qquad (18)$$

$$X_{ij}^4 \geq 0 \qquad \forall i,j \qquad (19)$$

$$X_{ij}^2 - X_{ij}^1 \geq 0 \qquad \forall i,j \qquad (20)$$

$$X_{ij}^3 - X_{ij}^2 \geq 0 \qquad \forall i,j \qquad (21)$$

$$X_{ij}^1 - X_{ij}^4 \geq 0 \qquad \forall i,j \qquad (22)$$

$$X_{ij}^5 - X_{ij}^3 \geq 0 \qquad \forall i,j \qquad (23)$$

Considering Theorem 1, instead of constraints (13) and (14), constraints (17) and (18) are proposed. To satisfy the non-negativity assumption of the problem and the condition of Definition 2, Constraint (15) is replaced by constraints (19)–(23).

Step 3. As Objective function (18) is a TIFN, it is minimized when all its elements are minimized, simultaneously. Therefore, the below model is obtained instead of models (16)–(23); the model of Step 2 is converted to the following multi-objective crisp model:

$$\min \sum_{i=1}^{m} \sum_{j=1}^{n} c_{ij}^1 X_{ij}^1 \qquad (24)$$

$$\min \sum_{i=1}^{m} \sum_{j=1}^{n} c_{ij}^2 X_{ij}^2 \qquad (25)$$

$$\min \sum_{i=1}^{m} \sum_{j=1}^{n} c_{ij}^3 X_{ij}^3 \qquad (26)$$

$$\min \sum_{i=1}^{m} \sum_{j=1}^{n} c_{ij}^4 X_{ij}^4 \qquad (27)$$

$$\min \sum_{i=1}^{m} \sum_{j=1}^{n} c_{ij}^5 X_{ij}^5 \qquad (28)$$

subject to

$$\sum_{j=1}^{n} X_{ij}^k = a_i^k \qquad \forall i,k | k \in \{1,\ldots,5\} \qquad (29)$$

$$\sum_{i=1}^{m} X_{ij}^k = b_j^k \qquad \forall j,k | k \in \{1,\ldots,5\} \qquad (30)$$

$$X_{ij}^4 \geq 0 \qquad \forall i,j \qquad (31)$$

$$X_{ij}^2 - X_{ij}^1 \geq 0 \qquad \forall i,j \qquad (32)$$

$$X_{ij}^3 - X_{ij}^2 \geq 0 \qquad \forall i,j \qquad (33)$$

$$X_{ij}^1 - X_{ij}^4 \geq 0 \qquad \forall i,j \qquad (34)$$

$$X_{ij}^5 - X_{ij}^3 \geq 0 \qquad \forall i,j \qquad (35)$$

Lemma 1. *The optimal solution of formulations (16)–(23) is a Pareto-optimal solution for formulations (24)–(35).*

Proof. The set of feasible solutions for both problems is the same. The proof is obtained by a contradiction-based method.

Assume that the solution $\widetilde{X}_{ij}^{I*} = \left(X_{ij}^{1*}, X_{ij}^{2*}, X_{ij}^{3*}; X_{ij}^{4*}, X_{ij}^{2*}, X_{ij}^{5*} \right)$ is the optimal solution of formulations (16)–(23) and not a Pareto-optimal solution for formulations (24)–(35). Therefore, there should be a solution as $\bar{X}_{ij}^{I} = \left(\bar{X}_{ij}^{1}, \bar{X}_{ij}^{2}, \bar{X}_{ij}^{3}; \bar{X}_{ij}^{4}, \bar{X}_{ij}^{2}, \bar{X}_{ij}^{5} \right)$, which holds one of the following cases:

- Case 1: $\sum_{i=1}^{m}\sum_{j=1}^{n} c_{ij}^{1}\bar{X}_{ij}^{1} < \sum_{i=1}^{m}\sum_{j=1}^{n} c_{ij}^{1}X_{ij}^{1*}$, $\sum_{i=1}^{m}\sum_{j=1}^{n} c_{ij}^{k}\bar{X}_{ij}^{k} \leq \sum_{i=1}^{m}\sum_{j=1}^{n} c_{ij}^{k}X_{ij}^{k*}$, $\forall k \in \{2,3,4,5\}$;
- Case 2: $\sum_{i=1}^{m}\sum_{j=1}^{n} c_{ij}^{2}\bar{X}_{ij}^{2} < \sum_{i=1}^{m}\sum_{j=1}^{n} c_{ij}^{2}X_{ij}^{2*}$, $\sum_{i=1}^{m}\sum_{j=1}^{n} c_{ij}^{k}\bar{X}_{ij}^{k} \leq \sum_{i=1}^{m}\sum_{j=1}^{n} c_{ij}^{k}X_{ij}^{k*}$, $\forall k \in \{1,3,4,5\}$;
- Case 3: $\sum_{i=1}^{m}\sum_{j=1}^{n} c_{ij}^{3}\bar{X}_{ij}^{3} < \sum_{i=1}^{m}\sum_{j=1}^{n} c_{ij}^{3}X_{ij}^{3*}$, $\sum_{i=1}^{m}\sum_{j=1}^{n} c_{ij}^{k}\bar{X}_{ij}^{k} \leq \sum_{i=1}^{m}\sum_{j=1}^{n} c_{ij}^{k}X_{ij}^{k*}$, $\forall k \in \{1,2,4,5\}$;
- Case 4: $\sum_{i=1}^{m}\sum_{j=1}^{n} c_{ij}^{4}\bar{X}_{ij}^{4} < \sum_{i=1}^{m}\sum_{j=1}^{n} c_{ij}^{4}X_{ij}^{4*}$, $\sum_{i=1}^{m}\sum_{j=1}^{n} c_{ij}^{k}\bar{X}_{ij}^{k} \leq \sum_{i=1}^{m}\sum_{j=1}^{n} c_{ij}^{k}X_{ij}^{k*}$, $\forall k \in \{1,2,3,5\}$;
- Case 5: $\sum_{i=1}^{m}\sum_{j=1}^{n} c_{ij}^{5}\bar{X}_{ij}^{5} < \sum_{i=1}^{m}\sum_{j=1}^{n} c_{ij}^{5}X_{ij}^{5*}$, $\sum_{i=1}^{m}\sum_{j=1}^{n} c_{ij}^{k}\bar{X}_{ij}^{k} \leq \sum_{i=1}^{m}\sum_{j=1}^{n} c_{ij}^{k}X_{ij}^{k*}$, $\forall k \in \{1,2,3,4\}$.

If the first case occurs, then $\sum_{i=1}^{m}\sum_{j=1}^{n} \widetilde{c}_{ij}^{I} \otimes \bar{X}_{ij}^{I} < \sum_{i=1}^{m}\sum_{j=1}^{n} \widetilde{c}_{ij}^{I} \otimes \widetilde{X}_{ij}^{I*}$, which is in contradiction with the optimality of $\widetilde{X}_{ij}^{I*} = \left(X_{ij}^{1*}, X_{ij}^{2*}, X_{ij}^{3*}; X_{ij}^{4*}, X_{ij}^{2*}, X_{ij}^{5*} \right)$. It is easy to show that the other cases will also result in the same contradiction and the lemma is proved. □

Step 4. Multi-objective formulations (24)–(35) are examined for their efficient solutions (Pareto-optimal solutions). For this aim, a hybrid fuzzy programming approach is modified in this step. The classical form of the fuzzy programming approach was introduced in [39]. However, it has been shown that this approach cannot always provide Pareto-optimal solutions [40]. Therefore, some modifications of this approach have been developed to improve its inefficiency. Authors [40–43] present some of the modifications of this approach (see also [35,44]). In this step, we modify the fuzzy programming approach in a new form in order to obtain the Pareto-optimal solutions of the Multi-objective formulations (24)–(35). This modification is presented by some sub-steps as below.

Step 4.1. First, for each objective function of formulations (24)–(35), the positive ideal solution (POS) and the negative ideal solution (NIS) are obtained. Therefore, the below formulations are proposed:

$$Z_1^{PIS} = \max \sum_{i=1}^{m}\sum_{j=1}^{n} c_{ij}^{1} X_{ij}^{1}$$
subject to
Constraints (29)–(35) \hfill (36)

$$Z_1^{NIS} = \max \sum_{i=1}^{m}\sum_{j=1}^{n} c_{ij}^{1} X_{ij}^{1}$$
subject to
Constraints (29)–(35) \hfill (37)

$$Z_2^{PIS} = \min \sum_{i=1}^{m}\sum_{j=1}^{n} c_{ij}^{2} X_{ij}^{2}$$
subject to
Constraints (29)–(35) \hfill (38)

$$Z_2^{NIS} = \max \sum_{i=1}^{m}\sum_{j=1}^{n} c_{ij}^{2} X_{ij}^{2}$$
subject to
Constraints (29)–(35) \hfill (39)

$$Z_3^{PIS} = \min \sum_{i=1}^{m} \sum_{j=1}^{n} c_{ij}^3 X_{ij}^3$$
subject to
Constraints (29)–(35) \hfill (40)

$$Z_3^{NIS} = \max \sum_{i=1}^{m} \sum_{j=1}^{n} c_{ij}^3 X_{ij}^3$$
subject to
Constraints (29)–(35) \hfill (41)

$$Z_4^{PIS} = \min \sum_{i=1}^{m} \sum_{j=1}^{n} c_{ij}^4 X_{ij}^4$$
subject to
Constraints (29)–(35) \hfill (42)

$$Z_4^{NIS} = \max \sum_{i=1}^{m} \sum_{j=1}^{n} c_{ij}^4 X_{ij}^4$$
subject to
Constraints (29)–(35) \hfill (43)

$$Z_5^{PIS} = \min \sum_{i=1}^{m} \sum_{j=1}^{n} c_{ij}^5 X_{ij}^5$$
subject to
Constraints (29)–(35) \hfill (44)

$$Z_5^{NIS} = \max \sum_{i=1}^{m} \sum_{j=1}^{n} c_{ij}^5 X_{ij}^5$$
subject to
Constraints (29)–(35) \hfill (45)

Step 4.2. According to the positive and negative ideal solutions of Step 4.1, for any feasible solution of formulations (24)–(35), the below linear membership function (MF) is considered (like [39]).

$$\mu_r(Z_r) = \begin{cases} 1 & Z_r \leq Z_r^{PIS} \\ \frac{Z_r^{NIS} - Z_r}{Z_r^{NIS} - Z_r^{PIS}} & Z_r^{PIS} \leq Z_r \leq Z_r^{NIS} \\ 0 & Z_r \geq Z_r^{NIS} \end{cases} \quad \forall r \in \{1, 2, \ldots, 5\} \quad (46)$$

Here, $\mu_r(Z_r)$ is the linear membership function of Z_r (for $r \in \{1, 2, \ldots, R\}$ ($R = 5$ in this paper)).

Step 4.3. (Proposed single-objective model step) The following integrated model is proposed to be solved instead of Multi-objective formulations (24)–(35):

$$\max \gamma \lambda_0 + (1 - \gamma) \sum_{r=1}^{R} \lambda_r$$
subject to $\quad \forall r \in \{1, 2, \ldots, R\}$
$\lambda_0 + \lambda_r \leq \mu_r(Z_r) \quad \forall r \in \{1, 2, \ldots, R\}$ \hfill (47)
$0 \leq \lambda_0, \lambda_r \leq 1$
Constraints (29)–(35)

In model (47), the compromise level and minimum satisfaction levels of the objective functions are controlled by the variables λ_0 and λ_r. The importance weight values of these variables are shown by γ ($0 \leq \gamma \leq 1$) and determined by the decision maker in advance. According to the literature, the value of γ is fixed as 0.4.

Lemma 2. *Single-objective formulation (47) is feasible and its optimal solution is a Pareto-optimal (efficient) solution for models (24)–(35).*

Proof. The proof can be easily obtained by a similar method to the study in [43]. □

Step 5. The solution achieved in Step 4, which is shown by $\left(X_{ij}^{1*}, X_{ij}^{2*}, X_{ij}^{3*}; X_{ij}^{4*}, X_{ij}^{2*}, X_{ij}^{5*}\right)$, is considered to calculate the objective function value of Formulations (8)–(11) as:

$$\widetilde{Z}^{I} = \sum_{i=1}^{m}\sum_{j=1}^{n}\left(c_{ij}^{1}, c_{ij}^{2}, c_{ij}^{3}; c_{ij}^{4}, c_{ij}^{2}, c_{ij}^{5}\right) \otimes \left(X_{ij}^{1*}, X_{ij}^{2*}, X_{ij}^{3*}; X_{ij}^{4*}, X_{ij}^{2*}, X_{ij}^{5*}\right) \quad (48)$$

According to the nature of the FIFTP, as explained before, any Pareto-optimal solution found for formulations (24)–(35) is a feasible solution for formulations (16)–(23) and (8)–(11). Clearly, according to Objective functions (24)–(28), a better Pareto-optimal solution for formulations (24)–(35) may give better objective function value when supplied in formulations (16)–(23) and (8)–(11).

In general, the proposed solution approach of Steps 1–5 has two main advantages: (1) the fuzzy nature of the FIFTP is respected and (2) the hybrid programming approach of Section 4 controls the compromise level and minimum satisfaction levels of the objective functions together and guarantees obtaining a Pareto-optimal solution.

5. Numerical Examples

The proposed solution methodology of Section 4 is experimented numerically by some numerical examples from the studies of [36–38]; they are considered and solved here. According to these common examples, some right comparisons can be made. For further comparisons, we also use some existing modified and hybrid versions of the fuzzy programming approach, such as [40–43], instead. In these approaches, the objective functions are equally weighted if necessary.

Before we start solving the numerical examples, it is necessary to mention that the concepts of Theorem 1 were only a tool for transforming the FIFTP into their clear multi-objective formulations, formulations (24)–(35), but not a tool for comparing the TIFNs of the objective function obtained by the solution approaches. This means that among the obtained objective function values (TIFNs), there may be some incomparable values where one fuzzy value may not be smaller than another value with all its elements. In such cases, any fuzzy ranking function can be used for comparison.

Example 1. *Here, a transportation problem with four sources and four destinations is considered where only the transportation costs are of TIFNs. The example is taken from [36] and its data are given in Table 1. Any crisp value of this table is converted to a TIFN value with similar values (for instance, $a_1 = 11$ is converted to $a_1^I = (11, 11, 11; 11, 11, 11)$). The solution methodology presented in this study and the existing methods, LH, TH, SO, and ABS, are used to solve this example. The results of this example are reported in Table 2 (in this table, $\widetilde{X}_{11}^{I*} = 5.53$ means that $\widetilde{X}_{11}^{I*} = (5.53, 5.53, 5.53; 5.53, 5.53, 5.53))$.*

Table 1. The crisp and triangular intuitionistic fuzzy costs, availabilities, and demands of Example 1.

		Destinations				a_i
		1	2	3	4	
Sources	1	(2, 4, 5; 1, 4, 6)	(2, 5, 7; 1, 5, 8)	(4, 6, 8; 3, 6, 9)	(4, 7, 8; 3, 7, 9)	11
	2	(4, 6, 8; 3, 6, 9)	(3, 7, 12; 2, 7, 13)	(10, 15, 20; 8, 15, 22)	(11, 12, 13; 10, 12, 14)	11
	3	(3, 4, 6; 1, 4, 8)	(8, 10, 13; 5, 10, 16)	(2, 3, 5; 1, 3, 6)	(6, 10, 14; 5, 10, 15)	11
	4	(2, 4, 6; 1, 4, 7)	(3, 9, 10; 2, 9, 12)	(3, 6, 10; 2, 6, 12)	(3, 4, 5; 2, 4, 8)	12
b_j		16	10	8	11	45

Table 2. The results obtained for Example 1.

Method	$\left(\tilde{X}_{11}^{I*}, \tilde{X}_{12}^{I*}, \ldots, \tilde{X}_{44}^{I*}\right)$	$\tilde{Z}^I$
TH	(5.53, 5.47, 0, 0, 6.47, 4.53, 0, 0, 3, 0, 8, 0, 1, 0, 0, 11)	(121.47, 204, 291.07; 73.47, 204, 361.07)
LH	(5.53, 5.47, 0, 0, 6.47, 4.53, 0, 0, 3, 0, 8, 0, 1, 0, 0, 11)	(121.47, 204, 291.07; 73.47, 204, 361.07)
SO	(1, 10, 0, 0, 11, 0, 0, 0, 3, 0, 8, 0, 1, 0, 0, 11)	(126, 204, 282; 78, 204, 352)
ABS	(1, 10, 0, 0, 11, 0, 0, 0, 3, 0, 8, 0, 1, 0, 0, 11)	(126, 204, 282; 78, 204, 352)
Proposed	(1, 10, 0, 0, 11, 0, 0, 0, 3, 0, 8, 0, 1, 0, 0, 11)	(126, 204, 282; 78, 204, 352)

According to the results of Table 2, the following can be concluded to prove the effectiveness of the proposed solution method of this paper:

- The shortcomings of literature, e.g., negative solutions, and demand dissatisfaction do not exist in the obtained solutions;
- The proposed multi-objective approach performs as well as the multi-objective approaches like SO and ABS;
- The TIFN for the objective function obtained by the solution approach is the same as that obtained by [36].

Example 2. *This example is a case study with three sources and four destinations where only the transportation costs are of TIFNs. The example is taken from [36] and its data are shown in Table 3. Any crisp value of this table is converted to a TIFN value with similar values (for instance, $a_1 = 4500$ is converted to $a_1^I = (4500, 4500, 4500; 4500, 4500, 4500)$). The solution methodology presented in this study and the existing methods, LH, TH, SO, and ABS, are used to solve this example. The results of this example are reported in Table 4 (in this table, $\tilde{X}_{11}^{I*} = 3500$ means that $\tilde{X}_{11}^{I*} = (3500, 3500, 3500; 3500, 3500, 3500)$).*

Based on the results of Table 4, the following points can be mentioned that demonstrate the effectiveness of the proposed solution method:

- The shortcomings of the literature, e.g., negative solutions, and dissatisfaction with demand are not present in the obtained solutions;
- Moreover, the proposed multi-criteria approach performs the same as the multi-criteria solution methods TH, SO, and ABS;
- It is worth noting that the TIFN obtained by the solution approach for the objective function is obviously better than that obtained by [36] (12,710,000, 13,425,000, 14,070,000; 12,400,000, 13,425,000, 14,605,000).

Table 3. The crisp and triangular intuitionistic fuzzy costs, availabilities, and demands of Example 2.

		Destinations				a_i
		1	2	3	4	
Sources	1	(210, 250, 270; 200, 250, 280)	(600, 700, 750; 600, 700, 800)	(950, 1000, 1050; 900, 1000, 1100)	(3500, 3700, 3900; 3400, 3700, 4100)	4500
	2	(650, 750, 800; 600, 750, 850)	(350, 400, 450; 340, 400, 480)	(1000, 1050, 1100; 950, 1050, 1150)	(3600, 3900, 4600; 3500, 3900, 4600)	3500
	3	(2600, 2800, 3000; 2500, 2800, 3100)	(2100, 2200, 2300; 2100, 2200, 2350)	(2900, 3100, 3300; 2800, 3100, 3400)	(5400, 5600, 5800; 5300, 5600, 6000)	2000
b_j		3500	3000	2000	1500	

Table 4. The results obtained for Example 2.

Method	$\left(\tilde{X}_{11}^{I*}, \tilde{X}_{12}^{I*}, \ldots, \tilde{X}_{34}^{I*}\right)$	$\tilde{Z}^I$
TH	(3500, 0, 0, 1000, 0, 1500, 2000, 0, 0, 1500, 0, 500)	(12,610,000, 13,375,000, 14,070,000; 12,310,000, 13,375,000, 14,625,000)
LH	(3500, 0, 0, 1000, 0, 1462.85, 2000, 37.15, 0, 1537.15, 0, 462.85)	(12,608,140, 13,378,720, 14,094,150; 12,308,510, 13,378,720, 14,642,460)
SO	(3500, 0, 0, 1000, 0, 1500, 2000, 0, 0, 1500, 0, 500)	(12,610,000, 13,375,000, 14,070,000; 12,310,000, 13,375,000, 14,625,000)
ABS	(3500, 0, 0, 1000, 0, 1500, 2000, 0, 0, 1500, 0, 500)	(12,610,000, 13,375,000, 14,070,000; 12,310,000, 13,375,000, 14,625,000)
Proposed	(3500, 0, 0, 1000, 0, 1500, 2000, 0, 0, 1500, 0, 500)	(12,610,000, 13,375,000, 14,070,000; 12,310,000, 13,375,000, 14,625,000)

Example 3. *This numerical example is taken from [38] and its data are depicted in Table 5. Any crisp value of this table is converted to a TIFN value with similar values (for instance, $c_{11} = 16$ is converted to $c_{11}^I = (16, 16, 16; 16, 16, 16)$). The solution methodology presented in this study and the existing methods, LH, TH, SO, and ABS, are used to solve this example. The results of this example are reported in Table 6.*

Table 5. The crisp and triangular intuitionistic fuzzy costs, availabilities, and demands of Example 3.

		Destinations				$\tilde{a}_i^I$
		1	2	3	4	
Sources	1	16	1	8	13	(2, 4, 5; 1, 4, 6)
	2	11	4	7	10	(4, 6, 8; 3, 6, 9)
	3	8	15	9	2	(3, 7, 12; 2, 7, 13)
	4	6	12	5	14	(8, 10, 13; 5, 10, 16)
$\tilde{b}_j^I$		(3, 4, 6; 1, 4, 8)	(2, 5, 7; 1, 5, 8)	(10, 15, 20; 8, 15, 22)	(2, 3, 5; 1, 3, 6)	(17, 27, 38; 11, 27, 44)

Table 6. The results obtained for Example 3.

Method	$\tilde{X}_{11}^{I*}, \tilde{X}_{12}^{I*}, \ldots, \tilde{X}_{44}^{I*}$	$\tilde{Z}^I$
TH		
LH	(0, 0, 0; 0, 0, 0), (2, 4, 5; 1, 4, 6), (0, 0, 0; 0, 0, 0), (0, 0, 0; 0, 0, 0), (0, 0, 0; 0, 0, 0), (0, 1, 2; 0, 1, 2), (4, 5, 6; 3, 5, 7),	
SO	(0, 0, 0; 0, 0, 0), (1, 2, 4; 1, 2, 4), (0, 0, 0; 0, 0, 0), (0, 2, 3; 0, 2, 3),	(84, 135, 191; 57, 135, 218)
ABS	(2, 3, 5; 1, 3, 6), (2, 2, 2; 0, 2, 4), (0, 0, 0; 0, 0, 0), (6, 8, 11; 5, 8, 12),	
Proposed	(0, 0, 0; 0, 0, 0)	

According to the contents of Table 6, the following points are drawn that demonstrate the effectiveness of the proposed solution method of this paper:

- The weaknesses of the approach of [38], e.g., negative solutions, dissatisfaction with demand, and a negative objective function value, do not occur in the solution obtained with the proposed approach;
- For comparison, all multi-objective solution approaches yield the same result;
- Further comparisons show that the TIFN of the objective function achieved by the solution method presented in this study may not be better than those of [38], which are $(-310, 131, 579; -506, 131, 775)$. This is because of the negative values in the intuitionistic objective function value obtained by the approach of [38]. The negative TIFN objective function value obtained by [38] is due to the negative values of the obtained solution.

Example 4. *This example is taken from [37], who proposed a transportation problem between some factories and some retail stores. The data are reported in Table 7. The solution methodology presented in this study and the existing methods, LH, TH, SO, and ABS, are used to solve this example. The results of this example are reported in Table 8.*

Table 7. The triangular intuitionistic fuzzy costs, availability, and demands of Example 4.

		Retail Stores			$\tilde{a}_i^I$
		Tirunelveli	Trichy	Chennai	
Factories	Sivakasi	(1, 4, 9; 0, 4, 12)	(3, 13, 14; 2, 13, 15)	(4, 6, 16; 1, 6, 33)	(6, 7, 10; 2, 7, 11)
	Kollam	(4, 5, 7; 1, 5, 9)	(5, 10, 15; 0, 10, 39)	(7, 16, 24; 0, 16, 41)	(6, 15, 23; 1, 15, 29)
	Nagercoil	(1, 3, 6; 0, 3, 10)	(5, 13, 21; 5, 13, 35)	(8, 18, 27; 6, 18, 48)	(2, 10, 16; 0, 10, 21)
$\tilde{b}_j^I$		(3, 8, 16; 0, 8, 19)	(1, 6, 7; 0, 6, 14)	(10, 18, 26; 3, 18, 28)	(14, 32, 49; 3, 32, 61)

Table 8. The results obtained for Example 4.

Method	$\tilde{X}_{11}^{I*}, \tilde{X}_{12}^{I*}, \ldots, \tilde{X}_{33}^{I*}$	$\tilde{Z}^I$
TH		
LH	(3, 3, 6; 0, 3, 6), (1, 2, 2; 0, 2, 3), (2, 2, 2; 2, 2, 2),	
SO	(0, 5, 10; 0, 5, 10), (0, 4, 5; 0, 4, 11), (6, 6, 8; 1, 6, 8),	(72, 391, 883; 2, 391, 1924)
ABS	(0, 0, 0; 0, 0, 3), (0, 0, 0; 0, 0, 0), (2, 10, 16; 0, 10, 18)	
Proposed	(0, 0, 0; 0, 0, 0), (0, 0, 1; 0, 0, 2), (6, 7, 9; 2, 7, 9), (1, 1, 3; 0, 1, 6), (1, 6, 6; 0, 6, 7), (4, 8, 14; 1, 8, 16), (2, 7, 13; 0, 7, 13), (0, 0, 0; 0, 0, 5), (0, 3, 3; 0, 3, 3)	(63, 310, 764; 2, 310, 1759)

The following conclusions can be drawn from Table 8, which demonstrates the effectiveness of the proposed solution method in Section 4:

- The shortcomings of the [37] approach, such as negative solutions, demand dissatisfaction, and negative objective function values, do not occur in the solution obtained with the proposed approach;
- For comparison, all multi-objective solution approaches, except the proposed one, yield the same result. The solution determined with the proposed solution method is significantly better than the other multi-objective solution approaches;
- Further comparison shows that the TIFN of the objective function achieved by the solution method proposed in this study is not better than those of [37], which are (137, 292, 502; 12, 292, 961). This is because of the negative values of the intuitionistic

objective function value of [37]. The negative TIFN of the objective function obtained by [37] is due to negative values in the obtained solution.

Example 5. *This example is also taken from [37]. It considers four sources and four destinations with the triangular intuitionistic fuzzy parameters of Table 9. The solution methodology presented in this study and the existing methods, LH, TH, SO, and ABS, are used to solve this example. The results of this example are reported in Table 10.*

Table 9. The triangular intuitionistic fuzzy costs, availability, and demands of Example 5.

		Destinations				$\tilde{a}_i^I$
		1	2	3	4	
Sources	1	(14, 16, 18; 12, 16, 20)	(0, 1, 2; −1, 1, 3)	(7, 8, 9; 6, 8, 10)	(11, 13, 15; 10, 13, 16)	(2,4,6; 1,4,7)
	2	(8, 11, 14; 7, 11, 15)	(3, 4, 5; 2, 4, 6)	(5, 7, 9; 4, 7, 10)	(8, 10, 12; 6, 10, 14)	(5,6,7; 4,6,8)
	3	(6, 8, 10; 5, 8, 11)	(13, 15, 17; 12, 15, 18)	(7, 9, 11; 6, 9, 12)	(1, 2, 3; 0, 2, 4)	(7,8,9; 5,8,11)
	4	(5, 6, 7; 4, 6, 8)	(11, 12, 13; 10, 12, 14)	(3, 5, 7; 1, 5, 9)	(12, 14, 16; 11, 14, 17)	(8,10,12; 6,10,14)
$\tilde{b}_j^I$		(3,4,5; 2,4,6)	(3, 5, 7; 1, 5, 9)	(10, 12, 14; 8, 12, 16)	(6, 7, 8; 5, 7, 9)	(22, 28, 34; 16, 28, 40)

Table 10. The results obtained for Example 5.

Method	$(x_{11}^*, x_{12}^*, \ldots x_{44}^*)$	$\tilde{Z}^I$
TH	(0, 0, 0; 0, 0, 0), (2, 4, 6; 1, 4, 7), (0, 0, 0; 0, 0, 0),	
LH	(0, 0, 0; 0, 0, 0), (0, 0, 0; 0, 0, 0), (0, 1, 1; 0, 1, 2),	
SO	(4, 5, 6; 4, 5, 6), (0, 0, 0; 0, 0, 0), (1, 1, 1; 0, 1, 2),	(63, 118, 189; 27, 118, 273)
ABS	(0, 0, 0; 0, 0, 0), (0, 0, 0; 0, 0, 0), (6, 7, 8; 5, 7, 9),	
Proposed	(2, 3, 4; 2, 3, 4), (0, 0, 0; 0, 0, 0), (6, 7, 8; 4, 7, 10), (0, 0, 0; 0, 0, 0)	

The below points are drawn from the results presented in Table 10, which demonstrate the effectiveness of the solution method proposed in this paper:

- The shortcomings of the [37] approach, such as negative solutions, demand dissatisfaction, and negative objective function values, do not occur in the solution obtained with the proposed approach;
- In comparison, all multicriteria solution approaches yield the same result;
- Further comparison shows that the TIFN of the objective function achieved by the solution method proposed in this paper may not be better than those of [37], which are (77, 118, 159; 42, 118, 194). This is because of the negative values of the intuitionistic objective function value of [37]. The negative TIFN of the objective function of [37] is due to the negative values in the obtained solution.

6. Concluding Remarks

In this study, a balanced form of the transportation problem was solved, with the variables and parameters all consisting of TIFNs (triangular intuitionistic fuzzy numbers). The existing approaches proposed for this intuitionistic fuzzy transportation problem have many shortcomings, such as using ranking functions, determining negative values for the variables, and calculating negative values for the objective function even when the unit transportation costs are positive. To overcome these difficulties, a new approach without a ranking function was proposed here. The proposed solution method converts the intuitionistic fuzzy transportation problem into a problem with multiple objective functions and proposes a new hybrid version of the fuzzy programming approach to solve the multi-objective problem. The computer experiments conducted have shown the superiority and effectiveness of the solutions achieved by the proposed solution method over the solutions obtained using the approaches of the literature based on the quality of the results. It is notable to mention that the proposed approach of this study may be useful to logistics and transportation analysts and managers and also the academic researchers of the field.

Author Contributions: Methodology, A.M.; Validation, S.S.; Formal analysis, L.M.; Data curation, L.M.; Writing—original draft, S.N.; Writing—review & editing, T.A. and A.A.; Supervision, S.S.; Funding acquisition, L.M. All authors have read and agreed to the published version of the manuscript.

Funding: This research received no external funding.

Data Availability Statement: The raw data supporting the conclusions of this article will be made available by the authors on request.

Conflicts of Interest: The authors declare no conflict of interest.

References

1. Aggarwal, S.; Gupta, C. Solving intuitionistic fuzzy solid transportation problem via new ranking method based on signed distance. *Int. J. Uncertain. Fuzziness Knowl. Based Syst.* **2016**, *24*, 483–501. [CrossRef]
2. Asunción, M.D.L.; Castillo, L.; Olivares, J.F.; Pérez, O.G.; González, A.; Palao, F. Handling fuzzy temporal constraints in a planning environment. *Ann. Oper. Res.* **2007**, *155*, 391–415. [CrossRef]
3. De, S.K.; Sana, S. S Backlogging EOQ model for promotional effort and selling price sensitive demand-an intuitionistic fuzzy approach. *Ann. Oper. Res.* **2013**, *233*, 57–76. [CrossRef]
4. Fard, A.F.; Gholian-Jouybari, F.; Paydar, M.M.; Hajiaghaei-Keshteli, M. A bi-objective stochastic closed-loop supply chain network design problem considering downside risk. *Ind. Eng. Manag. Syst.* **2017**, *16*, 342–362.
5. Hajiaghaei-Keshteli, M. The allocation of customers to potential distribution centers in supply chain networks: GA and AIA approaches. *Appl. Soft Comput.* **2011**, *11*, 2069–2078. [CrossRef]
6. Delavar, M.R.; Hajiaghaei-Keshteli, M.; Molla-Alizadeh-Zavardehi, S. Genetic algorithms for coordinated scheduling of production and air transportation. *Expert Syst. Appl.* **2010**, *37*, 8255–8266. [CrossRef]
7. Ganesan, K.; Veeramani, P. Fuzzy linear programs with trapezoidal fuzzy numbers. *Ann. Oper. Res.* **2006**, *143*, 305–315. [CrossRef]
8. Hosseinzadeh Lotfi, F.; Allahviranloo, T.; Alimardani Jondabeh, M.; Alizadeh, L. Solving a full fuzzy linear programming using lexicography method and fuzzy approximate solution. *Appl. Math. Model.* **2009**, *33*, 3151–3156. [CrossRef]
9. Mahmoodirad, A.; Pamucar, D.; Niroomand, S. A new intuitionistic fuzzy scheme of data envelopment analysis for evaluating rural comprehensive health service centers. *Socio-Econ. Plan. Sci.* **2024**, *95*, 102004. [CrossRef]
10. Ozel, M. Some consequences on the planar three-index transportation problem. *Int. J. Comput. Math.* **2010**, *87*, 2325–2331. [CrossRef]
11. Zadeh, L.A. Fuzzy sets. *Inf. Comput.* **1965**, *8*, 338–353. [CrossRef]
12. Bellman, R.; Zadeh, L.A. Decision making in fuzzy environment. *Manag. Sci.* **1970**, *17*, 141–164. [CrossRef]
13. Atanassov, K.T. Intuitionistic fuzzy sets. *Fuzzy Sets Syst.* **1986**, *20*, 87–96. [CrossRef]
14. He, Y.; He, Z.; Huang, H. Decision making with the generalized intuitionistic fuzzy power interaction averaging operators. *Soft Comput.* **2017**, *21*, 1129–1144. [CrossRef]
15. Mahmoodirad, A.; Allahviranloo, T.; Niroomand, S. A new effective solution method for fully intuitionistic fuzzy transportation problem. *Soft Comput.* **2019**, *23*, 4521–4530. [CrossRef]
16. Meng, F.; Tan, C. A method for multi-attribute group decision making based on generalized interval-valued intuitionistic fuzzy choquet integral operators. *Int. J. Uncertain. Fuzziness Knowl. Based Syst.* **2017**, *25*, 821–849. [CrossRef]
17. Nayagam, V.L.G.; Jeevaraj, S.; Dhanasekaran, P. An intuitionistic fuzzy multi-criteria decision-making method based on non-hesitance score for interval-valued intuitionistic fuzzy sets. *Soft Comput.* **2016**, *21*, 7077–7082. [CrossRef]
18. Niroomand, S.; Garg, H.; Mahmoodirad, A. An intuitionistic fuzzy two stage supply chain network design problem with multi-mode demand and multi-mode transportation. *ISA Trans.* **2020**, *107*, 117–133. [CrossRef]
19. Reiser, R.H.S.; Bedregal, B. Correlation in interval-valued Atanassov's intuitionistic fuzzy sets—conjugate and negation operators. *Int. J. Uncertain. Fuzziness Knowl. Based Syst.* **2017**, *25*, 787–819. [CrossRef]
20. Kumar Bind, A.; Rani, D.; Kumar Goyal, K.; Ebrahimnejad, A. A solution approach for sustainable multi-objective multi-item 4D solid transportation problem involving triangular intuitionistic fuzzy parameters. *J. Clean. Prod.* **2023**, *414*, 137661. [CrossRef]
21. Niroomand, S.; Hadi-Vencheh, A.; Mirzaei, M.; Molla-Alizadeh-Zavardehi, S. Hybrid greedy algorithms for fuzzy tardiness/earliness minimization in a special single machine scheduling problem: Case study and generalization. *Int. J. Comput. Integr. Manuf.* **2016**, *29*, 870–888. [CrossRef]

22. Shivani, R.D. Multi-objective multi-item four dimensional green transportation problem in interval-valued intuitionistic fuzzy environment. *Int. J. Syst. Assur. Eng. Manag.* **2024**, *15*, 727–744. [CrossRef]
23. Dempe, S.; Starostina, T. Optimal toll charges in a fuzzy flow problem. In Proceedings of the International Conference 9th Fuzzy Days, Dortmund, Germany, 18–20 September 2006.
24. Dinager, D.S.; Palanivel, K. The transportation problem in fuzzy environment. *Int. J. Algorithm Comput. Math.* **2009**, *12*, 93–106.
25. Nagoorgani, A.; Razak, K.A. Two stage fuzzy transportation problem. *J. Phys. Sci.* **2006**, *10*, 63–69.
26. Pandian, P.; Natarajan, G. A new algorithm for finding a fuzzy optimal solution for fuzzy transportation problem. *Appl. Math. Sci.* **2010**, *4*, 79–90.
27. Mohideen, I.S.; Kumar, P.S. A comparative study on transportation problem in fuzzy environment. *Int. J. Math. Res.* **2010**, *2*, 151–158.
28. Basirzadeh, H. An approach for solving fuzzy transportation problem. *Appl. Math. Sci.* **2011**, *5*, 1549–1566.
29. Kaur, A.; Kumar, A. A new approach for solving fuzzy transportation problem using generalized trapezoidal fuzzy number. *Appl. Soft Comput.* **2012**, *12*, 1201–1213. [CrossRef]
30. Jansi Rani, J.; Dhanasekar, S.; Micheal, D.R.; Manivannan, A. On solving fully intuitionistic fuzzy transportation problem via branch and bound technique. *J. Intell. Fuzzy Syst.* **2023**, *44*, 6219–6229. [CrossRef]
31. Beg, I.; Bisht, M.; Rawat, S. An approach for solving fully generalized intuitionistic fuzzy transportation problems. *Comput. Appl. Math.* **2023**, *42*, 329. [CrossRef]
32. Akram, M.; Umer, S.; Syed, M.; Tofigh, A. A new method to determine the Fermatean fuzzy optimal solution of transportation problems. *J. Intell. Fuzzy Syst.* **2023**, *44*, 309–328. [CrossRef]
33. Peng, Z.; Nikbakht, M.; Ebrahimnejad, A.; Hosseinzadeh Lotfi, F.; Allahviranloo, T. Fully interval-valued fuzzy transportation problems: Development and prospects. *Comput. Appl. Math.* **2024**, *43*, 15. [CrossRef]
34. Agrawal, A.; Singhal, N. An efficient computational approach for basic feasible solution of fuzzy transportation problems. *Int. J. Syst. Assur. Eng. Manag.* **2024**, *15*, 3337–3349. [CrossRef]
35. Falcón-Cardona, J.G.; Coello, C.A.C. A new indicator-based many-objective ant colony optimizer for continuous search spaces. *Swarm Intell.* **2017**, *11*, 71–100. [CrossRef]
36. Singh, S.K.; Yadav, S.P. A new approach for solving intuitionistic fuzzy transportation problem of type-2. *Ann. Oper. Res.* **2016**, *243*, 349–363. [CrossRef]
37. Kumar, P.S.; Hussain, R.J. Computationally simple approach for solving fully intuitionistic fuzzy real life transportation problems. *Int. J. Syst. Assur. Eng. Manag.* **2016**, *7*, 90–101. [CrossRef]
38. Singh, S.K.; Yadav, S.P. Efficient approach for solving type-1 intuitionistic fuzzy transportation problem. *Int. J. Syst. Assur. Eng. Manag.* **2015**, *6*, 259–267. [CrossRef]
39. Zimmermann, H.J. Fuzzy programming and linear programming with several objective functions. *Fuzzy Sets Syst.* **1978**, *1*, 45–55. [CrossRef]
40. Alavidoost, M.H.; Babazadeh, H.; Sayyari, S.T. An interactive fuzzy programming approach for bi-objective straight and U-shaped assembly line balancing problem. *Appl. Soft Comput.* **2016**, *40*, 221–235. [CrossRef]
41. Lai, Y.-J.; Hwang, C.-L. Possibilistic linear programming for managing interest rate risk. *Fuzzy Sets Syst.* **1993**, *54*, 135–146. [CrossRef]
42. Selim, H.; Ozkarahan, I. A supply chain distribution network design model: An interactive fuzzy goal programming-based solution approach. *Int. J. Adv. Manuf. Technol.* **2008**, *36*, 401–418. [CrossRef]
43. Torabi, S.A.; Hassini, E. An interactive possibilistic programming approach for multiple objective supply chain master planning. *Fuzzy Sets Syst.* **2008**, *159*, 193–214. [CrossRef]
44. Castro, O.R.; Pozo, A.; Lozano, J.A.; Santana, R. An investigation of clustering strategies in many-objective optimization: The I-Multi algorithm as a case study. *Swarm Intell.* **2017**, *11*, 101–130. [CrossRef]

Disclaimer/Publisher's Note: The statements, opinions and data contained in all publications are solely those of the individual author(s) and contributor(s) and not of MDPI and/or the editor(s). MDPI and/or the editor(s) disclaim responsibility for any injury to people or property resulting from any ideas, methods, instructions or products referred to in the content.

MDPI AG
Grosspeteranlage 5
4052 Basel
Switzerland
Tel.: +41 61 683 77 34

Mathematics Editorial Office
E-mail: mathematics@mdpi.com
www.mdpi.com/journal/mathematics

Disclaimer/Publisher's Note: The title and front matter of this reprint are at the discretion of the Guest Editors. The publisher is not responsible for their content or any associated concerns. The statements, opinions and data contained in all individual articles are solely those of the individual Editors and contributors and not of MDPI. MDPI disclaims responsibility for any injury to people or property resulting from any ideas, methods, instructions or products referred to in the content.